CONTRAST
DATA MINING

Concepts, Algorithms,
and Applications

Chapman & Hall/CRC
Data Mining and Knowledge Discovery Series

SERIES EDITOR
Vipin Kumar
University of Minnesota
Department of Computer Science and Engineering
Minneapolis, Minnesota, U.S.A.

AIMS AND SCOPE

This series aims to capture new developments and applications in data mining and knowledge discovery, while summarizing the computational tools and techniques useful in data analysis. This series encourages the integration of mathematical, statistical, and computational methods and techniques through the publication of a broad range of textbooks, reference works, and handbooks. The inclusion of concrete examples and applications is highly encouraged. The scope of the series includes, but is not limited to, titles in the areas of data mining and knowledge discovery methods and applications, modeling, algorithms, theory and foundations, data and knowledge visualization, data mining systems and tools, and privacy and security issues.

PUBLISHED TITLES

UNDERSTANDING COMPLEX DATASETS:
DATA MINING WITH MATRIX DECOMPOSITIONS
David Skillicorn

COMPUTATIONAL METHODS OF FEATURE SELECTION
Huan Liu and Hiroshi Motoda

CONSTRAINED CLUSTERING: ADVANCES IN ALGORITHMS, THEORY, AND APPLICATIONS
Sugato Basu, Ian Davidson, and Kiri L. Wagstaff

KNOWLEDGE DISCOVERY FOR COUNTERTERRORISM AND LAW ENFORCEMENT
David Skillicorn

MULTIMEDIA DATA MINING: A SYSTEMATIC INTRODUCTION TO CONCEPTS AND THEORY
Zhongfei Zhang and Ruofei Zhang

NEXT GENERATION OF DATA MINING
Hillol Kargupta, Jiawei Han, Philip S. Yu, Rajeev Motwani, and Vipin Kumar

DATA MINING FOR DESIGN AND MARKETING
Yukio Ohsawa and Katsutoshi Yada

THE TOP TEN ALGORITHMS IN DATA MINING
Xindong Wu and Vipin Kumar

GEOGRAPHIC DATA MINING AND KNOWLEDGE DISCOVERY, SECOND EDITION
Harvey J. Miller and Jiawei Han

TEXT MINING: CLASSIFICATION, CLUSTERING, AND APPLICATIONS
Ashok N. Srivastava and Mehran Sahami

BIOLOGICAL DATA MINING
Jake Y. Chen and Stefano Lonardi

CONTRAST DATA MINING

Concepts, Algorithms, and Applications

Edited by

Guozhu Dong and James Bailey

CRC Press
Taylor & Francis Group
Boca Raton   London   New York

CRC Press is an imprint of the
Taylor & Francis Group, an **informa** business

A CHAPMAN & HALL BOOK

CRC Press
Taylor & Francis Group
6000 Broken Sound Parkway NW, Suite 300
Boca Raton, FL 33487-2742

© 2005 by Taylor & Francis Group, LLC
CRC Press is an imprint of Taylor & Francis Group

No claim to original U.S. Government works
Printed on acid-free paper
Version Date: 2012907
International Standard Book Number: 978-1-4398-5432-7 (Hardback)

Cover Photo: Sunset over Mindil Beach, Darwin. Photo by Katherine Ramsay.

Library of Congress Cataloging-in-Publication Data

Contrast data mining : concepts, algorithms, and applications / [edited by] Guozhu Dong, James Bailey.
  Pages cm.--(Chapman & Hall/CRC data mining and knowledge discovery series)
  Includes bibliographical references and index.
  ISBN 978-1-4398-5432-7 (hardback : acid-free paper)
  1. Contrast data mining. I. Dong, Guozhu, 1957 - editor of compilation. II. Bailey,
  James, 1971 June 30-
QA76.9.D343C65   2013
006.3'12--dc23   2012025085

**Visit the Taylor & Francis Web site at
http://www.taylorandfrancis.com**

**and the CRC Press Web site at
http://www.crcpress.com**

Dedication

To my wife Diana and my children. {G.D.}

To my wife Katherine. {J.B.}

To all contributing authors of the book
and to all researchers of the contrast mining field. {G.D. and J.B.}

Contents

12 Using Emerging Patterns in Outlier and Rare-Class Prediction 171

Lijun Chen and Guozhu Dong

13 Enhancing Traditional Classifiers Using Emerging Patterns 187

Guozhu Dong and Kotagiri Ramamohanarao

16 Discriminating Gene Transfer and Microarray Concordance Analysis

233

Shihong Mao and Guozhu Dong

17 Towards Mining Optimal Emerging Patterns Amidst 1000s of Genes

241

Shihong Mao and Guozhu Dong

Foreword

Contrast data mining is an important and focused subarea of data mining. Its aim is to find interesting contrast patterns that describe significant differences between datasets satisfying various contrasting conditions. The contrasting conditions can be defined on class, time, location, other "dimensions" of interest, or their combinations. The contrast patterns can represent nontrivial differences between classes, interesting changes over time, interesting trends in space, and so on.

Contrast data mining has provided, and will continue to provide, a unique angle to examine certain challenging problems and to develop powerful methodologies for solving those challenging problems, both in data mining research and in various applications. For the former, contrast patterns have been used for classification, clustering, and discriminative pattern analysis. For the latter, contrast data mining has been used in a wide spectrum of applications, such as differentiating cancerous tissues from benign ones, distinguishing structures of toxic molecules from that of non-toxic ones, and characterizing the differences on the issues discussed in the blogs on U.S. presidential elections in 2008 and those discussed in 2012. Contrast data mining can be performed on many kinds of data, including relational, vector, transactional, numerical, textual, music, image, and multimedia data, as well as complex structured data, such as sequences, graphs, and networks.

There have been numerous research papers published in recent years, on contrast mining algorithms, on applying contrast patterns in classification, clustering, and discriminative pattern analysis, and on applying contrast patterns and contrast-pattern based classification and clustering to a wide range of problems in medicine, bioinformatics, chemoinformatics, crime analysis, blog analysis, and so on. This book, edited by two leading researchers on contrast mining, Professors Guozhu Dong and James Bailey, and contributed to by over 40 data mining researchers and application scientists, is a comprehensive and authoritative treatment of this research theme. It presents a systematic introduction and a thorough overview of the state-of-the-art for contrast data mining, including concepts, methodologies, algorithms, and applications.

I have high confidence that the book will appeal to a wide range of readers, including data mining researchers and developers who want to be informed about recent progress in this exciting and fruitful area of research, scientific researchers who seek to find new tools to solve challenging problems in their own research domains, and graduate students who want to be inspired on problem solving techniques and who want to get help with identifying and solving novel data mining research problems in various domains.

I find the book enjoyable to read. I hope you will like it, too.

Jiawei Han

University of Illinois, Urbana-Champaign

March 19, 2012

Preface

Contrasting is one of the most basic types of analysis. Contrasting based analysis is routinely employed, often subconsciously, by all types of people. People use contrasting to better understand the world around them and the challenging problems they want to solve. People use contrasting to accurately assess the desirability of important situations, and to help them better avoid potentially harmful situations and embrace potentially beneficial ones.

Contrasting involves the comparison of one dataset against another. The datasets may represent data of different time periods, spatial locations, or classes, or they may represent data satisfying different conditions. Contrasting is often employed to compare cases with a desirable outcome against cases with an undesirable one, for example comparing the benign and diseased tissue classes of a cancer, or comparing students who graduate with university degrees against those who do not. Contrasting can identify patterns that capture changes and trends over time or space, or identify discriminative patterns that capture differences among contrasting classes or conditions.

Traditional methods for contrasting multiple datasets were often very simple so that they could be performed by hand. For example, one could compare the respective feature means, compare the respective attribute-value distributions, or compare the respective probabilities of simple patterns, in the datasets being contrasted. However, the simplicity of such approaches has limitations, as it is difficult to use them to identify specific patterns that offer novel and actionable insights, and identify desirable sets of discriminative patterns for building accurate and explainable classifiers.

Contrast data mining, a special and focused area of data mining, develops concepts and algorithmic tools to help us overcome the limitations of those simple approaches. Recently, especially in the last dozen or so years, a large number of research papers on the concepts and algorithms of contrast data mining, and a large number of papers on successful applications of contrast mining in a wide range of scientific and business domains, have been reported. However, those results were only available in widely scattered places. This book presents the results in one place, in a comprehensive and coordinated fashion, making them more accessible to a wider spectrum of readers.

The importance and usefulness, and the diversified nature of contrast mining, have been indicated not only by the large number of papers, but also by the many names that have been used for *contrast patterns*. For example, the following names have been used: change pattern, characterization rule, class association rule, classification rule, concept drift, contrast set, difference pattern, discriminative association, discriminative interaction pattern, discriminative pattern, dissimilarity pattern, emerging pattern, gradient pattern, group difference, unusual subgroups, and generalized contrast patterns such as fuzzy/disjunctive emerging patterns and contrast inequalities/regressions.

This book is focused on the mining and utilization of contrast patterns. It is divided into seven parts.

Part I, Preliminaries and Measures on Contrasts, contains two chapters, on preliminaries and on statistical measures for contrast patterns, respectively.

Part II, Contrast Mining Algorithms, contains five chapters: Chapters 3 and 4 are on mining emerging patterns using tree-based structures or tree-based searches, and using Zero-Suppressed Binary Decision Diagrams, respectively. Chapter 5 is on efficient direct mining of selective discriminative patterns for classification. Chapter 6 is on mining emerging patterns from structured data, such as sequences and graphs. Chapter 7 is on incremental maintenance of emerging patterns.

Part III, Generalized Contrasts, Emerging Data Cubes, and Rough Sets, contains three chapters: Chapter 8 is on more expressive contrast patterns (such as disjunctive/fuzzy emerging patterns, and contrast inequalities). Chapter 9 is on emerging data cube representations for OLAP data mining. Chapter 10 relates jumping emerging patterns with rough set theory.

Part IV, Contrast Mining for Classification and Clustering, contains four chapters: Chapter 11 gives an overview and analysis of contrast pattern based classification. Chapter 12 is on using emerging patterns in outlier and rare-class prediction. Chapter 13 is on enhancing traditional classifiers using emerging patterns. Chapter 14 presents CPC — Contrast Pattern Based Clustering Algorithm — together with a brief discussion on the CPCQ clustering quality index, which is based on the quality, abundance, and diversity of contrast patterns.

Part V, Contrast Mining for Bioinformatics and Chemoinformatics, contains five chapters: Chapter 15 is on emerging pattern based rules characterizing subtypes of leukemia. Chapter 16 is on discriminating gene transfer and microarray concordance analysis. Chapter 17 is on mining optimal emerging patterns when there are thousands of genes or features. Chapter 18 is on the theory and applications of emerging chemical patterns. Chapter 19 is on emerging molecule patterns as structural alerts for computational toxicology.

Part VI, Contrast Mining for Special Application Domains, contains five chapters: Chapter 20 is on emerging patterns and classification for spatial and image data. Chapter 21 is on geospatial contrast mining with applications on vegetation, biodiversity, and election-voting analysis. Chapter 22 is on mining emerging patterns for activity recognition. Chapter 23 is on emerging pattern based prediction of heart diseases and powerline safety. Chapter 24 is on emerging pattern based crime spots analysis and rental price prediction.

Part VII, Survey of Other Papers, contains one chapter: Chapter 25 gives an overview of results on contrast mining and applications, with a focus on papers not already cited in the other chapters of the book. The chapter incudes citations of papers that present algorithms on mining changes and model shift, on mining conditional contrasts, on mining niche patterns, on discovering holes and bumps, on discovering changes and emerging trends in tourism and in music, on understanding retail customer behavior, on using patterns to analyze and improve genetic algorithms, on using patterns to preserve privacy and protect network security, and on summarizing knowledge level differences between datasets.

The 25 chapters of this book were written by more than 40 authors who conduct research in a diverse range of disciplines, including architecture engineering, bioinformatics, biology, chemoinformatics, computer science, life-science informatics, medicine, and systems engineering and engineering management. The cited papers of the book deal with topics in much wider range of disciplines. It is also interesting to note that the book's authors are from a dozen countries, namely Australia, Canada, China, Cuba, Denmark, France, Germany, Japan, Korea, Poland, Singapore, and the USA.

The 25 chapters demonstrate many useful and powerful capabilities of contrast mining. For example, contrast patterns can be used to characterize disease classes. They can capture discriminative gene group interactions, and can help define interaction based importance of genes, for cancers. They can be used to build accurate and explainable classifiers that perform well for balanced classification as well as for imbalanced classification, to perform outlier detection, to enhance traditional classifiers, to serve as feature sets of traditional classifiers, and to measure clustering quality and to construct clusters without distance functions. They can be used in compound selection for drug design and in molecule toxicity analysis, in crime spot analysis and in heart disease diagnosis, in rental price prediction and in powerline safety analysis, in activity recognition, and in image and spatial data analysis. In general, contrast mining is useful for diversified application domains involving many different data types.

A very interesting virtue of contrast mining is that contrast-pattern aggregation based classification can be effective when very few, as few as three, training examples per class are available. This virtue is especially useful for situations where training data may be hard to obtain, for instance for drug lead selection. Another interesting characteristic is that length statistics of minimal jumping emerging patterns can be used to detect outliers, allowing the use of one number as a measure to detect intruders. Using such a minimal model is advantageous, since it is hard for intruders to discover and emulate the model of the normal user in order to evade detection. A third interesting trait of contrast mining is the ability to use the collective quality and diversity of contrast patterns to measure clustering quality and to form clusters, without relying on a distance function, which is often hard to define appropriately in clustering-like exploratory data analysis. As you read the chapters of the book, you will notice many other powerful aspects of contrast patterns, which make them very useful in solving many challenging problems.

Perhaps the most important contribution of contrast mining will come when we no longer need to use the naive Bayes or similar simplifying approaches to handle the challenge of high dimensional data, when we have developed the methodology to systematically analyze, and accurately use, sets of multi-feature contrast patterns instead. We believe that contrast mining has made useful progress in this direction, and we hope that results reported in this book will help researchers make progress on this important problem. Success in this direction will have a large impact on the understanding and handling of intrinsically complex processes, such as complex diseases whose behaviors are influenced by the interaction of multiple genetic and environmental factors.

We envision that, in the not too distant future, the field of contrast data mining will become mature. Then, other disciplines such as biology, medicine, and physics will refer to contrast mining and use methods from the contrast mining toolbox, in the same way that they now use methods such as logistic regression and PCA. We also foresee that, as the world moves towards ubiquitous computing, people may some day have a *contrasting app* on their iPhone-like device, which, when pointed at two types of things, can answer the question "in what ways do these two types differ?"

This book demonstrates that contrast mining has been a fruitful field for research on data mining methodology and for research on utilizing contrast mining to solve real-life problems. There are still many interesting research questions that deserve our attention, both in developing contrast mining methodology within the realm of computer science and in utilizing contrast mining to solve challenging problems in domains outside of computer science. Let us join together in exploring the concepts, algorithms, techniques, and applications of contrast data mining, to quickly realize its full potential.

Guozhu Dong, Wright State University
James Bailey, The University of Melbourne
March 2012

Part I

Preliminaries and Statistical Contrast Measures

Chapter 1

Preliminaries

Guozhu Dong

Department of Computer Science and Engineering, Wright State University

1.1 Datasets of Various Data Types

This section presents preliminaries on two frequently used data types for data mining, namely transaction data and attribute-based vector/tuple data. Other special data types will be described in the chapters that require them.

For transaction data, one assumes that there is a universal set of items of interest for a given application. A *transaction t* is a non-empty set of items. A transaction may also be associated with a *transaction identifier* (TID). A *transaction dataset D* is a bag (multi-set) of transactions. Within D, the TIDs are unique; a transaction of D can occur multiple times. Transaction datasets are often used to describe market basket data, text data, discretized vector data, discretized image data, etc. Table 1.1 gives an example.

For vector/tuple data, there is a universal set $\{A_1, ..., A_m\}$ of attributes of interest. Each attribute A_i is associated with a domain $dom(A_i)$, and A_i can be *numerical* or *categorical* (which is a synonym of nominal), depending on whether its domain contains only numbers or not. It is assumed that the domain of a categorical attribute is finite. A *vector* or *tuple* is a function t mapping the attributes to their domains such that $t(A_i) \in dom(A_i)$ for each A_i. A vector t is often given in the form $(t(A_1), ..., t(A_m))$. Vectors are used

TABLE 1.1: A Transaction Dataset

T1	bread, cat food, cereal, egg, milk
T2	bread, juice, yogurt
T3	butter, cereal, diaper, juice, milk
T4	bread, juice, yogurt

TABLE 1.2: A Vector Dataset

Age	Gender	Education	BuyHybrid
32	female	phd	yes
52	female	bachelor	yes
62	male	phd	yes
29	male	bachelor	no
33	female	masters	no

to describe objects. A *vector dataset* is a set of vectors/tuples. Table 1.2 gives an example; the dataset has four attributes: Age, Gender, Education, and BuyHybrid; Age is numerical and the other three are categorical.

A transaction dataset can be represented as a binary vector dataset, where each item is viewed as a binary attribute, and the values 0 and 1 represent absence and presence respectively of the item in the given transactions.

A dataset D may be associated with classes. In this case, some number $k \geq 2$ of class labels $C_1, ..., C_k$ are given, and D is partitioned into k disjoint subsets $D_1, ..., D_k$ such that D_i is the dataset for class C_i. It is customary to directly use C_i to refer to D_i. Table 1.2 can be viewed as a dataset with two classes, where the class labels are the two BuyHybrid values; the dataset then has three attributes, namely Age, Gender, and Education, and the "yes" class consists of the first three tuples, and the "no" class consists of the last two.

1.2   Data Preprocessing

For pattern mining, it is common to transform numerical attribute values into "items". Let D be a vector dataset. The transformation is achieved using *binning*, also called *discretization*, of the numerical attributes. Binning of a numerical attribute has two steps: First, the domain of the attribute is partitioned into a finite number of disjoint intervals (bins). Then, each tuple t of D is transformed into a new tuple t' where, for each numerical attribute A, $t'(A)$ is set to the interval that $t(A)$ belongs to. The *discretized dataset* of D can now be viewed as a transaction dataset, where the items have the form (A, a), A is an attribute and a is either a value of A (if A is categorical) or an interval of A (if A is numerical). Here, the item (A, a) should be viewed as $A = a$ if A is categorical, and viewed as $A \in a$ if A is numerical. For the dataset in Table 1.2, as one possibility, one can discretize Age into three intervals, namely $[0, 30)$, $[30, 50), [50, 100]$. The first tuple is then transformed into the transaction $\{Age \in [30, 50), Gender = female, Education = phd, BuyHybrid = yes\}$.

The square brackets "[" and "]" are used denote closed ends of intervals, and the round brackets "(" and ")" are used to denote open ends. The end of an interval whose boundary value is $+\infty$ or $-\infty$ should be open.

Binning can be done either statically before performing pattern mining, or dynamically during pattern mining. We only discuss the static case below.

Many binning methods have been developed. They can be divided into two categories: A binning method is called *supervised* if the tuples have assigned classes and the method uses the class information, and it is called *unsupervised* otherwise [128]. Unsupervised binning methods include equi-width and equi-density. Supervised binning methods include the entropy based method.

Let A be a numerical attribute of a vector dataset D, and let k be the desired number of intervals for A.

The *active range* of A is given by $[a_{min}, a_{max}]$, where a_{min} and a_{max} are respectively the minimum and maximum values of A in D. The *implicit range* of A is given by $[a^*_{min}, a^*_{max}]$, where a^*_{min} is the minimal value (which can be a_{min} or $-\infty$ or some other value) and a^*_{max} is the maximum value (which can be a_{max} or $+\infty$ or some other value) of the domain of A.

The *equi-width* method divides A's active range into intervals of equal width. Specifically, the method uses the following intervals for A: $[a^*_{min}, a_{min} + w_e]$, $(a_{min} + w_e, a_{min} + 2w_e]$, ..., $(a_{min} + (k-1)w_e, a^*_{max}]$, where $w_e = \frac{(a_{max} - a_{min})}{k}$. a^*_{min} and a^*_{max} are used instead of a_{min} and a_{max}, to enure that the discretization applies to not only known data in D but also unseen future data. The method's name can be explained as follows: If only the "active" parts, namely $[a_{min}, a_{min} + w_e]$, $(a_{min} + w_e, a_{min} + 2w_e]$, ..., $(a_{min} + (k-1)w_e, a_{max}]$, are considered, then the intervals have the same width.

For the dataset in Table 1.2 and $k = 3$, the equi-width method discretizes the Age attribute into the following three intervals, $[0, 40]$, $(40, 51]$ and $(51, 150]$, assuming that the minimal and maximal age values are 0 and 150 respectively. The corresponding "active" intervals are $[29, 40]$, $(40, 51]$, and $(51, 62]$ and they have equal width.

The *equi-density* method divides A's active range into intervals all having the same number of matching tuples in D. Specifically, the method uses the intervals $[a^*_{min}, a_1]$, $(a_1, a_2]$, ..., $(a_{k-1}, a^*_{max}]$ such that the interval densities, $|\{t \mid t \in D, t(A) \in$ the ith interval$\}|$, are as close to $\frac{|D|}{k}$ as possible. It is customary to only use the mid-points of distinct consecutive values of the attribute, when the values are sorted, as the interval boundaries.

To illustrate, for the dataset in Table 1.2 and $k = 2$, the equi-density method may discretize the Age attribute into the following two intervals, $[0, 42.5]$ and $(42.5, 150]$, assuming that the minimal and maximal age values are 0 and 150 respectively. Densities of the two intervals are 3 and 2 respectively. The method may also discretize the Age attribute into the following two intervals, $[0, 32.5]$ and $(32.5, 150]$.

As suggested by the name, entropy based binning uses the entropy measure. Let D' be a dataset having κ classes C_1, ..., C_κ. Let $p_i = \frac{|C_i|}{|D'|}$ for each i. The *entropy* [362] of D' is defined by

$$\mathsf{entropy}(D') = -\sum_{i=1}^{\kappa} p_i \, log_2 \, p_i.$$

An entropy value is often viewed as an indication of the purity of D' – the smaller the entropy value the "purer" (or more "skewed") D' is.

The *entropy based binning* method iteratively splits an interval into two intervals, starting by splitting the active range of A in D. Specifically, to determine the split value in D, the method [145] first sorts the A values in D into an increasing list $a_1, ..., a_n$. Then each mid-point between two distinct consecutive A values in the list is a candidate split value. Each split value v divides D into two subsets, $D_1 = \{t \in D \mid t(A) \leq v\}$ and $D_2 = \{t \in D \mid t(A) > v\}$. The *information gain* of a split v is defined to be

$$\text{infoGain}(v) = \text{entropy}(D) - \sum_{i=1}^{2} \frac{|D_i|}{|D|} \text{entropy}(D_i).$$

The split value v' that maximizes $\text{infoGain}(v)$ is chosen as the split value for A. This splits the active range of A into two intervals. If more intervals are needed, this method is used to find the best split value for A in D_1 and the best split value for A in D_2; then the better one among the two is selected to produce one additional interval in D. This process is repeated until some stopping condition is satisfied.

For the dataset in Table 1.2 and $k = 2$, the entropy based method works as follows. The age values of D are sorted to yield the following list: $29, 32, 33, 52, 62$. The candidate split values are $30.5, 32.5, 42.5, 57$. It can be verified that 42.5 is the best split. Hence the method produces the following two intervals: $[0, 42.5], (42.5, 150]$. Intuitively, the D_1 and D_2 associated with the split value of 42.5 are the purest among the candidate split values.

1.3   Patterns and Models

Two major categories of knowledge that are often considered in data mining are patterns and models. Loosely speaking, a model is global, in the sense that it refers to the whole population of data under consideration, whereas a pattern is local and refers to a subset of that total population.

In general terms, a *pattern* is a condition on data tuples that evaluates to either *true* or *false*. Not all conditions are considered patterns though – only succinct conditions that are much simpler and much smaller in size than the data they describe are worthwhile to be returned as patterns of interest.

Patterns can be specified in different pattern languages. We discuss some commonly used ones below. More expressive pattern languages are used in the literature and in later chapters of this book.

For transaction data, patterns are frequently given as itemsets. An *itemset* is a finite set of items. A transaction t is said to *satisfy* or *match* an itemset X if $X \subseteq t$.

When vector data is discretized, the itemset concept carries over. Recall that the form of an item here is either $A = a$ or $A \in a$, depending on whether A is categorical or numerical. The *satisfaction* of an item $A = a$ or $A \in a$ by a vector t is defined in the natural manner. A vector t *satisfies* an itemset X if each item in X is satisfied by t. Equivalently, we say that t *satisfies* an itemset X if the discretized version of t satisfies X in the transaction sense. The word "matches" is often used as a synonym of "satisfies".

The *matching data* of an itemset X in a dataset D is given by $\mathsf{mt}(X, D) = \{t \in D \mid t$ satisfies $X\}$. The *count* and *support* of X in D are given by $\mathsf{count}(X, D) = |\mathsf{mt}(X, D)|$ and $\mathsf{supp}(X, D) = \frac{\mathsf{count}(X)}{|D|}$. The concepts of itemset, count and support given here are the same as in association mining [3].

An itemset X is *closed* [326] in a dataset D if there is no proper superset itemset Y of X satisfying $\mathsf{count}(Y, D) = \mathsf{count}(X, D)$. Closed patterns are often preferred since they reduce the number of frequent patterns and yet they can be used to recover the supports of all frequent patterns.

The *equivalence class* of an itemset X with respect to a dataset D is defined as the set of all itemsets Y satisfying $\mathsf{mt}(Y, D) = \mathsf{mt}(X, D)$. Such equivalence classes are often *convex*, meaning that Z is in a given equivalence class if there exist X and Y in the given equivalence class satisfying $X \subseteq Z \subseteq Y$.

Convex sets of patterns can be represented by *borders* of the form $< L, R >$, where L is the set of the minimal patterns (defined in terms of the set-containment relationship of the itemsets of the patterns) of the convex set and R is the set of maximal patterns of the convex set. (It is easy to see that L and R are both anti-chains with respect to the set containment relation, i.e. there are no patterns X and Y of L satisfying $X \subseteq Y$ and similarly for R.) In particular, an equivalence class has one maximal itemset (which is referred to as the closed pattern of the equivalence class) and a set of minimal itemsets (which are referred to as the minimal generators of the equivalence class).

We now turn to models. While many possibilities exist, here we focus on classifiers and clusterings.

A *classifier* is a function from data tuples to (predicted) class labels. Classifiers are often constructed from *training data*. A *classification algorithm* builds a classifier for each given training dataset. Many types of classifiers and classification algorithms have been studied. Different classifiers are defined using different approaches; some are easier to understand than others.

The evaluation of the quality of a classifier is an important issue. Several measures have been considered, including accuracy, precision, recall, and F-score. We discuss accuracy below.

The *accuracy* of a classifier reflects how often (as a percentage) the classifier is correct (i.e., the predicted class is the true class). For accuracy estimation, often a given dataset is divided into a *training* part and a *testing* part; a classifier is built from the training part and its accuracy is determined using the testing part. To reduce variability in accuracy evaluation, cross-validation is performed. In *k-fold cross validation*, where $k \geq 2$ is an integer, a given dataset D is randomly shuffled and partitioned into k parts/folds. *Stratified partitions*, partitions where the class ratios in each fold are roughly equal to those ratios in the whole dataset, are preferred. Then, each fold of the partition is used as a testing dataset and the other $k-1$ folds are used as training data. The average accuracy of the k classifiers built in this manner is considered as the accuracy of the classifier (more precisely, the accuracy of the classification algorithm). In practice, 5-fold or 10-fold cross validation is often used. To further reduce variability, k-fold cross validation can be repeated many times (using different shuffling results), and the average accuracy of the repeated k-fold cross validation is considered as the accuracy of the classifier.

A *clustering* of a dataset D is a partition (or grouping) of D into some desired number k of subsets $C_1, ..., C_k$. Each subset is called a *cluster* in the clustering. The quality of a clustering can be measured in many ways. Often distance based clustering quality measures are used, including the intra-cluster difference measure; clustering algorithms often attempt to minimize such quality measures. Given a distance function d on tuples and a clustering $C = (C_1, ..., C_k)$ of D, the *intra-cluster difference* measure is defined as

$$\mathsf{ICD}(C) = \sum_{i=1}^{k} \sum_{s \in C_i, t \in C_i, s \neq t} d(s,t).$$

Observe that the inter-cluster difference, defined as the sum of pairwise distance of tuples in different clusters, is maximized automatically when ICD is minimized. Average can be used in the definition instead of the sum. Many clustering algorithms and clustering quality measures have been studied.

It is interesting to note that contrast patterns can be used to define quality measures on clusterings and can be used as the basis of a clustering algorithm to form clusterings, without the use of distance functions, which can be difficult to define appropriately when performing clustering analysis. Chapter 14 will discuss a contrast pattern based quality measure (called CPCQ) and a contrast pattern based clustering algorithm (called CPC).

1.4   Contrast Patterns and Models

This section presents some basic definitions of contrast patterns and models. Specific variants will be discussed in various chapters of the book.

In general, contrasting can be performed on datasets satisfying statically defined conditions or on datasets satisfying dynamically defined conditions. For the former, two or more datasets are needed, and for the latter, just one dataset is required. Often each of the datasets corresponds to a class.

We first discuss the case for statically defined conditions. Given two or more datasets that one wishes to contrast, *contrast patterns and models* are patterns and models that describe differences and similarities between/among the given datasets. In this book, the focus is on the difference type, although we may discuss the similarity type occasionally.

The datasets under contrast can be subsets of a common dataset. For example, they can be the classes of a common underlying dataset, or subsets of a common underlying dataset satisfying various conditions. The datasets under contrast can also be datasets for a given application collected from different locations, or different time periods.

The datasets under contrast may also contain classes themselves. For example, one may contrast two datasets for two different diseases, where each dataset has two classes (e.g. normal and diseased).

According to the above, most classifiers are examples of contrast models. Clusterings that come with patterns/models characterizing the clusters, as is done in conceptual clustering [297, 151] (and also Chapter 14), can also be viewed as contrasting models. As mentioned in the preface, this book, and the discussion below, will focus on the mining and utilization of contrast patterns.

Contrast patterns are often defined as patterns whose supports differ significantly among the datasets under contrast. There are three common ways to define "supports differ significantly," one being growth-rate (or support-ratio) based, another being support-delta based, and the third using two thresholds.

Many chapters in this book refer to contrast patterns as emerging patterns [118].

We focus on the two datasets case below, and will note how to generalize to more datasets. Let D_1 and D_2 be two datasets to be contrasted.

The *growth rate* [118, 119], also commonly referred to as *support ratio* or *frequency ratio*, of a pattern X for dataset D_j is $\mathsf{gr}(X, D_j) = \frac{\mathsf{supp}(X, D_j)}{\mathsf{supp}(X, D_i)}$, where $i \in \{1, 2\} - \{j\}$. It is customary to define $\mathsf{gr}(X, D_j) = 0$ if $\mathsf{supp}(X, D_j) = \mathsf{supp}(X, D_i) = 0$, and define $\mathsf{gr}(X, D_j) = \infty$ if $\mathsf{supp}(X, D_j) > 0$ and $\mathsf{supp}(X, D_i) = 0$.

The *support delta* (or support difference) [42, 44] of a pattern X for dataset D_j is $\mathsf{supp}_\delta(X, D_j) = \mathsf{supp}(X, D_j) - \mathsf{supp}(X, D_i)$, where $i \in \{1, 2\} - \{j\}$.

Definition 1.1 *Given a growth-rate threshold $\sigma_r > 0$, a pattern X is a σ_r-contrast pattern for dataset D_j if $\mathsf{gr}(X, D_j) \geq \sigma_r$. Similarly, given a delta threshold $\sigma_\delta > 0$, a pattern X is a σ_δ-contrast pattern for dataset D_j if $\mathsf{supp}_\delta(X, D_j) \geq \sigma_\delta$. If X is a contrast pattern for D_j, then D_j is the home dataset (also called target dataset or positive dataset), and the other datasets are the opposing datasets (also called background datasets or negative datasets), of X. A contrast pattern whose support is zero in its opposing datasets but non-zero in its home dataset is called a jumping emerging pattern; its growth rate is ∞.*

When discussing σ_r- or σ_δ-contrast patterns, σ_r and σ_δ are often omitted.

Besides the support-ratio and support-delta based ways, one can also define contrast patterns using a *two-support based method*. More specifically, given a support threshold $\alpha \in [0, 1]$ for home dataset and a support threshold $\beta \in [0, 1]$

for the opposing dataset, a pattern X is a (α, β)-*contrast pattern* [34] for dataset D_j if $\mathsf{supp}(X, D_j) \geq \alpha$ and $\mathsf{supp}(X, D_i) \leq \beta$ $(i \in \{1, 2\} - \{j\})$.

Example 1.1 *To illustrate the three definitions, consider the data shown in Table 1.3, which can be viewed as the result of discretizing each gene G_i into two intervals, denoted by L (low) and H (high), of microarray gene expression data. For $X_0 = \{G_1 = L, G_2 = H\}$, we have $\mathsf{supp}(X_0, Cancer) = 0.75$, $\mathsf{supp}(X_0, Normal) = 0.25$, $\mathsf{supp}_\delta(X_0) = 0.5$, and $\mathsf{gr}(X_0, Cancer) = 3$; X_0 is a contrast pattern for $\sigma_\delta = 0.4$ using the support-delta definition and for $\sigma_r = 2$ using the growth rate definition. For $X_1 = \{G_1 = L, G_2 = H, G_3 = L\}$, we have $\mathsf{supp}(X_1, Cancer) = 0.50$, $\mathsf{supp}(X_1, Normal) = 0$, $\mathsf{supp}_\delta(X_1) = 0.5$, and $\mathsf{gr}(X_1, Cancer) = \infty$; X_1 is a contrast pattern for $\sigma_\delta = 0.4$ and for $\sigma_r = 100$. X_1 is a contrast pattern for $\alpha = 0.4$ and $\beta = 0$ using the two support definition.*

TABLE 1.3: Example Dataset for Contrast Patterns

Cancer Tissues				Normal Tissues			
G_1	G_2	G_3	G_4	G_1	G_2	G_3	G_4
L	H	L	H	H	H	L	H
L	H	L	L	L	H	H	H
H	L	L	H	L	L	L	H
L	H	H	L	H	H	H	L

Using a growth-rate as the only threshold to mine contrast patterns allows us to obtain contrast patterns without a minimum support threshold, and to obtain contrast patterns with high growth rate but low support. This is an advantage for classification applications (see Chapter 11), and for situations where we wish to identify emerging trends in time or space. Using a support-delta threshold implies a minimum support threshold in the home dataset.

Both growth rate and support delta are example interestingness measures on contrast patterns. Other interestingness measures such as relative risk ratio, odds ratio, and risk difference [247, 255] have been studied in the literature. Chapter 2 presents various measures on contrast patterns.

There are two ways to generalize to the case with more than two datasets. We can either replace $\mathsf{supp}(X, D_i)$ by $\max_{i \neq j} \mathsf{supp}(X, D_i)$, or replace it by $\mathsf{supp}(X, \cup_{i \neq j} D_i)$, in the definitions for $\mathsf{gr}(X, D_j)$ and $\mathsf{supp}_\delta(X, D_j)$.

So far the discussion is about the static case, where the datasets to be contrasted are predefined. We now consider a dynamic case. Let D be a given dataset and μ a given measure that can be applied to patterns, such as the support of itemsets, or the sum of a measure attribute as used in data cubes. We wish to mine *contrasting pairs* (X_1, X_2) such that X_1 and X_2 are very similar patterns syntactically and $\mu(\mathsf{mt}(X_1, D))$ and $\mu(\mathsf{mt}(X_2, D))$ differ significantly [117, 122]. Here the datasets $\mathsf{mt}(X_1, D)$ and $\mathsf{mt}(X_2, D)$ are discovered on the fly instead of given a priori. Observe that a contrasting pair (X_1, X_2) can also be given as a contrasting triple $(X_1 \cap X_2, X_1 - X_2, X_2 - X_1)$, as was done in [122]. Using the contrasting triple notation, we can see that a contrasting pair refers to a base condition X and two contrasting conditions $X_1 - X_2$ and $X_2 - X_1$ relative to the base.

Chapter 2

Statistical Measures for Contrast Patterns

James Bailey

Department of Computing and Information Systems, The University of Melbourne

2.1 Introduction

An important task when working with contrast patterns is the assessment of their quality or discriminative ability. In this chapter, we review a range of measures that may be used to assess the discriminative ability of contrast patterns. Some of these measures have their origins in association rules, others in statistics, and others in subgroup discovery. Our presentation is not exhaustive, since dozens of measures exist. Instead we present a selection that covers a number of the main types.

We will focus on the situation where just two classes are being contrasted. However, many of the measures can be extended in a straightforward way to deal with three or more classes. Work in [1] provides a useful survey of 16 different measures appropriate for the multi class case.

When considering how to assess discriminative ability, a key intuition is that a contrast pattern can be modeled as a binary feature (i.e. the pattern is either present or absent) of each instance/transaction in the data. Therefore, to assess discriminative ability, one may borrow from the large range of techniques which already exist for evaluating feature discrimination power between two classes.

2.1.1   Terminology

We first outline the scenario for transaction data. Let U_D be the universe of all items in the dataset D. A pattern is an itemset $I \subseteq U_D$. A transaction is a subset T of U_D and a dataset D is a set of transactions. A transaction T contains the contrast pattern I if $I \subseteq T$. The support of I in D is written as $support(I, D)$ and is equal to the percentage of transactions in D that contain I. The count of transactions in D that contain I is written as $count(I, D)$. For an itemset I in dataset D, we define $f_D(I) = \{T \in D | I \subseteq T\}$, that is all transactions in D containing I. Thus $|f_D(I)| = count(I, D)$.

An itemset X is a closed itemset in D if for every itemset Y such that $X \subset Y$, $support(Y, D) < support(X, D)$. X is a (minimal) generator in D if for every itemset Z such that $Z \subset X$, $support(Z, D) > support(X, D)$. Using these concepts, one may form equivalence classes for D, corresponding to sets of transactions. For each equivalence class, there is exactly one closed pattern and one or more generators. Both the closed pattern and the generators are contained in all transactions in their equivalence class.

For the case where the data is non-transactional (discrete attribute valued), then these definitions extend in the obvious way. A pattern I is then a conjunction of attribute values and $support(I, D)$ ($count(I, D)$) is the fraction (count) of instances in D for which I is true.

We will assume there exist two datasets, a positive dataset D_p and a negative dataset D_n. Given a pattern I, we need to assess its ability to contrast or discriminate between D_p versus D_n.

A useful structure we will need is the contingency table. Given I, one may construct a contingency table CT_{I, D_p, D_n}, representing the distribution of I across D_p and D_n:

	D_p	D_n	Sums
I	n_{11}	n_{12}	a_1
$\neg I$	n_{21}	n_{22}	a_2
Sums	$|D_p| = b_1$	$|D_n| = b_2$	$\sum_{ij} n_{ij} = N$

Here $n_{11} = count(I, D_p)$, $n_{12} = count(I, D_n)$, $n_{21} = |D_p| - n_{11}$ and $n_{22} = |D_n| - n_{12}$. Note that $support(I, D_p) = n_{11}/|D_p|$ and $support(I, D_n) = n_{12}/|D_n|$.

The *risk* of a contrast pattern I in a dataset D, denoted by $risk(I, D)$, is the probability that the pattern I occurs in D. It can be estimated using the ratio of the number of times I occurs in D to the size of D, i.e. equal to $support(I, D)$. The odds of a contrast pattern I in a dataset D, denoted by $odds(I, D)$, is the probability the pattern occurs in D divided by the probability it doesn't occur in D. It can be estimated by the ratio of the number of times the pattern occurs in D to the number of times it doesn't occur in D: $odds(I, D) = support(I, D)/(1 - support(I, D))$.

2.2 Measures for Assessing Quality of Discrete Contrast Patterns

We now examine measures of discrimination ability for the discrete case, where a contrast pattern either occurs or doesn't occur in each instance/transaction of D_p and D_n.

Confidence: This is a popular measure in the association rule community. It is aimed at assessing the predictive ability of the pattern for the positive class. Larger values are more desirable.

$$conf(I, D_p, D_n) = \frac{n_{11}}{N} = count(I, D_p)/count(I, D_p \cup D_n).$$

Here n_{11} is as defined in CT_{I,D_p,D_n}. Note that $conf$ is an estimate of the probability $Pr(D_p|I)$. When the sizes of D_p and D_n are very different, the confidence measure can be difficult to interpret.

Growth Rate or Relative Risk: This measure assesses the frequency ratio of the pattern between the two datasets. Larger values are more desirable.

$$GR(I, D_p, D_n) = support(I, D_p)/support(I, D_n).$$

It was used in [118] to measure the quality of emerging patterns. In [255] it is pointed out that growth rate is the same as the statistical measure known as *relative risk*, which is the ratio of the risk in D_p to the risk in D_n. i.e. $risk(I, D_p)/risk(I, D_n)$. It is shown in [197] that

$$GR(I, D_p, D_n) = \frac{conf(I, D_p, D_n)}{1 - conf(I, D_p, D_n)} \times \frac{|D_n|}{|D_p|}$$

and for fixed $\frac{|D_n|}{|D_p|}$ the growth rate increases monotonically with confidence (and vice versa). This helps explain why choosing patterns with high confidence values can be similar to choosing patterns with high growth rate.

Support Difference or Risk Difference: This assesses the absolute difference between the supports of the pattern in D_p and D_n. It was used in [42] as one of the measures for assessing the quality of contrast sets. Larger values are more desirable.

$$SD(I, D_p, D_n) = support(I, D_p) - support(I, D_n).$$

It is pointed out in [255] that this measure is the same as risk difference: $risk(I, D_p) - risk(I, D_n)$, that is popular in statistics.

Odds Ratio: This is analogous to the risk ratio and was proposed in [255, 239]. Odds ratios are popular for measuring effects in a clinical context. The odds ratio is the ratio of odds of the pattern I in D_p to the odds of the pattern I in D_n. Larger values are more desirable.

$$OddsRatio(I, D_p, D_n) = \frac{support(I, D_p)/(1 - support(I, D_p))}{support(I, D_n)/(1 - support(I, D_n))}.$$

Gain: This is a rule based measure that was used in the CPAR system [450]. Larger values are more desirable.

$$gain(I, D_p, D_n) = support(I, D_p) \times (\log \frac{support(I, D_p)}{support(I, D_p \cup D_n)} - \log \frac{|D_p|}{|D_p \cup D_n|}).$$

Length: This measure simply counts the number of items contained in the contrast pattern.

$$length(I, D_p, D_n) = |I|.$$

According to the minimum description length principle, it can be argued that shorter patterns are more desirable for discrimination [246]. From a clustering perspective, work in [277] argues that a cluster D_p which contains many short generator contrast patterns is good, since this implies it is significantly different from the other clusters D_n. Also, a cluster which contains many long closed contrast patterns is also good, since it is more likely to be coherent. Hence, one can assess the quality of a generator pattern of I in equivalence class e with a single value: the ratio [277] between the length of the (unique) closed pattern for e, divided by the length of I, i.e. $\frac{|I_e^c|}{|I|}$ (higher values are more desirable). Furthermore, one may also scale this according to the support value of the pattern, i.e. $support(I, D_p) \times \frac{|I_e^c|}{|I|}$.

Statistical Significance: Given the contingency table CT_{I,D_p,D_n} one may use classical statistical measures to test the null hypothesis that the occurrence of the pattern I and the dataset label are independent. One way to do this is by computing the chi-square statistic χ^2 and then deriving a p-value:

$$\chi^2 = \sum_{i=1}^{i=2} \sum_{j=1}^{j=2} \frac{(n_{ij} - E_{ij})^2}{E_{ij}},$$

where $E_{ij} = \frac{(\sum_{k=1}^{k=2} n_{ik}) \times (\sum_{k=1}^{k=2} n_{kj})}{N}$ is the expected frequency count in cell ij of the table. This test is used in [42] for assessing the significance of a contrast set. Smaller values of the statistic are more desirable.

Alternatively, for situations where the datasets are small or the counts in the contingency table are small, one may instead use the Fisher exact test [30]. This calculates the probability of finding a table where I is more positively associated with the dataset label.

$$p = \sum_{i=0}^{min(n_{12},n_{21})} \frac{a_1! a_2! |D_p|! |D_n|!}{N!(n_{11} + i)!(n_{12} - i)!(n_{21} - i)!(n_{22} + i)!}.$$

Smaller values of p are more desirable. When conducting significance tests for many contrast patterns, the issue of statistical correction for multiple testing arises. There are various approaches to this problem and a good discussion of the issues by Webb can be found in [430].

Mutual Information: This measures the information shared by the contrast pattern occurrence and the dataset label. It tells us how much knowing whether the contrast pattern occurs reduces our uncertainty about the dataset label and vice versa. Larger values are more desirable.

$$MI(I, D_p, D_n) = \sum_{i=1}^{i=2} \sum_{j=1}^{i=2} \frac{n_{ij}}{N} \log \frac{n_{ij}/N}{a_i b_j / N^2}.$$

Subgroup Discovery Measures: The field of subgroup discovery has investigated a number of interestingness measures for subgroups. These measures are similar to and can be used for assessment of contrast patterns and we mention two examples. The first is weighted relative accuracy [229], for which larger values are more desirable.

$$WRACC(I, D_p, D_n) = \frac{n_{11} + n_{12}}{|D_p| + |D_n|} \left(\frac{n_{11}}{n_{11} + n_{12}} - \frac{|D_p|}{N} \right).$$

It is shown in [319] that

$$\begin{aligned} &WRACC(I, D_p, D_n) \\ &= \frac{|D_p|}{(|D_p \cup D_n|)} \times \frac{|D_n|}{(|D_p \cup D_n|)} \times (support(I, D_p) - support(I, D_n)) \end{aligned}$$

thus closely connecting it to the support difference measure. Another subgroup interestingness measure is the generalization quotient [155], for which larger values are more desirable:

$$q_g(I, D_p, D_n) = \frac{n_{11}}{n_{12} + g},$$

where g is a user parameter. It is shown in [319] that

$$GR(I, D_p, D_n) = q_0(I, D_p, D_n) \times \frac{|D_n|}{|D_p|},$$

thus closely connecting the generalization quotient to the growth rate measure.

Assessing Sets of Contrast Patterns: Given a set of contrast patterns $I_1, \ldots, I_k$, an obvious approach for measuring their overall quality is to compute the average value of one of the above measures across all the patterns; for example, compute the average growth rate. Another approach is to compute the accuracy or area under the ROC curve when using the set of patterns for a supervised classification task. Alternatively, one may use a measure to assess the diversity of the pattern set (with higher diversity being desirable). Two metrics that have been proposed here [277] are item overlap between the contrast patterns (IO) and overlap of the data instances they are contained in (DO), for which lower values are more desirable:

$$IO(I_1, \ldots, I_k) = \frac{2}{k(k+1)} \sum_{i=1}^{k} \sum_{j=i+1}^{k} ovi(I_i, I_j)$$

where $ovi(I_i, I_j) = |I_i \cap I_j|$ (the number of items shared by I_i and I_j), and

$$DO(I_1, \ldots, I_k) = \frac{2}{k(k+1)} \sum_{i=1}^{k} \sum_{j=i+1}^{k} ovt(I_i, I_j)$$

where $ovt(I_i, I_j) = |f_D(I_i) \cap f_D(I_j)|$ (the number of transactions that both I_i and I_j are contained in).

2.3   Measures for Assessing Quality of Continuous Valued Contrast Patterns

We now examine the situation where the pattern corresponds to a continuous quantity. We refer to this as a contrast feature and the aim is to assess the discrimination ability of the contrast feature between D_p and D_n. We consider non-parametric measures. Let the values of the contrast feature in D_p be $x_1, \ldots, x_{|D_p|}$ and values in D_n be $y_1, \ldots, y_{|D_n|}$.

Signal to Noise Ratio: This is popular in the area of gene expression analysis [374]:

$$SNR = \frac{|\mu_{D_p} - \mu_{D_n}|}{\sigma_{D_p} + \sigma_{D_n}}$$

where μ_{D_i} is the mean value of the contrast feature in D_i and σ_{D_i} is its standard deviation. If the difference between the two means is large and the measure of variability (the denominator) is small, this indicates stronger discrimination or contrast.

Area under the ROC Curve (AUC): This views the contrast feature value as a ranking measure and assesses whether the instances in D_p tend to be ranked higher than those in D_n. In the simple case assuming no ties:

$$AUC = \frac{1}{|D_p| \times |D_n|} \sum_{i=1}^{|D_p|} \sum_{j=1}^{|D_n|} \mathbf{1}_{x_i > y_j}$$

where $\mathbf{1}_{x_i>y_j}$ is the indicator function equal to 1 if $x_i > x_y$ and 0 otherwise. It takes values in the range $[0, 1]$ where 0.5 corresponds to random performance. The value of the AUC is equivalent to the Wilcoxon Mann Whitney Statistic.

Kolmogorov Smirnov Test: This uses the maximal distance between cumulative frequency distributions of the feature in D_p and D_n as the statistic. Given the empirical distribution function for the contrast feature values in D_p $F_{D_p}(z) = \frac{1}{|D_p|} \sum_{i=1}^{i=|D_p|} \mathbf{1}_{x_i \leq z}$ and a similarly defined empirical distribution function for D_n, then the KS two sample test is defined as:

$$\sup_z |F_{D_p}(z) - F_{D_n}(z)|$$

where sup denotes the supremum operator.

Confidence Intervals: For these continuous contrast features, one often wishes to assess the reliability of measures. This may be done using by constructing intervals using methods such as bootstrap sampling or empirical likelihood [462].

2.4 Feature Construction and Selection: PCA and Discriminative Methods

One may also take a different perspective on discrimination ability and consider methods that select or construct groups of features that satisfy some discriminative objective function. Such methods include Principal Components Analysis (PCA), Linear Discriminant Analysis (LDA) and multivariate analysis of variance (MANOVA). We discuss each in turn.

The goal of PCA is to reduce the dimensionality of the data while retaining as much as possible of the variation present in the dataset. However, dimensionality reduction typically results in information loss. PCA produces a new feature space, where the features can be ranked according to the amount of variance they capture in the full feature space. PCA finds components that are useful for representing data. However, there is no basis to assume that the components have good ability to discriminate between classes, and interpretability of those components is an issue.

The goal of Linear Discriminant Analysis (LDA) is to perform dimensionality reduction whilst preserving as much of the class discriminatory information as possible. It seeks to find directions along which the classes are best separated and takes into consideration the scatter within-classes but also the scatter between-classes.

Discriminant function analysis (DA) is multivariate analysis of variance (MANOVA) reversed. In MANOVA, the independent variables are the groups and the dependent variables are the predictors. In discriminant analysis, the independent variables are the predictors and the dependent variables are the groups. DA is usually used to predict membership in naturally occurring groups; it answers the question: can a combination of variables be used to predict group membership? Discriminant function analysis is broken into a 2-step process: (1) testing significance of a set of discriminant functions, and (2) classification. The first step is computationally identical to MANOVA. There is a matrix of total variances and covariances; likewise, there is a matrix of pooled within-group variances and covariances. The two matrices are compared via multivariate F tests in order to determine whether or not there are any significant differences (with regard to all variables) between groups. One first performs the multivariate test, and, if statistically significant, proceeds to see which of the variables have significantly different means across the groups.

2.5   Summary

We have reviewed a range of measures for assessing the significance of contrasts. In our presentation, we have avoided "looking inside" the contrast pattern to assess the relationships between items or attribute values. Recent work in [144] presents an interesting approach in this direction and categorizes the different types of discrimination ability a pattern may possess. As one can see from our listing, many different measures for assessing contrast pattern quality exist and it is far from obvious which one(s) to prefer for a particular application. A possible heuristic here is to select one measure as the primary one for enumerating contrast patterns and then use other measures as filters for post processing the contrast pattern set that is mined. In general though, choosing appropriate interestingness measures is very challenging; it is likely to require domain knowledge insights and to require specifics of the nature of the problem/task at hand.

Part II

Contrast Mining Algorithms

Chapter 3

Mining Emerging Patterns Using Tree Structures or Tree Based Searches

James Bailey and Kotagiri Ramamohanarao

Department of Computing and Information Systems, The University of Melbourne

3.1 Introduction

In this chapter we consider the challenge of mining emerging patterns. In particular, we overview three approaches that can be used for mining a specific type of emerging pattern, known as a jumping emerging pattern. All approaches employ a tree structure to generate the patterns.

The idea to employ a tree for emerging pattern mining is natural, given the popularity and success of frequent pattern trees [180] for mining frequent patterns. One advantage is that the use of trees provides the ability to compress the input dataset(s) via sharing with common prefixes, thus allowing more data to be stored in memory for mining. The use of a tree contrasts with the generate and test approach for emerging pattern mining, as outlined in [464], which was based on the use of a set enumeration tree to explore the search space. Storing the datasets in a tree structure means that candidate assessment is only required for itemsets that are known to occur in the dataset and other parts of the itemset lattice need not be explored.

Compared to the task of mining frequent patterns though, mining emerging patterns brings some new challenges. Firstly, emerging patterns are defined with reference to both a positive and negative dataset. This necessitates the use of multiple counts to be kept per node, one per class (in contrast to frequent patterns which are defined using only a single dataset and thus only require a single count). Secondly, different pruning techniques are needed, since the a-priori property does not hold for emerging patterns. Thirdly, different methods for recursively processing conditional sub-trees may be needed, during search space exploration.

The first approach we mention is from [33] and we will refer to it as emerging pattern mining using a *ratio tree structure*. The second approach is from [141] and we refer to it as the *CP-tree structure* (contrast pattern tree structure). The third approach, *DPMiner*, is from [247] and employs concepts based on itemset equivalence classes (minimal generators and closed patterns) to enumerate emerging patterns. All three techniques use a tree structure inspired by the approach of [180] and we will assume familiarity with that work.

3.1.1   Terminology

We briefly review some definitions that will be required. If i is an itemset, then $support(i, D)$ is equal to the fraction of transactions in dataset D containing i. An *emerging pattern* is an itemset whose support in one set of data differs significantly from its support in another. Let z be an emerging pattern, let D_p be the positive dataset and let D_n be the negative dataset. The growth rate of z is $support(z, D_p)/support(z, D_n) = \rho$. If $suppport(z, D_p) = \xi$ and $support(z, D_n) = 0$, then z is called a ξ jumping emerging pattern (ξ-JEP). We say that z is a minimal ξ-JEP if there does not exist any other ξ-JEP z', for which $z' \subseteq z$. It is common to set ξ equal to $1/|D_p|$, which corresponds to mining all jumping emerging patterns occurring at least once in D_p and never in D_n. For the $\xi = 1/|D_p|$ case, we refer to the pattern simply as a jumping emerging pattern.

An itemset X is a closed itemset if for every itemset Y such that $X \subset Y$, $support(Y, D) < support(X, D)$. X is a (minimal) generator if for every itemset Z such that $Z \subset X$, $support(Z, D) > support(X, D)$. Using these concepts, one may form equivalence classes from a dataset D, corresponding to sets of transactions. For each equivalence class, there is exactly one closed pattern and one or more generators. Both the closed pattern and the generators are contained in all transactions in their equivalence class.

We will illustrate some of the ideas using the following simple transactional dataset:

ID	Class	Itemset (instance)
1	D_p	$\{v,x,y,z\}$
2	D_p	$\{v\}$
3	D_p	$\{w,z\}$
4	D_p	$\{w,x,y,z\}$
5	D_n	$\{v,w\}$
6	D_n	$\{x,z\}$
7	D_n	$\{v,w,x,y\}$
8	D_n	$\{y,z\}$

3.2 Ratio Tree Structure for Mining Jumping Emerging Patterns

As mentioned earlier, the first tree based data structure for mining JEPs that we examine is based on the frequent pattern tree [180]. A ratio tree is conceptually the same as a frequent pattern tree, except that extra counts are maintained in each node. Each node in the tree is associated with some itemset i and the node records the frequency of i in both D_p and D_n. At a high level, to mine all minimal emerging patterns, one traverses the tree, inspecting the counts at each node. When the node counts indicate a high disparity (ratio) between frequency in D_p and frequency in D_n, this means that there exists an itemset which is a candidate to be a JEP and then further assessment is recursively required.

An important choice in building a ratio tree is determining a global ordering for items, since this ordering will influence the shape of the tree. The quality of an ordering may be considered from two different angles: i) the ordering should minimize the total number of nodes in the tree (high compression), ii) the ordering should "push" JEPs higher up the tree, so that only shorter itemsets need to be examined during tree traversal. Three potential orderings that can be considered are:

- *Frequent tree ordering.* Order items according to their descending probability in $(D_p \cup D_n)$. This ordering aims to achieve high compression of the data via many shared prefixes in the tree.

- *Ratio ordering:* Let the probability of an item in D_p be p_1 and its probability in D_n be p_2. Order items in descending value of $p = p_1/p_2$. This ordering aims to "push" the JEPs higher up in the tree, compared to the frequent tree ordering, potentially allowing the JEPs to be discovered earlier, thus allowing more effective pruning of the bottom nodes in the tree.

- *Hybrid ordering:* This is a combination of the ratio tree ordering and the frequent tree ordering. Firstly, both the ratio tree ordering and frequent tree ordering are calculated. Then, given a user specified percentage α, the initial α percent of items are chosen according to the ratio tree ordering. All items not yet used are then ordered according to the frequent tree ordering. This ordering aims to create trees that possess a mix of both good compression characteristics and good tree pattern characteristics.

At a high level, the process for mining all jumping emerging patterns using the ratio tree is as follows: A ratio tree can be viewed as a forest of component trees, where each component tree is rooted by one of the items in $D_p \cup D_n$. Component trees are mined successively. Within a component tree, all prefixes (branches) in the tree are traversed in a depth first fashion. A prefix corresponds to some path in the component tree from its root item to some base node. If the base node contains a counter of at least 1 for D_p and a zero counter for D_n, then the itemset spanning from the root of the component tree to the base node is unique to D_p and hence is a potential JEP. In such a case, by projecting out all branches which share the same root item and base node within the component tree, we can obtain all the itemsets from D_p containing these two items, by traversing the side links of the tree. A diagram of the structure for the example dataset is shown in Figure 3.1.

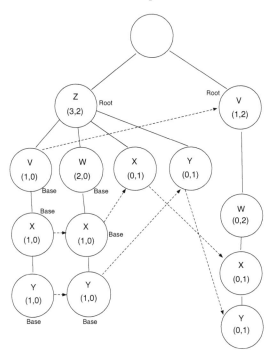

FIGURE 3.1: Ratio Tree for Example Dataset: Ordering is $z \prec v \prec w \prec x \prec y$. There is a root node for each component subtree. Base nodes correspond to nodes that can be reached following a path from the root and which have zero frequency in D_n and non zero frequency in D_p.

Once all negative itemsets for a given root and base node have been collected, they are then mined for JEPs using the border differential subroutine from [119]. This subroutine computes the minimal itemsets occurring in the itemset spanning from base to root and not occurring in any of these negative itemsets. Interestingly, this task is equivalent to computing all minimal transversals of a hypergraph using a classic technique first developed by Berge [35]. The border-differential approach of [119] can therefore be viewed as an optimized version of the Berge technique for minimal hypergraph transversal computation. Considering again Figure 3.1 when Z is the root and Y is the base. This is a potential JEP since Y has frequency 1 in D_p and 0 in D_n. The following transactions from D_n containing Z and Y are then projected out: $\{Z, Y\}$. The border differential procedure is then invoked to find the minimal itemsets containing both Z and Y, occurring in $\{Z, V, X, Y\}$ and not occurring in $\{Z, Y\}$. This yields $\{Z, V, Y\}$ and $\{Z, X, Y\}$ as JEPs. The item Z is then removed from $\{Z, V, X, Y\}$ and the itemset $\{V, X, Y\}$ is reinserted into the tree.

The ratio tree mining algorithm is designed to compute JEPs. For computing ξ-JEPs, it is necessary to perform post processing of the JEPs in order to check the ξ constraint. In practice, experimental analysis in [33] found that a hybrid ordering ($\alpha = 30\%$) was the most effective choice in reducing mining time.

3.3 Contrast Pattern Tree Structure

We now review a second algorithm from [141], for mining emerging patterns, based on the use of a contrast pattern tree. This algorithm discovers the complete set of ξ-JEPS.

A CP-tree is a tree storing all instances from both D_p and D_n. Items in the CP-tree are ordered according to the ratio ordering that was discussed in the previous ratio tree algorithm. Each instance corresponds to a path in the CP-tree from root to leaf and each node contains a set of items and counts for each item with respect to the frequency of the induced prefixes in D_p and D_n. Different from the ratio tree, children that share the same prefix are stored within the one node. Figure 3.2 shows the CP-tree for our example dataset, assuming the items have been ordered according to $z \prec v \prec w \prec x \prec y$. Note how at the second level from the top of the tree, the items v, w, x, and y are all placed in the same node, since they share the common prefix z. Compare this with the ratio tree in Figure 3.1, where each of these items occupies its own node.

Mining ξ-JEPs is accomplished by a depth first traversal of the tree, examining the candidates: $\{z\}, \{z, v\}, \{z, v, x\}, \{z, v, x, y\}, \{z, w\}, \{z, w, x\}, \{z, w, x, y\}, \{z, x\}, \{z, y\}, \{v\}, \{v, w\}, \{v, w, x\}, \{v, w, x, y\}$. The counts for each candidate may need to be computed by merging subtrees. For example, the counts for $\{z, y\}$ must be computed by examining both the $\{z, y\}$ path and the $\{z, w, x, y\}$ path. So when considering the candidate $\{z, y\}$, a merging operation is performed in order to correctly compute the counts for this itemset. We do not describe the details of the merge procedure here. Once the correct counts have been computed, it is then straightforward to determine whether the itemset is a ξ-JEP.

Experiments from [141] show that the CP-tree approach can outperform

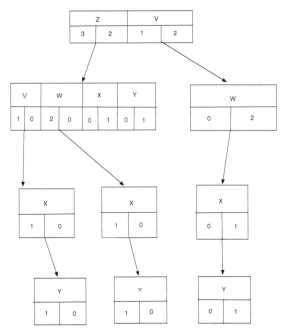

FIGURE 3.2: Contrast Pattern Tree for Example Dataset: Ordering is $z \prec v \prec w \prec x \prec y$. Based on [141], Copyright 2006, with permission from IEEE.

the ratio tree approach when ξ is approx. $\geq 1\%$ and it is somewhat slower when $\xi \leq 1\%$.

3.4 Tree Based Contrast Pattern Mining with Equivalence Classes

The third approach we mention was proposed in [247]. At a high level, they propose the DPMiner algorithm, which operates by enumerating the equivalence classes that are discriminative between D_p and D_n, using depth first traversal of the frequent pattern tree. Enumeration based on equivalence classes brings with it the advantage of a compressed representation. Each discriminative equivalence class can represented using its (unique) closed pattern and its generators. For an equivalence class, its associated patterns occur in exactly the same transactions for $D_p \cup D_n$ and one can also assess the frequencies in D_p and D_n separately, in order to measure discriminative power. DPMiner operates by enumerating the generators in parallel with the closed itemsets. By using an appropriate choice of thresholds and an appropriate measure of statistical significance, the generators of the equivalence classes correspond to precisely the ξ-jumping emerging patterns discriminating between D_p and D_n.

Similar to the algorithms we saw in Sections 3.2 and 3.3, nodes in the tree contain counters for the two classes D_p and D_n. Processing of the tree is somewhat similar to algorithms for mining closed patterns with frequent pattern trees, such as FPclose [167]. One interesting optimization is that the header table does not contain items which appear in every transaction of the database (or conditional projected database), because such items cannot be generators. This can substantially reduce the size of the tree that is needed. Also, unlike [167], techniques are used to avoid the need for extra checking of whether or not patterns are closed. In addition, to speed up computation, two hash tables are used. One hash table is used for storing generators and checking their minimality. The other hash table is used for storing closed itemsets, since each generator needs to be associated with the closed itemset that represents its equivalence class. Whenever a generator is identified, its closure is generated and a check is performed to determine whether or not the closure is already in the hash table. Otherwise the closure needs to be inserted. Due to its strategy of enumerating closed itemsets, DPMiner can also be used to efficiently enumerate the frequent closed itemsets and its performance in this regard is highly competitive with other algorithms for frequent closed pattern mining.

3.5   Summary and Conclusion

We have briefly reviewed three approaches for mining jumping emerging patterns based on the use of tree structures. All approaches are based on the use of a frequent pattern tree data structure. The key idea is that counts for both classes must be stored in each node of the tree. During tree traversal, it may be necessary to examine multiple branches of the tree in order to correctly compute the counts of the itemset prefix of the branch. The three approaches we have examined have been found to work well in practice, with DPMiner being the fastest overall, due to its sophisticated enumeration and search through the tree. DPMiner may also be deployed for mining more general patterns than ξ JEPs, known as δ discriminative patterns. Another approach that can be used for JEP mining is to adopt a more complex structure than a tree, known as a binary decision diagram. This will be discussed in the following chapter.

Chapter 4

Mining Emerging Patterns Using Zero-Suppressed Binary Decision Diagrams

James Bailey and Elsa Loekito

Department of Computing and Information Systems, The University of Melbourne

4.1 Introduction

In this chapter, we study the computation of emerging patterns using a sophisticated data structure, known as a zero-suppressed binary decision diagram (ZBDD). We will see how the ZBDD data structure can be used to enumerate emerging patterns. The advantage of ZBDDs lies in their ability to store input data or output patterns in a highly compressed form. This is particularly advantageous for high dimensional datasets, such as gene expression data, where the number of features is very large and the number of emerging patterns that are output can be huge. The ZBDD data structure provides an interesting alternative to popular structures such as the frequent pattern tree [180], whose variants have previously been proposed as an effective emerging pattern mining method [33, 141], and which were reviewed in Chapter 3. The presentation is based on our work in [283].

ZBDDs [298] are an extension of binary decision diagrams [61]. Binary decision diagrams are a graph based data structure that allows efficient representation and manipulation of boolean formulae, and they have proved extremely useful in a number of areas of computer science, such as SAT solvers [78], VLSI and reliability [352].

ZBDDs are an important type of binary decision diagrams and are particularly appropriate for compactly representing sparse data. From a data mining angle, ZBDDs have been shown to be useful for representing and manipulating input databases, and for storing output frequent patterns. Work in [301] showed that using ZBDDs for maintaining output patterns can improve the LCM algorithm for mining frequent itemsets. Work in [300] showed that ZBDDs are useful for post-processing operations on the patterns, such as pattern matching, and extracting length-k patterns. Work in [287, 284] showed how ZBDDs can be used for mining frequent patterns and frequent subsequences. In the following, we will first review background about the ZBDD data structure and then examine how it can be used for mining emerging patterns.

4.2   Background on Binary Decision Diagrams and ZBDDs

Binary Decision Diagrams are directed acyclic graphs which are compact representations of boolean formulae and they allow logical operations (AND, OR, XOR, etc.) to be performed in polynomial time with respect to the number of nodes. A Binary Decision Diagram is similar to a binary decision tree, except that identical sub-trees are merged, and node fan-in is allowed as well as fan-out. Binary Decision Diagrams have been widely used in the area of VLSI/CAD, and in the field of reliability engineering for fault-tree analysis.

More formally, a binary decision diagram, BDD, is a canonical directed acyclic graph consisting of one source node, multiple internal nodes, and two sink nodes which are labelled as 0 and 1 respectively. Every node is labelled. An internal node N with a label x, denoted by $N = node(x, N_1, N_0)$, encodes the boolean formula $N = (x \wedge N_1) \vee (\overline{x} \wedge N_0)$, where N_1 (resp. N_0) is the 1-child (resp. 0-child) of N. The edge connecting a node to its 1-child (resp. $0 - child$) is also called the true-edge (false-edge). In the illustrations shown shortly, the solid lines correspond to true-edges whereas dotted lines correspond to false-edges. Each path from the root node to sink-1 (resp. sink-0) gives a true (resp. false) assignment for the represented formula.

Two important properties of a BDD which explain the efficiency of its operations include: (1) identical subtrees are shared, (2) intermediate results from past computations are stored as much as possible. So in general, a high degree of node sharing is achieved by the BDD and this helps ensure that the worst-case complexity of most operations is polynomial with respect to the number of nodes.

A Zero-suppressed Binary Decision Diagram is a special type of BDD, introduced by Minato in [298] for set-manipulation in combinatorial problems. A survey on the applications of ZBDDs can be found in [299]. ZBDDs are particularly appropriate for compactly representing sparse data, such as itemsets, making them attractive for itemset enumeration tasks in data mining.

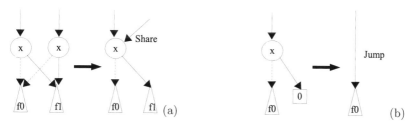

FIGURE 4.1: (a) Merging rule; (b) Zero-suppression rule. Based on [283], Copyright 2006, with permission from ACM.

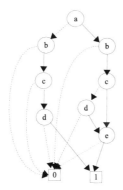

FIGURE 4.2: ZBDD representation of a set of itemsets $\{\{a, b, c, e\}, \{a, b, d, e\}, \{b, c, d\}\}$. Based on [283], Copyright 2006, with permission from ACM.

A ZBDD imposes a variable ordering such that the label of each node must be of lower index than the labels of its children. ZBDDs employ the following two reduction rules (see illustrations in Fig 4.1):

1. Merging rule: share all equivalent subtrees (to obtain canonicity).

2. Zero-suppression rule: eliminate all nodes whose true-edge points to the sink-0 node, and bypass the incoming links to the node's 0-child.

The zero-suppression rule is effective, since the characteristic functions represented by ZBDDs are monotonic boolean functions, i.e. do not contain negated variables or terms. Thus, negative variables are not necessary and their corresponding nodes may be eliminated.

Using these rules allows a boolean formula to be represented with high compression. An n variable formula has a space of 2^n truth values. However, the corresponding ZBDD can have exponentially fewer nodes.

A collection of itemsets can be mapped into a Boolean space. Given a domain of n items, a set of itemsets can be represented as a Boolean function by using n input boolean variables for each bit in the itemset. The output

TABLE 4.1: Primitive operations on ZBDDs P and Q. Based on [283], Copyright 2006, with permission from ACM.

0	The empty set, $\emptyset$
1	The set of an empty itemset, $\{\emptyset\}$
$P \bigcup_Z Q$	Union of P and Q
$P \cap_Z Q$	Intersection of P and Q
$P \bigcup_{Z_{min}}$	Minimal union of P and Q
$P \setminus Q$	Subtraction of Q from P
$notSupSet(P, Q)$	Subtraction from P of any itemset which is is a superset of an itemset in Q

value, 1 or 0, expresses whether each item-combination specified by the input variables is included in the set or not. Formally, an itemset p is represented by a n-bit binary vector $X = (x_1; x_2; \ldots; x_n)$, here $x_i = 1$ if item i is contained in p. The characteristic function for a set S of itemsets is the function $X_S : \{0,1\}^n \to \{0,1\}$. Here $X_S(p) = 1$ if $p \in S$, and $X_S(p) = 0$ otherwise.

In ZBDD semantics, a node $N = (x, N_1, N_0)$ represents a set S of itemsets such that $S = S_0 \cup (S_1 \times \{x\})$, where S_1 and S_0 are the sets of itemsets encoded by N_1 and N_0, respectively. An itemset p in S is interpreted as a conjunction of the items contained in p and yields a true assignment for the boolean formula encoded by N. A ZBDD consisting of only the sink-0 node encodes the empty set ($\emptyset$), and a ZBDD consisting of only the sink-1 node encodes the set of empty itemsets ($\{\emptyset\}$).

Basic set and itemset operations for ZBDDs that we will use are *union* $(A \cup B)$, *difference* $(A \setminus B)$, and *intersection* $(A \cap B)$. They have been defined formally in [298] and are polynomial in the number of nodes in the ZBDD. They are listed in Table 4.1.

Example 4.1 *The ZBDD encoding for a set of itemsets:* $\{\{a, b, c, e\},$ $\{a, b, d, e\}, \{b, c, d\}\}$ *is shown in Figure 4.2 (assume lexicographic variable ordering). This set can also be expressed as a DNF formula:* $(a \wedge b \wedge c \wedge e) \vee (a \wedge b \wedge d \wedge e) \vee (b \wedge c \wedge d)$.

Variable Ordering: Depending on the function being represented, the number of nodes in a ZBDD may be highly sensitive to its variable ordering. Work in [299] showed that a good variable ordering for compact BDDs (and ZBDDs) has two properties: i. groups of inputs that are closely related should be kept near to each other; ii. inputs that greatly affect the function should be located at higher positions in the structure.

It is highly challenging to find an optimal variable ordering. One pragmatic approach is to find an appropriate ordering before generating the binary decision diagram by adopting some heuristics [154]. Another approach is to start with an initial ordering and permute the variables as the BDD is constructed [356]. The latter approach is usually more effective than the former, but it consumes much of the computation time. In the algorithm we show shortly, we use the former approach, by computing statistics about the frequency of the variables in the input datasets.

4.3   Mining Emerging Patterns Using ZBDDs

We will next describe how ZBDDs can be used for mining emerging patterns. Before doing so though, we need to formally specify the type of emerging pattern that will be mined.

Given a positive dataset D_p, a negative dataset D_n, and support thresholds α and β, an Emerging Pattern (EP) is an itemset p satisfying two support constraints, i) $support(p, D_n) < \beta$ and ii) $support(p, D_p) \geq \alpha$. Furthermore, p is a minimal EP if p is minimal in the sense that it does not contain any other itemset that also satisfies constraints i) and ii). Note that in [118], emerging patterns were defined using an α threshold and a growth rate ρ. We choose instead to use a β threshold, rather than ρ. This can capture the most popular important type of emerging pattern, known as the jumping emerging pattern, for which $\alpha = 1$ and $\rho = \infty$, or equivalently $\alpha = 1$ and $\beta = 1$. (Here α and β should be viewed as support counts.)

We next describe a ZBDD based algorithm for mining emerging patterns. Characteristics of the ZBDD that make it particularly suitable for data mining are its compact structure and its efficiency in performing set operations. We can use it as a generator for pattern candidates and also for storage of the output patterns (i.e. the itemsets which satisfy the given constraints). This is similar to existing data mining methods which use structures such as FP-trees [180] and Pattern trees [141]. The search space is dictated by the contents of the negative dataset and patterns are extended in a depth-first fashion. We will refer to the partially extended patterns as *prefixes*. The output ZBDD stores the minimal emerging patterns and it is constructed bottom-up. To increase the efficiency of the algorithm, a number of pruning strategies are employed within the mining algorithm.

Early pruning of invalid candidates: In principle, a mining algorithm could examine a search space covering all possible itemset combinations. However, this is unnecessary and instead we traverse a search space which avoids generating candidate patterns which could never satisfy the β constraint. For any given prefix p (candidate), we can partition D_n into the set of transactions definitely not containing p ($D_n^{\overline{p}}$) and transactions which do contain p (D_n^p). At each step, if p needs extending, then it only needs to be extended by an item which is not from at least one of the transactions in D_n^p, i.e. from the complement of one of the transactions in D_n^p (otherwise a non minimal pattern will result). It is therefore profitable for the input ZBDD to consist of the complements of the transactions in D_n (i.e. $\overline{D_n}$). Traversing a ZBDD based on $\overline{D_n}$ ensures that the candidate generation space is much smaller. This pruning method is particularly effective if $|D_n|$ is relatively small, as is often the case for biological data.

α **constraint pruning**: This strategy is based on the well-known anti-monotonicity, or a-priori principle. Any prefix which doesn't satisfy the α constraint should have its supersets pruned. Also, as a pre-processing step, any item whose $support(D_p) < \alpha$ can be deleted from D_p and D_n.

β **constraint pruning**: This strategy is based on the monotonicity of the β constraint. If a prefix satisfies the β constraint, then it is not necessary to extend it any further, since a non-minimal pattern would result.

Non minimal pattern pruning: Since the final output is required to only consist of minimal patterns, it is profitable to immediately prune any non-minimal patterns, once it can be determined that they are not globally minimal.

The ZBDD algorithm for finding minimal emerging patterns is shown in Algorithm 1. We explain the algorithm line by line. The first parameter to the algorithm, P, is stored as a ZBDD. $prefix$ is the partially extended pattern; it satisfies the α constraint, but fails the β constraint. D_p and D_n correspond to the bitmaps from the respective dataset and are used as the method for computing $support$.

The algorithm is invoked by calling $mineEP(\overline{D_n}, prefix = \{\}, D_p, D_n, \alpha, \beta)$. It is called recursively on projections of $\overline{D_n}$ as the pattern candidates are explored.

Lines $1-8$ in the algorithm state the terminal condition of the recursion. When it reaches a sink node, 0 or 1, it has reached the end of the search space for extending the given $prefix$. If $prefix$ passes the β constraint, i.e. $support(prefix, D_n) \le \beta$, then accept $prefix$ as a minimal emerging pattern. Otherwise $prefix$ cannot be part of the output ZBDD (and so the the sink-0 node is returned).

The two core operations in the algorithm are computing $zOut_x$, which extends $prefix$ with the next item found in the candidates, and computing $zOut_{\overline{x}}$ which explores the remainder of the search space. They will each be the subtrees in the resulting ZBDD output.

Before attempting to extend $prefix$ with the next item, x, the algorithm first tests whether the α and β prunings can be performed. Line 14 prunes $prefix \cup \{x\}$ and its supersets by the α-constraint pruning. Lines 17 uses β-constraint pruning to stop $prefix$ from being extended. Finally, if none of these two cases is applicable, x is appended to the $prefix$ and instances of P which do not contain x are explored, storing the output in $zOut_x$.

Line 26 computes $zOut_{\overline{x}}$. The generated patterns in $zOut_x$ and in $zOut_{\overline{x}}$ are locally minimal, but may not be globally minimal. Non-minimal pattern elimination is performed by a primitive ZBDD operation $notSupSet$ (Line 29).

Optimizations: For the case where $\beta = 1$ (which corresponds to the common and important case of jumping emerging patterns), the computation of $zOut_x$

Algorithm 1: mineEP(P, $prefix$, D_p, D_n, α, β)

---

1 Invoke mineEP($D_n^{\overline{p}}$, {}, D_p, D_n, α, β) to begin mining initially.

Require: P : a ZBDD of the search space containing a complemented projection of the negative dataset

$prefix$: a prefix itemset which project P

D_p : Bitmap of the positive dataset

D_n : Bitmap of the negative dataset

α : a min support (wrt. D_p) threshold

β : a max support (wrt. D_n) threshold

Ensure: $zOut$: a ZBDD representing the set of minimal emerging patterns i satisfying $support(i, D_p) \geq \alpha$ and $support(i, D_n) < \beta$.

1: **if** P is a ZBDD sink node, **then**
2:     // Terminal case
3:     // Reaches end of the search space for extending $prefix$
4:     // return $prefix$ as a minimal EP if it passes β constraint
5:     **if** $support(prefix, D_n) < \beta$ **then**
6:         **return** 1
7:     **else**
8:         **return** 0 // Remove $prefix$ from the output ZBDD
9:     **end if**
10: **else**
11:     // Let $P = node(x, P_1, P_0)$
12:     // Grow $prefix$ with the next item in the search space
13:     $prefix_{new} = prefix \cup \{x\}$
14:     **if** $support(prefix_{new}, D_p) < \alpha$, **then**
15:         // α constraint pruning: prune $prefix_{new}$
16:         $zOut_x = 0$
17:     **else if** $support(prefix_{new}, D_n) < \beta$ **then**
18:         // β constraint pruning: stop extending $prefix_{new}$
19:         $zOut_x = 1$
20:     **else**
21:         // Explore supersets of $prefix_{new}$ from instances not containing x
22:         $zOut_x = mineEP(P_0, prefix_{new}, D_p, D_n, \alpha, \beta)$
23:     **end if**
24:
25:     // Explore candidates from the remaining search space
26:     $zOut_{\overline{x}} = mineEP(P_0 \bigcup_Z P_1, prefix, D_p, D_n, \alpha, \beta)$
27:
28:     // Non-minimal patterns elimination
29:     $zOut_x = notSupSet(zOut_x, zOut_{\overline{x}})$
30:     $zOut = getNode(x, zOut_x, zOut_{\overline{x}})$
31: **end if**

(line 26 in the algorithm) can be optimized by passing it the minimal union between P_0 and P_1, i.e. $P_0 \bigcup_{Z_{min}} P_1$. As a result, the computed $zOut_x$ only contains patterns which may be non-minimal by the item $\{x\}$. Thus, line 29 in the algorithm can be replaced by a set-difference operation $zOut_x \setminus zOut_{\overline{x}}$ which is a less complex operation. This optimization cannot be used in the general case when $\beta > 0$, since it could eliminate valid pattern candidates.

Optimal variable ordering: One may investigate a number of heuristics for finding the optimal variable ordering for an efficient performance of $mineEP$, using information about the item frequencies in D_p and D_n. Two alternative ordering strategies are natural starting points.

The first heuristic places the least frequent item in D_p at the top of the ZBDD, with subsequent items being ordered by increasing support in D_p. This aims to achieve early α support threshold pruning based on D_p, by locating items which are more likely to be pruned, higher up in the structure.

The second heuristic places the least frequent item in D_n (i.e. occurring most frequently in $\overline{D_n}$) as the first item in the ZBDD, with other items being ordered by increasing frequency in D_n This can be justified on two levels. Firstly, consider line 22 in the algorithm. Having a smaller P_0 here is likely to be advantageous, particularly when the ZBDD at that point is large. Using the most frequent item in $\overline{D_n}$ at the top of the tree, means that P_0 is likely to be small for the early recursive calls. Secondly, this heuristic gives higher preference to the β constraint, in a similar manner to that for the α constraint in the first heuristic, the aim being to achieve early β-constraint pruning.

4.4   Discussion and Summary

We have described a ZBDD based approach for mining emerging patterns. We saw how the ZBDD data structure could be used for storing both input transactions and output patterns and presented a search procedure for traversing the ZBDD, using various pruning techniques. Experimental results in [283] show this approach is highly effective for computing emerging patterns and outperforms a tree based approach from [141]. It performs particularly strongly for gene expression datasets, which are challenging to mine due to their high dimensionality.

It is interesting to note that the ZBDD data structure may also be used for mining other types of emerging patterns. Loekito et al. in [283] show how it can be used for mining disjunctive emerging patterns. These generalize emerging patterns by allowing disjunctions, as well as conjunctions in pattern descriptions and correspond to a restricted class of CNF formulae. This is discussed in Chapter 8 and explored in [286]. Other variants of ZBDDs, known as weighted ZBDDs may also be used for mining emerging patterns and these are further described in [282].

Chapter 5

Efficient Direct Mining of Selective Discriminative Patterns for Classification

Hong Cheng

Department of Systems Engineering and Engineering Management, The Chinese University of Hong Kong

Jiawei Han

Department of Computer Science, University of Illinois at Urbana-Champaign

Xifeng Yan

Department of Computer Science, University of California at Santa Barbara

Philip S. Yu

Department of Computer Science, University of Illinois at Chicago

This chapter considers the efficient direct mining of discriminative patterns. Here, by discriminative patterns we mean those patterns that can be used as features by some classification algorithms, to produce highly accurate classifiers. The direct mining approach pushes the constraints implied by "to serve as feature set" for classification into the mining process. As will be discussed below, direct mining algorithms can significantly outperform two-step algorithms (which first mine patterns and then select a subset of the mined patterns as discriminative patterns). More specifically, this chapter will discuss two direct mining algorithms, in addition to giving an overview of some recent results in this direction.

5.1 Introduction

Frequent pattern based classification has been explored in recent years and its power was demonstrated by multiple studies in several domains, including (1) associative classification [270, 126, 258, 95, 421] on categorical data, where a classifier is built based on high-support, high-confidence association rules; and (2) frequent pattern based classification [221, 106, 88] on data with complex structures such as sequences and graphs, where discriminative frequent patterns are taken as features to build high quality classifiers. A frequent itemset (pattern) is a set of items that occur in a dataset no less than a user-specified minimum support *min_sup*, which can be the absolute minimum support count, or the relative minimum support ratio. Discriminative patterns are those patterns that can be used as features by some classification algorithms, to produce highly accurate classifiers.

The above mentioned studies achieve promising classification accuracy and demonstrate the success of frequent patterns (or association rules) in classification. For example, in [270, 258, 421], associative classification was found to be competitive with traditional classification methods, such as C4.5 and SVM, sometimes even better on categorical datasets [95]. In addition, frequent patterns are also promising for classifying complex structures such as graphs [221, 106, 88] with high accuracy.

Most of these studies [270, 126, 258, 95, 88, 106] take a *two-step* process: First mine all frequent patterns or association rules whose supports $\geq$ *min_sup* and then perform a feature selection or rule ranking procedure. Figure 5.1 (A)

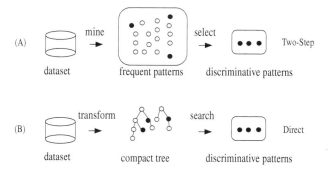

FIGURE 5.1: Two-Step Approach (A) vs. Direct Pattern Mining (B). Source: Reprinted from Ref. [89], Copyright 2008, with permission from IEEE.

shows the flow of the two-step framework, where a dark circle represents one discriminative pattern. Although the approach is straightforward and achieves high classification accuracy, it could incur high computational cost. The efficiency issues exist in the following two aspects.

First, frequent pattern mining could take a long time to complete due to the exponential combinations among items, which is common for dense datasets or high-dimensional data. When the problem scale is large or min_sup is low, it could take a long time to complete the mining. It often turns out that the mining results, even those for closed frequent itemsets, grow exponentially.

More importantly, the classification tasks attach great importance to the frequent itemsets that are highly discriminative w.r.t. the class labels. Since frequent itemsets are generated solely based on support information, not based on discriminative power, a large number of indiscriminative itemsets can be generated during the mining step. When the complete mining results are prohibitively large, yet only the highly discriminative ones are of real interest, it is inefficient to wait for a long time for the mining algorithm to finish and then apply feature selection to post-process the huge set of mining results. Even for a feature selection algorithm with linear complexity, it could be very expensive to process a large number, such as millions, of features which is a common scale in frequent patterns.

The computational cost raised by the two-step framework motivates researchers to investigate an alternative approach: *Instead of generating the complete set of frequent patterns, directly mine highly selective discriminative patterns for classification.* Figure 5.1 (B) illustrates the direct mining methodology which first transforms data into a compact search tree, e.g., FP-tree [180], and then searches discriminative patterns directly. In this chapter, we review two direct discriminative pattern mining approaches, DDPMine by Cheng et al. [89] and HARMONY by Wang and Karypis [421], and a few follow-up works [142, 207, 160]. The direct discriminative pattern mining approaches are shown to outperform the two-step method with significant speedup.

5.2   DDPMine: Direct Discriminative Pattern Mining

In the DDPMine approach, there are two objectives we want to achieve: (1) for efficiency concerns, we want to directly mine a set of highly discriminative patterns; and (2) for accuracy consideration, we impose a *feature coverage* constraint: every training instance has to be covered by one or more features.

DDPMine developed two modules to meet these two objectives: (1) a branch-and-bound search method to identify the most discriminative pattern in a data set; (2) an instance elimination process to remove the training instances that are covered by the patterns selected so far. The branch-and-bound search algorithm is based on the upper bound estimation of discriminative measures derived from previous work [88], which is able to prune the search space effectively.

DDPMine progressively reduces the dataset size by iteratively eliminating training instances. This expedites the mining process since the mining complexity is closely related to the dataset size.

Both processes are actually implemented in a compact tree structure, FP-Tree, and are able to avoid the generation of the complete pattern set.

5.2.1   Branch-and-Bound Search

An upper bound of discriminative measures such as *information gain* was derived by [88] which is a function of pattern frequency. The discriminative power of low-frequency patterns is upper bounded by a small value. Based on this conclusion, we design a branch-and-bound search for directly mining discriminative patterns and pruning the indiscriminative ones. We adopt FP-growth [180] as the basic mining methodology and show how to incorporate the theoretical upper bound to facilitate a branch-and-bound search. For details of FP-growth mining, please refer to [180].

The basic idea is, during the recursive FP-growth mining, we use a global variable to record the most discriminative itemset discovered so far and its information gain score. Before proceeding to construct a conditional FP-tree, we first estimate the upper bound of information gain, given the size of the conditional database. Since the support of any itemset from this conditional database cannot be greater than the conditional database size, the information gain of any itemset from this conditional database is bounded by the upper bound value. If the upper bound value is no greater than the current best value, we can safely skip this conditional FP-tree as well as any FP-tree recursively constructed from it. Algorithm 1 shows the branch-and-bound mining algorithm. $IG(\beta)$ on line 6 is the information gain of frequent pattern β and $IG_{ub}(|D_\beta|)$ on line 10 is the information gain upper bound given the conditional database D_β. The upper bound formulae were derived in [88].

We will illustrate this method through the following example. Table 5.1

Algorithm 1 The Branch-and-bound Mining Algorithm

Input: An FP-tree P, min_sup s, a prefix α
Output: The most discriminative feature $bestPat$
Global variable: $maxIG := 0$, $bestPat := null$

Procedure $branch\_and\_bound(P, s, \alpha)$
1: **if** $P = \emptyset$
2:     **return**;
3: **for** each item a_i in P **do**
4:     generate pattern $\beta = a_i \cup \alpha$ with $\mathsf{supp}(\beta) = \mathsf{supp}(a_i)$;
5:     compute information gain $IG(\beta)$;
6:     **if** $IG(\beta) > maxIG$
7:         $maxIG := IG(\beta)$;
8:         $bestPat := \beta$;
9:     construct pattern β's conditional database D_β;
10:    $IG_{ub}(|D_\beta|) := upper\_bound(|D_\beta|)$;
11:    **if** $maxIG \geq IG_{ub}(D_\beta)$
12:       skip mining on D_β;
13:    **else**
14:       construct β's conditional FP-tree P_β;
15:       $branch\_and\_bound(P_\beta, s, \beta)$;

---

shows a training database which contains eight instances and two classes. Let $min\_sup = 0.25$. The global FP-tree is illustrated in Figure 5.2. The FP-tree is a compact prefix-tree structure. A node represents an item with the count and a path represents a transaction.

TABLE 5.1: A Sample Training Database D. Source: Reprinted from Ref. [89], Copyright 2008, with permission from IEEE.

TID	Set of Items	Class Label
100	a, b, c	1
200	a, b, c, d	1
300	a, b, c	1
400	a, b, d	1
500	c, d	0
600	b, c	0
700	a, b, c	1
800	a, b, c	1

The first frequent itemset generated is d with an information gain value $IG(d) = 0.016$. Then $maxIG$ is assigned 0.016. The conditional database and FP-tree on d is shown in Figure 5.3. Given the size of the conditional database is 3, the information gain upper bound is $IG_{ub}(3) = 0.467$. Since $IG_{ub}(3) >$

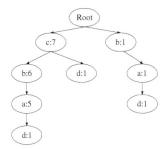

FIGURE 5.2: The Global FP-tree. Source: Reprinted from Ref. [89], Copyright 2008, with permission from IEEE.

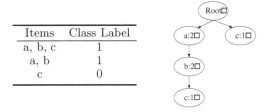

Items	Class Label
a, b, c	1
a, b	1
c	0

FIGURE 5.3: Conditional DB and FP-tree on d. Source: Reprinted from Ref. [89], Copyright 2008, with permission from IEEE.

$maxIG$, we cannot prune the conditional FP-tree on d. Therefore, we perform recursive mining on the conditional FP-tree and get ad, bd, cd, and abd, with $IG(ad) = 0.123$, $IG(bd) = 0.123$, $IG(cd) = 0.074$ and $IG(abd) = 0.123$.

As the mining proceeds to the frequent itemset a, we can compute its information gain $IG(a) = 0.811$ which is assigned to $maxIG$ as well. The conditional database and FP-tree on a is shown in Figure 5.4. Given the size of the conditional database is 6, the information gain upper bound is $IG_{ub}(6) = 0.811$. Since $maxIG = IG_{ub}(6)$, any itemset generated from the conditional FP-tree will have an information gain no greater than $maxIG$. Therefore, the conditional FP-tree can be pruned without any mining. To confirm our analysis, we could double check the actual mining results from this conditional FP-tree: ab, ac, ad, abd, and abc. A careful verification shows that the information gain of all these itemsets is no greater than $maxIG$, which is consistent with our pruning decision.

5.2.2   Training Instance Elimination

The branch-and-bound search directly mines the discriminative patterns and effectively prunes the search space. To achieve the feature coverage objective that ensures every training instance is covered by one or multiple features, we propose a feature-centered approach to generate features and shrink the feature search space.

Items	Class Label
b, c	1
b, c, d	1
b, c	1
b, d	1
b, c	1
b, c	1

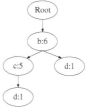

FIGURE 5.4: Conditional DB and FP-tree on a. Source: Reprinted from Ref. [89], Copyright 2008, with permission from IEEE.

Algorithm 2 The DDPMine Algorithm

Input: An FP-tree P, *min_sup s*
Output: A set of selected features F_s

Procedure DDPMine(P, s)
1: **if** $P = \emptyset$
2:     **return**;
3: $\alpha := branch\_and\_bound(P, s, null)$;
4: **if** $\alpha = null$
5:     **return**;
6: Compute the transaction id list $T(\alpha)$ containing α;
7: $P' := update\_tree(P, T(\alpha))$;
8: $F_s := \{\alpha\} \cup$ DDPMine(P', s);
9: **return** F_s;

The basic idea is, a branch-and-bound search produces the most discriminative itemset α. Then we eliminate the set of transactions which contain the itemset α, i.e., $T(\alpha)$, from the FP-tree and repeat the branch-and-bound search on the updated tree. This process iterates until all transactions are removed from the FP-tree. This approach is feature-centered in the sense that the mining process only concerns mining the most discriminative pattern.

The DDPMine algorithm, which integrates the branch-and-bound search and the feature-centered approach, is presented in Algorithm 2. It takes two inputs: an FP-tree and *min_sup*. An initial FP-tree is constructed from the training database. *branch_and_bound* searches the most discriminative feature α. Then the transaction set $T(\alpha)$ containing α is computed and removed from P. The resulting FP-tree is P'. Then DDPMine is recursively invoked on P' until the FP-tree becomes empty. If the *branch_and_bound* search function fails to discover any feature w.r.t. *min_sup* in the current FP-tree, the whole procedure terminates. The final output is the set of frequent itemsets generated by the iterative mining process.

Correspondingly, the running-time cost associated with DDPMine is

$$Cost = n \cdot (T_{mining} + T_{check\_db} + T_{update}) \qquad (5.1)$$

where n is the number of iterations which is usually very small. We will derive an upper bound of n in Section 5.2.3. T_{update} is the time to update the FP-tree. We design an efficient method for the update operation in Section 5.2.2.1.

5.2.2.1 Progressively Shrinking FP-Tree

One step in the DDPMine algorithm is *update_tree*, which removes the set of training instances $T(\alpha)$ containing the feature α from the FP-tree. We design an efficient method for update_tree operation with the corresponding data structure.

When we insert a training instance into an FP-tree, we register the transaction id of this instance at the node which corresponds to the very last item in the instance. Accordingly, the FP-tree carries training instance id lists. Due to efficiency concerns, the id lists are only registered with the global FP-tree, but not propagated in the conditional FP-trees when performing the recursive FP-growth mining.

When a frequent itemset α is generated, the training instances $T(\alpha)$ have to be removed from the global FP-tree. Then we perform a traversal of the FP-tree and examine the id lists associated with the tree nodes. When an id in a node appears in $T(\alpha)$, this id is removed. Correspondingly, the count on this node is reduced by 1, as well as the count on all the ancestor nodes up to the root of the tree. When the count reaches 0 at any node, the node is removed from the FP-tree. Clearly, the *update* operation basically is a traversal of the FP-tree. Thus, the complexity of this operation is

$$T_{update} = O(|V| + |D|) \qquad (5.2)$$

where $|V|$ is the number of nodes in the FP-tree and $|D|$ is the number of training instances in the database.

In our previous example, when we discover the itemset a with $T(a) = \{100, 200, 300, 400, 700, 800\}$, $T(a)$ are removed from the FP-tree. Figure 5.5 shows the updated tree where the gray nodes are the nodes with 0 count and will be removed from the updated tree. The rectangle boxes are the transaction id lists associated with the nodes. Since the global FP-tree is updated incrementally in each iteration, we call it the *progressively shrinking FP-tree*.

5.2.2.2 Feature Coverage

In the DDPMine algorithm, when a feature is generated, the transactions containing this feature are removed. In real classification tasks, we may want to generate multiple features to represent a transaction for accuracy consideration. To realize this purpose, we introduce a feature coverage parameter δ: A transaction is eliminated from further consideration when it is covered

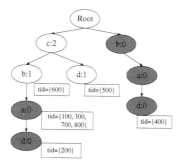

FIGURE 5.5: The Updated FP-tree with TID. Source: Reprinted from Ref. [89], Copyright 2008, with permission from IEEE.

by at least δ features. This feature could be easily integrated into DDPMine with some minor changes in the data structure: We keep a counter for each transaction. Whenever a feature is generated, the counter for each transaction containing this feature is incremented by one. When a counter reaches δ, the corresponding transaction is removed from the tree. The counters are stored in an array of integers, called *CTable*.

Besides the counter, we need to keep a global hash table, called *HTable*, to keep track of the features that are already discovered. When $\delta > 1$, a transaction will not be eliminated unless the counter reaches δ. As a result, the FP-tree may remain unchanged when no transactions are eliminated in one iteration. In such a case, we need to use a hash table to keep track of the features that are already discovered and thus avoid generating the same features multiple times. Let's follow the example in Table 5.1 and assume $\delta = 2$. In the first iteration, we generate the feature a. The CTable and HTable are shown in Figure 5.6. Since no counter reaches $\delta = 2$, no transaction is removed from the FP-tree. Thus, it remains unchanged.

TID	Count
100	1
200	1
300	1
400	1
500	0
600	0
700	1
800	1

FID	Items	Info Gain
1	a	0.811

FIGURE 5.6: CTable and HTable at Iteration 1. Source: Reprinted from Ref. [89], Copyright 2008, with permission from IEEE.

In the following iterations, the HTable will be checked for duplication whenever a new feature is discovered. If there is a "hit" in the HTable, the new feature will be ignored and the mining proceeds. In the second itera-

TID	Count
100	2
200	2
300	2
400	2
500	0
600	0
700	2
800	2

FID	Items	Info Gain
1	a	0.811
2	ab	0.811

FIGURE 5.7: CTable and HTable at Iteration 2. Source: Reprinted from Ref. [89], Copyright 2008, with permission from IEEE.

tion of this example, the mining algorithm first discovers a which exists in HTable already. Then the algorithm ignores it and proceeds. Finally, it generates ab as the most discriminative feature. After ab is generated, the CTable and HTable are changed and shown in Figure 5.7. Accordingly, transactions $\{100, 200, 300, 400, 700, 800\}$ are removed from the FP-tree.

5.2.3   Efficiency Analysis

DDPMine works in an iterative way and terminates when the training database becomes empty. We derive an upper bound of the number of iterations DDPMine has to go through.

Assume $min\_sup = \theta_0$, and DDPMine produces a frequent itemset α_i in the i-th iteration satisfying $\mathsf{supp}(\alpha_i) \geq \theta_0$. Clearly, DDPMine eliminates, before further processing, the training instances in $T(\alpha_i)$ from the current set of training instances since they are covered by the feature α_i. Then, we have the equation below which specifies the reduction of the training instance database:

$$|D_i| = |D_{i-1}| - |T(\alpha_i)| \tag{5.3}$$

where D_i is the training instances remaining after the i-th iteration, $T(\alpha_i)$ is the id list of transactions which contain α_i, and D_0 is the complete set of training instances.

Since $\mathsf{supp}(\alpha_i) \geq \theta_0$, we have $|T(\alpha_i)| \geq \theta_0 |D_{i-1}|$. Then we have

$$|D_i| = |D_{i-1}| - |T(\alpha_i)| \leq (1 - \theta_0)|D_{i-1}| \tag{5.4}$$

According to Eq. (5.4), we have

$$|D_i| \leq (1 - \theta_0)^i |D_0| \tag{5.5}$$

Assume after n iterations, the training database reduces to $|D_n| = 1$. Since $(1 - \theta_0)^n |D_0| \geq |D_n| = 1$, we can derive

$$n \leq \frac{\log |D_0|}{\log \frac{1}{1-\theta_0}} = \log_{\frac{1}{1-\theta_0}} |D_0| \tag{5.6}$$

According to Eq. (5.6), if $\theta_0 = 0.5$, $n \leq \log_2 |D_0|$. If $\theta_0 = 0.2$, $n \leq \log_{1.25} |D_0|$. If the training database has 1 million instances, then $n \leq 20$ if $\theta_0 = 0.5$; $n \leq 62$ if $\theta_0 = 0.2$.

The above bound analysis assumes the feature coverage parameter $\delta = 1$. If $\delta > 1$, the bound of n becomes

$$n \leq \delta \cdot \frac{\log |D_0|}{\log \frac{1}{1-\theta_0}} = \delta \cdot \log_{\frac{1}{1-\theta_0}} |D_0| \tag{5.7}$$

Eqs. (5.6) and (5.7) provide an upper bound of the number of iterations. In each iteration, the major computational cost is the frequent itemset mining. But it is more efficient than the original FP-growth mining, since it has the branch-and-bound pruning mechanism. In addition, the mining becomes more and more efficient as the training database shrinks. Combining Eqs. (5.1) and (5.7), the running-time cost of DDPMine is

$$Cost \leq \delta \cdot \log_{\frac{1}{1-\theta_0}} |D_0| \cdot (T_{mining} + T_{check\_db} + T_{update}) \tag{5.8}$$

5.2.4 Summary

The main technical features and contributions of DDPMine are:

(a) DDPMine avoids generating a large number of indiscriminative patterns, and also incrementally reduces the problem size by eliminating training instances and progressively shrinking the FP-tree, which further speeds up the mining process.

(b) Instead of mining a set of discriminative patterns in a batch, the "feature-centered" mining approach exploited by DDPMine could single out patterns sequentially in the progressively shrinking FP-tree which is shown to be very efficient.

(c) Time complexity analysis is provided for the DDPMine algorithm. An upper bound is derived on the number of iterations it has to go through, showing the computational cost analytically.

5.3 Harmony: Efficiently Mining The Best Rules For Classification

HARMONY [421] is an accurate and efficient rule-based classifier with good scalability, where the classifier contains a set of high confidence classification rules with a class label as the rules right hand side. The key idea behind HARMONY is to build a classifier that instead of using various heuristic methods to discover and/or select rules, it uses the most discriminative rules for each training instance. It takes an instance-centric view and directly mines the database of training instances to find at least one of the highest confidence frequent covering rules (if there are any) and include it in the final set of classification rules. By maintaining the highest confidence among the covering rules mined so far for each instance, HARMONY can employ some effective search strategies and pruning methods to speed up the model learning.

The rule-discovery problem in HARMONY is defined as follows. Given a training database D and a minimum support threshold min_sup, the problem is to find one of the highest confidence covering rules (abbreviated as $HCCR$) for each of the training instances in D.

5.3.1   Rule Enumeration

Given a training database D and a minimum support min_sup, HARMONY first computes the frequent items by scanning D once, and sorts them to get a list of frequent items (denoted by f_list), according to a certain ordering scheme. Assume $min\_sup = 0.25$ and the lexicographical ordering is the default ordering scheme, the f_list computed from D in Table 5.1 is $\{a, b, c, d\}$. HARMONY applies the divide-and-conquer method plus the depth-first search strategy. In this example, HARMONY first mines the rules whose body contains item 'a', then mines the rules whose body contains 'b' but no 'a', ..., and finally mines the rules whose body contains only 'd'. In mining the rules with item 'a', item 'a' is treated as the current prefix, and its conditional database (denoted by $D|_a$) is built and the divide-and-conquer method is applied recursively with the depth-first search strategy. To build conditional database $D|a$, HARMONY first identifies the instances in D containing 'a' and removes the infrequent items, then sorts the left items in each instance according to the f_list order, finally $D|_a$ is built as $\{\langle 100, bc, 1\rangle, \langle 200, bcd, 1\rangle, \langle 300, bc, 1\rangle, \langle 400, bd, 1\rangle, \langle 700, bc, 1\rangle, \langle 800, bc, 1\rangle\}$. Following the divide-and-conquer method, HARMONY first mines the rules with prefix 'ab', then mines rules with prefix 'ac' but no 'b', and finally mines rules with prefix 'ad' but no 'b' nor 'c'. During the mining process, when HARMONY gets a new prefix, it will generate a set of classification rules w.r.t. the training instances covered by the prefix. For each training instance, it always maintains one of its currently highest confidence rules mined so far. Assume the current prefix P is 'a' (i.e., $P = $ 'a'). As shown in the above example, P covers six instances with TIDs 100, 200, 300, 400, 700, and 800. HARMONY computes the covering rules according to the class distribution w.r.t. the prefix P. In this example, $\mathsf{count}(P, C_0) = 0$ and $\mathsf{count}(P, C_1) = 6$ (the support counts of P in class 0 and 1 respectively), and HARMONY generates two classification rules:

$$Rule\ 1 : a \to 0 : 0, \frac{0}{6}$$

$$Rule\ 2 : a \to 1 : 6, \frac{6}{6}$$

Rule 1 covers no instance, while Rule 2 covers the instances with TIDs 100, 200, 300, 400, 700, and 800. Up to this point, we have $HCCR_{100} = HCCR_{200} = HCCR_{300} = HCCR_{400} = HCCR_{700} = HCCR_{800} = Rule\ 2$.

5.3.2 Ordering of the Local Items

Many projection-based frequent itemset mining algorithms use the item support to order the local frequent items. However, when the goal is to mine the highest confidence rules w.r.t. the training instances, the support-based ordering schemes may not be the most efficient and effective way. As a result, the following three new ordering schemes are proposed as the alternatives.

Let the current prefix be P, its support be $\mathsf{supp}(P)$, the support and confidence of the classification rule w.r.t. prefix P and class label c_i, '$P \rightarrow c_i$', be $\mathsf{supp}(P, c_i)$ and $conf_P^{c_i}$, respectively, the set of local frequent items be $\{x_1, x_2, ..., x_m\}$, the number of prefix P's conditional instances containing item x_j $(1 \leq j \leq m)$ and associated with class label c_i $(1 \leq i \leq k)$ be $\mathsf{count}(P \cup \{x_j\}, c_i)$, and the support of $P \cup \{x_j\}$ be $\mathsf{supp}(P \cup \{x_j\}) = \sum_{i=1}^{k} \mathsf{supp}(P \cup \{x_j\}, c_i)$.

Maximum confidence descending order. Given a local item x_j $(1 \leq j \leq m)$ w.r.t. P, we can compute k rules with body $P \cup \{x_j\}$, among which, the i-th rule with rule head c_i is:

$$P \cup \{x_j\} \rightarrow c_i : \mathsf{count}(P \cup \{x_j\}, c_i), \frac{\mathsf{supp}(P \cup \{x_j\}, c_i)}{\mathsf{supp}(P \cup \{x_j\})}$$

The highest confidence among the k rules with body $P \cup \{x_j\}$ is called the maximum confidence of local item x_j, and is defined as the following:

$$\frac{\max_{1 \leq i \leq k} \mathsf{supp}(P \cup \{x_j\}, c_i)}{\mathsf{supp}(P \cup \{x_j\})} \tag{5.9}$$

To mine the highest confidence covering rules as quickly as possible, a good heuristic is to sort the local frequent items in their maximum confidence descending order.

Entropy ascending order. The widely used entropy measure assesses the purity of a cluster of instances. If the entropy of the set of instances containing $P \cup \{x_j\}$ $(1 \leq j \leq m)$ is small, it is highly possible to generate some high confidence rules with body $P \cup \{x_j\}$. Thus another good ordering heuristic is to rank the set of local frequent items in their entropy ascending order, and the entropy w.r.t. item x_j is defined as follows:

$$-\frac{1}{\log k} \sum_{i=1}^{k} \left(\frac{\mathsf{supp}(P \cup \{x_j\}, c_i)}{\mathsf{supp}(P \cup \{x_j\})}\right) \log\left(\frac{\mathsf{supp}(P \cup \{x_j\}, c_i)}{\mathsf{supp}(P \cup \{x_j\})}\right) \tag{5.10}$$

Correlation coefficient ascending order. Both the maximum confidence descending order and entropy ascending order do not consider the class distribution of the conditional database w.r.t. prefix P, which may cause some problems in some cases. To illustrate, assume the number of class labels $k = 2$, $\mathsf{count}(P, c_1) = 12$, and $\mathsf{count}(P, c_2) = 6$, then we can get two rules with body P as follows:

$$Rule \; 3 : P \rightarrow c_1 : 12, \frac{12}{18}$$

$$Rule \; 4 : P \rightarrow c_2 : 6, \frac{6}{18}$$

Suppose there are two local items, x_1 and x_2, and $\mathsf{count}(P \cup \{x_1\}, c_1) = 2$, $\mathsf{count}(P \cup \{x_1\}, c_2) = 1$, $\mathsf{count}(P \cup \{x_2\}, c_1) = 1$, and $\mathsf{count}(P \cup \{x_2\}, c_2) = 2$. According to Eqs 5.9 and 5.10, the maximum confidence and entropy w.r.t. item x_1 are equal to the corresponding maximum confidence and entropy w.r.t. x_2. Thus we cannot determine which one of x_1 and x_2 should be ranked higher. However, because the conditional database $D|_{P \cup \{x_1\}}$ has the same class distribution as conditional database $D|_P$, we cannot generate rules with body $P \cup \{x_1\}$ and a confidence higher than those with body P (i.e., Rule 3 and Rule 4). The two rules with body $P \cup \{x_1\}$ are shown as the following.

$$Rule \; 5 : P \cup \{x_1\} \rightarrow c_1 : 2, \frac{2}{3}$$

$$Rule \; 6 : P \cup \{x_1\} \rightarrow c_2 : 1, \frac{1}{3}$$

If we examine the rules generated from prefix itemset $P \cup \{x_2\}$ as shown in Rule 7 and Rule 8, we can see Rule 8 has higher confidence than Rule 4, and can be used to replace Rule 4 for the instances covered by Rule 8. In this case, item x_2 should be ranked before item x_1.

$$Rule \; 7 : P \cup \{x_2\} \rightarrow c_1 : 1, \frac{1}{3}$$

$$Rule \; 8 : P \cup \{x_2\} \rightarrow c_2 : 2, \frac{2}{3}$$

This example suggests that the more similar the class distribution between conditional databases $D|_P$ and $D|_{P \cup \{x_j\}}$ ($1 \leq j \leq m$), the lower is the possibility to generate higher confidence rules from $D|_{P \cup \{x_j\}}$. Because the correlation coefficient is a good metric in measuring the similarity between two vectors (the larger the coefficient, the more similar the two vectors), it can be used to rank the local items. In HARMONY, the correlation coefficient ascending order is by default adopted to sort the local items.

Let $\overline{\mathsf{supp}(P)}$ be $\frac{1}{k} \sum_{i=1}^{k} \mathsf{supp}(P, c_i)$, $\overline{\mathsf{supp}(P \cup \{x_j\})}$ be $\frac{1}{k} \sum_{i=1}^{k} \mathsf{supp}(P \cup \{x_j\}, c_i)$, σ_P be $\sqrt{\frac{1}{k} \sum_{i=1}^{k} (\mathsf{supp}(P, c_i))^2 - \overline{\mathsf{supp}(P)}^2}$, and then $\sigma_{P \cup \{x_j\}}$ be $\sqrt{\frac{1}{k} \sum_{i=1}^{k} (\mathsf{supp}(P \cup \{x_j\}, c_i))^2 - \overline{\mathsf{supp}(P \cup \{x_j\})}^2}$, the correlation coefficient between prefix P and $P \cup \{x_j\}$ ($1 \leq j \leq m$) is defined as follows.

$$\frac{\frac{1}{k}\sum_{i=1}^{k}(\text{supp}(P, c_i) \times \text{supp}(P \cup \{x_j\}, c_i) - \overline{\text{supp}(P)} \times \overline{\text{supp}(P \cup \{x_j\})})}{\sigma_P \times \sigma_{P \cup \{x_j\}}}$$

(5.11)

5.3.3 Search Space Pruning

Unlike the previous association-based algorithms [270, 258], HARMONY directly mines the final set of classification rules. By maintaining the current highest confidence among the covering rules for each training instance during the mining process, some effective pruning methods can be proposed to improve the algorithm efficiency.

Support equivalence item elimination. Given the current prefix P, among its set of local frequent items $\{x_1, x_2, ..., x_m\}$, some may have the same support as P. We call them support equivalence items and can be safely pruned according to the following Lemma 5.1.

Lemma 5.1 *(Support equivalence item pruning) Any local item x_j w.r.t. prefix P can be safely pruned if it satisfies* $\text{supp}(P \cup \{x_j\}) = \text{supp}(P)$.

Unpromising item elimination. Given the current prefix P, any one of its local frequent items, x_j $(1 \le j \le m)$, any itemset Y that can be used to extend $P \cup \{x_j\}$ (where Y can be empty and $P \cup \{x_j\} \cup Y$ is frequent), and any class label c_i $(1 \le i \le k)$, the following equation must hold:

$$\begin{aligned} conf_{P\cup\{x_j\}\cup Y}^{c_i} &= \frac{\text{supp}(P \cup \{x_j\} \cup Y, c_i)}{\text{supp}(P \cup \{x_j\} \cup Y)} \\ &\le \frac{\text{supp}(P \cup \{x_j\} \cup Y, c_i)}{min\_sup} \\ &\le \frac{\text{supp}(P \cup \{x_j\}, c_i)}{min\_sup} \end{aligned}$$

(5.12)

Because $conf_{P\cup\{x_j\}\cup Y}^{c_i} \le 1$ also holds, we have the following equation:

$$conf_{P\cup\{x_j\}\cup Y}^{c_i} \le \min\{1, \frac{\text{supp}(P \cup \{x_j\}, c_i)}{min\_sup}\}$$

(5.13)

Lemma 5.2 *(Unpromising item pruning) For any conditional instance* $\langle t_l, X_l, c_i \rangle \in D|_{P\cup\{x_j\}}$ $(1 \le l \le |D|_{P\cup\{x_j\}}|$, *and* $1 \le i \le k)$, *if the following always holds, item x_j is called an unpromising item and can be safely pruned.*

$$HCCR_{t_l}^{conf} \ge \min\{1, \frac{\text{supp}(P \cup \{x_j\}, c_i)}{min\_sup}\}$$

(5.14)

Unpromising conditional database elimination. Given the current prefix P, any itemset Y (where Y can be empty and $P \cup Y$ is frequent), any class label c_i ($1 \le i \le k$), the confidence of rule '$P \cup Y \to c_i$', $conf_{P \cup Y}^{c_i}$, must satisfy the following equation:

$$conf_{P \cup Y}^{c_i} = \frac{\mathsf{supp}(P \cup Y, c_i)}{\mathsf{supp}(P \cup Y)} \le \frac{\mathsf{supp}(P \cup Y, c_i)}{min\_sup} \le \frac{\mathsf{supp}(P, c_i)}{min\_sup} \qquad (5.15)$$

Moreover, because $conf_{P \cup Y}^{c_i} \le 1$ also holds, we have the following equation:

$$conf_{P \cup Y}^{c_i} \le \min\{1, \frac{\mathsf{supp}(P, c_i)}{min\_sup}\} \qquad (5.16)$$

Lemma 5.3 *(Unpromising conditional database pruning) For any conditional instance $\langle t_l, X_l, c_i \rangle \in D|_P$ ($\forall l, 1 \le l \le |D|_P|$, and $1 \le i \le k$), if the following always holds, the conditional database $D|_P$ can be safely pruned.*

$$HCCR_{t_l}^{conf} \ge \min\{1, \frac{\mathsf{supp}(P, c_i)}{min\_sup}\} \qquad (5.17)$$

HARMONY enumerates the classification rules following the projection-based frequent itemset mining framework. Given a prefix itemset pi and its corresponding conditional database cdb, for a training instance, it checks if a classification rule with higher confidence can be computed from the current prefix pi. If so, it replaces the corresponding instance's current highest confidence rule with the new rule. It then finds the frequent local items by scanning cdb, prunes invalid items based on the *support equivalence item pruning* method and the *unpromising item pruning* method. If the set of valid local items is empty or the whole conditional database cdb can be pruned based on the *unpromising conditional database* pruning method, it returns directly. Otherwise, it sorts the left frequent local items according to the correlation coefficient ascending order, and grows the current prefix, builds the conditional database for the new prefix, and recursively calls itself to mine the highest confidence rules from the new prefix.

5.3.4   Summary

In summary, HARMONY proposes different local item ordering schemes in the projection-based frequent itemset mining framework and designs several search space pruning strategies to achieve high computational efficiency. All these pruning methods preserve the completeness of the resulting rule-set in the sense that they only remove from consideration rules that are guaranteed not to be of high quality. HARMONY mines the classification rules for all the classes simultaneously and directly mines the final set of classification rules by pushing the pruning methods deeply into the frequent itemset mining process.

5.4 Performance Comparison Between DDPMine and Harmony

In [89], a classification performance comparison was conducted on a series of UCI datasets in terms of both efficiency and accuracy, by comparing DDPMine [89] with HARMONY [421] and PatClass [88], which are the state-of-the-art associative classification methods. PatClass is a representative of the two-step procedure by first mining a set of frequent itemsets followed by a feature selection step. LIBSVM [77] is used as the classification model by PatClass and DDPMine, while HARMONY uses the mined association rules to build a CAEP [126] style classifier, i.e., aggregating the confidence of multiple matching rules with the same class label for classification.

Table 5.2 shows the running time (in seconds) of the three methods. For both DDPMine and PatClass we compute the running time for both frequent itemset mining and feature selection; whereas for HARMONY, we compute the running time for association rule mining. The running time was averaged over 5-fold cross validation.

From Table 5.2, we can see that, DDPMine is the most efficient algorithm, followed by HARMONY while PatClass is the least efficient one. On average, DDPMine outperforms HARMONY by an order of magnitude and outperforms PatClass by two orders of magnitude.

Table 5.3 shows the accuracy comparison between these three methods. On average, DDPMine has comparable accuracy with PatClass, and both outperform HARMONY by 9.8%, which is a significant improvement.

TABLE 5.2: Runtime Comparison (seconds). Source: Reprinted from Ref. [89], Copyright 2008, with permission from IEEE.

Dataset	HARMONY	PatClass	DDPMine
adult	60.78	1070.39	**8.75**
chess	37.09	113.98	**1.20**
crx	0.71	7.56	**0.57**
hypo	52.19	66.09	**0.66**
mushroom	**0.63**	34.42	0.83
sick	53.45	170.94	**1.70**
sonar	5.53	15.83	**0.83**
waveform	8.06	85.23	**4.34**
total	218.44	1564.44	**18.88**

TABLE 5.3: Accuracy Comparison. Source: Reprinted from Ref. [89], Copyright 2008, with permission from IEEE.

Dataset	HARMONY	PatClass	DDPMine
adult	81.90	84.24	**84.82**
chess	43.00	91.68	**91.85**
crx	82.46	**85.06**	84.93
hypo	95.24	**99.24**	**99.24**
mushroom	99.94	99.97	**100.00**
sick	93.88	97.49	**98.36**
sonar	77.44	**90.86**	88.74
waveform	87.28	91.22	**91.83**
average	82.643	92.470	**92.471**

5.5   Related Work

Several studies [142, 207, 160] considered further extending the direct discriminative pattern mining methodology to handle different problem settings.

5.5.1 M^bT: Direct Mining Discriminative Patterns via Model-based Search Tree

To avoid the mining cost in the two-step approach, Fan et al. [142] proposed M^bT, a divide-and-conquer based approach to directly mine discriminative patterns as features vectors. M^bT builds a model-based search tree in a top-down manner. It starts with the whole dataset and mines a set of frequent patterns from the data. The best pattern is selected as the discriminative feature in the current search tree node according to some criterion, e.g., information gain, and used to divide the data set into two subsets, one containing this pattern and the other not. The mining and pattern selection procedure is repeated on each of the subsets until the subset is small enough or the examples in the subset have the same class label. After the algorithm completes, a small set of informative features are uncovered and the corresponding model-based search tree is constructed. Since the number of examples towards leaf level is relatively small, M^bT is able to examine patterns with extremely low global support that could not be enumerated on the whole dataset by the two-step method.

5.5.2   NDPMine: Direct Mining Discriminative Numerical Features

Most existing frequent pattern based classification methods assume that feature values of the mined patterns are binary, i.e., a pattern either exists or not. Kim et al. [207] consider the numerical feature values, i.e., the number of times a pattern appears which can be more informative. Reference [207] proposed NDPMine, a numerical discriminative pattern mining approach, which employs a mathematical programming method that directly mines discriminative patterns as numerical features for classification. A linear programming problem is defined to learn a classification hyperplane (i.e., a bound with maximum margin) and solved by column generation, a classic optimization technique. The column generation technique starts with an empty set of constraints in the dual problem and iteratively adds the most violated constraints. When there are no more violated constraints, the optimal solution under the set of selected constraints is equal to the optimal solution under all constraints. In NDPMine, each constraint in the dual corresponds to a class-dependent pattern (p, c). Thus, the column generation finds a class-dependent pattern at each iteration whose corresponding constraint is violated the most. A gain function is defined to measure the discriminative power of class-dependent patterns. Similar as DDPMine, NDPMine uses branch-and-bound to search for the optimal pattern and prune the search space based on the gain function upper bound. NDPMine is shown to be an order of magnitude faster, significantly more memory efficient and more accurate than current approaches.

5.5.3 uHarmony: Mining Discriminative Patterns from Uncertain Data

Gao and Wang [160] proposed an algorithm uHARMONY which mines discriminative patterns directly and effectively from uncertain data as classification features/rules. uHARMONY adopts the same framework as HARMONY. On uncertain data, fields of uncertain attributes no longer have certain values, but use probability distribution functions to represent the possible values and their corresponding probabilities. Expected support of the mined patterns is adopted to represent pattern frequentness, while expected confidence is used as the measurement of discrimination. The calculation of expected confidence is non-trivial and requires careful consideration. Given an itemset x and a class c, on uncertain database expected confidence $E(conf_x^c) = E(\mathsf{supp}(x, c)/\mathsf{supp}(x))$ is not simply equal to $E(\mathsf{supp}(x, c))/E(\mathsf{supp}(x))$, although we have $conf_x^c = \mathsf{supp}(x, c)/\mathsf{supp}(x)$ on certain database. Actually expected confidence is related with the probabilities of the possible worlds and is very expensive to compute due to the extremely large number of possible worlds. Thus [160] developed a theorem to compute the upper bound of expected confidence to speedup the calculation.

5.5.4 Applications of Discriminative Pattern Based Classification

The direct discriminative pattern mining methodology has also found broad applications in classifying high dimensional gene expression data [95], chemical compounds and proteins [444, 200], software behaviors [280, 87], malwares [448], and trajectories [235]. These research results demonstrate the success of discriminative frequent patterns in classifying both transactional and non-transactional data with complex structures, and open a new direction for frequent pattern mining.

5.5.5 Discriminative Frequent Pattern Based Classification vs. Traditional Classification

Traditional classification models have demonstrated their power in many challenging classification tasks, for example, support vector machines in classifying very high-dimensional text data. Compared with these traditional classification models, the discriminative frequent pattern based classification approach exploits the strong association between individual features to form higher-order features which usually reflect the underlying semantics of the data. The discriminative frequent pattern based approach is especially useful in classifying data with complex structures, e.g., sequences and graphs, where the simple features like sequence elements or graph vertices and edges are not discriminative enough to express the temporal or structural patterns. In such problems the discriminative pattern based classification method can show its power. In [95], association rule based classifier was found to outperform C4.5 and SVM in classifying high-dimensional gene expression data, and in [444], discriminative pattern based classification was shown to outperform graph kernel approach in classifying chemical compounds. It remains a future research topic to extend the discriminative pattern based approach to many other domains, e.g., high-dimensional text data, as well as the emerging ones.

5.6 Conclusions

In this chapter, we introduced some state-of-the-art methods, including DDPMine, HARMONY, M^bT, NDPMine, and uHARMONY, that directly mine a compact set of discriminative patterns for classification, without generating the complete set of frequent patterns. The proposed mining and pruning techniques were discussed in detail. These methods greatly reduce the computational time, while not sacrificing the classification accuracy. These research results advance the frequent pattern mining techniques and open new applications in frequent pattern based classification.

Chapter 6

Mining Emerging Patterns from Structured Data

James Bailey

Department of Computing and Information Systems, The University of Melbourne

6.1 Introduction

In Chapters 3 and 4, we have reviewed methods for mining contrast patterns from transaction or vector (matrix) data. In this chapter, we now consider the problem of mining emerging patterns for more complex types of objects. In particular, we examine extensions of emerging patterns for the case when objects may be either sequences or graphs. Two primary issues are i) how to define emerging patterns that distinguish between sets of sequences or graphs, and ii) how to to mine such patterns. We will initially consider the case for sequences and then look at the situation for graphs.

6.2   Contrasts in Sequence Data: Distinguishing Sequence Patterns

Databases of sequences can be found across many diverse areas and making comparisons between sets of sequences is an important knowledge discovery challenge. For example, in biology, huge sets of DNA sequences and protein sequences are being collected. A set of protein sequences, for example, may correspond to a protein family or to a collection of co-regulated genes. It is interesting to compare such sets of sequences with the aim of uncovering subsequences (motifs) that characterize and distinguish a particular family or phenotype. For example, in [363], it is observed that biologists are very interested in identifying the most significant subsequences that discriminate between outer membrane proteins and non-outer-membrane proteins. Another important type of sequence can be found in the domain of information retrieval. Web pages and books consist of sequences of words and comparisons can be made across collections of sentences to identify distinguishing phrases. Such phrases can be useful for improving search and indexing. Other examples of sets of sequences can be found in weblogs, workflow histories and time series data. Reference [124] gave a detailed coverage on sequence data analysis and mining and on feature selection/construction approaches.

Emerging patterns for sequence data have been studied in a number of works. In [74] emerging substrings were introduced. These are strings of items used to differentiate between two classes of sequences. A suffix tree is used to store all the substrings. Each tree node contains two support counters, recording the support of the candidate from one class. Traversal on the tree yields all the emerging substring patterns. Substring patterns satisfying a conjunction of constraints have also been mined using version space trees [149]. Work in [150] uses suffix arrays to find emerging substring patterns with a minimum growth rate constraint and minimum frequency constraint in the positive dataset. This algorithm operates in linear time to the size of the input datasets.

In biology, there is a large amount of literature devoted to discovering motifs. In their basic form, motifs are similar to frequent substrings or frequent subsequences. However, they typically require very high support, are not computed by distinguishing against a set negative set of sequences (they focus on the positive sequences and they often use some distribution to approximate the negative dataset) and they also take into account various biological constraints.

The description that follows is based on the presentation of the framework in [198], which describes a technique for discovering emerging subsequences, that satisfy certain gap constraints. Hereafter, in line with [198], we will refer to an emerging sequence pattern as a distinguishing sequence.

6.2.1 Definitions

Consider two datasets D_p and D_n, each containing a set of sequences. A distinguishing sequence corresponds to a sequence that is frequently found in D_p, but not frequently found in D_n. Compared to tabular (matrix) data, finding patterns which distinguish one set of sequences from another is challenging, since the number of dimensions is not fixed. Also, the order/position of items is significant and the same item can be repeated within a sequence.

Given two datasets of sequences D_p and D_n, two support thresholds δ and α and a maximum gap g, a pattern p is a minimal distinguishing subsequence with g-gap constraint (g-MDS), if the following conditions are met:

1. Frequency condition: $support(p, D_p, g) \geq \delta$.

2. Infrequency condition: $support(p, D_n, g) \leq \alpha$.

3. Minimality condition: There is no subsequence of p satisfying 1 and 2.

Here $support(p, D_i, g) = count(p, D_i, g)/|D_i|$ and $count(p, D_i, g)$ denotes the number of sequences in D_i for which the subsequence pattern p is contained having a gap of at most g between successive elements of p. Given D_p, D_n, α, δ and g, the g-MDS mining problem is to discover all the g-MDSs.

We will use the following sequence database from [198] as an example:

Sequence ID	Sequence	Class label
1	*CBAB*	D_p
2	*AACCB*	D_p
3	*BBAAC*	D_p
4	*BCAB*	D_n
5	*ABACB*	D_n

For the case of $g = 0$, the distinguishing subsequences correspond to emerging substrings [74]. In such a situation, it is preferable from an efficiency perspective to use a specialized approach for mining, such as a prefix tree. For $g \geq 1$, the situation is more complex, since the maximum gap constraint is neither monotone nor anti monotone and thus pruning is not straightforward.

Consider our example database and suppose $\delta = 1$, $\alpha = 0$, and $g = 1$. The 1-MDSs are *bb*, *cc*, *baa*, and *cba*. Note that *bb* is a subsequence of all the negative sequences, if no gap constraint is used. However, all occurrences of *bb* in D_n fail the 1-gap constraint, so *bb* becomes a distinguishing subsequence when $g = 1$. Observe that every super sequence of an 1-MDS fulfilling the 1-gap constraint and support thresholds is also distinguishing. However, these are excluded from the MDS set, since they are non-minimal and contain redundant information.

The imposition of a minimality condition for g-MDSs has similar rationale to imposing a minimality requirement for emerging patterns. It reduces output volume and means that the patterns discovered are shorter (more succinct).

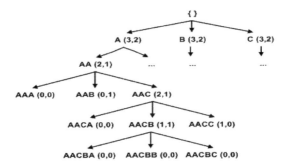

FIGURE 6.1: The lexicographic tree for sequence enumeration. Based on [198], Copyright 2005, with permission from IEEE.

6.2.2   Mining Approach

In order to mine g-MDSs, it is difficult (though not impossible) to directly adapt the data structures we saw in Chapters 3 and 4. Instead, a simpler and cleaner approach is to use a generate and test strategy. Subsequences are enumerated using depth-first search in a lexicographic sequence tree, in a manner similar to frequent subsequence mining techniques such as [29]. In the lexicographic sequence tree, each node contains a sequence s, a value for $support(s, D_p, g)$ and a value for $support(s, D_n, g)$. During the depth-first search, one extends the current node by a single item from the alphabet, according to some given lexicographic order. For (the sequence of) each newly-generated node n, its supports in D_p and D_n are calculated.

A key challenge relates to how support checking is performed. This is non-trivial, due to presence of gaps. The work in [198] proposes an efficient bitset technique that leverages a bitvector representation of itemsets and uses efficient bitwise operations on these bitvectors to optimize support checking.

6.3   Contrasts in Graph Datasets: Minimal Contrast Subgraph Patterns

We now consider how to compute emerging patterns that can differentiate between sets of graphs. We will refer to such patterns as a *contrast subgraph*. At a high level, a contrast subgraph is the smallest graph that appears in one graph dataset but never appears in another graph dataset. Contrast subgraphs are appealing, since they can capture structural differences between graphs. For example, a chemical compound can be represented as a graph. Given two classes of chemical compounds, one active and the other inactive, contrast subgraphs can then identify distinguishing characteristics between

Algorithm 3 Candidate_Gen(c,g,I,δ,α): Generate new candidates from sequence c. Based on [198], Copyright 2005, with permission from IEEE.

Require: c: sequence, g: maximum gap, I: alphabet, δ: minimal support in D_p, α: maximum support in D_n.
Ensure: MDS is a global variable containing all distinguishing subsequences generated from the entire tree.
1: $ds = \emptyset$ {to contain all distinguishing children of c}
2: **for all** $i \in I$ **do**
3:    **if** $c + i$ is not a supersequence of any sequence in ds **then**
4:      $nc = c + i$
5:      $supp_{D_p}$=Support(nc,D_p,g)
6:      $supp_{D_n}$=Support_Count(nc,D_n,g)
7:      **if** $supp_{D_p} \geq \delta$ AND $supp_{D_n} \leq \alpha$ **then**
8:        $ds = ds \cup nc$ {nc is distinguishing}
9:      **else if** $supp_{D_p} \geq \delta$ **then**
10:        Candidate_Gen(nc,g,I,δ,α)
11:      **end if**
12:    **end if**
13: **end for**
14: $MDS = MDS \cup ds$

---

the two classes. Alternatively, given two social networks, contrast subgraphs can highlight the differences between the two networks. Discriminative subgraphs may also be useful in other contexts, such as search and indexing [81] and querying image databases that are represented as attributed relational graphs. The aim here is to efficiently find all objects from the database contained in a given scene (query). For indexing, contrast features that have high pruning power (save most isomorphism tests) are selected. They are features that are contained by many graphs in the database, but are unlikely to be contained by a query graph.

Other graph contrasting approaches include [367] which examines how change in a time series of graphs can be determined using global distance measures. Contrasts between graphs are a focus of [150]. They propose a language that is able to query for fragments that are frequent in one class of graphs, but infrequent in another.

The task of discovering contrast subgraphs is similar to the task of discovering frequent subgraphs. Pioneering work in this area includes algorithms such as gSpan [445], AGM [195], and FSG [223]. Some aspects which make contrast subgraphs potentially different from frequent subgraph lies in the definitions, including:

- Must the contrast subgraph be connected, or may we allow disconnected subgraphs?

- May the contrast subgraph have isolated vertices (vertices that are connected with no edges)?

- Should the contrast subgraph possess any special structure (e.g. linear or tree)?

- May two graphs that are isomorphic both be output as contrast subgraphs, or is only one allowed?

- Is minimality an important factor?

In the case that isolated vertices are prohibited, the contrast subgraph may be referred to as an *edge set*. In what follows, we will review the key ideas from [406]. This work proposes an approach for discovering the set of contrast subgraphs, where each contrast may be disconnected, does not contain any isolated vertices and is minimal. Also, the contrast subgraphs in the output set are not required to be non-isomorphic from each other (i.e. a contrast subgraph appearing in two different locations will be output twice).

6.3.1   Terminology and Definitions for Contrast Subgraphs

A labeled graph G is a 4-tuple (V, E, α, β), V is a vertex set, $E \subseteq V \times V$ is a set of edges, α is a function assigning labels to vertices, and β is a function assigning labels to edges. $S = (W, F, \alpha, \beta)$ is the subgraph of $G = (V, E, \alpha, \beta)$ iff (1) $W \subseteq V$ and (2) $F \subseteq E \cap (W \times W)$. Equivalently, G is said to be the supergraph of S.

Given $G' = (V', E', \alpha', \beta')$ and $G = (V, E, \alpha, \beta)$, a subgraph isomorphism is an injective function $f : (V') \to V$ such that (1) $\forall e' = (u, v) \in E'$, there exists $e = (f(u), f(v)) \in E$, (2) $\forall u \in V', \alpha'(u) = \alpha(f(u))$ and (3) $\forall e' \in E', \beta'(e') = \beta(f(e'))$. If there exists such a function, then G' is subgraph isomorphic to G. If $f : (V') \to V$ is bijective, G' is isomorphic to G. Given the graphs G_p and G_n, $C \subseteq G_p$ is a common subgraph iff it is subgraph isomorphic to G_n.

An edge set is a graph with no isolated vertex. C is a common edge set iff (1) it is an edge set and (2) a common subgraph. C is a maximal common edge set iff it is a common edge set and there does not exist any strict superset which is a common edge set. C is a maximum common edge set if it is a common edge set and no other common edge set has more edges than C.

A minimal contrast subgraph is defined as follows. Given a set of positive graphs $\{G_{p_1}, \ldots, G_{p_l}\}$, and a set of negative graphs $\{G_{n_1}, \ldots, G_{n_k}\}$,

- C is a contrast subgraph if

   - C is not subgraph isomorphic to any of $\{G_{n_1}, \ldots, G_{n_k}\}$, and
   - C is subgraph isomorphic to one or more of $\{G_{p_1}, \ldots, G_{p_l}\}$.

C is minimal if all of its strict subgraphs are not contrast subgraphs.

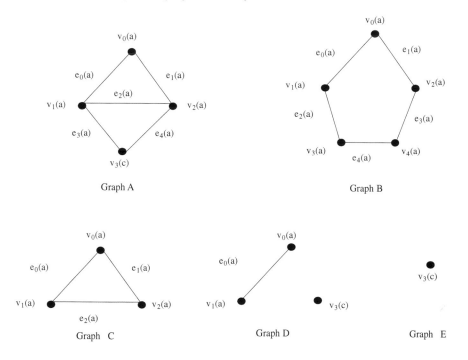

FIGURE 6.2: Examples of Contrast Subgraphs: C, D, and E are all contrast subgraphs contained in A and not in B. Based on [406], Copyright 2006, with permission from SIAM.

- C is a contrast edge set if (1) it is an edge set and (2) a contrast subgraph. It is minimal if all proper subsets of C do not form contrast subgraphs.

Figure 6.2 shows some examples: Graphs C, D, and E are all contrast subgraphs of Graph A when compared with Graph B.

6.3.2   Mining Algorithms for Minimal Contrast Subgraphs

We now describe the approach of [406] for mining minimal contrast subgraphs. In particular, the algorithm actually mines the minimal contrast edge sets. Contrast subgraphs containing isolated vertices can be enumerated separately.

Given a particular positive graph G_p, the algorithm operates in three main stages. In the first stage, it discovers the maximal common edge sets between G_p and each given negative graph G_{n_i}, using a backtracking tree. Next, the maximal common edge sets for all G_{n_i} are then unioned together and the minimal hypergraph transversals of their complements computed. This yields the minimal contrast edge sets for G_p, with respect to the set of negative graphs.

More formally, the connection between minimal contrast and maximal common edge sets is as follows. Suppose $S = \{S_1, S_2, ..., \}$ is a set of sets, then $\bar{S}$, the complement of S, is the set of complements of each of the sets, i.e. $\bar{S} = \{\bar{S}_1, \bar{S}_2, ..., \}$. Let $A = A_1, A_2, ..., A_n$ be a set of sets. We say a set P is a transversal of A if $(P \cap A_1 \neq \emptyset) \wedge (P \cap A_2 \neq \emptyset) \wedge .... \wedge (P \cap A_n \neq \emptyset)$. We say that P is a minimal transversal of A, if P is a transversal of A and each $P' \subset P$ is not a transversal of A. We define $MinTrans(A)$ to be the set of all the minimal transversals of A. The key idea is that the maximal common edge sets and the minimal contrast edge sets are dual of one another. Given a set of maximal common edge sets S, then the minimal transversals of S is equal to the collection of the smallest edge sets which are not contained in any edge sets from S (i.e. the minimal contrast edge sets).

For a particular positive graph G_p, the task of finding minimal contrast edge sets is thus equivalent to computing the set of maximal common edge sets between G_p and each of the negative graphs.

Given G_p and $\{G_{n_1}, \ldots, G_{n_k}\}$, let M_i be the set of maximal common edge sets between G_p and G_{n_i}. Then $MinTrans(\bar{M}_1 \cup \bar{M}_2 \cup \ldots \cup \bar{M}_k)$ is the set of all minimal contrast edge sets between G_p and $\{G_{n_1}, \ldots, G_{n_k}\}$.

One can compute the minimal hypergraph transversals (using a technique such as [35]) of the complements of the edge sets to derive the complete set of minimal contrast edge sets. This process can then be repeated for each positive graph. Combining the minimal contrast edge sets of all the positive graphs yields the entire set of minimal contrast edge sets of $\{G_{n_1}, \ldots, G_{n_k}\}$ versus $\{G_{p_1}, \ldots, G_{p_l}\}$. A full description of all the details and discussion of alternative approaches can be found in [405].

6.4   Summary

We have reviewed two quite different scenarios for computation of contrast patterns in more structured data. The first scenario was related to the discovery of subsequence patterns that are distinguishing between two sets of sequences. The second scenario was related to the discovery of subgraphs that are contained in a set of positive graphs, but not contained in a set of negative graphs.

Although these two scenarios are superficially quite different from mining emerging patterns in tabular (matrix) data, we can identify some common themes. Firstly, minimality is an important technique for reducing the number of contrast patterns that need to be mined and can be defined using a pattern inclusion (border) relationship. Secondly, contrast patterns may be enumerated by either using existence in D_p as the primary constraint or existence in D_n as the primary constraint. Contrast patterns are required to appear in D_p and not to appear in (or have minimal appearances in) the negative dataset D_n. This can be achieved by either i) enumerating patterns contained in D_p and then explicitly checking their support for each object in D_n (as we saw for distinguishing subsequence mining), or ii) enumerating minimal patterns not contained in any object in D_n and ensuring they occur in some object in D_p (as we saw for minimal contrast subgraph mining, as well as the ratio tree algorithm from Chapter 3).

In addition to sequences and graphs, there are other types of structured data such as images, time series, and so on. Chapter 20 studies approaches to represent emerging patterns for contrasting images, utilizing occurrence count features and utilizing spatial relationship features. Chapter 25 gives pointers to other papers on related topics.

Chapter 7

Incremental Maintenance of Emerging Patterns

Mengling Feng

Data Mining Department, Institute for Infocomm Research

Guozhu Dong

Department of Computer Science and Engineering, Wright State University

Due to advances in data acquisition, storage and transfer technologies, data is nowadays dynamically updated all the time. In addition, in many interactive data mining applications, data is often modified repeatedly. Re-generating the corresponding emerging patterns from scratch every time when the underlying data is updated/modified is obviously inefficient. It is more advantageous to incrementally maintain the emerging patterns.

In this chapter, we first present the motivations and potential applications for incremental maintenance of emerging patterns. We then formally define the maintenance problem, and discuss the challenges associated with solving the problem. After that, we discuss how an emerging pattern space can be concisely represented by its *border* [118]. Finally, we demonstrate how an emerging pattern space, represented by its *border*, can be effectively maintained under various data updates or modifications [249].

7.1   Background & Potential Applications

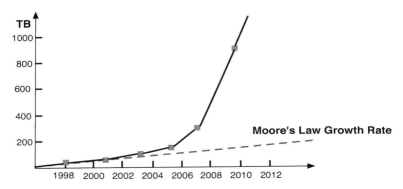

FIGURE 7.1: Projected average size of data warehouses [50].

Due to advances in data generation and collection technologies, the increased popularity of the Internet and the invention of cloud computing, the amount of available data has exploded in recent years. Figure 7.1 shows the projected sizes of data warehouses over the coming years. As pointed out by the vice president of *Google*, Marissa Mayer, "data explosion is bigger than Moore's law." According to various studies, the amount of available data has grown over 15-fold in the past few years, and the annual data growth rate is projected to increase to 45-fold by 2020 [11]. In this era of data explosion, data is no longer static. Data is dynamically updated all the time: new records are inserted, obsolete records are removed, and records containing errors are corrected. When the underlying data is updated, the corresponding emerging patterns also need to be updated. The most straightforward approach is to re-discover the emerging patterns. However, as graphically illustrated in Figure 7.2, the size of data affected by the updates is usually much smaller than the overall data size, and the original and the updated emerging pattern spaces have very large overlap. Moreover, the re-discovery approach also leads to large computational overheads, and it is likely to be practically infeasible. A more practical solution is to incrementally maintain the emerging patterns to reflect updates in the underlying data. In real-life applications, incremental maintenance of emerging patterns has been employed for real-time monitoring of critical assets [236] and diagnosis of medical conditions [323]. This chapter discusses how emerging patterns can be incrementally maintained when the pattern space is concisely represented by its *border*.

Incremental maintenance of emerging patterns is also a useful tool for interactive mining applications. One potential application is to answer hypothetical queries, including, the *"what if"* queries. Data analyzers are often interested in finding out *"what"* might happen to the discovered emerging

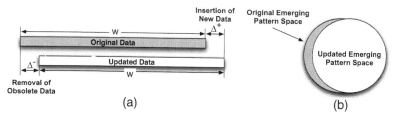

(a)

(b)

FIGURE 7.2: (a) A graphical illustration of dynamic data updates. (b) Overlaps between the original and the updated emerging pattern spaces.

patterns "*if*": some new transactions were inserted to the dataset, some existing transactions were removed, some existing transactions were replaced, or some sets of items are included or excluded, etc. Useful insights can often be discovered with interactive hypothetical queries.

Figure 7.3 (a) illustrates the naïve approach to answer *what if* hypothetical queries. First, the naïve approach requires the re-discovery of emerging patterns, which involves large amount of repeated computation effort. Moreover, to answer *what if* queries, the naïve approach needs to compare the original and updated pattern spaces. Since the size of emerging pattern spaces is usually very large, the comparison is computationally expensive.

As illustrated by Figure 7.3 (b), incremental maintenance of emerging patterns can be used to efficiently support the query answering process, without using the pattern re-generation and comparison steps of the naïve approach.

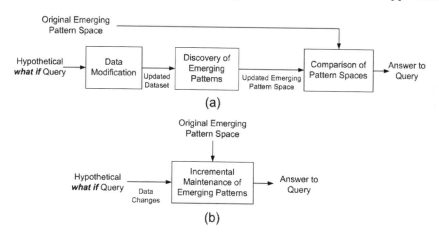

FIGURE 7.3: (a) The naïve approach and (b) the incremental maintenance approach to answer hypothetical *what if* queries.

7.2   Problem Definition & Challenges

Following the definitions in Chapter 1, given two contrasting datasets D_P and D_N and a *support ratio threshold*, σ_r, a pattern (or an itemset) P is an "emerging pattern" for the *positive* dataset D_P if and only if $SuppRatio(P, D_P, D_N) = \frac{Supp(P, D_P)}{Supp(P, D_N)} \geq \sigma_r$, where $Supp(P, D_x)$ denotes the support of P in dataset D_x. In some applications, the differences between the contrasting datasets are measured based on *support delta*. In this case, a pattern P is an emerging pattern for the *positive* dataset if and only if $SuppDelta(P, D_P, D_N) = Supp(P, D_P) - Supp(P, D_N) \geq \sigma_d$, where σ_d is the *minimum support delta threshold*. Given σ_r or σ_d, the "space of emerging pattern" or "emerging pattern space", denoted as $EP(D_P, D_N, \sigma_r)$ or $EP(D_P, D_N, \sigma_d)$, is the set of all valid emerging patterns. Since the *support ratio* threshold, σ_r, is more commonly used, for ease of discussion, in this chapter we will assume σ_r is used unless otherwise stated.

Types of Updates

Insertion of new instances is an update where new *positive* instances, Δ_P, and/or new *negative* instances, Δ_N, are inserted into the original contrasting datasets. Suppose the original contrasting datasets are D_P and D_N. The updated datasets then are $D'_P = D_P \cup \Delta_P$ and $D'_N = D_N \cup \Delta_N$, and $|D'_P| = |D_P| + |\Delta_P|$ and $|D'_N| = |D_N| + |\Delta_N|$. (We assume that $D_P \cap \Delta_P = \emptyset$ and $D_N \cap \Delta_N = \emptyset$.) Insertion of new instances is the most common data management operation. It allows new data to be included in the data analysis.

Deletion of existing instances is an update where existing *positive* instances, Δ_P, and/or *negative* instances, Δ_N, are removed from the current contrasting datasets. Suppose the original contrasting datasets are D_P and D_N. The updated datasets then are $D'_P = D_P - \Delta_P$ and $D'_N = D_N - \Delta_N$, and $|D'_P| = |D_P| - |\Delta_P|$ and $|D'_N| = |D_N| - |\Delta_N|$. (We assume that $\Delta_P \subset D_P$ and $\Delta_N \subset D_N$.) Deletion of existing instances is a data management operation that allows obsolete and invalid instances to be removed. It ensures the generated emerging patterns are not undesirably influenced by out-of-date or invalid instances that contain error.

> When the original contrasting datasets, D_P and D_N, are updated into D'_P and D'_N by inserting or removing instances, the task of incremental maintenance is to obtain the updated emerging pattern space, $EP(D'_P, D'_N, \sigma_r)$, by updating the original pattern space, $EP(D_P, D_N, \sigma_r)$.

Expansion of query item space is an update where new items are included in the existing "*query item space*".

Definition 7.1 *Given the positive and negative datasets, D_P and D_N, let $\mathcal{I} = \{i_1, i_2, \cdots\}$ be the "complete item space" that includes all the items in D_P and D_N. The "query item space", denoted as $\mathcal{I}_Q$, defines an item subspace where $\mathcal{I}_Q \subseteq \mathcal{I}$. In the context of $\mathcal{I}_Q$, only items in $\mathcal{I}_Q$ will be considered for the formation of emerging patterns, and all other items will be ignored.*

In the context of *query item space*, $\mathcal{I}_Q$, the emerging pattern space, $EP_{\mathcal{I}_Q}(D_P, D_N, \sigma_r)$, is defined as the set of emerging patterns P that $P \subseteq \mathcal{I}_Q$.

Expansion of *query item space* is an update where the existing *query item space*, $\mathcal{I}_Q$, expands with new items $\mathcal{I}_\Delta$. $\mathcal{I}_\Delta \neq \emptyset$ and $\mathcal{I}_\Delta \subset \mathcal{I}$. The updated *Query Item Space* becomes $\mathcal{I}'_Q = \mathcal{I}_Q \cup \mathcal{I}_\Delta$. Therefore, $\mathcal{I}_Q \subset \mathcal{I}'_Q \subseteq \mathcal{I}$.

Shrinkage of query item space is an update where the existing *query item space*, $\mathcal{I}_Q$, shrinks by removing items $\mathcal{I}_\Delta$. $\mathcal{I}_\Delta \neq \emptyset$ and $\mathcal{I}_\Delta \subset \mathcal{I}_Q$. The updated *query item space* becomes $\mathcal{I}'_Q = \mathcal{I}_Q - \mathcal{I}_\Delta$. This implies that $\mathcal{I}'_Q \subset \mathcal{I}_Q$.

When the original *query item space*, $\mathcal{I}_Q$, expands or shrinks into $\mathcal{I}'_Q$, the task of incremental maintenance is to obtain the updated emerging pattern space, $EP_{\mathcal{I}'_Q}(D_P, D_N, \sigma_r)$, by updating the original pattern space, $EP_{\mathcal{I}_Q}(D_P, D_N, \sigma_r)$.

We note that, for the insertion and removal of instance updates, the *query item space* is assumed to remain unchanged.

7.2.1 Potential Challenges

Data updates may invalidate existing emerging patterns and introduce new emerging patterns. As a result, the incremental maintenance of emerging patterns consists of two main computational tasks: to update existing patterns and to generate new emerging patterns.

To update the existing emerging patterns, the naïve way is to scan through all the existing patterns to find out which patterns are affected by the data updates and then update the patterns accordingly. Suppose the dataset is incrementally updated with m new instances. The computational complexity of the naïve approach is $O(N_{EP} \times m)$, where N_{EP} refers to the number of the existing emerging patterns. Since N_{EP} can often be very large, the naïve approach is often computationally too expensive to be practically feasible. Therefore, how to update the existing patterns effectively is one of the major challenges in incremental maintenance of emerging patterns.

The generation of new emerging patterns is also technically challenging. In theory, the number of possible candidates for the new emerging patterns equals to $(2^n - N_{EP})$, where n is the total number of items (attribute-value pairs) and N_{EP} is the number of existing emerging patterns. In most applications, the number of items can be around $500 \sim 1,000$. Suppose there are $1,000$ items in the contrasting datasets. The potential search space for the new emerging patterns will consist of over 10^{300} candidates. Given such a large search space, effective techniques are needed to extract the new emerging patterns.

In the subsequent sections, we will investigate how the emerging patterns can be effectively maintained by concisely representing the pattern space with its *border*. The concept of *border* was first introduced in [118] as a concise representation of emerging patterns.

7.3   Concise Representation of Pattern Space: The *Border*

ID	Outlook	Temp.	Humidity	Windy	AvoidOutdoor
1	rain	mild	high	false	Yes
2	rain	mild	normal	false	Yes
3	sunny	Hot	high	false	No
4	sunny	Hot	normal	true	No

(a)

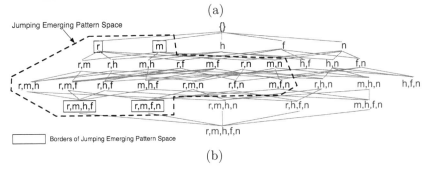

(b)

FIGURE 7.4: (a) Sample dataset; "AvoidOutdoor" is the class label; "Yes" indicates the positive class, and "No" indicates the negative class. (b) Emerging pattern space and its border. Here, we represent the attribute values using their first letters. The JEP space for the sample dataset, marked with a dotted line, includes 18 patterns; it can be concisely represented by its *border*, which consists of only 4 patterns highlighted in solid boxes.

This section discusses how the space of emerging patterns can be concisely represented. To illustrate the concept, we focus on a special type of emerging patterns — the "Jumping Emerging Patterns" (JEPs) .

Definition 7.2 *Given the positive and negative contrasting datasets D_P and D_N, a pattern P is a jumping emerging pattern for the positive dataset if and only if $Supp(P, D_P) > 0$ and $Supp(P, D_N) = 0$, or equivalently, $SuppRatio(P, D_P, D_N) = \infty$.*

A jumping emerging pattern for the *positive* dataset is a pattern P that appears only in *positive* instances and does not appear in any *negative* instances. For ease of discussion, when we mention "jumping emerging pattern" in subsequent discussion, it refers to the jumping emerging pattern for the *positive* dataset. The "space of jumping emerging pattern", in short *JEP* space, is then the pattern space that includes all valid jumping emerging patterns. We denote the space of jumping emerging patterns as $JEP(D_P, D_N)$. Jumping emerging patterns are most commonly used in the applications of classification, because they are often the most discriminative emerging patterns.

Figure 7.4 (a) shows a sample dataset on the relationship between the weather conditions and whether one should avoid staying outdoors. ("Yes" and "No" respectively denote the positive and negative classes.) Observe that, for this simple dataset consisting of only 4 instances and 4 attributes, the corresponding *JEP* space consists of 18 patterns. In the theoretical worse case, the size of the *JEP* space can grow exponentially with respect to the number of attributes. Updating and maintaining the *JEP* space can be computationally expensive. Luckily, the *JEP* space has a useful property: it is a convex space.

Definition 7.3 *A pattern space S is a convex space if, for all X, $Y \in S$, where $X \subseteq Y$, it is the case that $Z \in S$ whenever Z satisfies $X \subseteq Z \subseteq Y$.*

The convexity of the *JEP* space implies that, given any jumping emerging patterns X and Y, where $X \subseteq Y$, any pattern Z such that $X \subseteq Z \subseteq Y$ is also a jumping emerging pattern. This property forms the theoretical foundation for the concise representation of the *JEP* space.

Given a *JEP* space, we define the most general emerging patterns as the *left bound* of the pattern space, denoted as $\mathcal{L}$; and we define the most specific emerging patterns as the *right bound* of the pattern space, denoted as $\mathcal{R}$. The combination of the *left* and *right* bounds forms the *border* of the *JEP* space, denoted as $< \mathcal{L}, \mathcal{R} >$.

Based on the convexity of the *JEP* space, we observe the following four properties of its *border*. (a) Both the *left* and *right* bounds, $\mathcal{L}$ and $\mathcal{R}$, are *antichains*. Here, an *antichain* refers to a collection of patterns in which it is true for any two patterns X and Y that $X \not\subseteq Y$ and $Y \not\subseteq X$. (b) For each pattern X in $\mathcal{L}$, there exists at least one pattern Y in $\mathcal{R}$ such that $X \subseteq Y$. (c) For each pattern Y in $\mathcal{R}$, there exists at least one pattern X in $\mathcal{L}$ such that $X \subseteq Y$. (d) Most importantly, all patterns in the *JEP* space are completely covered by $\mathcal{L}$ and $\mathcal{R}$.

As a result, the *JEP* space can be concisely represented by its *border*, $< \mathcal{L}, \mathcal{R} >$. For the sample dataset of Figure 7.4, the *JEP* space (consisting of 18 patterns) can be concisely summarized by its *border*, which consists of only 4 patterns: $\mathcal{L} = \{\{r\}, \{m\}\}$ and $\mathcal{R} = \{\{r, m, h, f\}, \{r, m, n, f\}\}$.

Moreover, based on the notations of the *left* and *right* bounds, $\mathcal{L}$ and $\mathcal{R}$, we can re-interpret the *JEP* space as a collection of patterns that are supersets of some patterns in $\mathcal{L}$ and subsets of some patterns in $\mathcal{R}$. The *JEP* space can be expressed as $[\mathcal{L}, \mathcal{R}] = \{Z | \exists X \in \mathcal{L}, \exists Y \in \mathcal{R} \text{ such that } X \subseteq Z \subseteq Y\}$. Note that notations $< \mathcal{L}, \mathcal{R} >$ and $[\mathcal{L}, \mathcal{R}]$ are different from each other. $< \mathcal{L}, \mathcal{R} >$ denotes the *border* of the *JEP* space, which consists of only the *left* bound, $\mathcal{L}$, and the *right* bound, $\mathcal{R}$. On the other hand, $[\mathcal{L}, \mathcal{R}]$ refers to the entire *JEP* space that are bounded by the *border*, $< \mathcal{L}, \mathcal{R} >$.

Recall that a jumping emerging pattern is a pattern that occurs only in the *positive* instances, D_P, but not in the *negative* instances, D_N. Therefore, one can obtain all the jumping emerging patterns by subtracting all patterns, which have *non-zero* support in D_N, from the collection of patterns that have *non-zero* support in D_P. This idea is graphically demonstrated in Figure 7.5. Based on the concept of *border*, the collection of non–zero support patterns in D_P can be expressed as $[\{\emptyset\}, \mathcal{R}_\mathcal{P}]$, where $\mathcal{R}_\mathcal{P}$ is the *right* bound of the pattern space. Similarly, the collection of non-zero support patterns in D_N can be expressed as $[\{\emptyset\}, \mathcal{R}_\mathcal{N}]$, where $\mathcal{R}_\mathcal{N}$ is the *right* bound of the pattern space. As a result, the *JEP* space for the contrasting data D_P and D_N, denoted as $JEP(D_P, D_N)$, can be re-written as:

$$JEP(D_P, D_N) = [\{\emptyset\}, \mathcal{R}_\mathcal{P}] - [\{\emptyset\}, \mathcal{R}_\mathcal{N}] \qquad (7.1)$$

This expression of the *JEP* space will be used in subsequent discussions. By concisely representing the *JEP* space with its *border*, one only needs to incrementally update the *border* patterns instead of the entire pattern space, which effectively reduces the computational complexity.

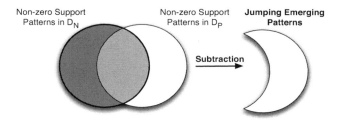

FIGURE 7.5: Pattern space subtraction to obtain the *JEP* space.

7.4   Maintenance of *Border*

This section investigates how the *border* of the *JEP* space can be incrementally maintained. First, Section 7.4.1 introduces some basic *border* operations, including *Subtraction*, *Union*, and *Intersection*. The subsequent sections then demonstrate, based on the basic operations, how the *border* can be effectively maintained under various data updates. Section 7.4.2 addresses the insertion of new instances, Section 7.4.3 the removal of existing instances, and Sections 7.4.4 and 7.4.5 the expansion and shrinkage of the *query item space*.

7.4.1 Basic *Border* Operations

***Border* Subtraction**: Recall that, the *JEP* space can be obtained by subtracting the non-zero support patterns in D_N, represented by $[\{\emptyset\}, \mathcal{R}_N]$, from the set of non-zero support patterns in D_P, represented by $[\{\emptyset\}, \mathcal{R}_P]$; see Figure 7.5. That is, $JEP(D_P, D_N) = [\{\emptyset\}, \mathcal{R}_P] - [\{\emptyset\}, \mathcal{R}_N]$ (Eq 7.1). Based on this formula, the *border* subtraction operation generates the *JEP* space with respect to the given $\mathcal{R}_P$ and $\mathcal{R}_N$. Figure 7.6 describes the detailed algorithm of the *border* subtraction operation, where $\mathcal{R}_P = \{A_1, ..., A_k\}$. The subroutine of the operation, *BorderDiff*, is described in Figure 7.7.

Input: Two pattern spaces given by $< \{\emptyset\}, \{A_1, ..., A_k\} >$ and $< \{\emptyset\}, \mathcal{R}_N >$
Output: $< \mathcal{L}, \mathcal{R} >$ such that $[\mathcal{L}, \mathcal{R}] = [\{\emptyset\}, \{A_1, ..., A_k\}] - [\{\emptyset\}, \mathcal{R}_N >$
Method:
1: $\mathcal{L} \leftarrow \{ \ \}, \mathcal{R} \leftarrow \{ \ \}$;
2: **for** j from 1 to k **do**
3: $\quad border = BorderDiff(< \{\emptyset\}, \{A_j\} >, < \{\emptyset\}, \mathcal{R}_N >)$;
4: $\quad \mathcal{L} = \mathcal{L} \cup$ left bound of *border*;
5: $\quad \mathcal{R} = \mathcal{R} \cup$ right bound of *border*;
6: **end for**
7: **return** $< \mathcal{L}, \mathcal{R} >$;

FIGURE 7.6: Operation *Border* Subtraction.

Input: Two pattern spaces given by $< \{\emptyset\}, \{U\} >$ and $< \{\emptyset\}, \{S_1, ..., S_k\} >$
Output: $< \mathcal{L}, \mathcal{R} >$ such that $[\mathcal{L}, \mathcal{R}] = [\{\emptyset\}, \{U\}] - [\{\emptyset\}, \{S_1, ..., S_k\}]$
Method:
1: $\mathcal{L} = \{\{x\} | x \in U - S_1\}$;
2: **for** i from 2 to k **do**
3: $\quad \mathcal{L} \leftarrow \{X \cup \{x\} | X \in \mathcal{L}, x \in U - S_i\}$;
4: $\quad$ remove patterns in $\mathcal{L}$ that are not most general;
5: **end for**
6: **return** $< \mathcal{L}, \{U\} >$;

FIGURE 7.7: Procedure *BorderDiff*.

***Border* Union**: Suppose D_N is a set of *negative* instances, D_P is a set of *positive* instances, and D_P is partitioned into two sets, D_{P_1} and D_{P_2}. It is interesting to know how the *JEP* space $JEP(D_P, D_N)$ is related to the *JEP* spaces $JEP(D_{P_1}, D_N)$ and $JEP(D_{P_2}, D_N)$. We have the following answer to that question:

Fact 7.4 *Given a negative dataset D_N and a positive dataset D_P and a partition of D_P into D_{P_1} and D_{P_2}, we have $JEP(D_P, D_N) = JEP(D_{P_1}, D_N) \cup JEP(D_{P_2}, D_N)$. This fact is illustrated in Figure 7.8.*

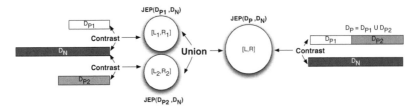

FIGURE 7.8: Union of two *JEP* spaces: given D_N and $D_P = D_{P_1} \cup D_{P_2}$, $JEP(D_P, D_N) = JEP(D_{P_1}, D_N) \cup JEP(D_{P_2}, D_N)$.

In the notion of *border*, suppose $JEP(D_P, D_N) = [\mathcal{L}, \mathcal{R}]$, $JEP(D_{P_1}, D_N) = [\mathcal{L}_1, \mathcal{R}_1]$ and $JEP(D_{P_1}, D_N) = [\mathcal{L}_2, \mathcal{R}_2]$. Then, $[\mathcal{L}, \mathcal{R}] = [\mathcal{L}_1, \mathcal{R}_1] \cup [\mathcal{L}_2, \mathcal{R}_2]$. Based on Fact 7.4, the *border* union operation in Figure 7.9 obtains the *JEP* space *border* $< \mathcal{L}, \mathcal{R} >$ from the *borders* $< \mathcal{L}_1, \mathcal{R}_1 >$ and $< \mathcal{L}_2, \mathcal{R}_2 >$.

Input: $< \mathcal{L}_1, \mathcal{R}_1 >$ representing $JEP(D_{P_1}, D_N)$ and $< \mathcal{L}_2, \mathcal{R}_2 >$ representing $JEP(D_{P_2}, D_N)$, for some datasets D_{P_1}, D_{P_2}, and D_N
Output: $< \mathcal{L}, \mathcal{R} >$ representing $JEP(D_{P_1} \cup D_{P_2}, D_N)$
% $< \mathcal{L}, \mathcal{R} >$ satisfies $[\mathcal{L}, \mathcal{R}] = [\mathcal{L}_1, \mathcal{R}_1] \cup [\mathcal{L}_2, \mathcal{R}_2]$
Method:
1: $\mathcal{L} = \mathcal{L}_1 \cup \mathcal{L}_2$;
2: $\mathcal{R} = \mathcal{R}_1 \cup \mathcal{R}_2$;
3: remove patterns in $\mathcal{L}$ that are not most general;
4: remove patterns in $\mathcal{R}$ that are not most specific;
   return $< \mathcal{L}, \mathcal{R} >$;

FIGURE 7.9: Operation *Border* Union.

Border Intersection: The *border* intersection operation addresses the opposite scenario compared with the *border* union operation. We have the following relationship between the underlying JEP spaces.

Fact 7.5 *Suppose we have a positive dataset D_P and a negative dataset D_N, and a partition of D_N into D_{N_1} and D_{N_2}. Then we have $JEP(D_P, D_N) = JEP(D_P, D_{N_1}) \cap JEP(D_P, D_{N_2})$. This is illustrated in Figure 7.10.*

In the notion of *border*, suppose $JEP(D_P, D_N) = [\mathcal{L}, \mathcal{R}]$, $JEP(D_P, D_{N_1}) = [\mathcal{L}_1, \mathcal{R}_1]$ and $JEP(D_P, D_{N_2}) = [\mathcal{L}_2, \mathcal{R}_2]$. Then, $[\mathcal{L}, \mathcal{R}] = [\mathcal{L}_1, \mathcal{R}_1] \cap [\mathcal{L}_2, \mathcal{R}_2]$. The *border* intersection operation in Figure 7.11 gives the *JEP* space *border* $< \mathcal{L}, \mathcal{R} >$ based on the *borders* $< \mathcal{L}_1, \mathcal{R}_1 >$ and $< \mathcal{L}_2, \mathcal{R}_2 >$.

7.4.2   Insertion of New Instances

Suppose we have D_P and D_N as the original contrasting *positive* and *negative* datasets, and the corresponding non-zero support pattern spaces are

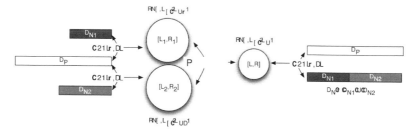

FIGURE 7.10: Intersection of two *JEP* spaces: given D_P and $D_N = D_{N_1} \cup D_{N_2}$, $JEP(D_P, D_N) = JEP(D_P, D_{N_1}) \cap JEP(D_P, D_{N_2})$.

Input: $< \mathcal{L}_1, \mathcal{R}_1 >$ representing $JEP(D_P, D_{N_1})$ and $< \mathcal{L}_2, \mathcal{R}_2 >$ representing $JEP(D_P, D_{N_2})$, for some datasets D_P, D_{N_1}, and D_{N_2}
Output: $< \mathcal{L}, \mathcal{R} >$ representing $JEP(D_P, D_{N_1} \cup D_{N_2})$
% $< \mathcal{L}, \mathcal{R} >$ satisfies $[\mathcal{L}, \mathcal{R}] = [\mathcal{L}_1, \mathcal{R}_1] \cup [\mathcal{L}_2, \mathcal{R}_2]$
Method:
1: $\mathcal{R} = \mathcal{R}_1 \cap \mathcal{R}_2$;
2: $\mathcal{L} = \{A \cup B | A \in \mathcal{L}_1, B \in \mathcal{L}_2\}$;
3: remove patterns in $\mathcal{L}$ that are not most general;
4: remove patterns P in $\mathcal{L}$ if $\nexists Q \in \mathcal{R}$ such that $P \subseteq Q$;
    return $< \mathcal{L}, \mathcal{R} >$;

FIGURE 7.11: Operation *Border* Intersection.

$[\{\emptyset\}, \mathcal{R}_\mathcal{P}]$ and $[\{\emptyset\}, \mathcal{R}_\mathcal{N}]$. Thus, the original *JEP* space can be expressed as $JEP(D_P, D_N) = [\{\emptyset\}, \mathcal{R}_\mathcal{P}] - [\{\emptyset\}, \mathcal{R}_\mathcal{N}]$. When new instances are inserted, there can be two scenarios, where new *positive* instances are inserted or new *negative* instances are inserted. We discuss these two scenarios separately.

Insertion of New *Positive* Instances: Suppose a set of new *positive* instances, Δ_P, is inserted, where $\Delta_P \cap D_P = \emptyset$. The updated set of *positive* instances is $(D_P \cup \Delta_P)$. Let $[\{\emptyset\}, \mathcal{R}_P^\Delta]$ denote the non-zero support pattern space of Δ_P. The updated *JEP* space with respect to $(D_P \cup \Delta_P)$ and D_N can be precisely defined by the following formula.

$$
\begin{aligned}
& JEP((D_P \cup \Delta_P), D_N) \\
=\ & ([\{\emptyset\}, \mathcal{R}_\mathcal{P}] \cup [\{\emptyset\}, \mathcal{R}_P^\Delta]) - [\{\emptyset\}, \mathcal{R}_\mathcal{N}] \\
=\ & ([\{\emptyset\}, \mathcal{R}_\mathcal{P}] - [\{\emptyset\}, \mathcal{R}_\mathcal{N}]) \cup ([\{\emptyset\}, \mathcal{R}_P^\Delta] - [\{\emptyset\}, \mathcal{R}_\mathcal{N}]) \\
=\ & JEP(D_P, D_N) \cup JEP(\Delta_P, D_N) \qquad (7.2)
\end{aligned}
$$

By Equation 7.2, the updated *JEP* space, $JEP((D_P \cup \Delta_P), D_N)$, is the union of the original *JEP* space, $JEP(D_P, D_N)$, and the *JEP* space contrasting Δ_P and D_N, $JEP(\Delta_P, D_N)$. Let $< \mathcal{L}, \mathcal{R} >$ be the *border* of the original *JEP* space. We can obtain the *border* of the updated *JEP* space in two steps:

Step 1. Discover the border of the *JEP* space contrasting Δ_P and D_N. Let $< \mathcal{L}', \mathcal{R}' >$ denote the resulting *border*.

Step 2. Apply the *border* union operation (Figure 7.9) on $< \mathcal{L}, \mathcal{R} >$ and $< \mathcal{L}', \mathcal{R}' >$.

Insertion of New *Negative* Instances: Suppose a set of new *negative* instances, Δ_N, is inserted, where $\Delta_N \cap D_N = \emptyset$. Thus, the updated *negative* instances are $(D_N \cup \Delta_N)$. Let $[\{\emptyset\}, \mathcal{R}_N^\Delta]$ denote the non-zero support pattern space of Δ_N. The updated *JEP* space with respect to D_P and $(D_N \cup \Delta_N)$ can be precisely defined as:

$$
\begin{aligned}
& JEP(D_P, (D_N \cup \Delta_N)) \\
= \ & [\{\emptyset\}, \mathcal{R}_P] - ([\{\emptyset\}, \mathcal{R}_N] \cup [\{\emptyset\}, \mathcal{R}_N^\Delta]) \\
= \ & ([\{\emptyset\}, \mathcal{R}_P] - [\{\emptyset\}, \mathcal{R}_N]) \cap ([\{\emptyset\}, \mathcal{R}_P] - [\{\emptyset\}, \mathcal{R}_N^\Delta]) \\
= \ & JEP(D_P, D_N) \cap JEP(D_P, \Delta_N) \qquad\qquad (7.3)
\end{aligned}
$$

We observe that, upon insertion of *negative* instances, Δ_N, the updated *JEP* space, $JEP(D_P, (D_N \cup \Delta_N))$, can be expressed as the intersection of the original *JEP* space, $JEP(D_P, D_N)$, and the *JEP* space contrasting D_P and Δ_N, $JEP(D_P, \Delta_N)$. Let $< \mathcal{L}, \mathcal{R} >$ be the *border* of the original *JEP* space. We can obtain the *border* of the updated *JEP* space in two steps:

Step 1. Discover the border of the *JEP* space contrasting D_P and Δ_N. Let $< \mathcal{L}', \mathcal{R}' >$ denote the resulting *border*.

Step 2. Apply the intersection operation (Figure 7.11) on $< \mathcal{L}, \mathcal{R} >$ and $< \mathcal{L}', \mathcal{R}' >$.

7.4.3   Removal of Existing Instances

When removing existing instances, there are also two scenarios: removing existing *positive* instances or removing existing *negative* instances. Different from the insertion case, the maintenance of the *JEP* space under the two removal scenarios is very distinct from each other.

Removal of Existing *Positive* Instances: Suppose a set of *positive* instances, Δ_P, is removed from the original data D_P. The *JEP* space will shrink upon the removal. The updated *JEP* space can be obtained by removing all non-zero support patterns in Δ_P. Let $[\{\emptyset\}, \mathcal{R}_P^\Delta]$ denote the non-zero support pattern space of Δ_P. The updated *JEP* space with respect to $(D_P - \Delta_P)$ and D_N is:

$$
JEP((D_P - \Delta_P), D_N) = JEP(D_P, D_N) - [\{\emptyset\}, \mathcal{R}_P^\Delta] \qquad (7.4)
$$

Let $< \mathcal{L}, \mathcal{R} >$ be the *border* of the original *JEP* space, $JEP(D_P, D_N)$. The subtraction in Eq 7.4 can be performed in the following steps:

Step 1. Discover the *border* of the non-zero support pattern space of $(D_P - \Delta_P)$. Let $< \{\emptyset\}, \mathcal{R}'_P >$ denote the resulting *border*.
Step 2. Let $\mathcal{L}' = \mathcal{L}$.
Step 3. Remove all patterns P in $\mathcal{L}'$ satisfying $\nexists Q \in \mathcal{R}'_P$ satisfying $P \subseteq Q$.

The resulting $< \mathcal{L}', \mathcal{R}'_P >$ is then the *border* of the the updated *JEP* space.
Removal of Existing *Negative* Instances: Suppose a set of *negative* instance, Δ_N, is removed. Upon the removal of existing *negative* instances, the *JEP* space will expand, as new emerging patterns will appear [249]. Under this case, the maintenance of the *JEP* space is much more complicated. We illustrate the process mathematically with the following formula. For ease of discussion, we denote $\mathcal{A} = [\{\emptyset\}, \mathcal{R}_P]$, the non-zero pattern space of the *positive* instances D_P, $\mathcal{B} = [\{\emptyset\}, \mathcal{R}'_N]$, the non-zero pattern space of the updated *negative* instances $(D_N - \Delta_N)$, and $\mathcal{C} = [\{\emptyset\}, \mathcal{R}^\Delta_N]$, the non-zero pattern space of the removed *negative* instances Δ_N.

$$
\begin{aligned}
& JEP(D_P, (D_N - \Delta_N)) \\
= {} & \mathcal{A} - \mathcal{B} = \mathcal{A} - \mathcal{B} - \mathcal{A} \cap \mathcal{B} \\
= {} & \mathcal{A} - \mathcal{B} - \mathcal{A} \cap \mathcal{B} - \mathcal{C} \cup \mathcal{A} \cap \mathcal{C} \\
= {} & (\mathcal{A} - \mathcal{B} \cup \mathcal{C}) \cup (\mathcal{A} \cap (\mathcal{C} - \mathcal{B})) \\
= {} & JEP(D_P, D_N) \cup (\mathcal{A} \cap (\mathcal{C} - \mathcal{B}))
\end{aligned} \tag{7.5}
$$

We observe that the first term of the union, $(\mathcal{A} - \mathcal{B} \cup \mathcal{C})$, is equivalent to the original *JEP* space, $JEP(D_P, D_N)$. The term $(\mathcal{C} - \mathcal{B}) = ([\{\emptyset\}, \mathcal{R}^\Delta_N] - [\{\emptyset\}, \mathcal{R}'_N])$ is then the *JEP* space contrasting Δ_N and D_N, $JEP(\Delta_N, D_N)$. Let $< \mathcal{L}, \mathcal{R} >$ be the *border* of the original *JEP* space, $JEP(D_P, D_N)$. The *border* of the updated *JEP* space can be obtained as follows.

Step 1. Discover the *border* of $JEP(\Delta_N, D_N)$.
    Let $< \mathcal{L}', \mathcal{R}' >$ denote the resulting *border*.
Step 2. Remove all patterns P in $\mathcal{L}'$ that does not appear in D_P.
Step 3. Apply the *border* union operation on $< \mathcal{L}, \mathcal{R} >$ and $< \mathcal{L}', \mathcal{R}' >$.

7.4.4 Expansion of Query Item Space

Let D_P and D_N denote the *positive* and *negative* datasets respectively. Let $\mathcal{I}$ be the *complete item space* that includes all the items in D_P and D_N and $\mathcal{I}_Q$ be the original *query item space*. Suppose a new item $e \in \mathcal{I}$ is inserted in the *query item space*, $\mathcal{I}_Q$. The *query item space* expands. The updated *query item space* becomes $\mathcal{I}'_Q = \mathcal{I}_Q \cup \{e\}$.

Let $[\{\emptyset\}, \mathcal{R}_P]$ be the non-zero support patterns in D_P under the original *query item space*, $\mathcal{I}_Q$, and let $[\{\{e\}\}, \mathcal{R}'_P]$ be the non-zero support patterns in D_P containing item e. Under the updated updated *query item space*, $\mathcal{I}'_Q = \mathcal{I}_Q \cup \{e\}$, the non-zero support patterns in D_P can then be expressed as $[\{\emptyset\}, \mathcal{R}_P] \cup [\{\{e\}\}, \mathcal{R}'_P]$.

Similarly, let $[\{\emptyset\}, \mathcal{R}_N]$ be the non-zero support patterns in D_N under $\mathcal{I}_Q$, and let $[\{\{e\}\}, \mathcal{R}'_N]$ be the non-zero support patterns in D_N containing item e. Under the updated updated *query item space*, $\mathcal{I}'_Q = \mathcal{I}_Q \cup \{e\}$, the non-zero support patterns in D_N can then be expressed as $[\{\emptyset\}, \mathcal{R}_N] \cup [\{\{e\}\}, \mathcal{R}'_N]$.

Based on Equation 7.1, the updated *JEP* space for the expanded *query item space*, $\mathcal{I}'_Q$, can be expressed as:

$$
\begin{aligned}
& JEP_{\mathcal{I}'_Q}(D_P, D_N) \\
=\ & ([\{\emptyset\}, \mathcal{R}_P] \cup [\{\{e\}\}, \mathcal{R}'_P]) - ([\{\emptyset\}, \mathcal{R}_N] \cup [\{\{e\}\}, \mathcal{R}'_N]) \\
=\ & ([\{\emptyset\}, \mathcal{R}_P] - [\{\{e\}\}, \mathcal{R}'_N] - [\{\emptyset\}, \mathcal{R}_N]) \cup \\
& ([\{\{e\}\}, \mathcal{R}'_P] - [\{\emptyset\}, \mathcal{R}_N] - [\{\{e\}\}, \mathcal{R}'_N]) \\
=\ & ([\{\emptyset\}, \mathcal{R}_P] - [\{\emptyset\}, \mathcal{R}_N]) \cup ([\{\{e\}\}, \mathcal{R}'_P] - [\{\{e\}\}, \mathcal{R}'_N]) \\
=\ & JEP_{\mathcal{I}_Q}(D_P, D_N) \cup ([\{\{e\}\}, \mathcal{R}'_P] - [\{\{e\}\}, \mathcal{R}'_N]) \quad (7.6)
\end{aligned}
$$

According to Equation 7.6, the updated *JEP* space can be obtained based on the *border*, $< \mathcal{L}, \mathcal{R} >$, of the original *JEP* space, and it can be achieved in two steps:

Step 1. Apply *border* subtraction operation to obtain the border of $[\{\{e\}\}, \mathcal{R}'_P] - [\{\{e\}\}, \mathcal{R}'_N]$. Let $< \mathcal{L}', \mathcal{R}' >$ be the resulting *border*.
Step 2. Apply the *border* union operation on $< \mathcal{L}, \mathcal{R} >$ and $< \mathcal{L}', \mathcal{R}' >$.

7.4.5   Shrinkage of Query Item Space

Shrinkage of *query item space* is the opposite operation of the expansion of *query item space*. Let $\mathcal{I}_Q$ be the original *query item space*. Suppose an item $e \in \mathcal{I}_Q$ is removed from $\mathcal{I}_Q$. The *query item space* shrinks, and the updated *query item space* becomes $\mathcal{I}'_Q = \mathcal{I}_Q - \{e\}$. Following the notations in Section 7.4.4, the updated *JEP* space for the shrunken *query item space* can then be formulated as:

$$
\begin{aligned}
& JEP_{\mathcal{I}'_Q}(D_P, D_N) \\
=\ & ([\{\emptyset\}, \mathcal{R}_P] - [\{\{e\}\}, \mathcal{R}'_P]) - ([\{\emptyset\}, \mathcal{R}_N] - [\{\{e\}\}, \mathcal{R}'_N]) \\
=\ & ([\{\emptyset\}, \mathcal{R}_P] - [\{\{e\}\}, \mathcal{R}'_P] - [\{\emptyset\}, \mathcal{R}_N]) \cup \\
& (([\{\emptyset\}, \mathcal{R}_P] - [\{\{e\}\}, \mathcal{R}'_P]) \cap [\{\{e\}\}, \mathcal{R}'_N]) \\
=\ & [\{\emptyset\}, \mathcal{R}_P] - [\{\emptyset\}, \mathcal{R}_N] - [\{\{e\}\}, \mathcal{R}'_P] \\
=\ & JEP_{\mathcal{I}_Q}(D_P, D_N) - [\{\{e\}\}, \mathcal{R}'_P] \quad (7.7)
\end{aligned}
$$

By Equation 7.7, the updated *JEP* space can be obtained by removing all existing emerging patterns that contain item e. Suppose the *border* of the original *JEP* space is $< \mathcal{L}, \mathcal{R} >$. The *border* of the updated *JEP* space, $< \mathcal{L}', \mathcal{R}' >$, can be effectively obtained as follows:

Step 1. $\mathcal{L}' = \{P|P \in \mathcal{L} \text{ and } e \notin P\}$.
Step 2. $\mathcal{R}' = \{P|P \in \mathcal{R} \text{ and } e \notin P\}$.
Step 3. Remove all patterns P in $\mathcal{R}'$ that are not most specific.
Step 4. Remove all patterns P in $\mathcal{R}'$ that do not contain any pattern in $\mathcal{L}'$.

7.5 Related Work

Incremental maintenance of emerging patterns has not received as much research attention as its discovery task. However, considerable amount of research effort has been committed to the incremental maintenance of *frequent patterns*. "Frequent Patterns" [3] are patterns that appear frequently in the data. The spaces of frequent patterns and emerging patterns share many similarities. For instance, both pattern spaces grow exponentially with the number of items, and both pattern spaces are convex [249, 239]. Therefore, ideas in frequent pattern maintenance can often be extended to the incremental maintenance of emerging patterns.

In the literature, the frequent pattern maintenance algorithms can be classified into four main categories: the 1) *Apriori-based* algorithms, 2) *Partition-based* algorithms, 3) *Prefix-tree-based* algorithms and 4) *Concise-representation-based* algorithms [147].

FUP [91] is the first *Apriori*-based maintenance algorithm. Inspired by Apriori [3], FUP updates the space of frequent patterns iteratively based on the candidate-generation-verification framework. The key technique of FUP is to make use of support information in previously discovered frequent patterns to reduce the number of candidate patterns. Since the performance of candidate-generation-verification based algorithms heavily depends on the size of the candidate set, FUP outperforms Apriori. Similarly, the partition-based algorithm SWF [233] also employs the candidate-generation-verification framework. However, SWF applies different techniques to reduce the size of candidate set. SWF slices a dataset into several partitions and employs a filtering threshold in each partition to filter out unnecessary candidate patterns. Even with all the candidate reduction techniques, the candidate-generation-verification framework still leads to the enumeration of large number of unnecessary candidates. This greatly limits the performance of both *Apriori*-based and partition-based algorithms.

To address this shortcoming of the candidate-generation-verification framework, tree-based algorithms have been proposed. Examples include FP-growth [180], a *prefix-tree* based algoirhtm, and Apriori-TFP [94], a *Total Support Tree (T-tree)* based algorithm. In [236] and [323], Apriori-TFP was extended to incrementally maintain emerging patterns. Apriori-TFP enumerates and generates patterns with the *T-tree*. A *T-tree* is basically a *set-enumeration tree*; it ensures a complete and non-redundant enumeration of patterns. *Apriori-TFP* (Total From Partial) efficiently constructs the *Total Support Tree, T-tree,* based on the *Partial Support Tree, P-tree*. P-tree is a summarized set-enumeration tree with partial support information of patterns [236]. Benefiting from the "Total From Partial" idea, Apriori-TFP achieves a good balance between time and memory efficiency. However, tree based algorithms still suffer from the undesirably large size of the pattern space.

To break this bottleneck, concise representations of the frequent pattern space have been proposed. The commonly used representations include "maximal patterns" [46], "closed patterns" [326], and "equivalence classes" [146]. Algorithms, such as Moment [92], ZIGZAG [415], and PSM (Pattern Space Maintainer) [146] have been proposed to maintain these concise representations.

Concise representations are also employed to summarize the pattern space of emerging patterns. The concept of *border* was first introduced in [118] to summarize the emerging pattern space with its *left* and *right* bounds — its border. Based on the concept of *border*, an effective method for incremental maintenance of emerging patterns was proposed in [249]. This method has been discussed in Sections 7.3 and 7.4. Reference [32] further extended the method to address the maintenance of emerging patterns for data streams. Since a data stream is a continuous stream of data, emerging pattern discovery in data streams, as defined in [32], is to contrast the updated data with the obsolete data. As illustrated in Figure 7.12, the contrasting *positive* dataset, D_P, refers to the relatively newer segment of the data stream, and the contrasting *negative* dataset, D_N, refers to the more obsolete segment. Suppose the data stream is updated in a sliding window manner. We can observe from Figure 7.12 that: newly updated data, Δ_P^+, will be included in the updated *positive* dataset, D_P'; some originally *positive* data, Δ_P^-, will become obsolete and will be converted into the *negative* dataset, D_N'; and, according to the concept of sliding window, the most obsolete data, Δ_N^-, will be removed.

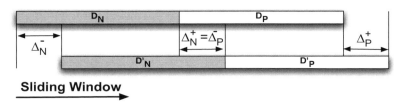

Sliding Window

FIGURE 7.12: Maintenance of emerging patterns over data streams. Note: $\Delta_P^+ = \Delta_P^- = \Delta_N^+ = \Delta_N^-$

7.6   Closing Remarks

In the current era of data explosion, data is dynamically updated all the time. In addition, data is also often modified to perform interactive mining. Re-generating emerging patterns every time when the underlying data is updated or modified involves large amount of redundancy and is practically infeasible. The practical solution is to incrementally maintain the discovered emerging patterns.

The pattern space of emerging patterns is usually very large. Updating every single pattern in the pattern space can be computationally expensive. This bottleneck can be addressed by summarizing the emerging pattern space using a concise representation. Compared with the entire pattern space, the concise representation consists of a much smaller number of patterns, thus it can be maintained with much lower computational cost.

To illustrate the concept, we focused on the jumping emerging patterns — the most discriminative emerging patterns. In Section 7.3, we discussed how the jumping emerging pattern space can be summarized with its concise representation, its *border*. In Section 7.4, we further discussed how the *border* of the jumping emerging pattern space can be effectively maintained under various data updates. The types of data updates that we have addressed include: insertion of new instances, removal of existing instances, expansion, and shrinkage of the *query item space*.

Part III

Generalized Contrasts, Emerging Data Cubes, and Rough Sets

Chapter 8

More Expressive Contrast Patterns and Their Mining

Lei Duan

School of Computer Science, Sichuan University

Milton Garcia Borroto

Centro de Bioplantas, Universidad de Ciego de Avila

Guozhu Dong

Department of Computer Science and Engineering, Wright State University

8.1 Introduction

This chapter presents the definition and mining of several types of generalized contrast patterns, including disjunctive emerging patterns, fuzzy emerging patterns, inequality contrasts, and contrast equations. The generalized contrast patterns use more expressive constructs, including disjunction (OR),

D_p				D_n			
A	**B**	**C**	**Class**	**A**	**B**	**C**	**Class**
a_1	b_2	c_1	Positive	a_1	b_3	c_1	Negative
a_1	b_1	c_3	Positive	a_2	b_1	c_2	Negative
a_2	b_3	c_2	Positive	a_2	b_3	c_2	Negative
a_3	b_2	c_2	Positive	a_3	b_2	c_1	Negative

TABLE 8.1: A small example dataset for disjunctive emerging patterns

fuzzy concepts, equality and inequality involving arithmetic expressions over multiple attributes. In comparison, the standard contrast patterns are often limited to conjunctions (AND) of simple single-attribute conditions. The more powerful constructs give the generalized contrast patterns more modeling power. The generalized contrast patterns may also be more intuitive. The disjunctive emerging patterns are generalized contrast patterns defined for nominal features, whereas the other three are generalized contrast patterns defined for numerical features.

8.2   Disjunctive Emerging Pattern Mining

8.2.1   Basic Definitions

To motivate the concept of disjunctive emerging pattern, consider the D_p and D_n datasets given in Table 8.1. While EPs (e.g. $\{a_1, b_2\}$) exist for ($\alpha = 0.25$, $\beta = 0$), no EP exists for ($\alpha = 0.5$, $\beta = 0$). (Here we consider emerging patterns (EPs) defined using two support thresholds α and β; EPs are itemsets X satisfying $\mathsf{supp}(X, D_p) \geq \alpha$ and $\mathsf{supp}(X, D_n) \leq \beta$.)

It is natural to ask: Can we generalize the concept of EPs so that discriminative patterns at the ($\alpha = 0.5$, $\beta = 0$) level can be captured?

It is worth noting that EPs are conjunctions of simple single-attribute conditions. For the data in Table 8.1, $\{a_1, b_2\}$ actually represents $A = a_1 \wedge B = b_2$. One natural way to generalize is to also use disjunction, in addition to conjunction. This leads to the following definitions from [283].

A *disjunctive item* is the disjunction of a set of items on one common attribute. For the data in Table 8.1, $a_1 \vee a_3$ is a disjunctive item but $a_1 \vee b_1$ is not. A *disjunctive itemset* X is the conjunction of the disjunctive items in X. The support of a disjunctive itemset X in a dataset D is defined in the natural manner, as the fraction of tuples of D that satisfy X.

Given a positive dataset D_p, a negative dataset D_n, and support thresholds α and β, a *disjunctive emerging pattern* (*disjunctive EP*) is a disjunctive itemset X satisfying $\mathsf{supp}(X, D_p) \geq \alpha$ and $\mathsf{supp}(X, D_n) \leq \beta$.

For the data in Table 8.1, both $X = (a_1 \lor a_3) \land (b_1 \lor b_2 \lor b_3) \land (c_2 \lor c_3)$ and $(a_1 \lor a_2) \land (b_1 \lor b_2) \land (c_1 \lor c_3)$ are disjunctive EPs at the ($\alpha = 0.5$, $\beta = 0$) level. The support of X in D_p is 0.5 and its support in D_n is 0.

Some disjunctive items are trivial – they are satisfied by all possible tuples in the data. For example, for the data in Table 8.1, $(b_1 \lor b_2 \lor b_3)$ is a trivial disjunctive item. Trivial disjunctive items can be removed from disjunctive itemsets without causing any changes to the statistics of the disjunctive itemsets. So, there is no need to include the requirement that each disjunctive EP contain a disjunctive item for each attribute (which was included in [283]).

As discussed earlier, for given thresholds α and β, it can happen that many disjunctive EPs exist but no EP exists. Below, we discuss other relationships/differences between EPs and disjunctive EPs. Generally speaking, disjunctive EPs are more expressive, allowing them to capture contrast patterns of greater complexity. These are indicated by observations given below.

Theorem 8.1 *Given support thresholds α and β and datasets D_p and D_n, each emerging pattern X is a disjunctive emerging pattern.*

The converse of this theorem does not hold.

Sometimes disjunctive EPs can represent multiple EPs in a concise manner. This happens when several EPs of lower support can be merged together to form a disjunctive EP. For example, $\{a_1, b_1\}$ ($\equiv a_1 \land b_1$) and $\{a_1, b_2\}$ ($\equiv a_1 \land b_2$) are EPs for Table 8.1 and ($\alpha = 0.25$, $\beta = 0$). Both have $\mathsf{supp}(D_p) = 0.25$ and $\mathsf{supp}(D_n) = 0$. These two EPs can be "unioned" to yield the disjunctive EP $X = a_1 \land (b_1 \lor b_2)$ having $\mathsf{supp}(X, D_p) = 0.5$ and $\mathsf{supp}(X, D_n) = 0$.

An interesting special case exists when each attribute's domain contains exactly two values. In this case, the two types of EPs coincide.

It can be argued that disjunctive EPs are especially suitable for data which calls for contrasts involving disjunctions of items within specific dimensions.

Being more expressive, disjunctive EPs are harder to compute. Below we present one algorithm for mining disjunctive EPs.

8.2.2   ZBDD Based Approach to Disjunctive EP Mining

Reference [283] gives a ZBDD (Zero-suppressed Binary Decision Diagram) based method, called *mineDEP*, for mining EPs and disjunctive EPs. The key ideas of *mineDEP* include using ZBDD for generating pattern candidates, and also for storing the output patterns. Below we present that method.

We use Figure 8.1 to illustrate ZBDD (see Chapter 4 for details on ZBDD). Each root-to-sink-1 path π from the root to the sink-1 node represents a set S_π as follows: The meaning of a "solid edge" in π is that the item of the parent node is "in" S_π, and that of a "dotted edge" is that the item of the parent node is "not in" S_π. Observe that edges leading to the sink-1 node are always solid, whereas edges leading to the sink-0 node are always dotted. So, the path a_2–b_3–c_2–1 represents the itemset $\{a_2, b_3, c_2\}$, and the path a_2–b_3··c_2–

b_1–1 represents the itemset $\{a_2, c_2, b_1\}$. Paths from the root to the sink-0 node always represents $\{\}$.

The search space of *mineDEP* is dictated by the contents of the negative dataset. For efficiency purposes, *mineDEP* works with pattern complements, which are likely to contain fewer items, rather than the patterns themselves. Candidate patterns are generated by growing prefixes in the complemented pattern space. For each prefix P, the complement of P (denoted by $\bar{P}$) represents a disjunctive itemset; for the example data in Table 8.1, $\overline{\{a_2, c_1\}} = \{a_1, a_3, b_1, b_2, b_3, c_2, c_3\}$, representing the disjunctive itemset $(a_1 \vee a_3) \wedge (b_1 \vee b_2 \vee b_3) \wedge (c_2 \vee c_3)$ (the conjunction of the disjunctive items each defined by the disjunction of the items for one attribute).

The initial input of *mineDEP* includes: a ZBDD Z_D representing a projection of the negative dataset D_n, a prefix itemset P (with initial value of $\{\}$) which defines a projection of Z_D, bitmaps of the positive and negative datasets D_p and D_n, a min support threshold α, a max support threshold β.

Mining proceeds by calling *mineDEP* on recursive projections of D_n, starting from D_n. Before attempting to grow a prefix P with the next item, x, the algorithm first tests whether the α and β pruning can be performed; that is, exploration of the search space stops if one of the following conditions is satisfied: (a) $\mathsf{supp}(\overline{P \cup \{x\}}, D_p) < \alpha$, (b) $\mathsf{supp}(\overline{P \cup \{x\}}, D_n) \leq \beta$. For (a), exploration stops since no expansion of $P \cup \{x\}$ will get a desired disjunctive EP. For (b), we stop expanding $P \cup \{x\}$ with $\overline{P \cup \{x\}}$ as a maximal disjunctive EP (more expansion will only find non-maximal disjunctive EPs). (Note: we want to mine the maximal disjunctive EPs.) If no pruning is applicable, x is appended to the P. Then instances which do not contain x are explored (following the left child of x), with the output stored in $zOut_x$. The next routine is to compute $zOut_{\bar{x}}$ from a projection of the database of instances containing x, namely the set obtained by following the right child of x. Some itemsets in $zOut_{\bar{x}}$ may be contained by some itemsets in $zOut_x$; the non-minimal patterns are pruned. $zOut_{\bar{x}}$ and $zOut_x$ will be the two subtrees of the ZBDD output.

When the prefix P reaches a sink node, it has reached the end of the search space for growing. If P passes the β constraint, it is a satisfying maximal disjunctive EP and the ZBDD sink-1 node is returned. Otherwise, prefix cannot be part of the output ZBDD, so the sink-0 node is returned.

Finally, the output ZBDD stores the maximal disjunctive EPs.

Figure 8.1 gives a ZBDD for D_n, and the bitmaps of D_p and D_n, of Table 8.1. As stated before, $(a_1 \vee a_3) \wedge (b_1 \vee b_2 \vee b_3) \wedge (c_2 \vee c_3)$ is a disjunctive EP for that dataset at the $(\alpha = 0.5, \beta = 0)$ level. Below, we demonstrate how *mineDEP* discovers this and other maximal disjunctive EPs.

Initially, the prefix P is $\{\}$ and the first candidate item x is a_2. The bitmaps show that neither α nor β pruning is applicable for a_2. Thus, a_2 is appended to P, yielding $P = \{a_2\}$. Next, $zOut_x$ of a_2 is produced by exploring the left subtree of a_2, which represents instances not containing a_2. When growing the prefix with the next item c_1, we see that $\mathsf{supp}(\overline{\{a_2, c_1\}}, D_p) = \alpha$ and $\mathsf{supp}(\overline{\{a_2, c_1\}}, D_n) = \beta$. So β constraint pruning is preformed for the prefix

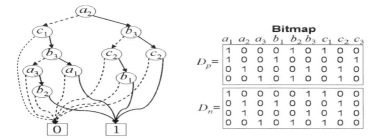

					Bitmap			
a_1	a_2	a_3	b_1	b_2	b_3	c_1	c_2	c_3
1	0	0	0	1	0	1	0	0
1	0	0	1	0	0	0	0	1
0	1	0	0	0	1	0	1	0
0	0	1	0	1	0	0	1	0

$D_p =$ (rows above)

1	0	0	0	0	1	1	0	0
0	1	0	1	0	0	0	1	0
0	1	0	0	0	1	0	1	0
0	0	1	0	1	0	1	0	0

$D_n =$ (rows above)

FIGURE 8.1: The ZBDD of D_n and bitmaps of D_p and D_n of Table 8.1.

$\{a_2.c_1\}$, and the $zOut_x$ of c_1 is assigned 1. So there is now a solid path a_2-c_1-1 in the output ZBDD of $mineDEP$, and hence $\overline{\{a_2, c_1\}} = (a_1 \vee a_3) \wedge (b_1 \vee b_2 \vee b_3) \wedge (c_2 \vee c_3))$ becomes a newly discovered maximal disjunctive EP.

In another case, with prefix $P = \{a_2\}$ and when growing with the item b_3, $\mathsf{supp}(\overline{\{a_2, b_3\}}, D_p) > \alpha$, and $\mathsf{supp}(\overline{\{a_2, b_3\}}, D_n) > \beta$. So, we grow P to $P = \{a_2, b_3\}$. Then, $zOut_x$ of b_3 is obtained by exploring the left subtree of b_3 (instances containing neither a_2 nor b_3). When growing the prefix with a_3, $\mathsf{supp}(\overline{\{a_2, a_3, b_3\}}, D_p) > \alpha$, but $\mathsf{supp}(\overline{\{a_2, a_3, b_3\}}, D_n) = \beta$. So, β constraint pruning is preformed. The prefix stops growing and the $zOut_x$ of c_1 is assigned 1. The path $\{a_2, b_3, a_3\}$ is a solid path to sink-1 node in the output ZBDD of $mineDEP$. So $\overline{\{a_2, a_3, b_3\}} = (\{a_1, b_1, b_2, c_1, c_2, c_3\})$ becomes a discovered maximal disjunctive EP. For growing the prefix $P = \{a_2, b_3\}$ with b_2, $\mathsf{supp}(\overline{\{a_2, b_3, b_2\}}, D_p) < \alpha$. So $\{a_2, b_2, b_3\}$ becomes a dotted path to sink-0 node in the output ZBDD ($\overline{\{a_2, b_2, b_3\}}$ is not a maximal disjunctive EP).

Similarly, the other two maximal disjunctive EPs $\{(a_1 \vee a_2 \vee a_3) \wedge (b_1 \vee b_2 \vee b_3) \wedge c_3, (a_1 \vee a_2) \wedge (b_1 \vee b_2) \wedge (c_1 \vee c_3)\}$ can be discovered.

A number of pruning strategies were also presented in [283] to further optimize the algorithm.

8.3 Fuzzy Emerging Pattern Mining

This section discusses fuzzy emerging patterns (FEPs), a mixture of the concepts of fuzzy logic [456] and emerging patterns [118]. After motivating and defining the basic concepts, this section presents an algorithm for mining FEPs, and briefly discusses a method for using FEPs in classification.

8.3.1 Advantages of Fuzzy Logic

Since its inception in 1965 [456], fuzzy logic has had a significant impact on science and technology because it allows computers to reason in a manner similarly the way people do, and because fuzzy systems allow us to model systems in a way closer to the way people understand them.

A fuzzy set S is specified by a fuzzy membership function $\mu_S : X \rightarrow [0,1]$ that maps each value $x \in X$ to its degree of membership $\mu_S(x)$ in the set S. A fuzzy set defines a fuzzy concept. For example, the first diagram in Figure 8.2 shows three fuzzy sets for three fuzzy concepts of temperature. We note that 10°C has membership of 0.5 in both fuzzy sets "cool" and "warm", while it has no membership at all in fuzzy set "hot". The fuzzy sets allows us to say that 10°C is somewhat cool and somewhat warm, but it is not hot at all.

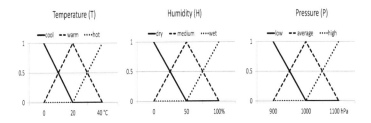

FIGURE 8.2: Fuzzy sets describing temperatures, humidity, and pressure.

The fuzzy curve of Figure 8.2 describes the concept "hot" more meaningfully and accurately than the crisp condition $Temperature > 40$. Using the crisp condition, the temperature 39.5°C is not hot at all, but 40.5°C is fully hot. In contrast, using the fuzzy curve, 39.5°C is very close to being *hot*, and 39.5°C and 40°C are very close to each other regarding *hot*ness, which is very similar to the way people understand the concept "hot".

The concepts of fuzzy emerging patterns were introduced to alleviate some drawbacks of crisp patterns which rely on crisp boundaries on numerical features, to make the pattern fulfillment relation more flexible, and to make it easier to read and explain patterns.

8.3.2   Fuzzy Emerging Patterns Defined

A *fuzzy pattern* is a fuzzy conjunction of *fuzzy items* of the form $[A \in FS]$, where A is an attribute, FS is a fuzzy set, and $\in$ refers to the membership of (the value of) A to FS.

Example 8.1 $[Temperature \in hot] \wedge [Humidity \in normal]$ *is a fuzzy pattern. It can be read and understood in plain English as "Temperature is hot and Humidity is normal".*

Additionally, fuzzy sets can be modified by *linguistic hedges* like "very", "somewhat", and "above". Linguistic hedges modify the meaning (and shape) of fuzzy sets like adverbs modify verbs and adjectives in natural languages. These hedges are very important because they modify in different ways the semantic and shape of the original fuzzy sets, making the modified sets closer to the intended concepts in the problem domain.

Example 8.2 $[Temperature \in very(hot)] \wedge [Humidity \in somewhat(normal)]$ *is a fuzzy pattern using linguistic hedges "very" and "somewhat". The semantic of the expression can be easily understood based on the definition of "hot" and "normal".*

Instead of the simple 0-1 approach to defining "support" for crisp patterns where an object supports a pattern either 100% or 0%, an object supports every fuzzy pattern to some *degree* according to its membership to the fuzzy items of the fuzzy pattern. The individual fuzzy support of an object o for a given fuzzy pattern F is defined as the minimum membership (μ) of all its attribute values in their respective fuzzy sets:

$$fsup(o, F) = \min_{f \in F} \{\mu_f(o)\}.$$

The support of a fuzzy pattern F in a class C_i as the sum of the individual fuzzy support for all objects in C_i:

$$FSup(F, C_i) = \sum_{o \in C_i} fsup(o, F).$$

We measure the relevance of a fuzzy pattern using the concept of *Trust*. The *Trust* of a fuzzy pattern F measures the ratio of F's support in the class with the highest support, with respect to F's total support in all the classes:

$$Trust(F) = \frac{\max_{C_i} FSup(F, C_i)}{\sum_{C_i} FSup(F, C_i)}.$$

We can view $Trust(F)$ as a measure on F's discriminating power between the classes. A *Trust* above 0.5 means the pattern has higher support in the highest supported class than in the other classes. *Trust* can be used as voting weight of fuzzy emerging patterns in classification.

Based on the above discussion, we can now define a *fuzzy emerging pattern* (FEP) as a fuzzy pattern F with $Trust(F) > 0.5$.

8.3.3 Mining Fuzzy Emerging Patterns

Fuzzy emerging patterns can be mined using a diversified decision tree based approach [161]. This approach first induces a diverse collection of decision trees, and then extracts fuzzy emerging patterns from the decision trees. This method avoids the global discretization step, and allows patterns to be expressed with a rich set of properties that include operators such as $<, \geq, \neq$.

Diversified decision tree based pattern miners have the following steps:

1. Induce a set of decision trees, using a technique to ensure diversity among the trees.
2. Extract patterns from each induced decision tree. Each extracted pattern corresponds to the conjunction of the properties in the path from the root node to a leaf node.
3. Merge the set of patterns extracted from all induced decision trees.
4. Filter the set of the patterns.

The algorithm for mining fuzzy emerging pattern, named FEPM [162], is based on fuzzy decision trees. FEPM uses a variant of ID3 [344] tailored for the fuzzy case, with the following five differences (a–e):

(a) The candidate splits include the following fuzzy sets and their fuzzy negation: (a1) all the fuzzy sets obtained in the fuzzyfication[1] step, and (a2) all fuzzy sets in (a1), modified by all different predefined hedges. The hedges should be defined by the user according to the problem domain.

Observe that one attribute can contribute multiple splits. This differs from standard decision trees, where an attribute contributes exactly one split. (Some decision trees use a nominal value and its complement to split nodes.)

(b) In classical ID3, each object in a decision node is assigned to a single child node. In the fuzzy version, each object is assigned to all children nodes with appropriate membership values. Hence, every object belongs to every node in the fuzzy tree with a different membership value. To calculate the object membership in a child node, the FEPM algorithm applies a fuzzy AND between the object membership in the parent node and the membership of the object to the fuzzy set associated to the child node.

(c) If the membership of an object to a node is below a given threshold μ_{min} (usually μ_{min} is set to 0.05), the object is deleted from the node.

(d) Let $\mu_N(o)$ denote the membership of an object o to a node N. The quality of a split is evaluated using *fuzzy information gain* [127]:

$$fig(N) = fimp(N) - \sum_{N_c \in child(N)} fimp(N_c) \times \frac{\sum_{o \in N_c} \mu_{N_c}(o)}{\sum_{o \in N} \mu_N(o)}$$

where $fimp(N')$, the *fuzzy impurity* of a node N', is defined as:

$$fimp(N') = - \sum_{C \in classes(N')} \frac{\sum_{o \in C} \mu_{N'}(o)}{\sum \mu_{N'}(o)} \times \log(\frac{\sum_{o \in C} \mu_{N'}(o)}{\sum \mu_{N'}(o)})$$

(e) The following stop criteria are used: (e1) The node is pure, i.e. all the objects in the node belong to the same class. (e2) The node is empty. (e3) No split provides an improvement in the fuzzy information gain.

To guarantee diversity among the trees used to extract the fuzzy emerging patterns, FEPM produces a set of trees using a trade-off between computing

---

[1] Fuzzification transforms a numerical variable into a collection of fuzzy sets covering the variable domain. See Figure 8.2 for examples.

only the best tree (by always selecting the split with the highest fuzzy information gain at each node) and building all possible trees (which may be hard to apply to nontrivial problems because of its time complexity). Specifically, FEPM expands the best k candidate splits[2] for the root node, $k - 1$ for its children, $k - 2$ for its grandchildren, and so on. For nodes at level k or higher, FEPM expands only the best candidate split. This allows higher diversity in upper nodes, where there are often more good splits, reducing the diversity in lower nodes, where there are fewer good splits. The total number of generated decision trees might be less than $k!$, since some of the trees might be identical because its induction procedure ends before the tree level k.

From each tree, FEPM extracts all the fuzzy patterns, and assigns each pattern to the class with the highest fuzzy support. Finally, FEPM removes duplicated patterns and patterns which are not emerging (with $Trust \leq 0.5$).

To illustrate, consider the dataset containing exactly the three objects given in Table 8.2, using the membership functions given in Figure 8.2.

Object	Temperature (°C)	Humidity (%)	Pressure (hPa)	Class
o1	20	0	1095	BadDay
o2	37	12	1005	GoodDay
o3	18	60	975	BadDay

TABLE 8.2: Description of the objects used in the example

For $k = 5$, the diversified tree generation procedure generates $k! = 120$ fuzzy decision trees, for the level-diversity vectors starting from $(1, 1, 1, 1, 1)$ and ending at $(5, 4, 3, 2, 1)$.

For example, the tree for $(2, 1, 3, 2, 1)$ is built using the second best split for the root node, the best split for nodes at the second level, the third best split for nodes at the third level, and so on.

The candidate splits for each node are given by the set $\{(A, h(f_A), not(h(f_A))) \mid A \in \{T, H, P\}$, f_A is a fuzzy concept for A, h is a linguistic hedge for $A\}$. There are 9 candidate spits if there are no linguistic hedges.

Figure 8.3 shows the complete fuzzy decision tree. As this tree has four leaves, four fuzzy emerging patterns are extracted, as shown in Table 8.3. In this case, no pattern is discarded, because they all have $Trust > 0.5$. It is important to appreciate the expressivity and ease to understand the extracted patterns.

To illustrate, the following are three representative fuzzy emerging patterns with very high trust mined from the *Iris* of UCI Machine Learning Repository:

$[petallength \in extremely(low)] \bigwedge [petalwidth \in low]$,
    class: **iris-setosa**, $Trust = 0.99$
$[petalwidth \in extremely(high)]$,
    class: **iris-virginica**, $Trust = 0.95$

---

[2]k is a fixed positive number

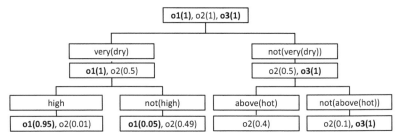

FIGURE 8.3: A fuzzy tree for data in Table 8.2. The membership of the objects to each node are given, in addition to the split condition for the node.

Class	FEP	Trust
BadDay	$[Hum \in very(dry)] \wedge [Pres \in high]$	0.99
	$[Hum \in not(very(dry))] \wedge [Temp \in not(above(hot))]$	0.91
GoodDay	$[Hum \in very(dry)] \wedge [Pres \in not(high)]$	0.90
	$[Hum \in very(dry)] \wedge [Temp \in above(hot)]$	1.00

TABLE 8.3: Fuzzy emerging patterns extracted from the tree in Figure 8.3. Hum: Humidity; Temp: Temperature; Pres: Pressure.

$$[petallength \in positively(medium)] \bigwedge [petalwidth \in medium]$$
$$\bigwedge [petallength \in not(extremely(high))],$$
class: **iris-versicolor**, $Trust = 0.96$

In experiments reported here and in the next subsection, shapes using straight lines similar to those used in Figure 8.2 are used to define the fuzzy concepts. The split values were determined using equi-width binning.

8.3.4   Using Fuzzy Emerging Patterns in Classification

Below we briefly discuss how FEPC [162] uses fuzzy emerging patterns in classification, in the CAEP [126] style. Since the fuzzy hedges complicate the relationship among the patterns, we need to extend the concepts regarding the specific vs general relationship among patterns to the fuzzy case.

Definition 8.1 *A fuzzy item* $f_1 \equiv [Attr_1 \in FS_1]$ *is more specific than another fuzzy item* $f_2 \equiv [Attr_2 \in FS_2]$ *if* $Attr_1 = Attr_2$ *and*[3] $FS_1 \subset FS_2$.

The concept is similar to that in the crisp case. For the fuzzy case it helps to think in the relation between extensions of the concepts (i.e. which objects belong to the concept), and not the subset inclusion of the items. A pattern

---

[3]This is the fuzzy subset relation. A fuzzy set S_1 is subset of another fuzzy set S_2 if S_1 has lower or equal membership values than S_2 for all values in the domain.

is then more specific if it covers a subset of the other concept. For example, pattern "hot and high" is more specific than "hot" and than "high", which are more general. For fuzzy patterns, we substitute crisp subset by fuzzy subset. Hence, the pattern "very(hot)" is more specific than "hot" because the degree to very(hot) is always below the membership to hot. (In English, every very-hot temperature is always hot, but the contrary is not true.)

Definition 8.2 *Let F_1 and F_2 be two fuzzy emerging patterns. F_1 is more specific than F_2, and F_2 is more general than F_1, if for each fuzzy item f_2 in F_2, F_1 contains an equal or more specific fuzzy item f_1.*

If two patterns contain linguistic hedges, we use the fuzzy subset inclusion between them to determine which is more general. For example, the fuzzy item $very(high)$ is more general than $extremly(high)$, but less general than $somewhat(high)$. The "more general" relation is antisymmetric, and two patterns may be incomparable with each other. By Definition 8.2, an object supports a more general pattern with higher degree than a less general pattern.

To select which patterns to use for classification is a complex task [161]. Using more specific patterns reduces duplicate pattern contribution and provides more information about relationships between features, but specific patterns occur less often in query objects, causing abstention[4]. On the other hand, general patterns are more resistant to noise and can be mined with less computational effort. Nevertheless, aggregating many minimal (most general) patterns may cause duplicate contributions and decrease in classification accuracy.

FEPC organizes all available patterns in a pattern graph, where (1) each node represents a fuzzy emerging pattern, and (2) there is an arc from node N_1 to node N_2 if the pattern for N_1 is more specific than the pattern for N_2. In this graph, nodes with no ancestors are maximal patterns (most specific), and nodes with no descendants are minimal patterns (most general).

The following simplification procedure is applied to the graph, to help avoid considering a more general pattern while a more specific one has not been examined in the classification process: Discard an arc A from node N_1 to node N_2 if there is a longer path connecting N_1 and N_2 in the same direction.

To compute the votes per class of a query object O, FEPC starts by evaluating the patterns with no ancestors. If an evaluated pattern matches O (with a fuzzy support above a certain threshold) the vote to its class is increased with its $Trust$, while all its descendants are discarded. Otherwise, all immediate descendants are evaluated in the same way. The process ends when every node has been evaluated or discarded. Finally, FEPC assigns to O the class with the highest total vote.

Example 8.3 *Consider the following patterns **ABE**, **ABD**, **DE**, **AB**, **A**, and **D**. Here **A**, **B**, **C**, **D**, and **E** represent fuzzy items. The pattern graph*

---

[4]Abstention happens when no emerging pattern matches the query object, thus giving no evidence for the classifier to select a class.

contains the following edges: $ABE \rightarrow AB$, $ABD \rightarrow AB$, $AB \rightarrow A$, $ABD \rightarrow$
D, *and* $DE \rightarrow D$. *Observe that* $ABE \rightarrow A$ *is not in the graph due to the
presence of a longer path from* ABE *to* A. *To classify an object* $Q = ABC$
(which is a short way of saying that Q *has positive membership in* A, B, *and
* C *and zero membership in* D *and* E), *FEPC first considers the patterns with
no ancestors:* ABE, ABD, *and* DE. *None of them matches* Q, *so FEPC
considers their immediate descendants:* AB *and* D. *Since* Q *matches* AB,
the pattern A *is discarded. Finally,* AB *is the only pattern that contributes
a vote for the classification of* Q. *FEPC classifies the object* ADE *using the
votes of* DE *and* A.

FEPC tries to classify each object O with fuzzy emerging patterns that
are as specific as possible. The classifier uses a more general pattern Y that
matches O only if none of the more specific patterns of Y matches O. This
allows us to combine specific patterns having low errors with general patterns
with low abstention, and helps us to avoid vote duplication by similar patterns.

Experiments on a range of numerical datasets from the UCI repository
show that FEPC has very good performance and often significantly outperforms other classifiers such as Boosting, Bagging, C4.5, Random Forest, and
SVM; the outperformance over the best of those classifiers is at least 5% (absolute improvement) on average, on a selection of 16 UCI datasets. (See [161].)
As in the last subsection, in experiments reported here, fuzzy concepts were
defined using straight line shapes similar to those used in Figure 8.2, and the
split values were automatically extracted using equi-width binning.

8.4   Contrast Inequality Discovery

8.4.1   Basic Definitions

Informally speaking, a contrast inequality describes a discriminating condition concerning several numerical attributes, which is frequently satisfied by
objects of one class but is seldom satisfied by objects of the other classes.

We first give some examples before defining the formal concepts.

Example 8.4 *Consider the data in Table 8.4, concerning the average
monthly salary of five economic sectors in three coastal and three inland cities (in some given year). The following two inequalities are satisfied by all coastal cities but are not satisfied by any inland city:*
$$Insurance < Catering,$$
$$IT > Retailing + Finances.$$

Inequality based contrasting relationships such as the two above occur
frequently in the real world. For example, the condition "$\frac{w}{h^2} \leq 25$", where

TABLE 8.4: Income in industry sectors in coastal and inland cities

	IT	$Insurance$	$Retailing$	$Finances$	$Catering$	**Class**
$city_1$	2200	1100	400	1300	2200	coastal
$city_2$	3100	1300	590	1400	1500	coastal
$city_3$	3200	1250	630	690	1600	coastal
$city_4$	2000	1500	830	1200	1400	inland
$city_5$	1900	1800	970	930	1800	inland
$city_6$	1500	1350	840	700	1300	inland

w and h are respectively a person's weight in kg and height in meters, is a contrast inequality discriminating "not-obese" persons and other persons. ($\frac{w}{h^2}$ is the well known Body Mass Index (BMI)). As another example, the driving safety tip that says, "If your car travels the distance between you and the car in front in less than 3 seconds, then you are not driving safely" can be expressed as a contrast inequality discriminating unsafe driving and safe driving.

We consider inequalities of the form of $exp_1 \; \theta \; exp_2$, where each exp_i is an expression and θ is a relational operator. Expressions are constructed from terms and functions; a term is either an attribute or a constant, and the terms in an expression are connected by functions; the functions can include addition (+), subtraction (-), multiplication (*), division (/), log, sine, and so on. (The set of functions for use in inequalities can vary depending on the application.) The number of arguments or operands of a function will be called the arity of the function. A relational operator is one of $<$ and $\leq$. ($>$ and $\geq$ are not needed, since inequalities involving them can be expressed using $<$ and $\leq$. For example, $A > B$ is equivalent to $B < A$.) An inequality with n terms is called a n-term inequality. For example, $A > B + C$ is a 3-term inequality.

The concept of satisfaction of inequalities by data objects is defined in the natural manner. For example, in Table 8.4, the relationship $IT > Retailing + Finances$ is satisfied by all coastal cities but not satisfied by any inland cities.

Let η be an inequality. The support of η in dataset D, denoted as $\mathsf{supp}_D(\eta)$, is defined in the standard way. A *contrast inequality* is an inequality η whose support changes significantly from one dataset, D_1, to another, D_2. The contrast significance of η from D_1 to D_2 is evaluated by the support ratio of the supports between D_1 and D_2, denoted as $CS_{D_1 \to D_2} = \mathsf{supp}_{D_2}(\eta) \; / \; \mathsf{supp}_{D_1}(\eta)$. (The value of $CS_{D_1 \to D_2}$ is ∞, if $\mathsf{supp}_{D_2}(\eta) \neq 0$ and $\mathsf{supp}_{D_1}(\eta) = 0$.) The goal of contrast inequality mining is finding all contrast inequalities from D_1 to D_2 *satisfying* the *given support ratio threshold*. We refer to D_1 as the opposing dataset and D_2 as the home dataset of the contrast inequality, and the contrast inequality is called a contrast inequality of D_2. When applied to datasets with classes, contrast inequalities can capture useful contrasts between the classes.

We note that each contrast inequality with 100% support in D_2 and 0% support in D_1 can be converted into a contrast inequality with 100% support in D_1 and 0% support D_2, by reversing the direction of the relational operator.

While the concept of contrast inequality is similar to that of EPs (both capture distinguishing characteristics between two datasets/classes), there are differences. The main differences are that EPs are composed of single-attribute conditions and discretization of numeric attributes is often needed before EP mining, whereas contrast inequalities typically describe non-decomposable contrasting relationships involving multiple attributes and discretization on numerical attributes is not needed before contrast inequality mining.

Compared with EP mining, contrast inequality mining is more challenging since the construction of inequalities involves not only a set of attributes, but also a set of functions and a multitude of ways to combine the attributes and functions. Naive enumeration based search is way too expensive.

Below we discuss a heuristic method to discover some high quality contrast inequalities. Since contrast inequalities can be arbitrarily long and it is not feasible to examine all contrast inequalities of arbitrary lengths, we impose a length constraint n on the maximal number of terms the inequalities can use.

8.4.2   Brief Introduction to GEP

As mentioned above, the space of candidate contrast inequalities is large and complex, especially for a high dimensional dataset. It makes sense to use some heuristic methods in order to be able to efficiently find some high quality contrast inequalities. Below we present a contrast inequality mining algorithm using a recently developed variation of Genetic Algorithms (GA) and Genetic Programming (GP), namely Gene Expression Programming (GEP). This method can find *multiple* high quality contrast inequalities, when used multiple times using different seeds.

GEP uses both linear symbolic strings of fixed length (similar to the chromosomes of GA) and tree structures of different sizes and shapes (similar to the parse trees of GP). This allows GEP to provide flexible and efficient ways to program evolutionary computation [148]. GEP offers great potential for solving complex modeling and optimization problems, and has been used in many applications concerning symbolic regression, classification, time series analysis, cellular automata, and neural network design, etc. The details of GEP are beyond the scope of this chapter; a brief introduction is given below.

The main steps of GEP are very similar to those of GA and GP: GEP uses populations of individuals to represent candidate solutions, GEP selects preferred individuals based on their fitness, and GEP uses genetic modification to generate individuals of successive generations.

In GEP, an individual is given by some fixed number of genes. Unlike GA and GP, each GEP gene has access to a genotype and a corresponding phenotype. The genotype is a symbolic string of some fixed length, and the phenotype is the tree structure for the expression coded by that string. The string 'is divided into a head part and a tail part, both having fixed lengths; the tail can only contain term symbols. The length of the head (h) and the length of the tail (t) were selected such that $t = h * (\alpha - 1) + 1$, where α is the maximal arity of the functions under consideration. The values of h and t remain unchanged in the middle of an execution of a given GEP algorithm.

Although the length ($= h + t$) of the genes is fixed, the tree structures constructed from the coding region of the genes can have different sizes and shapes. (The coding region is determined by the level based traversal of the tree for the gene that produces a valid mathematical expression.) The constraints described in the above paragraph are used to ensure that each gene produces a valid mathematical expression.

The four genes given in Figure 8.4 all have the same head and tail lengths of 4 and 5 respectively, but their expression trees (the children of the topmost + operators) have different sizes and shapes. Only the first 5 symbols for gene 2 ("-a/eb????") are in the coding region of the corresponding gene. (We use '?' to denote a symbol in the non-coding region.)

GEP starts with a random generation of some number of seed individuals. Then GEP selects some individuals according to their fitness, and reproduces new individuals by modifying the selected individuals. Genetic modification, which creates the necessary genetic diversity, ensures that GEP can eventually produce some optimal solution in the long evolutionary process.

There are three kinds of genetic modifications, namely mutation, transposition, and recombination. Mutation and transposition operate on a single individual, and recombination takes place on two individuals. A mutation can change a symbol in a gene into another symbol, as long as it does not introduce function symbols in the tail. Transposition rearranges short fragments within a gene, under some limitations. Recombination exchanges some elements between two randomly chosen individuals to form two new individuals. All newly created GEP individuals are syntactically correct candidate solutions. This feature distinguishes GEP from GP, where some genetic modifications can produce invalid solutions. More details can be found in [148].

The individuals of each new generation undergo the same processes of selection and reproduction with modification as in the preceding generation. The evolution process repeats until some stop condition (given in terms of number of generations, quality of solutions, and so on) is satisfied.

8.4.3 GEP Algorithm for Mining Contrast Inequalities

Two-genome Individual for Contrast Inequality Mining: For contrast inequality mining, we need to ensure that each GEP individual represents a valid inequality. This can be done by using the two-genome individual structure [131]. A two-genome individual is a triple (G_1, G_2, θ), where G_1 and G_2 are genomes and θ is a relational operator and G_1 and G_2 respectively correspond to the left and right operands of θ. A genome consists of $k \geq 1$ genes, which are connected by a linking function, where k is the arity of the function. Each two-genome individual is guaranteed to represent a valid inequality.

Figure 8.4 gives an example of a two-genome individual $(G_1, G_2, <)$ representing an inequality. Each G_i is a genome with two genes which are connected by +. For each of the four genes, the head length is 4, the tail length is 5, the function set is {+, -, *, /}, and the term set is {a, b, c, d, e, f}.

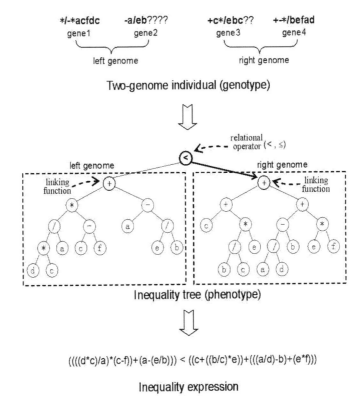

FIGURE 8.4: Inequality tree of a two-genome individual.

Fitness Function Design: The fitness function is important for GEP algorithms since it measures the goodness of candidate solutions and controls the direction of evolution. Since the aim of contrast inequality mining is finding highly discriminative inequalities between the classes, we can measure the fitness of an individual η using the ratio between the supports of η in the datasets/classes. To mine contrast inequality between D_1 and D_2 having D_2 as the home dataset, the fitness of individual η is defined by Equation 8.1.

$$fit(\eta) = (\text{supp}_{D_2}(\eta) * |D_2| + 1) / (\text{supp}_{D_1}(\eta) * |D_1| + 1) \qquad (8.1)$$

The pseudo-count of 1 is used to avoid division by zero. Clearly, all fitness values are positive, with maximum of $(|D_2| + 1)$ and minimum of $1/(|D_1| + 1)$. Equation 8.1 appears to be more likely to guide GEP to find contrast inequalities with zero occurrence in D_1, than the fitness function definition using support-difference of $\text{supp}_{D_2}(\eta) - \text{supp}_{D_1}(\eta)$.

Input: (1) the opposing dataset: D_1; (2) the home dataset: D_2
Output: a contrast inequality with highest fitness value
Method:
1: $pop \leftarrow CreateSeedIndividuals(\ )$;
2: $FitEval(pop, D_1, D_2)$;
3: $bestIndividual \leftarrow GetBestIndividual(pop)$;
4: repeat steps (5-8) until the stop condition is satisfied
5: $\quad pop \leftarrow Select(pop)$;
6: $\quad GeneticModification(pop)$;
7: $\quad FitEval(pop, D_1, D_2)$;
8: $\quad bestIndividual \leftarrow GetBestIndividual(pop)$;
9: return contrast inequality represented by $bestIndividual$;

FIGURE 8.5: The pseudocode of GEPCIM.

GEPCIM: The GEP based algorithm for mining contrast inequality, GEPCIM, is given in Figure 8.5. Step 1 of GEPCIM creates the initial population. Steps 2 and 7 calculate the fitness of each individual in *pop*. In Steps 3 and 8, function $GetBestIndividual(\ )$ selects the best individual discovered so far. From Step 5 to Step 6, the selected individuals are modified by genetic operations. The algorithm stops when the stop condition is satisfied and the individual with highest fitness discovered is returned.

The individuals in the initial population are generated by randomly selecting function/term symbols for different positions in the genes, under the restriction that functions cannot be used in the gene tails. Due to the randomness, the initial populations in different executions of the algorithm tend to be different. Moreover, the selection of individuals as input to genetic modifications is also performed randomly among the fitting individuals. As a result, different contrast inequalities can result from different GEPCIM executions.

In each run of a GEP based algorithm, the number of individuals in the population remains the same in the whole evolution process. So memory space consumption will not increase no matter how many generations are produced.

Combining the above two paragraphs, we see that GEPCIM is a useful tool for efficiently mining a diversified set of highly discriminative contrast inequalities from high dimensional data. Experiments, discussed next, confirm this.

8.4.4 Experimental Evaluation of GEPCIM

We now discuss an experimental evaluation of the GEPCIM algorithm. We selected two microarray datasets, Colon Tumor [9] and ALL/AML [166], which have often been used in previous EP mining studies.

For each of Colon Tumor and ALL/AML, 20 attributes with highest information gain are selected for contrast inequality mining. In Colon Tumor, the

TABLE 8.5: Contrast inequalities mined from Colon Tumor

$(g_{513} + g_{1227}) * g_{267}/(g_{245} + g_{1293}) + (g_{897} - g_{652})/(g_{780} - g_{1293})$
$< (g_{493} - g_{625} * g_{1293}/g_{652} + g_{249}/g_{245} * g_{1227})$
supports in D_p and D_n: 22 and 0; # generations: 15518
$g_{780} + g_{1772}/(g_{652} - g_{625}) * g_{493}$
$\geq g_{1042}/g_{1227} * (g_{625} + g_{399}) + g_{267} - g_{765} + g_{652} - g_{493} - g_{1423}$
supports in D_p and D_n: 22 and 0; # generations: 14507

TABLE 8.6: Contrast inequalities mined from ALL/AML

$g_{760}/g_{2354}/g_{248} - g_{1882} + g_{2354} > g_{2020} + g_{6218} - g_{1745}$
supports in ALL and AML: 27 and 0; # generations: 0
$g_{5772} + g_{6041}/g_{6376} \geq g_{4847} + g_{4499}$;
supports in ALL and AML: 27 and 0; # generations: 1

positive and the negative classes are respectively used as the home dataset (D_p) and the opposing dataset (D_n); in ALL/AML, the ALL and the AML classes are respectively used as the home dataset (D_p) and the opposing dataset (D_n). We set the maximal number of generations at 20000, and run GEPCIM 20 times per dataset. For Colon Tumor, the average fitness of the mined contrast inequalities is 24.8, using on average 9908.7 generations for finding them. For ALL/AML, the average fitness of the contrast inequalities is 28, using on average 3.2 generations to find them. Two of the best discovered contrast inequalities for each dataset are listed in Tables 8.5 and 8.6; variable g_i represents the i-th gene of the original microarray dataset.

We now compare the results of GEPCIM against the results of EP mining [253]. Tables 8.5 and 8.6 show that GEPCIM can find contrast inequalities from the 20 genes with highest information gain whose discriminativeness is higher than the discriminativenes of EPs from the 35 genes with highest information gain. For Colon Tumor, among the jumping EPs of the positive class mined from the 35 genes, the highest support in the positive class is 17; in contrast, among the discovered contrast inequalities with zero support in the negative class, the highest support in the positive class is 22.

8.4.5   Future Work

Many interesting questions remain for contrast inequality mining, including: How to design efficient algorithms to discover all contrast inequalities from a given dataset? How to discover diversified sets of contrast inequalities when it is too hard to mine all contrast inequalities? How to make use of contrast inequalities to construct accurate classifiers? How to use domain knowledge in efficient mining of actionable contrast inequalities? How to design a simplification routine in GEP to find compact contrast inequalities equivalent to given contrast inequalities?

TABLE 8.7: Example data for contrast equation

	A_1	A_2	A_3	A_4	A_5	Class
s_1	2	4	4	9	5	C_1
s_2	1	1	2	4	9	C_1
s_3	4	3	1	8	3	C_1
s_4	3	4	3	8	1	C_2
s_5	4	5	2	6	8	C_2
s_6	6	2	4	7	9	C_2

8.5 Contrast Equation Mining

Sometimes, mathematical equations can provide elegant and easy-to-understand descriptions of discriminating relationships among classes. For example, $arm\_span = height$ is an equation differentiating normal persons from professional basketball players, since it is well known the equation is true for most people but it is not true for professional basketball players.

We consider equations of the form of $\eta = c$, where η is a mathematical expression built from attributes and functions, and c is a constant. Let $\eta(s)$ denote the value of η on data object s, and let $Err(\eta(s), c) = |\eta(s) - c|$ denote the absolute difference between $\eta(s)$ and c. (One can also consider the relative difference.) For a given dataset D, let $AvgErr(\eta(D, c)) = (\Sigma_{s \in D} Err(\eta(s), c))$ / $|D|$ be the average error of η on D. A *contrast equation* is an equation whose average error changes significantly from one dataset, D_1, to another, D_2. More specifically, for a given error threshold t ($t > 0$) and an error ratio threshold ϵ ($0 < \epsilon < 1$), a *contrast equation* from D_1 and D_2 is an equation $\eta = c$ satisfying $AvgErr(\eta(D_2, c)) < t$ and $AvgErr(\eta(D_2, c))$ / $AvgErr(\eta(D_1, c))$ $< \epsilon$; we refer to D_2 as the home dataset and D_1 as the opposing dataset of the contrast equation. When applied to datasets with classes, contrast equations can capture useful contrasts between the classes.

Example 8.5 *Consider the 6 samples of classes c_1 and c_2 of Table 8.7. Let η be $a_1 + a_2 + a_3 - a_4$ and $c = 0$. The average error of η in C_1 and C_2 are 0.3333 and 4.0 respectively. If the error threshold (t) is 0.4 and the error ratio threshold (ϵ) is 0.25, $\eta = 0$ is a contrast equation.*

Similar to contrast inequality mining, contrast equation mining is also very challenging and naïve enumeration based search is clearly way too expensive. As a result, heuristic methods are desirable for discovering some high quality contrast equations. Like contrast inequalities, contrast equations can be arbitrarily long and it is not feasible to examine all contrast equations of arbitrary lengths, we also impose a length constraint n in the form of an upper bound on the number of terms. The set of functions that are to be used in the equation construction also needs to be fixed.

Below we discuss a GEP-based algorithm similar to that of GPCIM for mining high quality contrast equations. Many of the ideas of GEPCIM can be easily modified for mining contrast equations. We only discuss how to design an appropriate fitness function here. Let *pErr* denote the average error of the individual f under consideration in the home dataset of f (as a contrast equation), and *nErr* the average error of f in the opposing dataset. Suppose t is the given error threshold. The fitness of f is defined [130] as follows.

$$fit(f) = \begin{cases} 1/pErr * t * 0.5 & pErr > t \\ (1 - pErr/nErr) * 0.5 + 0.5 & pErr \leq t \end{cases}$$

The fitness value falls into $(0, 0.5]$ when $pErr > t$, and it falls into $[0.5, 1.0]$ when $pErr \leq t$. Using this fitness function, a GEP individual will get high fitness value if its *pErr* is not greater than t and its error ratio $(pErr/nErr)$ is small. Such individuals will have more opportunities to survive and produce offspring, contributing the high quality of the final solution.

Experiments indicate that the GEP based algorithm can efficiently find contrast equations [130]. The details are omitted here.

If we define the concept of satisfaction of an equation by a data object in the contrast inequality manner, the discriminativeness of a contrast equation can also be evaluated by the support ratio of the supports between any two datasets. In this case, the problem of contrast equation mining is a special case of contrast inequality mining when the relational operator is equal. GEPCIM can be applied to the contrast equation discovery directly.

There are many questions worthy of future study, such as how to discover all contrast equations efficiently for a given dataset? How to design a mining method that can adjust the error threshold adaptively without human intervention? How to find the most compact contrast equations?

8.6   Discussion

Reference [342] studied the mining of generalized emerging patterns in the presence of hierarchies/taxonomies in attribute domains.

In addition to using expressive constructs in defining more expressive contrast patterns as discussed in this chapter, one can also use structural properties of data (e.g. spatial/directional relationships for image data; see Chapter 20) in defining more expressive contrast patterns. Other possibilities can also be explored. For contrast inequality mining and contrast equation mining, future research questions are also presented in Section 8.4.5 and at the end of Section 8.5.

Chapter 9

Emerging Data Cube Representations for OLAP Database Mining

Sébastien Nedjar, Lotfi Lakhal, and Rosine Cicchetti

Laboratoire d'Informatique Fondamentale de Marseille (LIF), Aix-Marseille Université - CNRS

9.1 Introduction

Decision makers are generally interested in discovering interesting trends by using a data warehouse to analyze data collected from a "population". The data warehouse contains data concerning various measures which are observed with respect to different attributes called dimensions. More precisely, all the possible combinations of dimensions can be relevant and considered at all possible granularity levels. In order to meet decision makers' needs, the concept of a data cube was introduced [168]. It groups the tuples according to all the dimension combinations along with their associated measures. The main interest of this structure is to support an interactive analysis of data, because all the possible trends are not yet computed. Of course, due to its very nature (the very great volume of original data and exponential number of dimension combinations), a data cube can be very large.

Let us assume that we have a data cube computed from a set of data accumulated so far in a data warehouse, and imagine that a refresh operation has to be performed in order to insert new collected data. Particularly interesting knowledge can be gained from the comparison between the cubes of these two datasets: which novelties does the refreshment bring? which trends, unknown until now, appear? or in contrast, which existing trends disappear? Similar knowledge can be obtained every time two semantically comparable data cubes are compared. For instance, if two datasets are collected in two different geographical areas or for two population samples, it is possible to highlight the behavior modifications, the contrast between their characteristics or the deviations with respect to a witness sample.

In order to capture trend reversals in data warehouses, we have proposed the concept of Emerging Cube [311, 309]. It results from coupling two interesting structures: the data cube [168] and the emerging patterns [119, 118]. From the cube of two database relations, the Emerging Cube gathers all the tuples satisfying a twofold emergence constraint: the value of their measure is weak in one relation (C_1 constraint) and significant in the other relation (C_2 constraint). Computing an Emerging Cube is a difficult problem because two data cubes have to be computed and then compared. As mentioned above, the computation of the cubes is costly and their comparison is likely to have a significant cost because their size is very large. Thus, to really take advantage of the new knowledge captured by the Emerging Cube, it is critical to avoid the computation of the two data cubes.

In data mining, various research works have studied reduced representations and shown their usefulness. For instance, the covers for frequent patterns which generally discard numerous patterns and keep only the most representative ones while preserving the same expressiveness [326, 333, 46, 459]. In a similar spirit, some approaches aim to provide reduced representations for the data cube in order to avoid the storage explosion problem [67, 227, 439, 302]. We have studied these kinds of representations in the Emerging Cube perspective.

Decision makers can have several uses of trend reversals. The first one is to know whether a certain trend is emerging or not. The underlying objective is to obtain an efficient classifier like in [119] but in an OLAP context. The second use is OLAP querying. In this case, the user wishes to retrieve the measure values associated with any emerging tuple. This kind of knowledge makes it possible to quantify the strength of the trend reversals. The third use is the navigation within the Emerging Cube at various granularity levels. For example, if a strong trend reversal appears in a very aggregated tuple, it is probably interesting for the user to understand the phenomenon's origin and drill down into the Emerging Cube for retrieving more detailed tuples which explain such a phenomenon.

There is a strong relationship between the three quoted uses. A representation with navigation capabilities also has querying capabilities, while a representation from which queries can be answered also has classification capacities. The more complex the use is, the richer the representation will be.

This chapter presents three types of representations, each one adapted to a specific use. These representations and their uses are the following:

(1) Borders are used to represent the boundaries of the solution space. They offer the the most reduced representations possible, but at the cost of losing the measure values. In addition to containing enough information for building classifiers, they place emphasis on certain particular tuples, which can be a good starting point of a navigation within the Emerging Cube. The first couple of borders group the lower and the upper frontiers corresponding to the most aggregated and the most detailed tuples satisfying the emergence constraint [309]. In the second couple of borders, we replace the lower border by a new one called $U^\sharp$ [310]. This new border encompasses the most detailed tuples which satisfy the C_2 constraint, but not the C_1 one.

(2) The second type of representations is the Emerging Closed Cube [313, 312, 311]. Its objective is to retrieve the values of the measures while eliminating most redundancies. Such redundancies are captured by subsets of aggregated tuples which share a similar semantics. In fact, they are computed from the very same data of the original relation but they differ from their granularity level or their involved dimensions. In the Emerging Closed Cubes, we only keep a representative tuple for these subsets of redundant tuples. The result is a set of emerging closed tuples. Nevertheless, these closed tuples are not sufficient to get a lossless representation and we have to add to them one of the borders. In this context, we show that $U^\sharp$ can be refined and reduced by removing another kind of redundancy.

(3) The third representation is the Emerging Quotient Cube [312]. In the same spirit as the Emerging Closed Cube, it aims to eliminate redundancies but it keeps enough information to preserve navigation capabilities. Obviously, the consequence is that the size of this representation is greater than the size of the previous one.

This chapter provides a synthesis of research work performed around the Emerging Cube and its representations. The remainder of this chapter presents the concepts related to the Emerging Cube, the representations of the Emerging Cube, and relationships between the representations.

9.2   Emerging Cube

In this section, we review and summarize the issue addressed when proposing the concept of Emerging Cube.

Let us consider a relation r with a set of dimensions (denoted by D_1, D_2, ..., D_n) and a measure (denoted M). The Emerging Cube characterization fits

TABLE 9.1: Relation example SALES₁

City	Month	Category	Quantity
Paris	11/06	Clothes	100
Paris	11/06	Video Game	100
London	11/09	Video Game	100
Berlin	11/09	Video Game	600
London	11/06	Video Game	100

TABLE 9.2: Relation example SALES₂

City	Month	Category	Quantity
London	11/06	Clothes	300
London	11/09	Video Game	300
London	11/06	Video Game	300
Paris	11/06	Clothes	300
Berlin	11/09	Video Game	200
Berlin	11/09	Clothes	200
Berlin	11/06	Video Game	100

in the more general framework of the Cube Lattice of the relation r: $CL(r)$ [67]. The latter is a suitable search space which is to be considered when computing the data cube of r. It organizes the multidimensional tuples, possible solutions of the problem, according to a generalization / specialization order, denoted by $\preceq_s$ [227][1]. These tuples are structured according to the dimensions of r and the special value ALL [168]. Moreover, we append to these tuples a virtual tuple which only encompasses empty values in order to close the structure. Any tuple of the Cube Lattice generalizes the tuple of empty values. For handling the tuples of $CL(r)$, the operator $+$ is defined. Given two tuples, it yields the most specific tuple in $CL(r)$ which generalizes the two operands.

Example 9.1 *Table 9.1 contains data about sales. The dimensions are: the customer's city, the sale month and the product category.*

In $CL(\text{SALES}_1)$, let us consider the June's sales in Paris, i.e. the multidimensional tuple (Paris, 11/06, ALL). This tuple is specialized by the following two tuples of the relation: (Paris, 11/06, Clothes) and (Paris, 11/06, Video Game). Furthermore, (Paris, 11/06, ALL) $\preceq_s$ (Paris, 11/06, Clothes) exemplifies the specialization order between tuples. Moreover we have (Paris, 11/06, Clothes) + (Paris, 11/06, Video Game) = (Paris, 11/06, ALL).

Definition 9.1 (Measure Function) *Let f be an aggregate function, r a database relation and t a multidimensional tuple. We denote by $f_{val}(t, r)$ the value of the aggregate function f for the tuple t in the relation r.*

---

[1]$t_1 \preceq_s t_2$ means that t_1 is less specific than t_2, i.e. it is less detailed.

Example 9.2 *In the* SALES$_1$ *relation, the total sale in Paris for the month 11/06 and any product category can be given by* SUM$_{val}$((*Paris, 11/06, ALL*), SALES$_1$) = 200.

In the remainder of the chapter, we only consider additive aggregate functions [332] such as COUNT, SUM, MIN, MAX.

Definition 9.2 (Emerging Tuple) *Let r_1 and r_2 be two compatible relations (same set of dimensions and measures). A tuple $t \in CL(r_1 \cup r_2)$ is said to be emerging from r_1 to r_2 if and only if it satisfies the following two constraints C_1 and C_2:*

$$\begin{cases} f_{val}(t, r_1) < MinThreshold_1 \ (C_1) \\ f_{val}(t, r_2) \geq MinThreshold_2 \ (C_2) \end{cases}$$

Example 9.3 *Let us consider the* SALES$_1$ *(cf. Table 9.1) and* SALES$_2$ *(cf. Table 9.2) relations. We suppose that they correspond to the datasets of two different websites. Let $MinThreshold_1 = 200$ be the threshold for the relation* SALES$_1$ *and $MinThreshold_2 = 200$ the threshold for* SALES$_2$.

Then the tuple t_1 =(London, 11/06, ALL) is emerging from SALES$_1$ *to* SALES$_2$ *because* SUM$_{val}$(t_1, SALES$_1$) $= 100$ ($< MinThreshold_1$) *and* SUM$_{val}$(t_1, SALES$_2$) $= 600$ ($\geq MinThreshold_2$). *In contrast, the tuple t_2 = (Berlin, 11/06, ALL) is not emerging because* SUM$_{val}$(t_2, SALES$_2$) $= 100$ ($< MinThreshold_2$).

Definition 9.3 (Emergence Rate) *Let r_1 and r_2 be two compatible relations, $t \in CL(r_1 \cup r_2)$ a tuple and f an additive function. The emergence rate of t from r_1 to r_2, denoted by $ER(t)$, is defined by:*

$$ER(t) = \begin{cases} 0 \text{ if } f_{val}(t, r_1) = 0 \text{ and } f_{val}(t, r_2) = 0 \\ \infty \text{ if } f_{val}(t, r_1) = 0 \text{ and } f_{val}(t, r_2) \neq 0 \\ \dfrac{f_{val}(t, r_2)}{f_{val}(t, r_1)} \text{ otherwise.} \end{cases}$$

We observe that when the emergence rate is greater than 1, it characterizes trends significant in r_2 and not so clear-cut in r_1. In contrast, when the rate is lower than 1, it highlights disappearing trends, relevant in r_1 and not in r_2.

Example 9.4 *From the two relations,* SALES$_1$ *and* SALES$_2$, *we compute $ER((London, 11/06, ALL)) = 600/100$. Of course, the higher the emergence rate is, the more distinctive the trend is. Therefore, the quoted tuple means a jump of the sales in London for the month 11/06 between* SALES$_1$ *and* SALES$_2$.

Definition 9.4 (Emerging Cube) *Let $C_1(t)$ and $C_2(t)$ be given emerging constraints (cf. definition 9.2). The set of all the tuples of $CL(r_1 \cup r_2)$ emerging from r_1 to r_2 is called the Emerging Cube, and is defined by $\text{EC}(r_1, r_2) = \{t \in CL(r_1 \cup r_2) \mid C_1(t) \wedge C_2(t)\}$.*

Example 9.5 *Figure 9.1 provides the Cube emerging from the relations* SALES$_1$ *to* SALES$_2$ *with the thresholds* $MinThreshold_1 = 200$ *and* $MinThreshold_2 = 200$. *The emerging tuples are the ones appearing in a rectangle. For the sake of readability, the dimension values are coded as follows:*

City		Month		Category	
Paris	$= P$	*11/06*	$= 1$	*Video Game*	$= V$
London	$= L$	*11/09*	$= 2$	*Clothes*	$= C$
Berlin	$= B$				

Moreover, '$*$' stands for the ALL value.*

9.3 Representations of the Emerging Cube

Like the data cube, the Emerging Cube is particularly large. Thus it is relevant to look for representations combining two qualities: they must be both reduced and adapted to the intended uses. This section presents three types of representations devoted to the three main uses of Emerging Cubes.

9.3.1 Representations for OLAP Classification

Borders provide a condensed representation of Emerging Cubes and have additional advantages. First of all, trend reversals, jumping or plunging down, can be very efficiently isolated and with lowest cost, because it is not necessary to compute and store the two underlying data cubes. Thus we save both execution time and storage space. Then we can immediately answer queries like "Is this trend emerging?" In order to systematically manage these kinds of queries, we can devise efficient classifiers to decide whether a trend is relevant or not. Moreover, the Emerging Cube borders, by focusing on particular tuples, provide an interesting starting point to navigate within cubes.

In this section we present the classical borders $[L; U]$ and introduce a new condensed representation: the borders $]U^\sharp; U]$.

9.3.1.1 Borders $[L; U]$

The C_1 and C_2 emergence constraints are monotone and anti-monotone respectively. Thus, for each tuple t satisfying the constraint C_1, we know that all the tuples more specific than t also satisfy C_1. Therefore the most general tuples (w.r.t $\preceq_s$) satisfying C_1 are the most useful. In contrast, for the C_2 constraint, the most specific tuples (w.r.t $\preceq_s$) are the most useful. These two sets of tuples stand at the boundaries of the Emerging Cube.

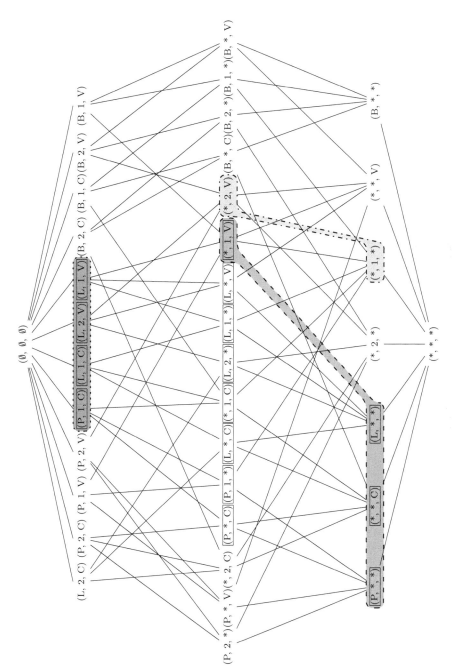

FIGURE 9.1: Representation of the Emerging Cube (from SALES₁ to SALES₂) and its borders.

Definition 9.5 (Borders $[L;U]$) *The Emerging Cube can be represented by the borders: U which encompasses the maximal emerging tuples and L which contains all the minimal emerging tuples according to the specialization order.*

$$\begin{cases} L = \min_{\preceq_s}(\{t \in CL(r_1 \cup r_2) \mid C_1(t) \wedge C_2(t)\}) \\ U = \max_{\preceq_s}(\{t \in CL(r_1 \cup r_2) \mid C_1(t) \wedge C_2(t)\}) \end{cases}$$

Proposition 9.1 *The borders $[L;U]$ are a representation for the Emerging Cube: $\forall \ t \in CL(r_1 \cup r_2)$, t is emerging from r_1 to r_2 if and only if $\exists (l, u) \in (L, U)$ such that $l \preceq_s t \preceq_s u$. In other words, t is emerging if and only if it belongs to the "range" $[L; U]$.*

Example 9.6 *With our example relations SALE_1 and SALE_2, Figure 9.1 gives the borders $[L;U]$ for the Emerging Cube. The L border is the set of tuples circled by a dashed line and the U border is the tuples circled by a dotted line.*

9.3.1.2   Borders $]U^\sharp;U]$

This section introduces a condensed representation: the borders $]U^\sharp;U]$. This representation is based on the maximal tuples satisfying the C_2 constraint (they are significant in r_2) without satisfying C_1 (thus they are also significant in r_1 and hence are not emerging). Moreover we provide an optimization of our search space because we no longer consider the Cube Lattice of $r_1 \cup r_2$, but only the Cube Lattice of r_2. Actually, by its very definition (cf. C_2 constraint) any emerging tuple is necessarily a tuple of $CL(r_2)$.

Definition 9.6 (Borders $]U^\sharp;U]$) *The Emerging Cube can be represented through two borders: U (cf. definition 9.5) and $U^\sharp$ encompassing all the maximal tuples not satisfying the C_1 monotone constraint but satisfying the C_2 anti-monotone constraint. Thus, we have:*

$$\begin{cases} U^\sharp = \max_{\preceq_s}(\{t \in CL(r_2) \mid \neg C_1(t) \wedge C_2(t)\}) \\ U = \max_{\preceq_s}(\{t \in CL(r_2) \mid C_1(t) \wedge C_2(t)\}) \end{cases}$$

Contrarily to the border L which belongs to the solution space, $U^\sharp$ encompasses the maximal tuples just below the solution space (because they do not satisfy C_1) thus just below the border L.

Example 9.7 *Figure 9.1 gives the borders $]U^\sharp;U]$ of the cube emerging from SALE_1 to SALE_2. The $U^\sharp$ border is the set of tuples circled by a dashed dotted line and the U border is the set of tuples circled by a dotted line.*

With the following proposition, we are provided with a simple mechanism to know whether a tuple is emerging or not by using the borders $]U^\sharp;U]$.

Proposition 9.2 *The borders $]U^\sharp;U]$ are a condensed representation for the Emerging Cube: $\forall \ t \in CL(r_2)$, t is emerging from r_1 to r_2 if and only if $\forall \ l \in U^\sharp$, $l \npreceq_s t$ and $\exists u \in U$ such that $t \preceq_s u$. Thus t is emerging if and only if it belongs to the "range" $]U^\sharp; U]$.*

Example 9.8 *With our example relations, the tuple (Paris, ALL, Clothes) is emerging because it generalizes the tuple (Paris, 11/06, Clothes) which belongs to the border U and does not generalize any tuple of the border $U^\sharp$. Moreover the tuple (ALL, ALL, Video Game) is not emerging because it generalizes the tuple (ALL, 11/09, Video Game) of the border $U^\sharp$.*

9.3.2   Representations for OLAP Querying

The idea of reducing the representations is popular in the contexts of frequent patterns [459] or OLAP [303]. We investigate it in the context of Emerging Cubes and propose three lossless representations: the **L**-Emerging Closed Cube, the $U^\sharp$-Emerging Closed Cube and the Reduced $U^\sharp$-Emerging Closed Cube.

The Closed Cube encompassing the set of the closed tuples is presently one of the most reduced representations for the data cube [67]. Thus it is interesting to propose a structure supported by the concepts associated with the Closed Cube for the Emerging Cube. Unfortunately a representation which is only based on emerging closed tuples is not sufficient to be a lossless representation. We show that for certain tuples the measure value cannot be retrieved. To avoid this drawback, we add the required information in order to obtain a new and lossless representation. This information is one of the borders.

9.3.2.1   L-Emerging Closed Cubes

The **L**-Emerging Closed Cube includes both *(i)* the set of emerging closed tuples and *(ii)* the L border. This approach is in the same spirit as the one proposed in [53] in the context of transaction databases and which encompasses the constrained closed patterns and the lower border (L).

The idea behind our representation is to remove redundancies existing within Emerging Cubes. Actually certain tuples S share a similar semantics with other tuples T which are more aggregated. In fact S and T are built up by aggregating the very same tuples of the original relation, but at different granularity levels. Thus a single tuple, the most specific of tuples with the same semantics, can stand for the whole set. The Cube Closure operator, introduced in [67], is intended for computing this representative tuple.

Definition 9.7 (Cube Closure) *The Cube Closure operator $\mathbb{C} : CL(r) \to CL(r)$ is defined, for each tuple $t \in CL(r)$ and each set of tuples $T \subseteq CL(r)$, as follows:*

$$\mathbb{C}(t, T) = \sum_{\substack{t' \in T, \\ t \preceq_s t'}} t'$$

where the $\sum$ operator has the very same semantics as the $+$ operator but operates on a set of tuples. Let us note that $\mathbb{C}(t, T) = (\emptyset, \dots, \emptyset)$ if $T = \emptyset$.

Let us consider aggregating all the tuples t' in T together by using the $+$ operator. We obtain a new tuple which generalizes all the tuples t' and which is the most specific one. This new tuple is the Cube Closure of t over T.

Example 9.9 *We get the Cube Closure of the tuple (London, ALL, ALL) in the relation* SALE$_1$ *by aggregating all the tuples which specialize it by using the operator* $+ : \mathbb{C}((L, *, *),$ SALE$_1) = (L, 1, V) + (L, 2, V) = (L, *, V).$

Definition 9.8 (Measure Function Compatible with the Cube Closure)
A measure function, f_{val}, relative to an aggregate function f, from $CL(r) \to \mathbb{R}$ is compatible with the closure operator $\mathbb{C}$ over T if and only if $\forall t,\ u \in CL(r)$, the following three properties are satisfied:

1. $t \preceq_s u \Rightarrow f_{val}(t, T) \geq f_{val}(u, T)$ *or* $f_{val}(t, T) \leq f_{val}(u, T)$,

2. $\mathbb{C}(t, T) = \mathbb{C}(u, T) \Rightarrow f_{val}(t, T) = f_{val}(u, T)$,

3. $t \preceq_s u$ *and* $f_{val}(t, T) = f_{val}(u, T) \Rightarrow \mathbb{C}(t, T) = \mathbb{C}(u, T)$.

This function is an adaptation, specific to the cube lattice framework, of the weight function introduced in [382] for any closure system of the power set. For example the measure functions COUNT and SUM are compatible with the Cube Closure operator.

Definition 9.9 (Emerging Closed Tuple) *A tuple $t \in CL(r)$ is an emerging closed tuple if and only if (1) t is an emerging tuple and (2) $\mathbb{C}(t, r_1 \cup r_2) = t$.*

Example 9.10 *The tuple (Paris, 11/06, Clothes) is an emerging closed tuple because:*

1. *(Paris, 11/06, Clothes) is an emerging tuple (cf. Figure 9.1)*

2. $\mathbb{C}((Paris, 11/06, Clothes),$ SALE$_1 \cup$ SALE$_2) = (Paris, 11/06, Clothes)$

The set of emerging closed tuples is not a lossless representation of the Emerging Cube because for certain tuples it is not possible to decide whether they are emerging or not. They are all the tuples more general than the most general emerging closed tuples.

For instance, let us consider the set of all emerging closed tuples (T) of the Figure 9.2. The tuples (ALL, ALL, Clothes) and (ALL, 11/06, ALL) share the same closure on T: (ALL, 11/06, Clothes) which is emerging. The former tuple is also emerging while the latter is not.

In order to achieve a lossless representation, we combine the set of emerging closed tuples from which the measure values can be retrieved and the borders which delimit the space of solutions. However, the border U is already included in the closed tuple set, because the elements of U are the most detailed (specific) emerging tuples. Thus they are necessarily closed tuples.

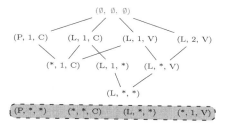

FIGURE 9.2: **L**-Emerging Closed Cube from SALES$_1$ to SALES$_2$.

Definition 9.10 (L-Emerging Closed Cube)
L-ECC$(r_1, r_2) = \{t \in CL(r_1 \cup r_2)$ *such that* t *is an emerging closed tuple*$\} \cup L$.

Example 9.11 *The **L**-Emerging Closed Cube is represented in Figure 9.2.*

To prove that the **L**-Emerging Closed Cube is a lossless representation for the Emerging Cube we introduce two propositions. The first shows that for any emerging tuple, we can compute its Cube Closure from either $r_1 \cup r_2$ or the **L**-Emerging Closed Cube, and obtain the same result. The second shows that two tuples having the same Cube Closure have the same emergence rate.

Proposition 9.3 *For all the emerging closed tuples* t, $\mathbb{C}(t, \text{L-ECC}(r_1, r_2)) = \mathbb{C}(t, r_1 \cup r_2)$.

Proposition 9.4 *Let* t *and* u *be two tuples of* $EC(r_1, r_2)$, *if* t *and* u *have the same Cube Closure over* $r_1 \cup r_2$, *then their emergence rate is the same:* $\forall t, u \in EC(r_1, r_2)$ *such that* $\mathbb{C}(t, r_1 \cup r_2) = \mathbb{C}(u, r_1 \cup r_2)$, *we have* $ER(t) = ER(u)$.

In order to make the **L**-Emerging Closed Cube a lossless representation, we have to compute the Cube Closure over $r_1 \cup r_2$, because two tuples can have the same Cube Closures on r_1 and on r_2, but different cube closure on $r_1 \cup r_2$. The next proposition makes sure that the **L**-Emerging Closed Cube is a lossless representation for the Emerging Cube.

Proposition 9.5 *The **L**-Emerging Closed Cube is a lossless representation for the Emerging Cube:*

$$\forall\, t \in CL(r_1 \cup r_2),\ t \in \text{EC} \Leftrightarrow \mathbb{C}(t, \text{L-ECC}(r_1, r_2)) \in \text{L-ECC}(r_1, r_2) \backslash L.$$

For instance, consider the emergence rate of $t =$ (Paris, ALL, ALL). We know that t is emerging because it is in the range $[L; U]$ (*cf.* Figure 9.1). By computing its Cube Closure over L-ECC(SALE$_1$, SALE$_2$), we obtain the tuple (Paris, 11/06, Clothes). Since the emerging rate of the previous tuple is 3 (*cf.* Figure 9.2), we know that the emerging rate of t is also 3.

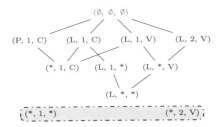

FIGURE 9.3: $U^\sharp$-Emerging Closed Cube from SALES$_1$ to SALES$_2$.

9.3.2.2 $U^\sharp$-Emerging Closed Cubes

In this section, we introduce a new structure, the $U^\sharp$-Emerging Closed Cube by using the $U^\sharp$ border instead of the L border.

Definition 9.11 ($U^\sharp$-Emerging Closed Cube)
$U^\sharp$-ECC$(r_1, r_2) = \{t \in CL(r_2)$ *such that t is an emerging closed tuple*$\} \cup U^\sharp$.

Example 9.12 *The $U^\sharp$-Emerging Closed Cube is represented in Figure 9.3.*

In order to prove that the $U^\sharp$-Emerging Closed Cube is a cover for the Emerging Cube we present a proposition showing that for any emerging tuple, we can compute its Cube Closure from either $r_1 \cup r_2$ or the $U^\sharp$-Emerging Closed Cube, and of course obtain the same result.

Proposition 9.6 *For all the emerging closed tuples t, $\mathbb{C}(t, U^\sharp$-ECC$(r_1, r_2)) = \mathbb{C}(t, r_1 \cup r_2)$.*

In order to make the $U^\sharp$-Emerging Closed Cube a lossless representation, we have to compute the Cube Closure over $r_1 \cup r_2$, because two tuples can have the same Cube Closure on r_1 and on r_2, but different Cube Closures on $r_1 \cup r_2$. In such cases it is impossible to compute the Cube Closure with only a single relation. The proposition below makes sure that the $U^\sharp$-Emerging Closed Cube is a cover for the Emerging Cube.

Proposition 9.7 *The $U^\sharp$-Emerging Closed Cube is a lossless representation for the Emerging Cube:*

$$\forall\, t \in CL(r_2),\ t \in \text{EC} \Leftrightarrow \mathbb{C}(t, U^\sharp\text{-ECC}(r_1, r_2)) \in U^\sharp\text{-ECC}(r_1, r_2) \backslash U^\sharp.$$

For instance, consider the emergence rate of $t = $ (Paris, ALL, Clothes). We know that t is emerging because it is in the range $]U^\sharp; U]$ (*cf.* Figure 9.1). By computing its Cube Closure over $U^\sharp$-ECC(SALES$_1$, SALES$_2$), we obtain the tuple (Paris, 11/06, Clothes). Since the emerging rate of the previous tuple is 3, we make sure that the emerging rate of t is also 3.

9.3.2.3 Reduced $U^\sharp$-Emerging Closed Cubes

In the previous section, we have shown that the border $U^\sharp$ must be appended to the emerging closed tuples in order to achieve a lossless representation of the Emerging Cube. By making use of the Cube Closure, we simplify the border $U^\sharp$ by discarding all the redundancies that it can encompass. In this way, we obtain a new cover: the Reduced $U^\sharp$-Emerging Closed Cube.

Definition 9.12 (Redundant Closed Tuple) *For all the tuples $t \in U^\sharp$, t is a redundant closed tuple if and only if $\mathbb{C}(t, U^\sharp\text{-}\mathrm{Ecc}(r_1, r_2)\backslash\{t\}) = t$.*

Example 9.13 *The tuple (London, ALL, Video Game) is a redundant closed tuple because:*

$$\mathbb{C}((L, *, V), U^\sharp\text{-}\mathrm{Ecc}(\mathrm{SALES}_1, \mathrm{SALES}_2)\backslash\{(L, *, V)\}) = (L, 2, V) + (L, 1, V)$$
$$= (L, *, V).$$

Definition 9.13 (Reduced $U^\sharp$ Border) *The Reduced $U^\sharp$ Border, denoted by $U^{\sharp\sharp}$, is composed of the tuples of $U^\sharp$ which are not redundant :*

$$U^{\sharp\sharp} = \{t \in U^\sharp \mid t \text{ is not a redundant closed tuple}\}.$$

Example 9.14 *With our example, the Reduced $U^\sharp$ Border only encompasses the tuple (ALL, 11/09, Video Game). The other tuple in $U^\sharp$ is discarded (cf. Definition 9.12).*

Let us recall that, like all the tuples of $U^\sharp$, all the tuples of $U^{\sharp\sharp}$ satisfy the C_2 anti-monotone constraint.

Definition 9.14 (Reduced $U^\sharp$-Emerging Closed Cubes) *The Reduced $U^\sharp$-Emerging Closed Cube, denoted by R-Ecc, is defined as follows:*

$$\text{R-Ecc}(r_1, r_2) = \{t \in CL(r_2) \mid t \text{ is an emerging closed tuple}\} \cup U^{\sharp\sharp}.$$

Example 9.15 *With our example relations, the Reduced $U^\sharp$-Emerging Closed Cube is composed of the emerging closed tuples given in Figure 9.3, and the Reduced $U^\sharp$ Border is limited to the single tuple (ALL, 11/09, Video Game).*

The following proposition shows that removing redundant closed tuples from the border $U^\sharp$ does not alter the closure computation for the emerging closed tuples. Thus the Reduced $U^\sharp$-Emerging Closed Cube is a lossless representation for the $U^\sharp$-Emerging Closed Cube and by transitivity it is a lossless representation for the Emerging Cube (*cf.* Proposition 9.9).

Proposition 9.8 $\forall\, t \in \text{R-Ecc}(r_1, r_2), \mathbb{C}(t, \text{R-Ecc}(r_1, r_2)) = \mathbb{C}(t, \mathrm{Ecc}(r_1, r_2))$.

Proposition 9.9 *The Reduced Emerging Closed Cube is a lossless representation for the Emerging Cube:*

$$\forall t \in CL(r_2),\ t \in \mathrm{Ec} \Leftrightarrow \mathbb{C}(t, \text{R-Ecc}(r_1, r_2)) \text{ is an emerging closed tuple.}$$

Example 9.16 *Let us derive the emergence rate of the tuple (Paris, ALL, Clothes). We know that this tuple is possibly emerging because it generalizes the tuple (Paris, 11/06, Clothes) of U. By computing its Cube Closure over* R-ECC(SALES$_1$, SALES$_2$)*, we obtain the tuple (Paris, 11/06, Clothes). Since this closed tuple is an emerging closed tuple, and its emergence rate is 3, we can assert that the emergence rate of (Paris, ALL, Clothes) is 3.*

For (ALL, 11/06, ALL), we can say that this tuple is possibly emerging because it generalizes the tuple (London, 11/06, Video Game) belonging to the U border. However, its Cube Closure over R-ECC(SALES$_1$, SALES$_2$)*, i.e. the tuple (ALL, 11/06, Video Game), does not belong to the set of emerging closed tuples. So we can say that (ALL, 11/06, ALL) is not emerging.*

9.3.3   Representation for OLAP Navigation

In a similar spirit, we study the Quotient Cube [227] which is also a reduced representation for Data Cubes. In this section, we state a link between the Quotient Cube and the Closed Cube, and use this property for proposing a new representation: the Emerging Quotient Cube; while the Emerging Quotient Cube is not as reduced as the **L**-Emerging Closed Cube, it has another advantage which is detailed later.

A Quotient Cube [227] provides a summary of a data cube for certain aggregate functions like COUNT, SUM, ... Moreover the Quotient Cube preserves the semantics of the operators ROLL-UP/DRILL-DOWN within the data cube [168]. Hence it is relevant to study this structure from the perspective of the Emerging Cube. Before giving our proposal, we revisit the original definitions of the Quotient Cube in the Cube Lattice environment.

The idea behind the Quotient Cube is to discard redundancies by gathering together tuples sharing an equivalent information. This results in a set of equivalence classes partitioning the tuples of the data cube. Such a partitioning can be performed in various ways. But, in order to preserve navigation capabilities, it is necessary to deal with convex classes.

Definition 9.15 (Convex Equivalence Class) *Let $\mathcal{C} \subseteq CL(r)$ be an equivalence class. We say that $\mathcal{C}$ is convex if and only if:*

$$\forall t \in CL(r) \text{ if } \exists t', t'' \in \mathcal{C} \text{ such that } t' \preceq_s t \preceq_s t'' \text{ then } t \in \mathcal{C}.$$

A partition $\mathcal{P}$ of $CL(r)$ which encompasses only convex equivalence classes is called a convex partition.

The convexity property makes it possible to represent each equivalence class through its maximal and minimal tuples. Intermediary tuples are no longer useful and the underlying representation is reduced. To ensure that the partition is convex, the following equivalence relation is used.

Definition 9.16 (Quotient Equivalence Relation) *Let f_{val} be a measure*

function. We define the $\equiv_f$ equivalence relation as the reflexive transitive clo-sure of the following relation τ: let t, t' be two tuples, $t \tau t'$ holds if and only if (i) $f_{val}(t, r) = f_{val}(t', r)$ and (ii) t is either a parent or a child of t'.
The equivalence relation $\equiv_f$ is said to be a quotient equivalence relation *if and only if it satisfies the property of weak congruence: $\forall t, t', u, u' \in CL(r)$, if $t \equiv_f t', u \equiv_f u', t \preceq_s u$ and $u' \preceq_s t'$, then $t \equiv_f u$.*

We denote by $[t]_{\equiv_f}$ the equivalence class of t ($[t]_{\equiv_f} = \{t' \in CL(r)$ such that $t \equiv_f t'\}$). Then the Quotient Cube is defined as the set of equivalence classes, each one being provided by the value of the measure.

Definition 9.17 (Quotient Cube) *Let $CL(r)$ be the Cube Lattice of the database relation r and $\equiv_f$ a quotient equivalence relation. The Quotient Cube of r, denoted by $QuotientCube(r, \equiv_f)$, is defined as follows:*

$$QuotientCube(r, \equiv_f) = \{([t]_{\equiv_f}, f_{val}(t, r)) \text{ such that } t \in CL(r)\}.$$

The Quotient Cube of r is a convex partition of $CL(r)$.

For two equivalence classes $\mathcal{C}, \mathcal{C}' \in QuotientCube(r, \equiv_f)$, $\mathcal{C} \preceq_{QC} \mathcal{C}'$ when $\exists t \in \mathcal{C}$ and $\exists t' \in \mathcal{C}'$ such that $t \preceq_s t'$.
The construction of a Quotient Cube depends on the chosen quotient equivalence relation. As a consequence for two quotient equivalence relations, their related Quotient Cubes can be different. Moreover, the most useful quotient equivalence relation is the cover equivalence relation. The cover of any tuple t is the set of all tuples aggregated together to achieve t.

Definition 9.18 (Cover) *Let $t \in CL(r)$ be a tuple. The cover of t is the set of tuples of r that are generalized by t (i.e. $cov(t, r) = \{t' \in r$ such that $t \preceq_s t'\}$). Two tuples $t, t' \in CL(r)$ are* cover equivalent *over r, $t \equiv_{cov} t'$, if they have the same cover, i.e. $cov(t, r) = cov(t', r)$.*

Using the cover equivalence relation as an instance of $\equiv_f$ in Definition 9.17, we can define the *Cover Quotient Cube*.
Now we show that the Cover Quotient Cube is strongly related to the Cube Closure. Two tuples $t, t' \in CL(r)$ are Cube Closure equivalent, $t \equiv_C t'$, if and only if $\mathbb{C}(t, r) = \mathbb{C}(t', r)$.

Proposition 9.10 *Let $t, t' \in CL(r)$. Then t is cover equivalent to t' over r if and only if t is Cube Closure equivalent to t'.*

The above proposition states the relationship between the Quotient Cube and the concepts related with the Cube Closure. Moreover it shows that it is possible to define a Cover Quotient Cube by using any aggregate function compatible with the Cube Closure.

Emerging Quotient Cubes

Motivated by the relevant properties of the Quotient Cube, such a representation can be used for condensing Emerging Cubes. Since the emergence rate is not a monotone measure function, the underlying adaptation is difficult to express using the original concepts. This is why we state the link between the Quotient Cube and the concepts related to Cube Closure. We underline that this link requires a measure function compatible with the Cube Closure operator. It is possible for two tuples, related by the generalization order, to have both an infinite emergence rate. Nevertheless, these two tuples can have a different closure. As a consequence, the emergence rate is not compatible with the Cube Closure because the third property of Definition 9.8 does not hold. Thus for defining the Emerging Quotient Cube, it is not possible to use the emergence rate as a measure function. Instead, we make use of the couple $(f_{val}(t, r_1), f_{val}(t, r_2))$ because it is composed of two functions which are themselves compatible with the Cube Closure.

Definition 9.19 (Emerging Quotient Cube) *The set of equivalence classes of $CL(r_1 \cup r_2)$ emerging from r_1 to r_2, denoted by $EQC(r_1, r_2)$, is called the Emerging Quotient Cube from r_1 to r_2:*

$$EQC(r_1, r_2) = \{([t]_{\equiv_f}, f_{val}(t, r_1), f_{val}(t, r_2)) \mid$$
$$[t]_{\equiv_f} \in QuotientCube(r_1 \cup r_2, \equiv_f) \wedge t \in \text{Ec}(r_1, r_2)\}.$$

Each equivalence class of the Emerging Quotient Cube is represented by its maximal element which is an emerging closed tuple. The next proposition shows that the U and L borders are included in the Emerging Quotient Cube. More precisely U contains the maximal element of the maximal classes (which are closed tuples) while L encompasses the minimal elements (or key tuples) of the minimal classes. Thus navigating within the Emerging Quotient Cube is possible.

Proposition 9.11 *The classical lower and upper borders are included in the Emerging Quotient Cube. The characterization of these borders based on the Emerging Quotient Cube is the following:*

1. *$U = \max_{\preceq_s}(\{\max_{\preceq_{QC}}(\{[t]_{\equiv_f}\})\})$ such that $([t]_{\equiv_f}, f_{val}(t, r_1), f_{val}(t, r_2)) \in EQC(r_1, r_2)$.*

2. *$L = \min_{\preceq_s}(\{\min_{\preceq_{QC}}(\{[t]_{\equiv_f}\})\})$ such that $([t]_{\equiv_f}, f_{val}(t, r_1), f_{val}(t, r_2)) \in EQC(r_1, r_2)$.*

The next proposition proves the correctness of the above representation.

Proposition 9.12 *The Emerging Quotient Cube is a summary of the Emerging Cube: $\forall\ t \in CL(r_1 \cup r_2)$, t is emerging if and only if $([t]_{\equiv_f}, f_{val}(t, r_1), f_{val}(t, r_2))$ belongs to the Emerging Quotient Cube.*

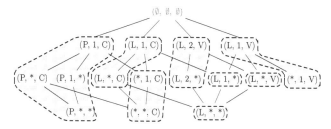

FIGURE 9.4: Illustration of the Emerging Quotient Cube.

Example 9.17 *With* SALES$_1$ *and* SALES$_2$, *Figure 9.4 presents the associated Emerging Quotient Cube. The equivalence classes are marked. All the tuples in an equivalence class share the same couple (*SUM$_{val}(t, r_2)$, SUM$_{val}(t, r_1)$*) of aggregated measures. The leftmost class is represented by its maximal and minimal tuples, intermediary tuples which are redundant must be discarded.*

9.4   Discussion

We have presented different representations intended to reduce the size of the Emerging Cube. Each of them has particular uses. The two pairs of borders provide accurate OLAP classifiers. The Emerging Closed Cube adds to classification tasks querying capabilities and the Emerging Quotient Cube enriches the quoted functionalities with navigation possibilities. The L based representations are also related through an inclusion link as shown below.

Theorem 9.1 *Let* $[L; U]$, L-ECC *and* EQC *be the different representations for the Emerging Cube (*EC*) of two relations* r_1 *and* r_2. *Then we have:*

$$[L; U] \subseteq \text{L-ECC} \subseteq \text{EQC} \subseteq \text{EC}.$$

Figure 9.5 illustrates the uses of the different structures and their relationships. It exemplifies the intuition that the more the users need functionalities, the more information is required.

We do not mention the representations encompassing the $U^\sharp$ border because of two reasons. Firstly, an inclusion link cannot be stated between the $U^\sharp$ based representations. Secondly, the sizes of L and $U^\sharp$ are theoretically equivalent. Nevertheless, experimental evaluations [311, 310] have shown that the $U^\sharp$ border is in practice more reduced than L. These experimental results lead to the following order between the size of all the representations:

$$|[U^\sharp; U]| \leq |[L; U]| \leq |\text{R-ECC}| \leq |U^\sharp\text{-ECC}| \leq |\text{L-ECC}| \leq |\text{EQC}| \leq |\text{EC}|.$$

Depending on the expected uses and the available computation tools, the user can choose the most suitable representation.

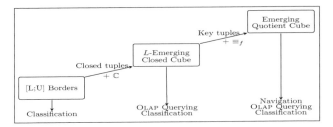

FIGURE 9.5: Relationships between and uses of the L based representations. Source: Reprinted from Ref. [307].

9.5 Conclusion

The users of OLAP systems are interested in great trends hidden in large datasets. We believe that the way in which trends evolve captures relevant knowledge for decision makers. In order to obtain such knowledge, we have proposed the concept of Emerging Cube. Around this concept, we have studied several related issues. For each of them, we make proposals in order to devise a global approach for dealing with trend reversals. This chapter aims to synthesize the research work about the main concern among the different issues, *i.e.* the reduced representations of the Emerging Cube. We propose three types of representations centered on three different uses. We start with the simplest and smallest one which supports a single use: OLAP classification. We follow with an intermediary representation requiring more information than the previous one but enriching the offered functionalities with OLAP querying. We end by proposing the most sophisticated and largest representation which adds, to previous capabilities, the navigation within the Emerging Cube. According to their needs, the decision makers can choose the most suitable representation.

In addition to these representations, we tackled another issue: size estimation of Emerging Cubes [308]. Providing such an estimation makes it possible, before any cube computation, to know the result size and therefore to best calibrate the emergence constraint. By predicting the result size, the user can know if the representation will be manageable. Then the size estimation can be seen as another criterion to choose the adequate representation. The tool devised for such a prediction is particularly efficient and yields an approximate size no more than 5% different from the true size.

In order to complement the described contributions, algorithms have to be devised with two important qualities: efficiency and integrability within RDBMSs. We are currently working on different algorithms computing the various representations and integrated within an homogeneous algorithmic platform [314]. By devising a seamless and integrated relational approach, it is possible to take advantage of existing ROLAP analysis tools. Then, contrary to [438], the Emerging Cube will be a particular data cube and like the original one it will be possible to express queries, explore and navigate within it.

Chapter 10

Relation Between Jumping Emerging Patterns and Rough Set Theory

Pawel Terlecki and Krzysztof Walczak

Institute of Computer Science, Warsaw University of Technology

10.1 Introduction

Since its introduction in 1982, rough set theory (RST) [328] has become a robust knowledge discovery framework that does well in handling incompleteness, vagueness, and uncertainty in data [331, 330, 103, 341]. RST research has revealed numerous connections and led to hybrid concepts in important fields, such as probability theory [469], Dempster-Shafer theory of evidence [370], neural networks [266], fuzzy sets, granular computing [263], or data mining [169].

Extensive work on rule induction, classification [329, 47], feature selection, and data reduction [385] overlaps with areas of application of emerging pat-

TABLE 10.1: A sample decision table $(\mathcal{U}, \mathcal{C}, d) = (\{u_1, ...u_8\}, \{a_1, ..., a_4\}, d)$

	a_1	a_2	a_3	a_4	d
u_1	0	0	2	4	0
u_2	0	1	0	1	0
u_3	0	1	1	3	0
u_4	0	1	1	3	1

	a_1	a_2	a_3	a_4	d
u_5	1	1	0	1	1
u_6	1	0	1	0	1
u_7	0	2	0	5	2
u_8	1	0	1	2	2

terns. While each approach uses a specific formal apparatus and a different representation of data, the fundamental objectives and notions are common.

RST considers a universe of objects characterized by means of functions called attributes. Furthermore, knowledge is interpreted as an ability to discriminate objects and, thus, each *attribute set* carries certain amount of information. Assuming that only certain attributes are available, indiscernibility of objects leads to the most fundamental concept of a *rough set*. It approximates a conventional set by means of two sets, a *lower* and an *upper approximation*, which refer to objects definitely included in the set and the ones it may contain, respectively.

The rough perspective on data reduction is built around *reducts* - highly informative attribute sets. The most generic reducts provide the same information as all available attributes and remain minimal with respect to the inclusion relation. This concept and its many variants have close relatives in the family of emerging patterns. Proofs of the relations given in this chapter are available in [398, 402, 400, 399].

10.2   Theoretical Foundations

Decision problems are often facilitated with a decision table in which each observation carries information on conditions and corresponding decisions. This notation corresponds to a vector dataset with a distinguished decision attribute. The decision attribute can be interpreted as a class label.

Definition 10.1 *A decision table is a triple $(\mathcal{U}, \mathcal{C}, d)$, where $\mathcal{U}$ is a non-empty finite set of objects called the* universe, $\mathcal{C}$ *is a non-empty finite set of* condition attributes *and d is a decision attribute. We will use $\mathcal{A}$ to denote $\mathcal{C} \cup \{d\}$. Each attribute $a \in \mathcal{A}$ is a function $a : \mathcal{U} \mapsto V_a$, where V_a is the domain for a.*

Example 10.1 *Table 10.1 gives a decision table $(\mathcal{U}, \mathcal{C}, d)$ (our running example), where a_1, a_2, a_3, a_4 are condition attributes and d is a decision one. Attributes map objects to values, for example $a_1(u_1) = 0$, $a_2(u_4) = 1$, $d(u_8) = 2$.*

Objects are comparable by means of available attributes. Indiscernibility of objects can be expressed by an equivalence relation based on attribute equality. This relation contains all pairs of objects that cannot be discerned with a given set of attributes. The rest of the definitions are formulated for a given decision table $\mathcal{DT} = (\mathcal{U}, \mathcal{C}, d)$.

Definition 10.2 *For $B \subseteq \mathcal{A}$, an* indiscernibility relation *is defined as*
$$IND_{\mathcal{DT}}(B) = \{(u, v) \in \mathcal{U} \times \mathcal{U} | \forall_{a \in B}\, a(u) = a(v)\}.$$
The indiscernibility relation defines a partition of the universe $\mathcal{U}$ denoted by $\mathcal{U}/IND_{\mathcal{DT}}(B)$. A block of this partition that contains an object $u \in \mathcal{U}$ is denoted by $B_{\mathcal{DT}}(u)$, or $B(u)$ if DT is understood from the context.

Example 10.2 *Fewer condition attributes often lead to more indiscernible pairs. For example, $IND(\mathcal{C}) = \{(u_i, u_i) \mid 1 \leq i \leq 8\} \cup \{(u_3, u_4), (u_4, u_3)\}$ generates the partition $\{\{u_1\}, \{u_2\}, \{u_3, u_4\}, \{u_5\}, \{u_6\}, \{u_7\}, \{u_8\}\}$; in contrast, $IND(\{a_1, a_2\}) = \{(u_i, u_i) \mid 1 \leq i \leq 8\} \cup \{(u_3, u_4), (u_4, u_3), (u_2, u_3), (u_3, u_2), (u_2, u_4), (u_4, u_2), (u_6, u_8), (u_8, u_6)\}$ generates the partition $\{\{u_1\}, \{u_2, u_3, u_4\}, \{u_5\}, \{u_6, u_8\}, \{u_7\}\}$.*

An attribute set $B \subseteq \mathcal{C}$ represents a certain amount of knowledge on the universe. Since each block of the corresponding partition $\mathcal{U}/IND_{\mathcal{DT}}(B)$ contains mutually indiscernible objects, one may use these blocks to approximate sets of objects.

Definition 10.3 *For $B \subseteq \mathcal{C}$, a B-lower approximation of a set $X \subseteq \mathcal{U}$ is defined as $\underline{B_{\mathcal{DT}}}(X) = \{u \in \mathcal{U} \mid B_{\mathcal{DT}}(u) \subseteq X\}$. Observe that $\underline{B_{\mathcal{DT}}}(X)$ is the union of equivalence classes contained in X.*

Example 10.3 *We have: $\underline{\{a_1, a_2\}}(\{u_1, u_2, u_3, u_4, u_5, u_6\}) = \{u_1\} \cup \{u_2, u_3, u_4\} \cup \{u_5\} = \{u_1, u_2, u_3, u_4, u_5\}$ and $\underline{\mathcal{C}}(\{u_4, u_5, u_6\}) = \{u_5\} \cup \{u_6\} = \{u_5, u_6\}$.*

The decision attribute allows us to partition the universe into blocks determined by possible decisions.

Definition 10.4 *For $k \in V_d$, a* decision class k *is defined by $U_k = \{u \in \mathcal{U} | d(u) = k\}$.*

If information on the objects is available through an attribute set $B \subseteq \mathcal{C}$, the decision classes can be approximated by means of the blocks of the partition $\mathcal{U}/IND(B)$. The lower approximations of the classes indicate objects that can be consistently classified. Note that, in general, this property does not hold. Some objects may be indiscernible with respect to B but belong to different decision classes.

Definition 10.5 *For $B \subseteq \mathcal{C}$, a B-positive region with respect to a decision attribute d is defined as*

$$POS_{\mathcal{DT}}(B, d) = \bigcup_{X \in \mathcal{U}/IND_{\mathcal{DT}}(\{d\})} \underline{B_{\mathcal{DT}}}(X).$$

Example 10.4 *The decision attribute generates the partition of the universe into decision classes: $\mathcal{U}/IND_{\mathcal{D}T}(\{d\}) = \{\{u_1, u_2, u_3\}, \{u_4, u_5, u_6\}, \{u_7, u_8\}\}$. The objects u_3 and u_4 are indiscernible by means of all the condition attributes and belong to different classes. Consequently, the positive region for $\mathcal{C}$ excludes these objects and is equal to $POS(\mathcal{C}, d) = \bigcup_{X \in \mathcal{U}/IND(\{d\})} \underline{\mathcal{C}}(X) = \underline{\mathcal{C}}(\{\{u_1, u_2, u_3\}\}) \cup \underline{\mathcal{C}}(\{\{u_4, u_5, u_6\}\})) \cup \underline{\mathcal{C}}(\{\{u_7, u_8\}\}) = \{u_1, u_2\} \cup \{u_5, u_6\} \cup \{u_7, u_8\} = \{u_1, u_2, u_5, u_6, u_7, u_8\}$.*

Definition 10.6 *For an object $u \in \mathcal{U}$, an attribute set $B \subseteq \mathcal{C}$ is a local super reduct iff $\forall(c \in V_d)(\mathcal{C}(u) \cap U_c = \emptyset \implies B(u) \cap U_c = \emptyset)$. B is a local reduct iff B is a local super reduct and none of its proper subset is a local super reduct. The set of all local reducts for the object u is denoted by $REDLOC_{\mathcal{D}T}(u, d)$.*

For objects from the positive region, the definition of a local reduct becomes simpler.

Lemma 10.1 ([385]) *For $u \in POS(\mathcal{C}, d)$, we have:*
$B \in REDLOC_{\mathcal{D}T}(u, d) \iff B$ is a minimal set such that $B(u) \subseteq U_{d(u)}$.

Example 10.5 *We have $REDLOC(u_2, d) = \{\{a_1, a_2, a_3\}, \{a_1, a_4\}\}$. Both attribute sets allow us to discern u_2 from all objects from other classes, i.e. $\{u_4, .., u_8\}$. Formally, from Lemma 10.1, the corresponding blocks for u_2 are subsumed by the class $d(u_2) = 0$: $\{a_1, a_2, a_3\}(\{u_2\}) = \{u_2\} \subseteq U_0$, $\{a_1, a_4\}(\{u_2\}) = \{u_2\} \subseteq U_0$. In addition, this property does not hold for any proper subset of these attribute sets, namely $\{\emptyset, \{a_1\}, \{a_2\}, \{a_3\}, \{a_1, a_2\}, \{a_1, a_3\}, \{a_2, a_3\}\}$ and $\{\emptyset, \{a_1\}, \{a_4\}\}$. In particular, we have $\emptyset(\{u_2\}) = \{u_1, u_2, u_3, u_4, u_5, u_6, u_7, u_8\}$, $\{a_1\}(\{u_2\}) = \{u_1, u_2, u_3, u_4, u_7\}$ and $\{a_4\}(\{u_2\}) = \{u_2, u_5\}$. On the other hand, $REDLOC(u_3, d) = REDLOC(u_4, d) = \emptyset$, since u_3 and u_4 are indiscernible and belong to different decision classes.*

For brevity of our discussion, we define a transactional equivalent for a decision table that specifies a domain of items for all transactions and uses decision items to encode class membership.

Definition 10.7 *A decision transaction system is a tuple $(\mathcal{D}, \mathcal{I}, \mathcal{I}_d)$, where $\mathcal{D}$ is a transaction dataset (multiset) over a universal set of items $(\mathcal{I} \cup \mathcal{I}_d))$ and $\forall(T \in \mathcal{D})(|T \cap \mathcal{I}_d| = 1)$. Elements of $\mathcal{I}$ and $\mathcal{I}_d$ are called condition and decision items, respectively.*

Similarly to decision tables, we introduce a notation for transactions corresponding to the same decision.

Definition 10.8 *For $k \in \mathcal{I}_d$, a decision class k is defined as $D_k = \{T \in \mathcal{D} | T \cap \mathcal{I}_d = \{k\}\}$. We use the symbols D_k and $D_{\{k\}}$ interchangeably.*

10.3 JEPs with Negation

Transactions express facts directly observed in the domain such as event occurrences or object characteristics. Consequently, itemsets from such transactions represent information that is observable. Further, we use the term *positive* to refer to this kind of knowledge. On the contrary, one may consider itemsets that complement positive transactions to a given itemspace. They cover information that is not available directly, but can be easily inferred. This approach leads to a type of knowledge referred to as *negative*.

A decision table can be easily transformed into a transaction database. Relations between reducts and emerging patterns for data given originally by a decision table [402, 398] allow us to use rough set methods to discover JEPs. One could ask if there is any relation to RST for input data provided in transactional form. Interestingly, this matter is closely related to negative knowledge in transaction databases.

We generalize JEPs to *JEPs with negation (JEPNs)* by taking into account both positive and negative items. It is shown that they correspond to classic JEPs in appropriately defined transaction databases [400]. At the same time, an information-preserving transformation of an input database to a binary decision table gives us a basis to consider relations to rough set reducts. In particular, we demonstrate that local reducts provide a way to identify minimal JEPNs.

Originally, negative relationships were introduced in [59], where a chi-square model was applied to estimate independence between two variables. As far as data mining is concerned, the vast majority of publications employ the idea of negation to formulate new interesting association rules. The proposed algorithms include variants of frequent itemset mining [357].

The extended pattern definition results in search space enlargement. Several approaches have been put forward to alleviate this effect. In [437, 18], the support-confidence framework is supplemented with additional measures of interestingness, thus, creating more pruning opportunities. Another option is to constrain the rule syntax. For example, in negative association rules [437] and confined association rules [18], only a complete antecedent or consequent can be negated, whereas in unexpected rules [322] and exception rules [192] negative items in antecedents are used to represent exceptions to regular associations. Some other approaches make use of domain knowledge to formulate valuable rules [455]. Last but not least, the problem of mining frequent itemsets with negation can be addressed with concise data representations [220].

10.3.1 Negative Knowledge in Transaction Databases

We propose a formal apparatus to deal with positive and negative information in classified transactional datasets. In our convention, new types of knowledge can be considered with the standard framework for emerging patterns, as long as the input data are appropriately transformed. Also, the new concepts provide a basis for pattern discovery approaches.

Hereinafter, we assume that our data are given by a decision transaction system $\mathcal{DTS} = (\mathcal{D}, \mathcal{I}, \mathcal{I}_d)$, where $\mathcal{D} = \{T_1, .., T_n\}$, $\mathcal{I} = \{I_1, .., I_m\}$, $\mathcal{I}_d = \{c_1, .., c_p\}$.

In order to express both positive and negative knowledge in the context of $\mathcal{DTS}$, we generalize the concepts of an itemspace, itemset, and item. In this section, the original meaning of these terms is preserved by preceding them with the adjective *positive*, e.g. a positive item.

Definition 10.9 *For a positive itemspace* $\mathcal{I}$, *a negative itemspace and an extended itemspace are defined as* $\overline{\mathcal{I}} = \{\bar{i} | i \in \mathcal{I}\}$ *and* $\mathcal{I} \cup \overline{\mathcal{I}}$, *respectively. The elements of these three itemspaces are called* positive, negative, *and* extended items, *respectively.*

A positive itemset with negation, a negative itemset with negation and an itemset with negation are any subsets of the respective itemspaces.

Our discussion pertains mostly to itemsets with negation. Thus, for brevity, we usually use short names: *itemsets* or *patterns*.

Negative items express the absence of the corresponding positive items in transactions. Consequently, itemsets that contain at least one positive item and its corresponding negative item have a self-contradictory interpretation. We distinguish a set of patterns that make sense in the considered setting.

Definition 10.10 The set of valid itemsets *is defined as* $\mathcal{P} = \{p \subseteq \mathcal{I} \cup \overline{\mathcal{I}} | \forall_{i \in \mathcal{I}} i \in p \Longrightarrow \bar{i} \notin p\}$. *Accordingly, each itemset from* $\mathcal{P}$ *is called* valid.

For brevity, we introduce the following notations.

Definition 10.11 *For an itemset* $X \in \mathcal{P}$, *we define: the* positive part $X_p = X \cap \mathcal{I}$, *the* negative part $X_n = X \cap \overline{\mathcal{I}}$, *the* negated pattern $\overline{X} = \{\bar{i} | i \in X\}$, *the* contradictory pattern $\widehat{X} = (\mathcal{I} \cup \overline{\mathcal{I}}) - X$, *the* extended pattern $\widetilde{X} = X \cup \widehat{X}$. *We assume that* $\bar{\bar{i}} = i$.

In other words, a positive (negative) part refers to the set of all positive (negative) items of a given pattern. A negated pattern is obtained by changing each positive item of a given pattern to the corresponding negative item and vice versa. A contradictory pattern is a complement of a negated pattern to the extended itemspace. Finally, an extended pattern is a sum of a given pattern and its contradictory pattern.

Now, we generalize basic measures defined for positive patterns, so that they can be used for itemsets with negation.

Definition 10.12 *The* extended support *of an itemset* $X \in \mathcal{P}$ *in a database* $D \subseteq \mathcal{D}$ *is defined as* $exsupp_D(X) = \frac{|\{T \in D | X_p \subseteq T \wedge X_n \subseteq \overline{\mathcal{I} - T}\}|}{|D|}$.

With this extended definition of support, we can accordingly introduce the notion of extended growth rate in terms of extended supports.

Definition 10.13 *The* extended growth rate *of an itemset* $X \subseteq \mathcal{I}$ *from* D_1 *to* D_2 *is defined as*

$$exgr_{D_1 \to D_2}(X) = \begin{cases} 0, & exsupp_{D_1}(X) = exsupp_{D_2}(X) = 0 \\ \infty, & exsupp_{D_1}(X) = 0 \text{ and } exsupp_{D_2}(X) \neq 0 \\ \frac{exsupp_{D_2}(X)}{exsupp_{D_1}(X)}, & otherwise. \end{cases}$$

Based on the above definitions, one may consider patterns analogous to positive emerging patterns. We focus solely on JEPs.

Definition 10.14 *A* jumping emerging pattern with negation (JEPN) *from* D_1 *to* D_2 *is an itemset* $X \in \mathcal{P}$ *with infinite extended growth rate.*

For convenience, we introduce the following sets of JEPNs.

Definition 10.15 *For* $D_1, D_2 \subseteq \mathcal{D}$, *we define (a) a* JEPN *space,* $JEPN_{\mathcal{DTS}}(D_1, D_2)$, *as the set of all JEPNs from* D_1 *to* D_2, *(b) a positive JEPN space as* $posJEPN_{\mathcal{DTS}}(D_1, D_2) = \{J \in JEPN_{\mathcal{DTS}}(D_1, D_2) | J \subseteq \mathcal{I}\}$, *and (c) a negative JEPNs space as* $negJEPN_{\mathcal{DTS}}(D_1, D_2) = \{J \in JEPN_{\mathcal{DTS}}(D_1, D_2) | J \subseteq \overline{\mathcal{I}}\}$.

Itemsets with negation are considered for a decision transaction system. We define two derivative systems to focus on just positive or negative itemsets.

Definition 10.16 *A* contradictory decision transaction system *based on* $\mathcal{DTS}$ *is a decision transaction system* $\widehat{\mathcal{DTS}} = (\{T_1', .., T_n'\}, \overline{\mathcal{I}}, \mathcal{I}_d)$, *where* $T_i' = \widehat{T}_i \cup (T_i \cap \mathcal{I}_d)$, *for each* $i = 1, .., n$.

To construct a contradictory decision transaction system, each transaction of $\mathcal{DTS}$ is replaced by its corresponding contradictory pattern, a decision item is excluded. Items complementing transactions of $\mathcal{DTS}$ to the positive itemspace can be directly observed in transactions of $\widehat{\mathcal{DTS}}$ as negative items.

Definition 10.17 *An* extended decision transaction system *based on* $\mathcal{DTS}$ *is a decision transaction system* $\widetilde{\mathcal{DTS}} = (\{T_1', .., T_n'\}, \mathcal{I} \cup \overline{\mathcal{I}}, \mathcal{I}_d)$, *where* $T_i' = \widetilde{T}_i \cup (T_i \cap \mathcal{I}_d)$, *for each* $i = 1, .., n$.

In other words, each transaction of $\mathcal{DTS}$ is extended to include its negated complements. All transactions of $\widetilde{\mathcal{DTS}}$ have the same size $|\mathcal{I}|$.

Example 10.6 *Let us consider the decision transaction system* $\mathcal{DTS}$ *in Table 10.2. We have* $\mathcal{I} = \{a, b, c, d, e, f\}$, $\mathcal{I}_d = \{c_0, c_1\}$, $\overline{\mathcal{I}} = \{\overline{a}, \overline{b}, \overline{c}, \overline{d}, \overline{e}, \overline{f}\}$ *and* $\mathcal{P} = \{p \subseteq \mathcal{I} \cup \overline{\mathcal{I}} | \forall_{i \in \mathcal{I}} i \in p \implies \overline{i} \notin p\}$. *Thus, for example, we have:* $ab\overline{b}c, a\overline{a}e \notin \mathcal{P}$. *Although transactions in* $\mathcal{DTS}$ *cannot contain negative items, they can still support patterns belonging to* $\mathcal{P}$, *when the extended definition of support is being used, e.g.* $exsupp_{D_0}(\overline{c}e) = 2$. *The contradictory and extended decision systems based on* $\mathcal{DTS}$ *are also given in Table 10.2.*

TABLE 10.2: Decision transaction systems: $\mathcal{DTS}$, $\widetilde{\mathcal{DTS}}$, $\widehat{\mathcal{DTS}}$

	$\mathcal{I}$	$\mathcal{I}_d$
T_1	cef	c_0
T_2	de	c_0
T_3	e	c_0
T_4	bcd	c_1
T_5	df	c_1
T_6	ace	c_1

	$\overline{\mathcal{I}}$	$\mathcal{I}_d$
T_1	$\overline{abd}$	c_0
T_2	$\overline{ab}\overline{c}\overline{f}$	c_0
T_3	$\overline{ab}\overline{c}d\overline{f}$	c_0
T_4	$\overline{ae}\overline{f}$	c_1
T_5	$\overline{abc}\overline{e}$	c_1
T_6	$\overline{bd}f$	c_1

	$\mathcal{I} \cup \overline{\mathcal{I}}$	$\mathcal{I}_d$
T_1	$cef\overline{abd}$	c_0
T_2	$de\overline{ab}\overline{c}\overline{f}$	c_0
T_3	$e\overline{ab}\overline{c}d\overline{f}$	c_0
T_4	$bcd\overline{ae}\overline{f}$	c_1
T_5	$df\overline{abc}\overline{e}$	c_1
T_6	$ace\overline{bd}f$	c_1

10.3.2   Transformation to Decision Table

Transactional data can be represented in the form of a decision table. We consider a transformation, in which objects are mapped to transactions and each item is assigned a binary attribute [179]. The attribute indicates the presence of the item in the respective transaction.

Definition 10.18 *A binary decision table based on $\mathcal{DTS}$ is a decision table $\mathcal{BDT}_{\mathcal{DTS}} = (\mathcal{U}, \mathcal{C}, d)$ where $\mathcal{U} = \{u_1, .., u_n\}$, $\mathcal{C} = \{a_1, .., a_m\}$, and $V_d = \{c_1, .., c_p\}$ such that $d(u_i) = c$ where $\{c\} = T_i \cap \mathcal{I}_d, \forall_{i \in 1..n}$, and*

$$a_j(u_i) = \left\{ \begin{array}{ll} 0, & I_j \notin T_i \\ 1, & I_j \in T_i \end{array} \right. , \forall_{i \in 1..n, j \in 1..m},$$

In this data representation, the fact whether an item belongs to a particular transaction or not is encoded by certain attribute values. Therefore, itemsets generated by an object and attribute set can contain negative items.

Definition 10.19 *For $\mathcal{BDT}_{\mathcal{DTS}}$, $u \in \mathcal{U}$, $B = \{a_k | k \in K\}$ and $K \subseteq \{1, .., m\}$, we define a binary pattern based on the object u and attribute set B as*

$$binPatt(u, B) = \{I_k \in \mathcal{I} | a_k(u) = 1\} \cup \{\overline{I}_k \in \mathcal{I} | a_k(u) = 0\}.$$

Example 10.7 *In order to describe the data in the decision transaction system $\mathcal{DTS}$, we can use the binary decision table $(\mathcal{U}, \mathcal{C}, d)$ based on $\mathcal{DTS}$, where $\mathcal{U} = \{u_1, u_2, u_3, u_4, u_5, u_6\}$, $\mathcal{C} = \{a_1, a_2, a_3, a_4, a_5, a_6\}$, $V_d = \{c_0, c_1\}$.*

Note that we use the same symbol to denote an item and the respective attribute, even though the latter is a function. Values of the attributes are given in Table 10.3.

TABLE   10.3:   The   corresponding   binary   decision   table $(\{u_1, u_2, u_3, u_4, u_5, u_6\}, \{a_1, a_2, a_3, a_4, a_5, a_6\}, d)$ based on $\mathcal{DTS}$

	a_1	a_2	a_3	a_4	a_5	a_6	d
u_1	0	0	1	0	1	1	0
u_2	0	0	0	1	1	0	0
u_3	0	0	0	0	1	0	0
u_4	0	1	1	1	0	0	1
u_5	0	0	0	1	0	1	1
u_6	1	0	1	0	1	0	1

10.3.3   Properties

This section looks at basic properties of JEPNs and their relation to rough set theory. We continue to consider the decision transaction system $\mathcal{DTS} = (\mathcal{D}, \mathcal{I}, \mathcal{I}_d)$.

The following two facts demonstrate equivalence of the support (growth rate) of a given pattern with negation in the extended decision transaction system $\widetilde{\mathcal{DTS}}$ as well as the extended support (extended growth rate) of this pattern in the original decision transaction system $\mathcal{DTS}$.

Theorem 10.1 *Let $D \subseteq \mathcal{D}$. Then $\forall_{X \subseteq \mathcal{I} \cup \widetilde{\mathcal{I}}} supp_{\widetilde{D}}(X) = exsupp_D(X)$.*

Remark 10.1 *Let $D \subseteq \mathcal{D}$. Then $\forall_{X \subseteq \mathcal{I} \cup \widetilde{\mathcal{I}}} gr_{\widetilde{D_1} \to \widetilde{D_2}}(X) = exgr_{D_1 \to D_2}(X)$.*

In light of these facts, it becomes evident that JEPNs in $\mathcal{DTS}$ are also JEPs in $\widetilde{\mathcal{DTS}}$ and vice versa.

Theorem 10.2 *Let $D_1, D_2 \subseteq \mathcal{D}$. Then $JEPN_{\mathcal{DTS}}(D_1, D_2) = JEP_{\widetilde{\mathcal{DTS}}}(D_1, D_2)$.*

Example 10.8 *Let us consider the patterns $\overline{a}\overline{b}\overline{c}, \overline{d}f \in P$. In the system $\widetilde{\mathcal{DTS}}$, we have $supp_{\widetilde{D_0}}(\overline{a}\overline{b}\overline{c}) = 2$, $supp_{\widetilde{D_1}}(\overline{a}\overline{b}\overline{c}) = 1$ and $gr_{\widetilde{D_1} \to \widetilde{D_0}}(\overline{a}\overline{b}\overline{c}) = 2/1 < +\infty$, which gives $\overline{a}\overline{b}\overline{c} \notin JEP_{\widetilde{\mathcal{DTS}}}(D_1, D_0)$. In the system $\mathcal{DTS}$, we have $exsupp_{D_0}(\overline{a}\overline{b}\overline{c}) = 2$, $exsupp_{D_1}(\overline{a}\overline{b}\overline{c}) = 1$ and $exgr_{D_1 \to D_0}(\overline{a}\overline{b}\overline{c}) = 2/1 < +\infty$, therefore, $\overline{a}\overline{b}\overline{c} \notin JEPN_{\mathcal{DTS}}(D_1, D_0)$. At the same time, in $\widetilde{\mathcal{DTS}}$, we have $supp_{\widetilde{D_0}}(\overline{d}f) = 2$, $supp_{\widetilde{D_1}}(\overline{d}f) = 0$ and $gr_{\widetilde{D_1} \to \widetilde{D_0}}(\overline{d}f) = +\infty$, thus, $\overline{d}f \in JEP_{\widetilde{\mathcal{DTS}}}(D_1, D_0)$. Now, in $\mathcal{DTS}$, we have $exsupp_{D_0}(\overline{d}f) = 2$, $exsupp_{D_1}(\overline{d}f) = 1$ and $exgr_{D_1 \to D_0}(\overline{d}f) = +\infty$, thus, $\overline{d}f \in JEPN_{\mathcal{DTS}}(D_1, D_0)$. Note that $\overline{d}f$ is also a minimal pattern.*

As we can see, extended support, extended growth rate and being a JEPN in $\mathcal{DTS}$ can be equivalently concluded in the extended decision transaction system $\widetilde{\mathcal{DTS}}$, which remains consistent with Theorems 10.1, 10.2 and Remark 10.1.

Since $JEPN_{\mathcal{DTS}}(D_1, D_2)$ is a JEP space, it is convex and can be concisely represented by a set interval. Throughout the rest of this section, we consider spaces $JEPN_{\mathcal{DTS}}(D'_k, D_k) = [\mathcal{L}_k, \mathcal{R}_k]$ for $k \in V_d$.

Itemsets with negation are closely related to attribute sets in the respective binary decision table. The following theorem demonstrates equivalence between a JEPN in $\mathcal{DTS}$ and a pattern generated by an attribute set and object from the positive region induced by this set in $\mathcal{BDT}_{\mathcal{DTS}}$.

Theorem 10.3 *Let $(\mathcal{U}, \mathcal{C}, d)$ be the binary decision table based on $\mathcal{DTS}$.*
$\forall_{k \in V_d} \forall_{P \subseteq \mathcal{C}} \forall_{u \in \mathcal{U}} u \in POS(P, k, d) \Longleftrightarrow binPatt(u, P) \in JEPN(D'_k, D_k)$.

In addition to the above, rough set theory provides a way of finding minimal JEPNs. In fact, the left bound of a JEPN space can be generated by means of local reducts induced for each object in the positive region of $\mathcal{BDT}_{\mathcal{DTS}}$.

Theorem 10.4 *Let $(\mathcal{U}, \mathcal{C}, d)$ be the binary decision table based on $\mathcal{DTS}$.*
$\forall_{P \subseteq \mathcal{C}} \forall_{u \in POS(\mathcal{C}, d)} P \in REDLOC(u, d) \Longleftrightarrow binPatt(u, P) \in \mathcal{L}_{d(u)}$.

Example 10.9 *Let us consider the decision transaction system DTS and corresponding binary decision table $\mathcal{BDT}_{\mathcal{DTS}}$, the itemset $P = \{a, b, c\}$ and the class $k = 0$. We have $POS(\{a, b, c\}, 0, d) = \{u_1, u_4, u_6\}$ and $binPatt(\{a, b, c\}, u_1) = \{\bar{a}, \bar{b}, c\}$. In addition, we have $exgr_{D_1 \rightarrow D_0}(\bar{a}\bar{b}c) = +\infty$, thus, $\bar{a}\bar{b}c \in JEPN_{\mathcal{DTS}}(D_1, D_0)$. Besides, $\{a, b, c\} \in REDLOC(u_1, d)$, $u_1 \in POS(\mathcal{C}, d)$ and $\bar{a}\bar{b}c \in \mathcal{L}_0$, where $[\mathcal{L}_0, \mathcal{R}_0]$ represents $JEPN_{\mathcal{DTS}}(D_1, D_0)$. Note that the situation is quite different for $binPatt(\{a, b, c\}, u_2) = \{\bar{a}b\bar{c}\}$. Here, we have $u_2 \notin POS(\{a, b, c\}, 0, d)$, thus, $\bar{a}b\bar{c}$ is not even a JEPN.*

On the other hand, the right bound can be derived directly from the positive region of a binary decision table.

Theorem 10.5 *Let $(\mathcal{U}, \mathcal{C}, d)$ be the binary decision table based on $\mathcal{DTS}$.*
$\mathcal{R}_k = \{binPatt(u, \mathcal{C}) \subseteq \mathcal{P} | u \in POS(\mathcal{C}, k, d)\}$.

Example 10.10 *Let us consider the decision transaction system DTS, corresponding binary decision table $\mathcal{BDT}_{\mathcal{DTS}}$ and class $k = 0$. We have $\{binPatt(u, \mathcal{C}) \subseteq \mathcal{P} | u \in POS(\mathcal{C}, 0, d)\} = \{binPatt(u, \mathcal{C}) \subseteq \mathcal{P} | u \in \{u_1, u_2, u_3\}\} = \{\bar{a}b\bar{c}de\bar{f}, \bar{a}\bar{b}\bar{c}de\bar{f}, \bar{a}b\bar{c}de\bar{f}\}$. Note that this collection is equal to the right bound $\mathcal{R}_0$.*

The theorems provided so far offer two ways of finding JEPNs. First - by finding JEPs in an extended decision transaction system, and second - by finding local reducts in a binary decision table. These methods allow us to indirectly find positive or negative JEPNs by means of filtering the bounds of the set interval of a JEPN space. The following theorem demonstrates that both collections can also be obtained directly, if an original or a contradictory database is considered, respectively.

Theorem 10.6 *Let $D_1, D_2 \in \mathcal{D}$. $posJEPN_{\widetilde{\mathcal{DTS}}}(D_1, D_2) = JEP_{\mathcal{DTS}}(D_1, D_2)$ and $negJEPN_{\widetilde{\mathcal{DTS}}}(D_1, D_2) = JEP_{\widetilde{\mathcal{DTS}}}(D_1, \bar{D}_2)$.*

Example 10.11 *The space $JEPN_{\mathcal{DTS}}(D_1, D_0)$ can be represented by the border $[\mathcal{L}_0, \mathcal{R}_0]$, where $\mathcal{L}_0 = \{ef, \overline{d}f, de, \overline{c}\overline{f}, \overline{c}e, \overline{c}\overline{d}, cf, \overline{b}\overline{d}\overline{f}, \overline{a}e, \overline{a}\overline{d}, \overline{a}\overline{b}\overline{f}, \overline{a}\overline{b}\overline{c}\}$ and $\mathcal{R}_0 = \{\overline{a}\overline{b}\overline{c}\overline{d}ef, \overline{a}\overline{b}\overline{c}de\overline{f}, \overline{a}\overline{b}\overline{c}\overline{d}e\overline{f}\}$.*

From the previous example, the set interval representing $JEP_{\mathcal{DTS}}(D_1, D_0)$ is equal to $[\{ef, de, cf\}, \{de, cef\}]$. This collection comprises all positive JEPNs, namely the collection $posJEPN_{\mathcal{DTS}}(D_1, D_0)$.

For the system $\widehat{\mathcal{DTS}}$, we obtain the space $JEP_{\widehat{\mathcal{DTS}}}(D_1, D_0)$ that is represented by the following set interval $[\{\overline{c}\overline{f}, \overline{c}\overline{d}, \overline{a}\overline{d}, \overline{a}\overline{b}\overline{f}\}, \{\overline{a}\overline{b}d, \overline{a}\overline{b}\overline{c}\overline{f}, \overline{a}\overline{b}\overline{c}\overline{d}f\}]$ and equal to the collection $negJEPN_{\mathcal{DTS}}(D_1, D_0)$.

As we can observe, $JEPN_{\mathcal{DTS}}(D_1, D_0)$ contains all the itemsets from both $posJEPN_{\mathcal{DTS}}(D_1, D_0)$ and $negJEPN_{\mathcal{DTS}}(D_1, D_0)$. Besides that, it includes itemsets that contain positive and negative items at the same time.

10.3.4 Mining Approaches

Let us consider a decision transaction system $\mathcal{DTS} = (\mathcal{D}, \mathcal{I}, \mathcal{I}_d)$. We are interested in finding the space of all jumping emerging patterns with negation, $JEPN_{\mathcal{DTS}}(D'_k, D_k)$, for each decision class $k \in V_Z$. Owing to the fact that, according to Theorem 10.2, each space of this kind is convex, our task can be defined as finding the respective set intervals $[\mathcal{L}_k, \mathcal{R}_k]$.

The relations studied in the previous section provide us with two methods of finding JEPNs. The first one, given in Figure 10.1, requires building the extended decision transaction system $\widehat{\mathcal{DTS}}$ based on $\mathcal{DTS}$. Then, for each decision class $k \in V_Z$, the databases D_k and D'_k are considered and the set interval for $JEP_{\widehat{\mathcal{DTS}}}(D'_k, D_k)$ is computed. According to Theorem 10.2, the resulting set intervals are also equal to $JEPN_{\mathcal{DTS}}(D'_k, D_k)$. For a database pair, a set interval can be obtained by means of one of the widely-known algorithms, like JEP-Producer [118] or CP-Tree mining [137].

Input: $\mathcal{DTS}$
Output: all minimal JEPs
Method:
1: $\mathcal{L}_k = \emptyset$ for each $k \in I_d$
2: for $(k = 1; 1 <= |\mathcal{I}_d|; k++)$
3:     Construct the extended decision transaction system $\widehat{\mathcal{DTS}}$
4:     Compute the set interval $[\widetilde{\mathcal{L}}_k, \widetilde{\mathcal{R}}_k]$ for a $JEP_{\widehat{\mathcal{DTS}}}(D'_k, D_k)$
5:     $\mathcal{L}_k = \widetilde{\mathcal{L}}_k$
6: return $\mathcal{L}_k | k \in I_d$

FIGURE 10.1: The JEPNBasic Algorithm. Adapted from Ref. [400], with kind permission from Springer Science+Business Media.

The second approach, given in Figure 10.2, involves building a binary decision table $\mathcal{BDT}_{\mathcal{DTS}} = (\mathcal{U}, \mathcal{C}, d)$ and applying the rough set framework to mine minimal patterns for each class. For each $u \in \mathcal{U}$, we compute the collection of local reducts $REDLOC(u, d)$. Then, by Theorem 10.4, the left bound of the respective set interval, for each class $k \in V_Z$, can be found by taking each object $u \in POS(\mathcal{C}, k, d)$ and generating patterns with all local reducts computed for u, i.e $\mathcal{L}_k = \{binPatt(u, P) | u \in POS(\mathcal{C}, k, d) \wedge P \in REDLOC(u, d)\}$. Moreover, from Theorem 10.5, the respective right bounds $\mathcal{R}_k$ are trivial, i.e. $\mathcal{R}_k = \{binPatt(u, \mathcal{C}) | u \in POS(\mathcal{C}, k, d)\}$. The most important step is to efficiently mine the complete sets of local reducts for each object. Several methods have been proposed in the literature, such as minimization of monotonous boolean functions [48, 219], traversing the lattice of all possible monoms [355, 403], identifying maximal monoms [219] and parallel approaches [384].

Input: $\mathcal{DTS}$
Output: all minimal JEPs
Method:
1: $\mathcal{L}_k = \emptyset$ for each $k \in I_d$
2: for$(i = 1; 1 <= |\mathcal{D}|; i + +)$
3:     Construct a binary decision table $\mathcal{BDT}_{\mathcal{DTS}}$
4: Compute $REDLOC(u_i, d)$ in $\mathcal{BDT}_{\mathcal{DTS}}$
5: $\mathcal{L}_k = \mathcal{L}_k \cup \{binPatt_{\mathcal{DTS}}(u_i, R) | R \in REDLOC(u_i, d)\}, k = T_i \cup \mathcal{I}_d$
6: return $\mathcal{L}_k | k \in I_d$

FIGURE 10.2: The JEPNRedLoc Algorithm. Adapted from Ref. [400], with kind permission from Springer Science+Business Media.

A JEPN space can be used to compute the corresponding JEP space. Indeed, according to Theorem 10.6, JEPs are equivalent to posJEPNs and the latter are all included in the JEPN space. From the definition, posJEPNs can be obtained by simple filtering out patterns with negative items from the bounds of the set interval representing the JEPN space. This filtering can be incorporated in the last step of the loop in either of the algorithm. For example, one may generate a pattern $binPatt_{\mathcal{DTS}}(u, R)$ only for an object $u \in \mathcal{U}$ and a local reduct $R \subseteq \mathcal{A}$, for which $\forall_{a \in R} a(i) = 1$.

Although this approach allows us to discover JEPs, it comes with a significant overhead of additionally generated patterns and, thus, remain impractical. In Section 10.4, more efficient variants of this method are presented.

TABLE 10.4: A sample decision transaction system $\mathcal{DTS}$ = $\{\{T_1, .., T_6\}, \{a, b, c, d, e, f, g, h\}, \{c_0, c_1\}\}$

T_1	adh	c_0
T_2	afg	c_0
T_3	ceg	c_0

T_4	ce	c_1
T_5	beh	c_1
T_6	bfg	c_1

TABLE 10.5: JEP and JEPN spaces for $\mathcal{DTS}$

Space	Set interval
$JEP(D_1, D_0)$	$[\{eg, d, cg, a\}, \{adh, afg, ceg\}]$
$JEP(D_0, D_1)$	$[\{eh, b\}, \{ce, beh, bfg\}]$
$JEPN(D_1, D_0)$	$[\{\overline{fg}, \overline{e}h, \overline{eg}, \overline{e}f, eg, d, cg, \overline{b}h, \overline{b}g, \overline{b}f, \overline{be}, \overline{bc}, a\},$ $\{a\overline{bcde}\overline{f}gh, a\overline{bcde}fgh, \overline{abc}degh\}]$
$JEPN(D_0, D_1)$	$[\{\overline{gh}, eh, e\overline{g}, dh, d\overline{g}, \overline{c}e, \overline{c}df, c\overline{g}, b, \overline{a}h, \overline{ag}, \overline{a}f, \overline{ae}, \overline{ac}\},$ $\{\overline{abcde}\overline{f}gh, a\overline{bcde}\overline{f}gh, \overline{abcde}fgh\}]$

10.4 JEP Mining by Means of Local Reducts

Transactional data can be transformed to the form of a binary decision table (see Section 10.3.2) and tackled by rough set methods. In particular, local reducts allow us to find JEPs as a side effect of JEPN discovery (Theorem 10.6). A major disadvantage of this approach is that itemspaces are usually large and result in high-dimensional decision tables. At the same time, much of the computation effort is wasted on finding undesirable patterns with negative items, that need to be filtered out anyway.

Example 10.12 *Consider the decision transaction system given in Table 10.4. A comparison of JEP and JEPN spaces given in Table 10.5 shows that the overhead of non-positive JEPNs can be overwhelming.*

This section discusses how to lower the dimensionality of decision tables by applying appropriate transformations. Our approaches are based on the fact that transactional data is usually sparse. Indeed, sometimes average transactions of real-life datasets can contain just a few items. Discovery methods may benefit from more concise data representations.

Hereinafter, we assume that our input data are represented by a decision transaction system $\mathcal{DTS} = (\mathcal{D}, \mathcal{I}, \mathcal{I}_d)$, where $\mathcal{D} = (T_1, .., T_n)$, $\mathcal{I} = \{I_1, .., I_m\}$, $\mathcal{I}_d = \{c_1, .., c_p\}$, $K = \{1, .., n\}$.

10.4.1   Global Condensation

In a binary decision table based on a decision transaction system, each binary attribute refers to a single item. One possible modification of this approach is to use multi-valued attributes to encode groups of items. The itemspace can be partitioned into blocks and each block is assigned a new attribute. We refer to this transformation as *global condensation*.

Local reducts in a binary decision table correspond to JEPNs. For a given target class, all the JEPNs constitute a convex space that also contains the JEPs. After performing global condensation, local reducts in the resulting decision table may no longer map to all the possible JEPNs. This fact is advantageous, since it diminishes the overhead of unnecessarily generated patterns. The method remains correct as long as the complete set of the positive JEPNs (JEPs) can be discovered.

10.4.1.1   Condensed Decision Table

In order to ensure that global condensation leads to a complete set of JEPs, we introduce a special type of a partition of an itemspace. Each transaction and each block are required to have at most one item in common.

Definition 10.20 *A partition* $\{p_1, .., p_r\}$ *of* $\mathcal{I}$ *is called* proper *iff* $\forall_{T \in \mathcal{D}} \forall_{j \in \{1,...,r\}} |T \cap p_j| <= 1$.

If a partition is proper, for each block p_i, we have at most $|p_i|$ different intersections of p_i with transactions of $\mathcal{D}$, where $i \in \{1, .., r\}$. Each of these intersections refers to at most one item and can be mapped to a distinct value of a single multi-valued attribute. We express the transformed dataset by means of a decision table.

Definition 10.21 *For a given a proper partition* $P = \{p_1, .., p_r\}$ *of* $\mathcal{I}$, *and a set* $F = \{f_1, .., f_r\}$ *where* $f_j : 2^{p_j} \mapsto \mathbb{N}$ *and* f_j *is a bijection for each* $j \in \{1, .., r\}$, *a condensed decision table based on* $\mathcal{DTS}$, P *and* F *is a decision table* $CDT_{\mathcal{DTS},P,F} = (\mathcal{U}, \mathcal{C}, d)$ *with* $\mathcal{U} = \{u_1, .., u_n\}$, $\mathcal{C} = \{a_1, .., a_r\}$, *and* $V_d = \{d_1, .., d_p\}$ *such that*

$$a_j(u_i) = f_j(T_i \cup p_j), \forall_{i \in 1..n, j \in 1..r}$$

$$d(u_i) = T_i \cap \mathcal{I}_d, \forall_{i \in 1..n}$$

The choice of the function F does not affect the structure of the decision table and is a matter of convention.

For the sake of convenience, we introduce a new notation to refer to patterns generated by an object and attribute set in a condensed decision table.

Definition 10.22 *For* $CDT_{\mathcal{DTS}}$, $u \in \mathcal{U}$, $B = \{a_k | k \in K\}$ *and* $K \subseteq \{1, .., m\}$, *a condensed pattern based on the object* u *and attribute set* B *is an itemset* $condPatt(u, B) = \bigcup_{k \in K} f_k^{-1}(a_k(u))$, *where* $u \in \mathcal{U}$, $B = \{a_k | k \in K\}$.

TABLE 10.6: The binary and condensed decision table based on $\mathcal{DTS}$ from Table 10.4 and the proper partition $\{\{a, b, c\}, \{d, e, f\}, \{g, h\}\}$

	a	b	c	d	e	f	g	h	d
u_1	1	0	0	1	0	0	0	1	0
u_2	1	0	0	0	0	1	1	0	0
u_3	0	0	1	0	1	0	1	0	0
u_4	0	0	1	0	1	0	0	0	1
u_5	0	1	0	0	1	0	0	1	1
u_6	0	1	0	0	0	1	1	0	1

	a_1	a_2	a_3	d
u_1	0	0	0	0
u_2	0	1	1	0
u_3	1	2	1	0
u_4	1	2	2	1
u_5	2	2	0	1
u_6	2	1	1	1

Example 10.13 *In Table 10.6 we present a transformation from a sample transactional dataset, through the respective binary table, to the condensed table that is generated for the proper partition* $\{\{a, b, c\}, \{d, e, f\}, \{g, h\}\}$. *Each attribute of the condensed table refers to a block of a partition and each attribute value to one item at most. In particular, for attribute* a_3 *we have:* $condPatt(u_4, a_3) = \emptyset$, $condPatt(u_5, a_3) = h$ *and* $condPatt(u_6, a_3) = g$. *Note that the partition* $\{\{a, b, c\}, \{d, e, f, g, h\}\}$ *is not proper, since* $|T_1 \cap \{d, e, f, g, h\}| = 2 > 1$.

Let us consider a condensed decision table $\mathcal{CDT}_{\mathcal{DTS}, P, F} = (\mathcal{U}, \mathcal{C}, d)$. The following theorem demonstrates that an object from the positive region of the condensed decision table can be used to generate a JEP, when one applies an attribute set whose each element maps to a non-empty itemset.

Theorem 10.7 $\forall_{R \subseteq \mathcal{C}} \forall_{u \in \mathcal{U}} (\forall_{j \in \{1, .., r\}} a_j \in R \Longrightarrow a_j(u) \neq f_j(\emptyset)) \Longrightarrow$
$(u \in POS(R, d) \cap \bar{U}_{d^{-1}(u)} \Longleftrightarrow condPatt(u, R) \in JEP(C'_{d^{-1}(u)}, C_{d^{-1}(u)}))$

Furthermore, the theorem below states that if such an attribute set is a local reduct, it generates a minimal JEP.

Theorem 10.8 $\forall_{R \subseteq \mathcal{C}} \forall_{u \in POS(C, d)} (\forall_{j \in \{1, .., r\}} a_j \in R \Longrightarrow a_j(u) \neq f_j(\emptyset)) \Longrightarrow$
$(R \in REDLOC(u, d) \Longleftrightarrow condPatt(u, R) \in \mathcal{L}_{d^{-1}(u)})$

10.4.1.2 Proper Partition Finding as Graph Coloring

The choice of a proper partition is critical for construction of a condensed decision table. This problem can be expressed in the language of the graph theory. We construct a graph in which each vertex corresponds to an item from an itemspace. Two vertices are connected with an edge only if there is at least one transaction that contains both corresponding items. From the definition, these two items cannot belong to the same block of a proper partition, which is substantial for JEP discovery. Otherwise, one attribute value would represent both items and patterns that contain only one of these items would not be considered in the further mining.

Definition 10.23 *An item-conflict graph based on $\mathcal{DTS}$ is an undirected graph $ICG_{\mathcal{DTS}} = (V, E)$ such that:*
$$\forall_{x,y \in \{1,..,m\}}\{v_x, v_y\} \in E \iff \exists_{T \in \mathcal{D}} i_x, i_y \in T, \text{ where } V = \{v_1, .., v_m\}.$$

Let us consider an item-conflict graph $ICG_{\mathcal{DTS}} = (V, E)$. In fact, every proper partition of the itemspace $\mathcal{I}$ corresponds to a coloring of this graph. For consistency, we represent colorings as partitions of the set of vertices V.

Theorem 10.9 *For a partition $\{w_1, .., w_r\}$ of V and partition $\{p_1, .., p_r\}$ of $\mathcal{I}$ such that $\forall_{j \in \{1,..,m\}} \forall_{k \in \{1,..,r\}} v_j \in w_k \iff i_j \in p_k$, we have:*
$$\{w_1, .., w_r\} \text{ is a coloring of } ICG_{\mathcal{DTS}} \iff$$
$$\{p_1, .., p_r\} \text{ is a proper partition for } \mathcal{DTS}$$

Example 10.14 *The item-conflict graph $ICG_{\mathcal{DTS}}$ based on $\mathcal{DTS}$ from Table 10.6 is presented in Figure 10.3. Vertices connected with an edge cannot have the same color. $\{\{a, b, c\}, \{d, e, f\}, \{g, h\}\}$ is one possible coloring. Note that this coloring also determines a proper partition in which colors correspond to blocks. Each of the transactions $T_1, .., T_6$ contains, at most, one of the items of each block.*

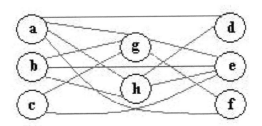

FIGURE 10.3: The item-conflict graph based on the decision transaction system $\mathcal{DTS}$ from Table 10.6. Adapted from Ref. [399], with kind permission from Springer Science+Business Media.

10.4.1.3   Discovery Method

We present how global condensation can be employed in identification of JEP spaces for the decision transaction system $\mathcal{DTS}$. The first stage of our method is to find a proper partition of the itemspace and use it to construct the respective condensed decision table. It is not obvious which partition is optimal for a given dataset and reduct finding algorithm. Since dimensionality is usually the most significant factor, we choose a criterion stating that fewer blocks of a partition lead to better performance. Following Theorem 10.9, one may consider an item-conflict graph $ICG_{\mathcal{DTS}}$ and reduce this optimization problem to graph coloring. Furthermore, since this is a preprocessing stage and suboptimal solutions are acceptable, widely known heuristics, like LF, SLR, RLF, SR [99], can be applied. The resulting partition allows us to transform $\mathcal{DTS}$ to a condensed decision table $\mathcal{CDT}_{\mathcal{DTS}}$.

Discovery of minimal patterns for the condensed decision table $\mathcal{CDT}_{\mathcal{DTS}} = \{\mathcal{U}, \mathcal{C}, d\}$ is the most expensive phase. A reduct finding method is used to identify $REDLOC(u, d)$ for each object $u \in \mathcal{U}$. Every local reduct $B \subseteq \mathcal{C}$ refers to the minimal pattern $condPatt(u, B)$. All the patterns found for the objects from a given class constitute the left bound of a respective JEP space.

Input: $\mathcal{DTS}$
Output: all minimal JEPs
Method:
1: $\mathcal{L}_c = \emptyset$ for each $c \in I_d$
2: Construct an item-conflict graph $ICG_{\mathcal{DTS}}$
3: Find a minimal coloring C in $ICG_{\mathcal{DTS}}$
4: Construct the condensed decision table $\mathcal{CDT}_{\mathcal{DTS},P,F} = \{\mathcal{U}, \mathcal{C}, d\}$, where P corresponds to the coloring C and F is any fixed mapping
5: for$(k = 1; k <= |\mathcal{U}|; k++)$
6:    Compute $REDLOC(u_k, d)$ in $\mathcal{CDT}_{\mathcal{DTS}}$
7:    $\mathcal{L}_c = \mathcal{L}_c \cup \{condPatt_{\mathcal{DTS}}(u_i, R) | R \in REDLOC(u_i, d)\}$, $c = d(u_i)$
8: return $\mathcal{L}_c | c \in I_d$

FIGURE 10.4: The JEPGlobalCond algorithm. Adapted from Ref. [399], with kind permission from Springer Science+Business Media.

10.4.2 Local Projection

Global condensation is performed once for a whole decision transaction system and generates an insignificant additional overhead while attribute values are translated back into items. Unfortunately, this method remains very sensitive to the distribution of items across transactions and, in the general case, finding a proper partition that substantially lowers the overall dimensionality may be very hard.

This problem can be alleviated by the following observation. Actual computation of local reducts is performed separately for each object and involves only a subset of the universe. Thus, instead of employing global condensation, one may want to focus only on transactions applicable to a particular reduct finding process. Conceivably, fewer transactions may lead to better partitions and overall efficiency, even though the pre-processing overhead is higher. We call this procedure *local condensation* [401].

Here, we present a different idea, *local projection*, that can potentially achieve much higher dimensionality reduction. It transforms input data with respect to each individual transaction. However, instead of grouping items into blocks, one takes into account only those from the considered transaction.

10.4.2.1   Locally Projected Decision Table

Let us consider a single transaction from $\mathcal{D}$. We construct a decision table that has binary attributes for all items from this transaction.

Definition 10.24 *For a transaction $T_i \in \mathcal{D}$, where $i = 1, .., |\mathcal{D}|$, a locally projected decision table based on $\mathcal{DTS}$ is a binary decision table $\mathcal{LPDT}_{\mathcal{DTS},T_i} = \mathcal{BDT}_{\mathcal{DTS}_i}$, where $\mathcal{DTS}_i = (\mathcal{D}_i, T_i, \mathcal{I}_d)$ and $\mathcal{D}_i = (T_k \cap T_i)_{k \in K}$.*

Hardness of an input decision system $\mathcal{DTS}$ can be characterized by the dimensionality of corresponding locally projected decision tables for all discernable transactions.

Definition 10.25 *The average and maximum dimensionality of locally projected decision tables based on $\mathcal{DTS}$ are defined as*

$$avgDim(\mathcal{DTS}) = |\{|T| | T \in \mathcal{R}_c \wedge c \in I_d\}| / \sum_{c \in I_d} |\mathcal{R}_c|$$

$$maxDim(\mathcal{DTS}) = max_{T \in \mathcal{R}_c \wedge c \in I_d} |T|, \text{ respectively.}$$

Note that, when all transactions are discernable, these parameters refer to the average (maximum) transaction length in $\mathcal{DTS}$.

Again, we introduce a concise notation to represent patterns generated by an object and attribute set in a locally projected decision table.

Definition 10.26 *For $T_i = \{I_k | k \in M'\}$, $u \in \mathcal{U}$, $B \subseteq C_i = \{a_k | k \in M'\}$, a locally projected pattern based on the object and attribute set is an itemset $itemPatt_{\mathcal{DTS},T_i}(u, B) = \{I_k \in T_i | a_k \in B \wedge a_k(u) = 1 \wedge k \in M'\}$, where $M' \subseteq \{1, .., m\}$ and $\mathcal{LPDT}_{\mathcal{DTS},T_i} = (\mathcal{U}, C_i, d)$.*

Note that $|itemPatt_{\mathcal{DTS},T_i}(u_i, B)| = |B|$. Whenever a decision transaction system is known from the context, the respective subscript is omitted.

Example 10.15 *In Table 10.7 we present the locally projected table based on the decision transaction system $\mathcal{DTS}$ (Table 10.6) and the transactions: T_1, T_2, T_3, respectively. In particular, the attribute set $\{d, h\}$ generates the following patterns: $itemPatt_{T_1}(u_1, \{d, h\}) = dh$, $itemPatt_{T_1}(u_5, \{d, h\}) = h$. For this dataset, we may calculate $avgDim = (3 + 3 + 3 + 2 + 3 + 3)/6 = 17/6 = 2.83$ and $maxDim = 3$, which gives 64.6% and 62.5% of a dimensionality gain comparing to a binary decision table.*

Theorem 10.10 states that the complete JEP space for a decision transaction system and given class can be obtained by finding the locally projected table for each discernable transaction and generating patterns for the object corresponding to this transaction and all attribute sets from this table.

TABLE 10.7: The locally projected tables: $\mathcal{LPDT}_{\mathcal{DTS},T_1}$, $\mathcal{LPDT}_{\mathcal{DTS},T_2}$, $\mathcal{LPDT}_{\mathcal{DTS},T_3}$

	a	d	h	d
u_1	1	1	1	0
u_2	1	0	0	0
u_3	0	0	0	0
u_4	0	0	0	1
u_5	0	0	1	1
u_6	0	0	0	1

	a	f	g	d
u_1	1	0	0	0
u_2	1	1	1	0
u_3	0	0	1	0
u_4	0	0	0	1
u_5	0	0	0	1
u_6	0	1	1	1

	c	e	g	d
u_1	0	0	0	0
u_2	0	0	1	0
u_3	1	1	1	0
u_4	1	1	0	1
u_5	0	1	0	1
u_6	0	0	1	1

Theorem 10.10 $\forall_{c\in\mathcal{I}_d}\{itemPatt_{\mathcal{DTS},T_i}(u_i,R)|i\in K\wedge u_i\in POS(\mathcal{C}_i,d)\cap U_c\wedge \mathcal{LPDT}_{\mathcal{DTS},T_i}=(\mathcal{U},\mathcal{C}_i,d)\wedge R\subseteq\mathcal{C}_i\}=JEP(\mathcal{C}'_c,\mathcal{C}_c)$.

The respective left bound of a JEP space can be found by applying local reducts for a given object rather than arbitrary attribute sets.

Theorem 10.11 $\forall_{c\in\mathcal{I}_d}\{itemPatt_{\mathcal{DTS},T_i}(u_i,R)|i\in K\wedge u_i\in POS(\mathcal{C}_i,d)\cap U_c\wedge \mathcal{LPDT}_{\mathcal{DTS},T_i}=(\mathcal{U},\mathcal{C}_i,d)\wedge R\in REDLOC(u_i,d)\}=\mathcal{L}_c$.

Example 10.16 *In order to illustrate Theorem 10.11, let us consider the class 0. For $\mathcal{LPDT}_{\mathcal{DTS},T_3}$ we have $REDLOC(u_3,d)=\{\{c,g\},\{e,g\}\}$. Each of these reducts refer to certain minimal patterns from $\mathcal{L}_0$. On the other hand, the pattern a is a minimal JEP, thus, we are able to find a respective set of local reducts and a respective locally projected table, namely: $\{a\}=REDLOC(u_1,d)$ for $\mathcal{LPDT}_{\mathcal{DTS},T_1}$.*

10.4.2.2   Discovery Method

Minimal jumping emerging patterns can be identified by local reduct computation in locally condensed tables based on consecutive transactions of a dataset. The actual procedure follows from Theorem 10.8.

Let us consider a decision transaction system $\mathcal{DTS}=(\mathcal{D},\mathcal{I},\mathcal{I}_d)$. For each transaction $T_k\in\mathcal{D}$, we build the locally projected decision table $\mathcal{LPDT}_{\mathcal{DTS},T_k}=(\mathcal{U},\mathcal{C}_k,d)$, where $k=1,..,|\mathcal{D}|$. Then, local reducts for the object u_k, that refers to T_k, are computed. Finally, each local reduct $R\in REDLOC(u_k,d)$ is mapped to the respective pattern $itemPatt_{T_k}(u,R)$ and added to the minimal JEP collection for the class $(T_k\cap\mathcal{I}_d)$. Once all transactions of $\mathcal{DTS}$ are processed, we obtain the complete collections $\{\mathcal{L}_c|c\in\mathcal{I}_d\}$.

Local projection can significantly reduce problem dimensionality, especially for sparse data. Although reduct computation remains the pivotal and

Input: $\mathcal{DTS}$
Output: all minimal JEPs
Method:
1: $\mathcal{L}_c = \emptyset$ for each $c \in \mathcal{I}_d$
2: for$(k = 1; k <= |\mathcal{D}|; k + +)$
3:     Construct the locally projected decision table $\mathcal{LPDT}_{\mathcal{DTS},T_k}$
4:     Compute $REDLOC(u_k, d)$ in $\mathcal{LPDT}_{\mathcal{DTS},T_k}$
5:     $\mathcal{L}_c = \mathcal{L}_c \cup \{itemPatt_{\mathcal{DTS},T_k}(u_k, R)|R \in REDLOC(u_k, d)\}, c = T_k \cup \mathcal{I}_d$
6:     return $\mathcal{L}_c|c \in \mathcal{I}_d$

FIGURE 10.5: The JEPLocalProj algorithm. Adapted from Ref. [397], with kind permission from Springer Science+Business Media.

hardest task, additional processing of polynomial complexity may start to have noticeable negative impact on overall efficiency of the algorithm. Below, we comment on five optimizations that can potentially alleviate this effect.

(a) It is not necessary to build tables $\mathcal{LPDT}_{\mathcal{DTS},T_i}$, for each $T_i \in \mathcal{D}$, explicitly. It suffices to construct respective discernibility sets. Note that, when local reducts are being computed for a certain object, one takes into account only objects from other classes from the class of this object. Consequently, for a given locally projected decision table, only the elements of the discernibility set that correspond to this object are meaningful for reduct finding.

(b) Transactions that are not maximal JEPs can be eliminated upfront, since they cannot introduce any new JEPs to the solution.

(c) A significant improvement can be achieved by grouping transactions by their classes. This allows us to iterate over only these objects that are necessary for particular processing.

(d) Discernibility sets for objects in one class share information on common attributes. Let us consider $\mathcal{BDT}_{\mathcal{DTS}} = (\mathcal{U}, \mathcal{C}, d)$. We have $\{X \cap \{a_i\}|DC_{\mathcal{DTS},T_1}\} = \{X \cap \{a_i\}|DC_{\mathcal{DTS},T_2}\}$, for each $c \in \mathcal{I}_d$, $T_1, T_2 \in D_c$, $T_1 \cap T_2 \neq \emptyset$ and $I_i \in T_1 \cap T_2$. This per-attribute information may be precomputed for each class and each attribute that belongs to some transaction in this class or computed lazily and stored when successive transactions are considered. As a result, one obtains a cache of the form $\{(c, I_i, \{u|u \in \mathcal{U} - \mathcal{U}_c \wedge a(i) = 0\})|c \in \mathcal{I}_d \wedge i \in \{1, .., m\}\}$, which is later used to build discernibility sets without examining the database every time. After construction from the cache, a set has to be reduced, since respective locally projected tables are different.

(e) For sparse datasets with a large number of transactions, elements of the discernibility collection of $LPDC_{\mathcal{DTS},T_i} = (\mathcal{U}, \mathcal{C}_i, d)$, for $i \in K$, are often close in size to $|C_i|$. Therefore, it may be more efficient to store their complements. In other words, for each object, one may generate an element consisting of attributes with values equal to 1.

Part IV

Contrast Mining for Classification & Clustering

Chapter 11

Overview and Analysis of Contrast Pattern Based Classification

Xiuzhen Zhang

School of Computer Science and IT, RMIT University

Guozhu Dong

Department of Computer Science and Engineering, Wright State University

11.1 Introduction

This chapter presents a high-level overview and analysis of contrast pattern (CP) based classification. It identifies two main issues for CP-based classification, namely CP model selection and CP-based classification strategy. It describes and compares representative CP-based classification algorithms, with respect to how they deal with the two main issues. It also discusses how and why CP-based classifiers can achieve high classification accuracy. Together, the presented algorithms use many of the important techniques that have been introduced in the general CP-based classification paradigm.

> **A contrast pattern based classification algorithm** builds a CP model in the training phase, and uses the CPs in the CP model according to some classification strategy to arrive at classification decisions.

This chapter also provides an analysis of the learning capability of CP-based classification models using the bias-variance decomposition (BVD) for classification errors, of the ability of those models to avoid overfitting, and of the ability of those models to solve the imbalanced classification problem.

It is widely recognized that CP-based classifiers often achieve high accuracy and offer various desirable properties (such as explainability, noise tolerance, suitability for imbalanced classification). This book contains several chapters related to CP-based classification, each dealing with a special way of CP-based classification, or a special application domain, including: using length statistics of emerging patterns[1] (EPs) in outlier and rare-class prediction (Chapter 12) and on using EPs to enhance traditional classifiers (Chapter 13); on EP-based rules for classifying/characterizing subtypes of leukemia (Chapter 15) in the field of bioinformatics; on emerging chemical pattern based classification of chemical compounds (Chapter 18) and emerging molecular pattern based analysis of toxicity of chemical molecules (Chapter 19) in the field of chemoinformatics; on EP-based classification for spatial/image data (Chapter 20); on EP-based crime spots analysis and rental price prediction (Chapter 24), on EP-based diagnosis of heart diseases and prediction of powerline safety (Chapter 23), and on EP-based activity recognition (Chapter 22).

CP-based classifiers, especially CAEP-style aggregation based classifiers, have been proven to be generally accurate and explainable, to perform well for imbalanced classification, and, as discussed in Chapter 18, to be useful for situations where few training examples are available.

11.2   Main Issues in Contrast Pattern Based Classification

Contrast patterns between data of different classes represent differences between the classes. (See Chapter 1 for more details regarding various preliminaries on contrast patterns.) CPs often capture class-discriminating signals with very high confidence (often 100%). However, a single CP by itself is often too weak as a prediction model to predict the class label for instances, as it typically occurs in only a small portion of data objects. Luckily, some carefully selected set of CPs can collectively form an accurate classification model for predicting the class label for query instances.

---

[1]Emerging patterns (EPs) are a special kind/name of CPs.

Two major issues must be addressed when developing CP-based classifiers. We give an overview on the two issues and their sub-issues below, and will give detailed explanations on, and approaches to address, those sub-issues later.

(1) **CP Model Selection**. What set of contrast patterns are selected for use in the classification process? We will refer to the set of CPs as a CP-based classification model. While including *all* CPs in the CP model is intuitively attractive, because the complete set of CPs describes the difference between the classes in all possible ways and this set gives the classifier more flexibility in selecting CPs in the classification process, it is not feasible in practical applications, since computing all possible CPs may be computationally infeasible and since the CP model may become too large. An ideal CP model should be a relatively small set of diversified representative high-quality CPs.

This issue can be either addressed in two separate processes, where pattern selection happens after pattern mining, or in a combined one where pattern selection is pushed into the pattern mining process. Pattern mining and selection can be performed in the eager manner, where a CP model is built once and used for the classification of all data objects, or in the lazy manner, where a CP model is built and used just for classifying a single data object.

When selecting CPs for inclusion in a CP model, the utility of individual patterns for predicting class labels is often considered; important factors include supports, support difference, support growth rate, and pattern length ratio (see Chapter 14 and Ref. [277]). Besides utility of individual CPs, relationships among patterns, such as item-based or matching-data based pattern similarity, improvement on discriminative power (similar to lift), or total coverage of selected patterns, are also important factors in CP model selection.

(2) **CP-Based Classification Strategy**. How are the contrast patterns in the CP model used in the classification process? We will refer to the approach designed to answer this question as a CP-based classification strategy.

Many choices are possible here: The classification strategy can use the "sequential-one-rule" approach, or use a method based on the "multi-pattern aggregation" approach. Moreover, there are many possible variations for each approach, especially for the "multi-pattern aggregation" one, regarding how the patterns are used to make classification decisions. Some methods even use length statistics of CPs to classify data objects (see [82] and Chapter 12).

Other problems need to be considered in designing a CP-based classification strategy, such as avoiding counting duplicate contributions (by similar CPs), and normalization (to counter pattern polarization – some classes's CPs are poorer in quantity and quality than others).

In general, the CP-based classification strategy issue has a bigger impact on constructing desirable classifiers.

11.3   Representative Approaches

The first contrast pattern based classification algorithms are CBA [270], and CAEP[2] [126]. Major representative CP-based classification systems after CBA and CAEP include iCAEP [465], JEP-C [244], DeEPs [245], CMAR [258], and CPAR [450]. CAEP was the first to use the multi-pattern aggregation way to make classification decisions. All of the above, except CBA, use the pattern aggregation approach; CBA is the only one that treats its CP model as a sequence. CBA, CMAR, and CPAR referred to CPs as class association rules.

The above representative CP-based classification models mine, select, and use CPs differently. Below we discuss how they deal with the two main issues.

11.3.1   Contrast Pattern Mining and Selection

The mining and selection of CPs for inclusion in the CP model typically rely on decisions on three factors.

(1) **Thresholds**. Thresholds are evaluated on individual patterns to determine if they are excluded. Commonly used thresholds include thresholds on pattern support in the whole dataset, on confidence, on supports in individual classes, and on growth rate (support ratio). Using thresholds on whole-dataset support may not be desirable for imbalanced classification or situations where some classes have many high support CPs, while some classes have few or no high support CPs. Almost all CP-based classification algorithms use support thresholds, although jumping emerging pattern based approaches only rely on thresholds on growth rates. (Recall that jumping EPs are EPs with infinite growth rate – they occur in their home class but never in other classes.) Mining with growth rate based thresholds allow us to mine CPs without support thresholds, and hence allow us to obtain useful CPs with high growth rate and low support. However, using ∞ as minimum growth rate threshold can also be undesirable in situations where few patterns satisfy this threshold.

(2) **Pattern Pruning Method**. By a pattern pruning method, we mean a method where certain patterns are excluded when certain other related patterns are already selected. Pattern pruning can be performed within or after the mining process. There are two general pattern pruning methods.

(2a) Only patterns in the left bounds of borders can be selected and patterns not in the left bounds of borders are all excluded. Recall that a border has the form $< L, R >$ where L and R are anti-chain sets of itemsets such that each $X \in L$ is a subset of some Y in R and vice versa; the border represents the set of all itemsets Z where there exist $X \in L$ and $Y \in R$ satisfying $X \subseteq Z \subseteq Y$. For example, $< \{ab, ac\}, \{abcd\} >$ is a border, representing

---

[2]The research on CAEP as reported in [126] was done during July 1998 — February 1999.

the set $\{ab, ac, abc, abd, acd, abcd\}$ of itemsets. Patterns in the left bound of a border for EPs are the most general and considered the most expressive, since they have the highest support among all patterns represented by the border, and since, in the case of jumping EPs, any proper subset of a jumping EP in the left bound is no longer a jumping EP. Several jumping EP based methods (e.g. DeEPs) use this method to mine/select CPs in the CP model. In one sense, EPs in the left bounds of borders are used to prune all superset EPs.

(2b) Patterns that do not offer significant improvement over related selected patterns are excluded. In general, a pattern X is related to a pattern Y if X is very similar to Y; similarity can be defined by item overlap ($\frac{|X \cap Y|}{|X \cup Y|}$), by matching tuple overlap ($\frac{|\mathsf{mt}(X) \cap \mathsf{mt}(Y)|}{|\mathsf{mt}(X) \cup \mathsf{mt}(Y)|}$), or simply by the subset-superset relationship ($X \subset Y$ and perhaps also $|Y - X|$ is small). The subset-superset relationship is often used, with some improvement thresholds on support, growth rate and other factors. For example, if Y is a superset of a selected CP X and $\mathsf{gr}(Y)$ is not significantly higher than $\mathsf{gr}(X)$, then Y is not selected.

CAEP and iCAEP both use the subset-superset (general-specific) based pruning method. (To our knowledge, the other similarity measures discussed above have not been considered in CP model determination.) CMAR defines a rank order on CPs (with high χ^2 value) in terms of confidence and support. Then CMAR uses higher ranked more general CPs to prune lower ranked more specific CPs, and also uses data coverage of CPs (somehow similar to the strategy of CBA) to prune CPs. CPAR's greedy approach to mining CPs using information gain improvement also belongs to this category. Sometimes "improvement" may be expressed as "the next best", as is the case for CBA. The "improvement based selection method" does not prune all supersets of selected CPs in general, unlike the "left bound" method.

(3) **Pattern Mining Time**. While most CP-based classification algorithms build the CP model in an eager manner, some builds the CP model in the lazy manner. For example, DeEPs builds the CP model after a test example is given for classification, using only the projection of training data limited to the items in the test example.

11.3.2   Classification Strategy

Many contrast pattern based classification strategies have been proposed. We analyze them with focus on how they deal with these four major issues:

(1) **The classification score formula**. This deals with how the discriminative power of CPs matching given test instances are used to arrive at a classification score for the classes.

(2) **Matching CP selection**. Should one use all matching CPs of an instance t in the CP model, or should one use a selective subset of matching CPs? Selecting a desirable subset can help avoid counting duplicate score contributions made by similar CPs (see item 4 below).

(3) **Classification score normalization**. Sometimes there is an imbal-

ance in the number and quality of CPs of different classes – some classes have many high quality CPs while some other classes have very few (high quality) CPs and instances of the CP-poor classes may be classified to the CP-rich classes. This problem is often related to the imbalanced classification problem defined in terms of the training set size imbalance, but not always. Normalization is one approach to solve the problem.

(4) **Duplicate score contribution avoidance**. Two CPs can be very similar to each other (when measured by their items or by the matching data) and it may be a good idea to count their discrimination signals only once.

CAEP makes classification decisions by aggregating support-weighted probabilities of all CPs (in its CP model) matching a test instance. (The CP model of CAEP is obtained using support and growth rate improvement between subset-superset EPs.) Each EP X can differentiate the class membership of a fraction of instances that match X, and the degree of X's support change in the classes signifies the odds that an instance matching X belongs to the class of X. For example, given an EP X with a support ratio of $5 : 1$ between class C_1 and class C_2, an instance matching X has a $5 : 1$ odds to belong to class C_1 if the two classes have roughly equal population sizes. The aggregation approach was proposed in [126], based on the intuition that combining (summing) those odds of all matching EPs can help make a more accurate classification. CAEP also considers the frequency of EPs, in addition to the odds; it favors high support EPs and lets such EPs give more influence on the classification scores. Let $\mathcal{E}(C_j)$ denote the EPs of a class C_j. Let t be a test case, and let $\mathcal{E}^t(C_j)$ be the set of EPs in $\mathcal{E}(C_j)$ that match t. The aggregate score of t for C_j is given by

$$score(t, C_j) = \sum_{X \in \mathcal{E}^t(C_j)} \mathsf{supp}(X, C_j) \times \frac{\mathsf{gr}(X)}{\mathsf{gr}(X) + 1}. \qquad (11.1)$$

Observe that the above can be rewritten as

$$score(t, C_j) = \sum_{X \in \mathcal{E}^t(C_j)} \mathsf{supp}(X, C_j) \times \frac{\mathsf{supp}(X, C_j)}{\mathsf{supp}(X, C_j) + \mathsf{supp}(X, \cup_{i \neq j} C_i)}. \qquad (11.2)$$

In Equation 11.1 the contribution of each CP X to $score(t, C_j)$ can be divided into two components: The first is the support of X in C_j, and the second is roughly the probability that t belongs to class C_j. Thus the score is the sum of frequency weighted probability of the matching EPs of t.

CAEP uses some fixed percentile of scores for training data in each class C_j to normalize the score for C_j as follows: Let $sc_1, ..., sc_{n_j}$ be the sorted list of $score(s, C_j)$ defined by Equation 11.1 for training instances s of C_j and class C_j; let $sc\_median(C_j)$ denote the median of $sc_1, ..., sc_{n_j}$. Then, we select the class C_i that maximizes the normalized score $\frac{score(t, C_j)}{sc\_median(C_j)}$ as the class of t. Normalization using other fixed percentile can also work. This was shown to help increase the odds for classifying instances of a CP-poor class (with few high quality EPs) to that class. To the best of our knowledge, CAEP was the first to use normalization to overcome the CP/class imbalance problem.

iCAEP adopts a minimum description/message length (MDL/MML) based approach to aggregate the discrimination signals of multiple selected EPs matching a test instance. MDL [354] and MML [417] assess the quality of model M for dataset D, using the total length needed to describe M and to describe D using M; the best model is one achieving minimum description length. Moreover, iCAEP uses ConsEPMiner [464] to mine EPs, hence growth rate improvement is used to prune EP Y if there exists some EP X in the CP model of iCAEP satisfying $X \subset Y$ and $\mathsf{gr}(Y) - \mathsf{gr}(X) <$ some given threshold.

Both the selection of EPs and classification score derivation pay attention to description length minimization.

Let t be a test case. iCAEP selects, for each class C_j, a subset $\mathcal{E}_j^t$ of EPs of class C_j that match t such that $\mathcal{E}_j^t$ gives a partition of t (when t is viewed as a set). The "partition" requirement is chosen to ensure that a small number of EPs are used to classify an instance, which helps avoid counting duplicate contributions made by similar patterns. To ensure that every instance has a partition by EPs, each singleton itemset is considered as an EP of every class; poor quality singleton EPs will give poor contribution to the classification score (see Equation 11.3). The heuristic of preferring "longer" EPs with more items (based on the intuition that such EPs capture important interaction among large number of items), and the heuristic of preferring EPs with high growth rate among EPs with equal length, are used in determining $\mathcal{E}_j^t$.

After $\mathcal{E}_j^t$ of EPs of class C_j is determined for each class C_j, the encoding length of t for class C_j is defined as follows:

$$L(t, C_j) = - \sum_{X \in \mathcal{E}_j^t} log_2 P(X|C_j). \tag{11.3}$$

The estimated probability of X given C_j is

$$P(X|C_j) = \frac{|\mathsf{mt}(X, C_j)| + 2|\mathsf{mt}(X, \cup_i C_i)|/|\cup_i C_i|}{|C_j| + 2}.$$

(Recall that $\mathsf{mt}(X, D) = \{t \in D \mid X \text{ matches } t\}$.) The instance t is assigned to the class C_i that minimizes $L(t, C_j)$.

We will use experiments to demonstrate the good performance of iCAEP.

The CP model of JEP-C contains the jumping EPs that belong to the left bounds of borders [118] of jumping EPs. Jumping EPs in the left bounds of borders of jumping EPs are considered as the most expressive jumping EPs, since they have the highest support among all jumping EPs and the results of removal of any item from such jumping EPs are not jumping EPs. Given a test instance t, let $\mathcal{E}_j^t$ be the set of the "left-bound" jumping EPs of class C_j that match t. Then the score of t for class C_j is given by

$$\sum_{X \in \mathcal{E}_j^t} \mathsf{supp}(X, C_j). \tag{11.4}$$

(Equation 11.4 is a special case of Equation 11.1, since $\frac{\text{gr}(X)}{\text{gr}(X)+1} = 1$ when $\text{gr}(X) = \infty$.) The instance t is classified to the class C_i that maximizes $\sum_{X \in \mathcal{E}_j^t} \text{supp}(X, C_j)$.

DeEPs adopts a lazy approach to classification using jumping EPs. Similarly to JEP-C, it uses only jumping EPs for classification and selects jumping EPs from the left bounds of borders of jumping EPs. Differently from JEP-C, where jumping EPs of the CP model are computed at the training stage, DeEPs computes the jumping EPs at the classification stage after a test instance t is given, from the projecting out the items of the instances that do not occur in t. Those mined "left-bound" jumping EPs are then used to match instances of the classes, and the sizes (normalized by the corresponding classes' sizes) of the matching data in the classes are used to decide the class of t – the class C_i that maximizes the normalized size is then deemed as the class of t. Specifically, let $\mathcal{E}^t(C_j)$ denote the set of "left-bound" jumping EPs for class C_j mined for t, the classification score of t for class C_j is defined as:

$$\frac{|\{x \in C_j | X \in \mathcal{E}^t(C_j), X \text{ matches } x\}|}{|C_j|} \tag{11.5}$$

The scoring strategy of DeEPs is motivated to avoid the duplicate contribution counting problem and to avoid the abstention problem (where a test instance may not match any mined CPs).

In CBA, the first rule (in a sequence of CPs representing the CP model) whose body matches an example t is used to classify t. Rules are ranked by their confidence, support, and number of conditions in the antecedent. CBA does not use aggregation of multiple CPs. While relying on a single rule for classification offers the ability to give straight forward explanation of classification decisions, the approach can suffer from low classification accuracy.

CMAR uses a weighted χ^2 approach to aggregate the combined effect of the multiple CPs for a class. Specifically, for each instance t, each matching CP X of t in a class C_j contributes the value of $\frac{v}{max\_v}v$, where v is the χ^2 value (for evaluating the correlation of X with class C_j) and max_v is an estimated maximum χ^2 value, to the score of t for class C_j.

CPAR uses the average probability of the best k patterns that matches a test instance t (for a fixed k). Specifically, the classification accuracy of a pattern X of class C_j is estimated as $\frac{\text{supp}(X, C_j)}{\text{supp}(X, \cup_i C_i)}$. The average accuracy of the k patterns for class C_j with the highest probabilities is then used as the score of t for C_j; and t is classified to the class with the highest average accuracy.

We now discuss how two other EP based classifiers select and aggregate multiple EPs. PCL (see [248] and Chapter 15) aggregates the discriminating power of multiple CPs using a normalized contribution: Let $\mathcal{E}_j$ be the set of EPs for class C_j in the CP model. Let $s_1(C_j), ..., s_{n_j}(C_j)$ be the sorted (descending order) list of $\text{supp}(X, C_j)$, the support of EPs X of class C_j. For a test instance t, let $\mathcal{E}_j^t$ be the subset of EPs in $\mathcal{E}_j$ that match t; let $s_1^t(C_j), ..., s_{m_j}^t(C_j)$ be the sorted list (descending order) of the supports for

EPs in $\mathcal{E}_j^t$. Then the score of t for class C_j is given by $\sum_{i=1}^{k} \frac{s_i^t(C_j)}{s_i^t(C_j)}$ (for a fixed k). This approach normalizes the supports of matching EPs of a class by the supports of the top-support EPs of the class. FEPC selects more specific fuzzy EPs and excludes more general ones of selected fuzzy EPs in the aggregation of multiple fuzzy matching EPs of test instances; see [162] and Chapter 8.

11.3.3 Summary

(1) For pattern mining, most classification algorithms use some heuristics when exploring the pattern space. Various heuristics have been proposed to reduce the number of patterns that need to be examined, including various improvement based pruning methods that prune more specific CPs after more general CPs have been mined. The jumping EP-based approaches (JEP-C and DeEPs) adopt border-based algorithms for mining patterns, hence avoiding exploring the huge pattern search space; they also allow us to mine useful CPs without support thresholds.

(2) For CP model selection, various improvement based methods have been used to prune more specific CPs after more general CPs have been selected.

(3) To select patterns from the CP model to classify a test instance t, most classifiers use all applicable CPs in the CP model, except iCAEP, CBA, PCL, and CPAR. CBA employs the first matching rule approach. iCAEP chooses a group of long CPs that partitions a given test instance, and PCL and CPAR use certain k best matching patterns.

(4) Classifiers differ greatly in their strategy of using patterns or rules for classification. The different classification strategies are all developed based on different intuitions of making use of patterns for classification. Different classification strategies can result in different classification accuracies. The following aggregation approaches have been considered: support weighted probability, minimal encoding length, support (of jumping EPs), χ^2-proportion weighted χ^2, average probability of best k patterns, and normalized support of best k patterns. Observe that some of these have impact on avoiding counting duplicate contribution, and some of these have impact on countering the CP-rich vs CP-poor imbalanced classification problem.

Contrast pattern based classifiers have been shown to make consistently more accurate predictions than popular classification models including the decision tree, Naive Bayes, Nearest Neighbor, bagging, boosting, even SVM. The good classification performance of CP-based classifiers can be attributed to: (a) CPs can describe sharp multi-dimensional contrasts between data classes which can reveal important discriminative interactions among attributes. (b) The matching-pattern based classification of CP-based classifiers allows us to use the conditions on multiple attributes contained a multi-dimensional discriminative pattern synergistically. (c) The CP models used by CP-based classifiers are more flexible and the CPs are mined from a search space much bigger than the search space of greedy search methods such as the decision tree approach. (d) Most importantly, the aggregation approach allows us to combine the discriminative power of multiple matching CPs for test instances.

Approaches having more flexibility in selecting the CPs and in the aggregation strategy can be applied to more applications, including situations where the difference between the contrasting classes is subtle (the CPs can have fairly small growth rates and/or they have fairly low support). Approaches with a more restricted CP model and a more restricted way of using the CPs may suffer when very few CPs with high support or high growth rate exist for inclusion in the CP model.

11.4   Bias Variance Analysis of iCAEP and Others

Bias-variance decomposition (BVD) has often been used to analyze classification algorithms [41, 216]. Below we present the BVD of a representative contrast patten based classifier, iCAEP, and compare its BVD against that of three popular classification schemes of C4.5, Naive Bayes, and kNN. This BVD analysis allows us to characterize the bias and variance of the iCAEP classifier. Moreover, using the BVD profile, we can identify opportunities to develop new strategies to further improve CP-based classification models.

The BVD analysis decomposes classification errors into three terms, namely bias, variance, and noise. To define them, we need some preliminaries. Let $D = \{(x_1, y_1), ..., (x_n, y_n)\}$ be a training dataset of (example, class label) pairs, and let $\{D_1, ..., D_m\}$ be a set of training datasets, with each D_j obtained from D by sampling with replacement. A given classification algorithm builds a classifier f_j for each D_j. A loss function $L(y_i, y)$ is used in the BVD analysis to measure the cost of predicting y when the true class is y_i. We consider the zero-one loss function L here: $L(y_i, y) = 0$ if $y = y_i$ and $L(y_i, y) = 1$ otherwise. For each x_i, let y_i^* denote the optimal prediction y minimizing $E_y[L(y_i^*, y)]$; the main prediction for the m classifiers $f_1, ..., f_m$ (and the zero-one loss function L) is the mode (most frequent) of $\{f_1(x_i), ..., f_m(x_i)\}$, denoted by y_i^m.

In BVD, bias is the loss incurred by the main prediction relative to the optimal prediction, defined by $E_i[L(y_i^*, y_i^m)]$. Variance is the average loss incurred by predictions relative to the main prediction, defined by $E_i E_j[L(y_i^m, f_j(x_i))]$. Noise measures the unavoidable component of the loss, incurred independently of the learning algorithm; it is defined as $E_i[L(y_i, y_i^*)]$.

We use the BVD methodology of Domingos' unified framework [111] (that article also describes how to decompose the prediction error on an example x_i into contributions to the bias, variance, and noise components). Also, following the procedure described in [429], ten-fold cross validation experiments were repeated 50 times to compute the bias and variance of iCAEP and the other classifiers. Table 11.1 lists the datasets used in our experiments.

It should be noted that, in empirical studies, classification errors are gen-

Dataset	Size	#classes	#attr
German	1,000	2	20
Hepatitis prognosis	155	2	19
Iris	150	3	4
Pima	768	2	8
Tic-tac-toe	958	2	9
Wine	178	3	13

TABLE 11.1: Datasets Used in BVD Experiments

erally decomposed into the bias and variance components only, with the bias component including the noise component (since it is hard to estimate the noise component). The discussion below also follows this treatment.

Dataset	Loss	Bias	Var	Varp	Varn	Varc
iris	0.139	0.060	0.079	0.102	0.025	0.023
german	0.261	0.248	0.013	0.041	0.028	0.028
hepatitis	0.163	0.154	0.009	0.021	0.012	0.012
pima	0.263	0.254	0.009	0.037	0.027	0.027
ttt	0.081	0.069	0.012	0.022	0.010	0.010
wine	0.015	0.011	0.004	0.005	0.001	0.001

TABLE 11.2: The BVD Result for iCAEP

Table 11.2 contains the BVD experimental results for iCAEP. Loss, Bias, and Var represent respectively the average loss, bias, and variance. Varp and Varn represent the average contribution to variance from the unbiased and biased instances respectively. (An instance x_i is biased if it gives a positive contribution to bias, i.e. the main prediction and the optimal prediction for x_i differ.) Varc represents the average contribution to variance from the biased instances, with the variance from each instance weighted by the probability that the class predicted is the optimal prediction, given that it is not the main prediction. Var = Varp − Varn and Varn = Varc in a two-class problem, whereas Var = Varp − Varc in non-two-class problems.

Clearly, Table 11.2 indicates that iCAEP tends to produce stable classification models in different application domains; it is not sensitive to variations in training data. This is true for contrast pattern based classification models in general. This may be partly attributable to the classification strategy of aggregating multiple contrast patterns for classifying test examples.

Moreover, Table 11.2 indicates that iCAEP as a classification model has high bias, since bias is almost always the main component for the overall classification loss. The average contribution of bias to classification errors varies from 43.2% (Iris) to 96.6% (Pima), with an average contribution of 81.3%.

Figure 11.1 compares the BVD performance of iCAEP with that of three other popular classification models, namely C4.5, kNN, and NB. In general, iCAEP achieves the lowest error (except on Iris) among all algorithms. This

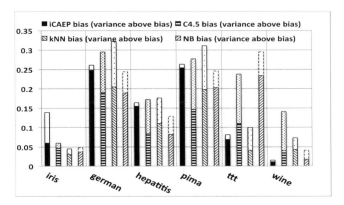

FIGURE 11.1: The BVD Results.

suggests that in general iCAEP is a more accurate classification scheme than C4.5, kNN, and NB. Comparing the contribution of the bias component towards the overall error, iCAEP has the highest relative bias component (81.3%); in contrast C4.5 has 53.5%, kNN has 59.4%, and NB has 70.2% contribution from the bias component, which are much lower than iCAEP's.

The experiments suggest that there is room to improve contrast pattern based classification algorithms. In general the multi-variate CPs and the aggregation style of classification provide more powerful ways to capture/utilize discriminative interactions among attributes, compared to the patterns formed and the way patterns are used, by the one-attribute-at-a-time decision trees, and therefore CP based classifiers achieve accurate classification. Nevertheless the high bias behavior in CP based classification schemes indicate that there is potential for finding low bias CP-based classification strategies to improve CP-based classification. Research in this direction may likely depend on more advanced approaches to aggregate the discriminating power of CPs, in addition to more advanced approaches to selecting CPs.

11.5   Overfitting Avoidance by CP-Based Approaches

Overfitting refers to the phenomenon where a classifier is much more accurate on the training data than on unseen testing data. Overfitting occurs if a model is developed to fit the training data precisely, to the extent that it loses generality for unseen test data. Overfitting is an important issue in classification model induction. It is believed that strategies to reduce overfitting can improve the generalizability of classification models and therefore improve their predictive accuracy. This section discusses ways to avoid overfitting in the induction of contrast pattern based classifiers.

There are three general approaches to avoid overfitting in the model development process. One approach is forward pruning or pre-pruning [433] — the process of searching for the best model is stopped when a sufficiently complex model is found, and hence models which are more complex than the current one are pruned before they are computed. An example is the early stopping strategy in decision tree learning [345]. Another approach to avoiding overfitting is backward pruning or post-pruning [433] – a complex model that fits the training data well is first developed and then pruned to simplify it. An example is the post-pruning strategy in decision tree learning [345], where a decision tree is first fully grown and then pruned to improve its generalization performance. The ensemble approach such as bagging [58] is a third approach to avoiding overfitting, which is especially effective since this reduces the variance of the component classifiers of the ensembles.

Contrast pattern based classifiers generally aggregated multiple patterns to reach a classification decision (except CBA). It has been reported in the literature that this induction strategy can achieve high classification accuracy and usually does not have the overfitting problem. The strategy of aggregating patterns for classification is similar in spirit to bagging predictors for classification, and thus can avoid overfitting.

In some sense, some CP-based classifiers also utilize pre-pruning in the CP mining process and post-pruning in selecting rules in the aggregation based scoring process. Generally the support and support growth rate thresholds are used as a simple measure to select the patterns. Moreover, some CP-based classifiers use some other strategies to select patterns; for example, "improvement based pruning" prunes a CP Y which is a superset of some selected CP X if the support and/or growth rate of Y are not much more desirable than those of X.

In iCAEP inter-pattern constraints are used to remove patterns, from the classification model, meeting given support and support growth rate thresholds if they are subsumed by any selected pattern. Moreover, patterns in the classification model are selectively used to classify test instances — long patterns are preferred over short ones, and among pattern sets that cover a test instance, those sets that have no item overlap between patterns are used.

In JEP-C and DeEPs, only patterns with infinite support growth rate are included in the model; no specific pre-pruning or post-pruning is performed. In CMAR, several strategies are used to prune less significant rules for classification, considering factors like the subsumption relationship between rules, and the coverage training instances of rules. In CPAR, only the best k rules for each class are selected to classify a test instance.

It has been reported that the heuristic-based forward pruning strategy, together with the aggregation approach to applying patterns for classification has achieved reasonably effective overfitting avoidance and has ensured high classification accuracy for unseen test examples.

11.6   Solving the Imbalanced Classification Problem

The class imbalance problem exists in many classification applications, where the examples of primary interest are from the minority class. In such applications, standard classification models tend to pay too much attention on the majority class and pay too little attention on the minority class. This section examines how contrast pattern based algorithms perform for imbalanced classification, using the example of iCAEP. The discussion below is focused on two-class problems, and the minority class is often referred to as the positive class and the majority class is referred to as the negative class.

We now give some background on studies on imbalanced classification. Re-sampling and cost-sensitive learning techniques are two popular techniques to combat imbalanced class distribution for classification. Various re-sampling strategies have been proposed, including random oversampling with replacement, random undersampling, focused oversampling, focused undersampling, and synthetic oversampling (see [80] for an overview). In the cost-sensitive learning approach, a weight is associated with the training examples to counter the imbalance of data distribution. Emerging patterns have been used to improve the re-sampling and cost-sensitive learning process for classifying rare classes [5, 8, 140]. However, the performance and properties of the associative classification models in general, and the contrast pattern based classification models in particular, have not been systematically studied for imbalanced classification. Recently [21] studied along this line and it was shown that classifiers based on contrast patterns can be effective for classifying rare examples.

11.6.1   Advantages of Contrast Pattern Based Classification

Rather than re-sampling or re-weighting in the original feature space, it may be better to work in the EP space and use CAEP-style classification to deal with imbalanced data distribution. There are three reasons for this:

(a) Each EP is a multi-variate condition involving several attributes. A set of EPs can more precisely capture discriminative conditions that exist in the minority class but rarely exist in the majority class, than other classifiers such as a decision tree or NB. It is also better than distance based classifiers such as kNN, since distance can become meaningless [51] in high dimensional spaces.

(b) For each EP of the minority class, its importance is relative to its support in the minority class, instead of relative to its absolute count. This implies that patterns that may be considered insignificant measured by support in the entire dataset can become significant now. This bias can help counter-balance the class imbalance issue. (In standard classifiers, patterns with small support relative to the whole dataset are simply discarded, which is likely a major reason why these classifiers' performance degrades significantly in the presence

Dataset	#features	#instances	# instances in minority class
CM1	21	498	49 (9.8%)
KC1	21	2109	326 (15.45%)
PC1	21	1109	77 (6.94%)
Labor	16	58	20 (35.09%)
Spambase	57	4601	1831 (39.80%)
Mushroom	22	8124	3916 (48.20%)

TABLE 11.3: Imbalanced and Balanced Datasets

of class imbalance.) Consider an imbalanced dataset of 10000 instances where the minority class C_1 has only 100 (1%) instances. Consider an EP e_1 of C_1 with $\mathsf{supp}(e_1, C_1) = 10\%$ and an EP e_2 of C_2 with $\mathsf{supp}(e_2, C_2) = 10\%$. They will be considered as equally important, since their relative support in the two classes is the same, even though their absolute support count is 10 and 990 respectively. We will show below that this simple but effective bias, combined with other strategies, can achieve accurate classification for rare examples.

(c) The CAEP-style classification aggregates all matching EPs of a test instance t in each class C to arrive at the classification score for t in C. This allows us to combine all available discriminative signals contained in t to classify it. Combined with (a) and (b), the CAEP-style classification can work well for imbalanced classification problems. This is confirmed by experiments.

11.6.2 Performance Results of iCAEP

Experiments were conducted to examine the performance of iCAEP, and to compare it against state-of-the-art re-sampling and cost-sensitive techniques for imbalanced classification. Meta-cost [110] is a technique that makes a base classifier cost-sensitive; it requires a misclassification cost measure, which is set to the inverse of class distribution in our experiments. SMOTE [79] re-samples a dataset by applying the synthetic minority oversampling technique.

For imbalanced classification, three real-world imbalanced datasets (see Table 11.3) from the software engineering discipline were used. They are available at the NASA IV&V Facility Metrics Data Program (MDP) repository (http://mdp.ivv.nasa.gov/index.html). They are software metrics data at the module (function/method) level for NASA software development projects. Using static software metrics at the module level to predict software defects has been shown useful [295]. Software defect prediction is a binary problem where a module is classified as having defects or not. A minority of modules (around 10% on average) contain defects.

Experiments were also conducted to test all algorithms for balanced classification, using three balanced datasets (Table 11.3) from the UCI repository.

Implementations in the data mining toolkit WEKA (version 3.6.0) [176] were used for Naive Bayes (NB), MetaCost-NB, SMOTE-NB, and Decision

Dataset	iCAEP	NB	Meta-NB	Smote-NB	DT	Meta-DT	Smote-DT
CM1	**0.71**	0.66	**0.71**	0.67	0.56	0.63	0.62
KC1	**0.79**	**0.79**	0.78	**0.79**	0.69	0.69	0.72
PC1	**0.69**	0.65	0.67	0.66	0.67	0.67	**0.70**

TABLE 11.4: AUC – Imbalanced Data. Bold: best results (AUC differing by ≤ 0.01 are considered equivalent). NB: Naive Bayes; DT: Decision Tree.

Tree (DT) (the J48 classifier in WEKA), MetaCost-DT and SMOTE-DT. Ten-fold cross validation tests were used to measure all algorithms.

While overall accuracy is used to evaluate performance in balanced classification, it is not suitable in imbalanced classification — a trivial classifier that predicts every instance as in the majority class can achieve very high overall accuracy yet its prediction for the rare class is extremely poor. Instead, the following evaluation metrics are used. (a) True positive rate (TP-rate) and true negative rate (FP-rate) measure respectively the prediction accuracy on positive and negative classes, and false positive rate (FP-rate) and false negative rate (FN-rate) measure the error rate on the positive and negative classes. (b) The Receiver Operating Characteristic (ROC) curve is a standard technique for summarizing classifier performance over possible tradeoffs between TP-rate and FP-rate. The x-y axes are the FP-rate and the TP-rate. A good classifier should have low FP-rates while maintaining high TP-rates. Area under ROC (AUC) is often used as a single comprehensive measurement for the performance for positive class prediction.

Table 11.4 shows the AUC for all classification algorithms on the 3 imbalanced datasets, and Figure 11.2 shows the corresponding ROC curves. In Table 11.4 the AUC for iCAEP compares favorably with all other algorithms on all three datasets. Figure 11.2 shows that iCAEP achieves steadily high TP-rate at very low FP-rate ($\leq 20\%$) on all datasets except PC1. Figure 11.2 (a–c) shows that iCAEP outperforms NB, MetaCost-NB, and Smote-NB on all datasets, confirming our belief that representative contrast patterns are powerful for classifying rare examples. NB performs reasonably well on imbalanced datasets, despite being a simple model; MetaCost and SMOTE did not improve the performance of NB significantly. In contrast, Figure 11.2 (d–f) shows that Decision Tree suffers significantly from class imbalance. However probably due to the above, Decision Tree responds well to MetaCost and SMOTE to produce significant improvement.

The overall accuracy of all classification algorithms on the balanced datasets is shown in Table 11.5. iCAEP obviously maintains a high overall accuracy on all three balanced datasets and performs steadily well. In contrast, MetaCost and SMOTE have varying performance on these datasets. Rather than maintaining the accuracy of base classifiers, on Labor, SMOTE decreases the accuracy of DT from 79% to 70.17%, whereas on Spambase,

Dataset	iCAEP	NB	Meta-NB	Smote-NB	DT	Meta-DT	Smote-DT
Labor	89.7	86.3	89.5	89.5	79.0	85.9	70.2
Spambase	91.2	89.9	80.6	79.7	93.0	93.1	92.9
Mushroom	99.8	99.7	92.9	96.0	100	100	100

TABLE 11.5: Accuracy – Balanced Data. NB and DT: see Table 11.4

MetaCost decreases the accuracy of DT from 89.87% to 79.72%. This may be due to the inherent randomness of both techniques, even when the balanced class distribution information is available to the model.

11.7   Conclusion and Discussion

Contrast pattern based classification has been proven to be both a fruitful direction of research and a desirable method to solve real world problems in many domains. Many highly effective CP-based classification algorithms have been proposed, and have been shown to have high accuracy and to perform well for imbalanced classification problems.

This chapter has provided a high level overview and analysis of contrast pattern based classification algorithms. This was done by considering how those algorithms handle the two main issues for contrast pattern based classification, namely contrast model selection and classification strategy using the contrast patterns. This chapter also provided experimental evaluation of contrast pattern based algorithms, with respect to the bias-variance decomposition and how they behave for imbalanced classification.

We now briefly discuss some related work. Several papers (e.g. [257, 38]) studied selecting representative patterns for the CBA-style classification. [121, 60, 351] gave overviews on pattern based classification. [71] considered EP based classification for relational data. [383, 139] studied noise tolerance of CAEP-style classifiers. [453] considered a "causal associative classification" approach. [428] considered using maximal EPs for classification.

There are many interesting problems to solve regarding improving CP-based classification. As mentioned earlier, an ideal CP model for a classifier should be a relatively small set of diversified representative high-quality CPs. The ideas proposed for measuring clustering quality and constructing clusters based on quality, abundance, and diversity of CPs (see [276, 152, 277] and Chapter 14) can be useful here. There are many challenging classification/prediction problems that require both high accuracy and highly explainable classification decisions; this book contains several chapters on using EP based classifiers to solve a range of classification/prediction problems of that kind (see Section 11.1), and other papers solving those problems will be cited in Chapter 25.

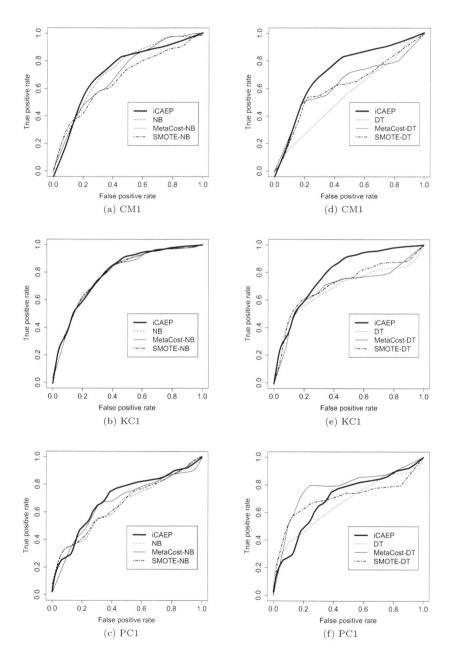

FIGURE 11.2: Performance on Imbalanced Datasets. (a–c): iCAEP vs MetaCost-NB and SMOTE-NB; (d–f): iCAEP vs MetaCost-DT and SMOTE-DT. NB: Naive Bayes; DT: Decision Tree.

Chapter 12

Using Emerging Patterns in Outlier and Rare-Class Prediction

Lijun Chen

Blue Systems Integration, BlueCross BlueShield of Tennessee

Guozhu Dong

Department of Computer Science and Engineering, Wright State University

12.1 Introduction

This chapter presents approaches that use length statistics of emerging patterns (EPs) to detect outliers, and use EPs in rare-class classification.

An outlier is "an observation which deviates so much from other observations as to arouse suspicion that it was generated by a different mechanism"

[184]. *Outlier detection* is a core task in data mining, and has attracted a great deal of attention from the research communities [189, 2, 215, 231].

Rare-class classification is concerned with classification when very little training data about the target class of interest (the rare class) is available. This is also a very challenging problem, since the lack of training data often implies a lack of high quality discriminative information for the rare class and often weakens the performance of main stream classification algorithms. Considerable attention has been given to this problem [182, 185, 2].

While the outlier detection and rare-class classification problems each have their unique challenges, they both face the common challenge of skewed data, i.e. with none or very little training data about an important class of interest.

Sections 12.2 and 12.3 are based on [82], whereas Section 12.4 is based on [5].

12.2   EP-length Statistic Based Outlier Detection

We now discuss the *OCLEP* approach for outlier detection. Roughly speaking, OCLEP uses the training data for a given class to build some EP length statistics, and uses the training data to derive the length statistics for each new test case and to classify the test cases based on the relationship of the length statistics for the test case and the length statistics of the training data.

OCLEP has several interesting features: (1) OCLEP achieves *one-class classification* by using EPs. This is the first time EPs are used in the one-class setting, although EPs have been used many times for multi-class classification. This becomes more interesting if one considers the way EPs are defined – EPs are patterns with significant support differences between classes. (2) OCLEP does not use the EPs themselves for classification; it uses some length statistics. This implies that OCLEP is virtually model free and that there is little need for keeping complex models for the normal and outlier classes; as a result, OCELP can have a better chance of performing well than complex model based outlier detection, since outlier cases such as intruders may change their behavior model in order to evade detection.

The discussion below on OCLEP will address these issues: (1) what kind of discriminative information can one-class EPs give, (2) how to mine EPs with one-class data, (3) how to define the EP length statistics, and (4) how to use length statistics to make the classification decision. The complete OCLEP method will be given after discussing those four issues.

We now briefly review the BorderDiff operation [118], which was used by the OCLEP approach. (Other emerging/contrast pattern mining algorithms can also be used.) Given a tuple (represented as transaction) t and a set T of tuples, BorderDiff(t, T) returns the set of minimal *jumping EPs* that occur in t but never occur in any tuples in T. For example, BorderDiff$(t, T) = \{\{1\}, \{2, 3, 4\}\}$ for $t = \{1, 2, 3, 4\}$ and $T = \{\{2, 3, 5, 6\}, \{2, 4, 7, 8\}, \{3, 4, 6, 8\}\}$.

12.2.1 EP Based Discriminative Information for One Class

We must first answer this question: What kind of EP based discriminative information can we use in one-class classification?

To answer that question, let's pretend that we have a two-class classification problem. Let D_i be the set of training data for class i, $i = 1, 2$. Suppose for the time being that D_i consists of transactions. Let us consider what kind of difference we may get between the following two invocations of BorderDiff: In one invocation we pick a transaction t_1 from D_1 and pick a subset T_1 of $D_1 - \{t_1\}$, and compute BorderDiff(t_1, T_1). In the other, we pick a t_2' from D_2 and pick a subset T_1' of D_1, and compute BorderDiff(t_2', T_1').

Naturally, data instances within a class are highly similar to each other and data instances of difference classes are highly different from each other. So BorderDiff(t_1, T_1) should contain long[1] patterns, while BorderDiff(t_2', T_1') should contain short patterns. The reasons are: Since t_1 is quite similar to the transactions in T_1 (they all come from class 1), we need long patterns to tell t_1 apart from instances in T_1. On the other hand, since t_2' is quite different from the transactions in T_1' (they come from different classes), we only need short patterns to tell t_2' apart from T_1'. This leads to the following key observation:

Property 12.1 *Provided that all transactions of T come from one class,* BorderDiff(t, T) *tends to contain long minimal EPs when t and T come from the same class, and it tends to contain short minimal EPs when t and T come from different classes.*

Experiments on the Mushroom data from UCI Machine Learning Repository also confirmed this observation. In fact, the average length of 1000 BorderDiff(t, T) invocations where t and T come from the same class is 7.78 (7.5 when t is from Edible, 8.05 when t is from Poisonous), and the average length of 1000 BorderDiff(t, T) invocations where t and T come from different classes is 3.03 (2.94 when t is from Edible and T are from Poisonous, 3.11 when t is from Poisonous and T are from Edible).

12.2.2 Mining EPs From One-class Data

The previous subsection also hinted on how to mine EPs from one-class.

One-class EP Mining Method: For each tuple t from a dataset D for one given class, pick a subset T of $D - \{t\}$ of suitable size k, and compute BorderDiff(t, T).

---

[1] We refer to the cardinality of an itemset as its length.

The suitable size k is determined as follows: If D is large, we choose k in the range of $[200, 800]$. If D is not very large, we choose k to be $|D|-1$. By choosing a larger k we use more tuples as background data to be compared against t. However, if k is too large, then more computation time is needed, without the benefit of additional discriminative information (compared against smaller k). A k in the hundreds range usually offers good speed-information tradeoff.

For training, we perform BorderDiff(t, T) for all $t \in D$ if D is small, and for a sample of several hundreds of t if D is large.

12.2.3   Defining the Length Statistics of EPs

For one-class classification, the individual EPs in BorderDiff(t, T) for all the t's may be too detailed/specific to be useful. We introduce a length statistic that allows us to make good use of Property 12.1 for one-class classification.

Definition 12.1 *The average length of a non-empty set S of patterns is*

$$\mathsf{avgLen}(S) = [\sum_i (N_i * i)]/|S|, \qquad (12.1)$$

where N_i is the count of EPs in S with length i for each i.

We compute the associated avgLen(BorderDiff(t, T)) for each BorderDiff(t, T) invocation, and use the average lengths for multiple BorderDiff(t, T) invocations for classification decision.

12.2.4   Using Average Length Statistics for Classification

Let D be the training data for a given class. In the training phase, we call BorderDiff(t, T) for a number of t's in D (and the associated T obtained as described in Section 12.2.2), and get the associated avgLen(BorderDiff(t, T)). This produces a set of average lengths. Let a and b be the minimum and maximum of those average lengths. Then any number c satisfying $a \le c \le b$ can be used as a cut-off threshold for classification decisions.

For classification, let s be a new case to be tested. We apply BorderDiff(s, T) to get the minimal jumping EPs for s against T as follows. If D is small, we let $T = D$ and let avgLen$(s) = $ avgLen(BorderDiff(s, D)). Otherwise, we use 20 random samples, $T_1, ..., T_{20}$, of D, and let avgLen$(s) = avg_{i=1}^{20}$(avgLen(BorderDiff(s, T_i))). If avgLen$(s) < c$ then we classify s as outlier; otherwise, we classify s as normal.

For outlier detection, there is always a trade-off between the hit rate (correctly identified outliers) and the *false positive (FP)* rate (mistakenly identified outliers). The distribution of avgLen(BorderDiff(t, T)) for the training phase can be used in selecting the cut-off to achieve a desired trade-off. A cut-off close to a will lead to low FP rate and low hit rate, while a cut-off close to b will lead to high hit rate but also high FP rate. Since a low FP rate is highly desired for outlier detection, we usually choose the cut-off point to be close to a.

12.2.5   The Complete OCLEP Classifier

Given training dataset D for the normal class, the *OCLEP classifier* for outlier detection is built and used as follows:

1. Preprocessing: Choose a feature construction strategy to transform the data in D into transactional format. The next section will discuss this for the intrusion detection scenario.

2. Mine the EPs from the training data: Call BorderDiff(t, T) m times for m distinct combinations of $t \in D$ and $T \subseteq D - \{t\}$ as follows. If D is small, randomly select $m = |D|$ different tuples $t \in D$ and let $T = D - \{t\}$ be t's corresponding T. If D is large, let $m = 100$, randomly select m different t from D, and let T be a random subset of $D - \{t\}$ such that $200 \le |T| \le 800$.

3. Get length statistics of the mined EPs: Compute the list of all average lengths for all BorderDiff(t, T) invocations of the last step. Sort the list into increasing order. Let a be the low and b the high in the sorted list.

4. Choose a classification cut-off point: A cut-off point c such that $a \le c \le b$ is chosen. (A smaller c will give low FP and hit rates, while a larger c will give high FP and high hit rates.)

5. Classification: Let s be a new case. If D is small, let $T = D$ and avgLen$(s) =$ avgLen(BorderDiff(s, D)). Otherwise, let $T_1, ..., T_{20}$ be 20 random samples of D and let avgLen$(s) = avg_i($avgLen(BorderDiff$(s, T_i)))$. If avgLen$(s) < c$ then we classify s as outlier; otherwise, we classify s as normal.

12.3   Experiments on OCLEP on Masquerader Detection

The OCLEP approach can be applied on many outlier detection or one-class classification problems. This section uses an empirical evaluation on masquerader detection to illustrate the effectiveness of the OCLEP approach.

There are five subsections, dealing with (1) some background about masquerader detection, (2) the data used in masquerader detection and the associated common training/testing methods, (3) the best one-class training method reported on the masquerader detection dataset, (4) our data preprocessing and feature selection approach, and (5) experimental results using OCLEP.

The experiments show that OCLEP can achieve very good detection accuracy while keeping the false positive rate low, it achieves slightly better area-under-the-curve than SVM, which is the best reported one-class approach. It can achieve good results when other approaches do not. OCLEP also shows promising results when used as OCLEP ensembles. OCLEP achieves all of the above by using a much simpler model, namely one number (length), for differentiating the normal and outlier classes.

12.3.1 Masquerader Detection

Masquerader attacks, in which an intruder pretends to be another person and uses another person's identity to do something, may be one of the most serious security problems.

Masquerader attacks often happen inside the protection of the firewalls, etc; study [100] shows that insiders can cause more damage, and are harder to catch, than outsiders. Authentication cannot detect masquerader attacks. Masqueraders are unknown ahead of their attacks. Masqueraders usually mimic a genuine user by stealing his/her identification, and the login details cannot distinguish between a legitimate user and masqueraders.

There are many efforts to build *masquerader detection* systems [28] in terms of user-command sequences. A common approach is to compare a user's recent behavior against his/her profile of typical behavior and to use deviation as indication of masquerading. There are several studies that model a user's behavior in order to detect anomalous misconduct, e.g. [133].

There have been several two-class training approaches [133, 294], which use information on both the legitimate user and the masqueraders. Such methods may not be realistic in practice since we usually do not have masqueraders' information and we may encounter unknown masqueraders.

A practical approach to detect masqueraders is to only use a legitimate user's own profile as training data, called one-class training, because it is easier to build a legitimate user's profile than a masquerader's and the masqueraders are unknown at training time. Studies in [422] show that the one-class training approach can achieve comparable performance to that achieved by two-class training approaches. It was noted that the one-class SVM performs better than one-class Naïve Bayes approaches, and even better than some two-class training approaches. However, the results reported were based on the theoretical optimal performance of SVM. It is hard to tune the system to discover the optimal parameters.

Studies in [82] and this chapter show that EP-based approach is very effective for masquerader detection.

12.3.2 Data Used and Evaluation Settings

The data for masquerader detection usually takes the form of *user-command sequences*. The detection system examines a block of (e.g. 100 of) a user's recent commands to decide if the user is a masquerader. The dataset provided by Schonlau et al [133], available at http://www.schonlau.net, is frequently used. It consists of sequences of "truncated" commands for 50 users; each user is represented by a sequence of 15,000 commands. The first 5,000 commands of each user are "clean data" (i.e. legitimately issued by the user), and the last 10,000 commands were probabilistically injected with commands issued by 20 users outside the community of the 50. The commands are grouped into blocks of 100 commands. The commands in one block are either all clean or all masquerade attacks, called "dirty blocks". The task is to accurately classify the user-command blocks into two categories: self (i.e. the clean blocks) and masqueraders (i.e. the dirty blocks).

The following three training/testing experiment settings have been used in the literature for evaluating detection methods; all consider a given user as the true "self," but they differ regarding whether they use the other users' information for training and what data is used for testing.

SEA: This is a two-class training experiment setting [133]. The training uses the first 5,000 commands of all users. When a given user is the self, the test data are the remaining 10,000 commands of the user; the 5,000 commands of the other 49 users can be used to build models/profiles of non-self.

1v49: This is a one-class training experiment setting [294]. Only the first 5,000 commands of self are used as training data, and the first 5,000 commands of the other 49 users (considered as masqueraders) are used as testing data.

1v49': This is also a one-class training experiment setting [422]. Only the first 5,000 commands of self are used as training data, and the first 5,000 commands of the other 49 users (considered as masqueraders), together with the rest of the 10,000 commands of the self, are used as testing data.

12.3.3 Data Preprocessing and Feature Construction

For preprocessing, we group the commands for a given user into blocks, with 100 commands per block, similarly to other studies. Each block is then converted into a feature vector, using a selected feature construction strategy.

There are many ways to construct features, depending on whether we treat the command blocks as sets, sequences, or bags. We studied the following six:

(1) *Binary.* Each command is a feature. The feature vector for a block B of commands contains, for each command C, a 1 or 0 to indicate whether or not C occurs in B. There are around 870 distinct commands in the dataset.

(2) *Frequency equal-length* and (3) *frequency equal-density*. For both methods, the frequency of each command in a block is considered. The frequency is transformed into binary format by using either equal length binning or equal density binning [179] approaches.

(4) *Pair.* In each block, each adjacent command pair is considered as a feature. There are a maximum of 99 features in a block.

(5) *Skip-one-pair.* We consider pairs of commands as features, if they are separated by exactly one command. For example, if $c_1 c_2 c_3$ is a subsequence in a block then $c_1 c_3$ is a feature. There are a maximum of 98 features in a block.

(6) *Triple.* In each block, each adjacent command triple is considered as a feature. There are a maximum of 98 features in a block.

As will be discussed in Section 12.3.5, the *binary* approach is the simplest and can achieve the best overall performance in terms of getting low FP rate.

The *frequency* approaches perform worst among the six approaches. The other approaches can improve the hit rate, but also lead to high FP rate.

12.3.4   One-class Support Vector Machine (ocSVM)

Support Vector Machines (SVM) [413] are *maximal margin* classifiers. In the two-class case, the basic idea is to map feature vectors to a high dimensional space via a kernel function and to compute a hyperplane in that space that (a) separates the training vectors from different classes and (b) maximizes the separation margin. One-class Support Vector Machine (ocSVM) uses examples from one-class, instead of multiple classes, for training. It treats the origin as the only example from "other classes", and finds the maximal margin hyperplane that best separates the training data from the origin. ocSVM has been shown to be very effective in document classification [289] and masquerader detection [422].

We used the LIBSVM 2.8 [77] with the default RBF kernel. We note that the ocSVM results reported here are the theoretically best: We simply let the SVM calculates all the distances, and the decision point (hyperplane) is then chosen by looking at all the test data together. The overall performance is the average over all the best solution for all users.

We considered different feature representations (see Section 12.3.3) for ocSVM. The results show that the *binary* approach achieved the best hit rate with FP rate similar to other feature approaches (all < 1%); the performance for the binary case is consistent with [422]. So the *binary* approach is used below for ocSVM unless mentioned otherwise.

12.3.5   Experiment Results Using OCLEP

We now present the empirical evaluation results of the OCLEP approach for masquerader detection. We will mainly compare OCLEP with the one-class SVM – the best one-class training method for this problem, and briefly mention reported results of other methods.

We will conduct the SEA and the 1v49' experiments mentioned above.

12.3.5.1   SEA Experiment

In this experiment setting, OCLEP and ocSVM are only trained on the first 5,000 commands of the user (the clean data), which is slightly different than the original SEA. The classifiers are tested on the remaining 10,000 commands of the user. The reported performance is the average performance over all 50 users.

In classification, we are often concerned with the trade-off between hits (or correct detection) and false positives (or false detection). This is often depicted on a *receiver operating characteristic (ROC)* curve where the percentages of hits and false positive are shown on the y-axis and x-axis respectively. The

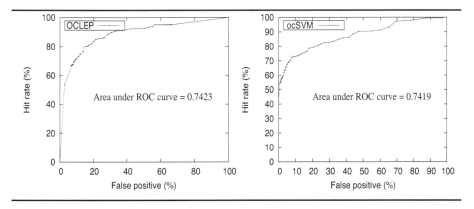

FIGURE 12.1: ROC curves for OCLEP and ocSVM.

area under the ROC curve (AUC) is often used to evaluate the overall performance of classification algorithms. Figure 12.1 shows ROC curves for OCLEP method and ocSVM. The AUC for OCLEP and ocSVM are 0.7423 and 0.7419, respectively. The AUC for OCLEP is slightly larger, although the two AUC values are very close.

For the masquerader detection problem, it is important to have a low false positive (FP) rate, say less than 1%. In this respect, ocSVM is a very promising method and is better than OCLEP. In fact, ocSVM is better than most of the two-class methods. ocSVM is the only method that can get the FP rate under 1% while still has reasonable hit rate. OCLEP can achieve 2.9% FP rate with 59.2% hits, which is ranged in the middle. Figure 12.2 gives a broad view of where the methods stands by including the ROC curves of OCLEP and ocSVM, and the best-outcome results[2] of other methods.

For each method, the best result is the one that achieves high hit rate and low false positive (FP) rate. Table 12.1 shows the result. We also note that no method completely dominates another method in term of the ROC curves, which is commonly used to show the trade-off between hits and FP rate.

Recall that the best result for ocSVM is the theoretical best, which is very hard (if not impossible) to obtain in real applications. But these results can be a good benchmark to compare with. In contrast, our OCLEP is parameter-free if we want to have the lowest FP possible: For each user, we simply pick the cut-off point as the minimum average length. This easy-to-use feature is very desirable for practical masquerader detection systems.

Table 12.2 shows the average performance over 50 users when different feature construction strategies are used in the OCLEP method. We can see that the *binary* approach has the best performance in terms of getting low

---

[2]The one-class version of Naïve Bayes classifiers was only used in the 1v49 experiment setting [294]. In [422], the performance was shown to be worse than ocSVM.

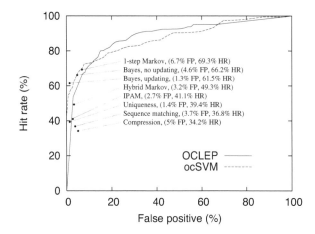

FIGURE 12.2: ROC curves for OCLEP, ocSVM; best reported results for other methods. Courtesy of IEEE from [82].

Methods	Hits %	FP %	One/two	Source
Uniqueness	39.4	1.4	Two	
IPAM	41.1	2.7	Two	
Hybrid Markov	49.3	3.2	Two	[133]
Sequence Matching	36.8	3.7	Two	
Compression	34.2	5.0	Two	
1-step Markov	69.3	6.7	Two	
N. Bayes (updating)	61.5	1.3	Two	[294]
N. Bayes (no updating)	66.2	4.6	Two	
ocSVM	42	0	One	[422]
OCLEP	59.2	2.9	One	[82]

TABLE 12.1: Best results of all methods

Feature Construction Strategy	Hits %	FP %
Binary	59.16	2.91
Frequency equal-length	44	2.92
Frequency equal-density	54.04	5.12
Pair	72.59	4.9
Skip-one-pair	69.96	5.06
Triple	70.85	4.62

TABLE 12.2: Average performance of OCLEP over 50 users when different feature construction strategies are used in the SEA experiment. Courtesy of IEEE from [82].

FP rate. The results of other approaches are also very appealing compared with other existing two-class approaches. For example, when using the *pair* approach, OCLEP can achieve 72.59% hits and 4.9% FP rate.

Feature Construction	OCLEP		ocSVM	
Strategy	Hits %	FP %	Hits %	FP %
Binary	25.67	2.9	42.92	0.82
Frequency equal-length	22.54	21.1	9.82	0.77
Frequency equal-density	16.8	14.07	11.87	0.82
Pair	43.65	5	34.73	0.82
Skip-one-pair	46.63	5.14	31.23	0.89
Triple	36.88	4.64	29.67	0.75

TABLE 12.3: Average performance over 50 users when different feature construction strategies are used in OCLEP and ocSVM in 1v49' experiment. Courtesy of IEEE from [82].

12.3.5.2 1v49' Experiment

Here, training is still based on the first 5,000 commands of a given user, similarly to the SEA experiment. The resultant classifier is tested not only on the rest of the 10,000 commands of the user, but also the first 5,000 commands of other 49 users. The data from other users are treated as masqueraders, yielding at least $50 * 49 = 2450$ masquerader blocks for each user.

Similarly to the SEA experiment, ocSVM theoretically performs better than OCLEP on average for 50 users. We also tested the impact of different feature construction strategies on both methods. Although the overall hit rates are low for all methods, from Table 12.3 we can see that *binary* approach is still the best for both methods. Notice that feature construction makes a difference for OCLEP. We can see that the *pair*, *skip-one-pair*, and *triple* approaches get much better hit rate only with slightly increased FP rate.

12.3.5.3 Situations When OCLEP is Better

Even though ocSVM outperforms OCLEP on average in terms of getting lower FP, OCLEP performed much better for several users. Table 12.4 lists several such users.

By analyzing the training data, we found that OCLEP performs better than ocSVM when there are more unique commands in each block. On the other hand, if there are many repeated commands in each block, ocSVM performs better. For example, for user5, there are more than 30 unique commands on average in each block, but the number is less than that for user2. This observation suggests that the performance of OCLEP could be improved if we use a different block size so that each block contains more distinct commands.

Users	OCLEP		ocSVM	
	Hits %	FP %	Hits %	FP %
User5	58.04	0	27.67	1
User15	27.24	1	20.48	1
User24	60.66	1.27	49.7	1.27
User34	66.65	1.1	30.99	1.1

TABLE 12.4: Some users where OCLEP performed much better than the ocSVM method when the *binary* feature construction was used in the 1v49' experiment. Courtesy of IEEE from [82].

We also note that there are more situations where OCLEP outperforms ocSVM when other feature construction strategies are used.

12.3.5.4   Feature Based OCLEP Ensemble

We examined the effectiveness of the *ensemble classifier* approach where we combine decisions of multiple OCLEP classifiers (where the ensemble for a set of feature selection methods contains exactly one OCLEP classifier per feature selection method). Table 12.5 lists some results in the SEA experiment setting. We see that this approach can improve the hit rate while keeping the FP rate at the same level. Notice that we can also achieve even lower FP in some cases; for example, we get 1.2% FP with 48.9% hit rate if we combine all six feature construction methods. This is a very encouraging result, and deserves further study.

Feature Construction Methods	Hits %	FP %
Binary, Pair, Skip-one-pair	66.5	3.4
Binary, Frequency ED, Skip-one-pair	53	2.2
Binary, Frequency EW, Pair, Skip-one-pair, Triple	64.3	2.7
All six	48.9	1.2

TABLE 12.5:   Results of the ensemble classifier approach in the SEA experiment, where we combine OCLEP decisions for different feature construction approaches. ED: equi-density; EW: equi-width. Courtesy of IEEE from [82].

12.4 Rare-class Classification Using EPs

Rare-class classification problems exist in many real-world applications across a wide range of domains, such as network intrusion detection, diagnosis of rare medical conditions, video surveillance, etc. All these applications share a common characteristic: samples of one class are extremely rare, while the number of samples of the other classes is large. In addition, it is more important to correctly classify the rare class samples than the other samples. The scarcity of the rare class cases makes it difficult to classify them correctly using traditional classifiers, especially for high dimensional data. References [182, 185, 2] studied techniques for rare class classification.

Reference [5] presented an approach called EPDT that combines emerging patterns (EPs) and decision trees for rare-class classification. The approach consists of two main steps in the EP enhanced decision tree building process: 1) using mined EPs for the rare class to create new rare-class instances, and 2) over-sampling important rare-class instances in decision tree building. (Reference [6] also considered expanding training data of rare class using EPs.)

The first step uses the rare-class EPs to create new rare-class instances. Given a training dataset D, let $\mathcal{E}$ be a set of mined rare-class EPs. $\mathcal{E}$ is divided into groups such that EPs of each group have values for most of the attributes of the dataset. The new rare-class instances are created by combining the EPs in each group, and also the attribute values with the highest support growth rate for attributes not occurring in the EP group. We use an example to illustrate the process. Suppose D has the seven attributes of $(A_1, ..., A_7)$, and suppose one EP group of the rare class contains the three EPs of $E_1 = \{(A_1 = 1), (A_2 = a_1)\}$, $E_2 = \{(A_5 = b_1), (A_6 = 2), (A_7 = 3)\}$, and $E_3 = \{(A2 = a_2), (A_3 = 4), (A_5 = b_2)\}$. For attribute A_4, there is no attribute value in the EP group; the A_4 value, say a_4, with the highest support growth rate from the major classes to the rare class is used. Combining the values in the EP group and the value a_4, the following four new instances are created and added to the training data of the rare class:

$$\{(A_1 = 1, A_2 = a_i, A_3 = 4, A_4 = a_4, A_5 = b_j, A_6 = 2, A_7 = 3) \mid 1 \leq i, j \leq 2\}.$$

The second step uses selective over-sampling of certain "important" rare-class instances to balance the rare-class dataset. The hope is that the *over-sampling* helps build better decision trees. However, over-sampling the rare-class instances randomly may affect the performance negatively [265] due to possible noise amplification. The selective over-sampling of EPDT overcomes this problem by duplicating the most important instances only: It only duplicates instances that contain rare-class EPs, based on the belief that these instances have the most important information that can aid the classification process and do not contribute noise in the space of rare-class instances.

Experiments on five previously studied rare-class classification datasets show that using EP-based new rare-class instance creation and selective EP-based over-sampling improves decision trees' performance for rare class classification. Specifically, EPDT gave significant improvement on weighted accuracy, recall, precision, and F-measure over methods such as C4.5 and Metacost, etc.

12.5   Advantages of EP-based Rare-class Instance Creation

EP-based rare-class instance generation has several advantages[3] over sampling based approaches.

In general, EP-based rare-class instance creation is an efficient way of generating new instances satisfying the implicit underlying multi-variate distributions of the training data. In some sense, EPs implicitly carry various conditional probabilities among the items and classes; using EPs allows us to generate new instances to better reflect the underlying distributions. Moreover, the EP-based new rare-class instance creation approach can give more diversity in the rare-class training data than other sampling based approaches.

Indeed, in a sampling approach we often sample instances from the original training data. Since the resulting training data is just like the original, this sampling approach does not add diversity to the training data. In case we use the naive Bayes method to generate new training instances, we have challenges since we need to estimate the parameters (using very small training data) and we need to rely on the independence assumption, and we may also need to rely on some simple distribution (e.g. the normal distribution). In case we use some model such as a Bayesian Network to guide the sampling process, we have an additional challenge of estimating many parameters using a very small training dataset.

On the other hand, EPs implicitly capture relationships on subsets of features. Such relationships can reflect joint distributions of those features. Using EPs to generate new instances is, in some sense, based on using the implicit joint distributions. The fact that EP-based classification (see Chapter 11) can achieve very high classification accuracy indicates that EPs are useful for estimating probabilities of tuples in classes (see [465, 138]). Perhaps it can be said that EP-based rare class instance creation can create new instances based on their probabilities to occur in the rare class. The above and the advantage of EP-based rare-class instance generation are reinforced by the fact that EP-based classification can generate very good classification results even when very few training instances (three instances per class) are available [25] (see also Chapter 18).

---

[3]We thank Kotagiri Ramamohanarao for some of the ideas of this section.

12.6   Related Work and Discussion

Here we provide more details for several masquerade detection methods that were compared against our OCLEP method. We already touched on other related works in previous sections.

Reference [133] identified six masquerade detection methods: Bayes 1-Step Markov, Hybrid Multi-Step Markov, Incremental Probabilistic Action Modeling (IPAM), Uniqueness, Sequence-Match, and Compression. These methods were trained to build a profile of self and a profile of non-self. The paper used the SEA experiment setting to evaluate the methods.

Reference [294] used the Naïve Bayes classification algorithm (two versions: one without updating, another one with updating) to solve the masquerader detection problem and obtained better results than those reported in [133]. In addition to evaluating the classifiers in the SEA experiment setting, the paper also designed the 1v49 experiment setting in order to (1) investigate the Naïve Bayes classification errors, and to (2) provide some insight on why some users are good masqueraders (i.e. hard to detect) and others are not.

Reference [422] used the one-class SVM algorithm on masquerader detection. It conducted experiments in both SEA and 1v49' experiment settings. The paper's experiments showed that the one-class training works as well as the multi-class training approaches, and the one-class SVM using binary features performs best among the one-class training approaches.

We have seen that EPs are a very powerful tool. EPs themselves have been used to solve many real-world problems, such as building robust and accurate classification, classification of cancer using microarray data, expanding training data, and so on. These are discussed in other chapters of the book.

This chapter showed that the length statistics of EPs can be used to detect outliers and to perform rare-class classification. Even though we only conducted experiments on the masquerader detection dataset, we believe that the OCLEP approach can also be used in other real-world applications, such as fraud detection, network intrusion detection, diagnosis of rare medical conditions, etc. It remains to be seen how OCLEP will perform on those domains.

In addition, we believe that EP length statistics and EP themselves can be used together to solve problems. In fact this was done for clustering and clustering quality evaluation (see [276, 277] and Chapter 14). Other possibilities still exist. We can also expect other interesting features (other than the length statistics) about EPs might be discovered and used to solve problems.

Regarding rare-class classification, Chapter 11 gives more background information on imbalanced classification and discusses how EP based classification (iCAEP) can give good performance results. It also compares iCAEP with popular approaches such as cost-sensitive learning techniques (represented by meta-cost [110]) and re-sampling learning techniques (represented by SMOTE [79]).

Chapter 13

Enhancing Traditional Classifiers Using Emerging Patterns

Guozhu Dong

Department of Computer Science and Engineering, Wright State University

Kotagiri Ramamohanarao

Department of Computing and Information Systems, The University of Melbourne

13.1 Introduction

This chapter discusses how emerging patterns can be used to help improve traditional classification algorithms. It focuses on two specific approaches, one [140, 461] using emerging patterns (EPs) [118] in weighted/fuzzy support vector machine (SVM) construction, and the other [8] using EPs in weighted decision tree construction. In the first approach, each training data instance is first given an EP based "relevance weight" to reflect its perceived importance for weighted SVMs (three weighting methods are discussed); in the second, each training data instance is first given a "class membership weight vector", of weighted membership for the classes. As will be seen below, the two approaches lead to significant improvement in classification accuracy and other benefits.

Chapter 12 has a related section on improving rare-class classification using emerging patterns.

The discussion below assumes that a dataset D with $k \geq 2$ classes $(C_1, ..., C_k)$ is given.

13.2   Emerging Pattern Based Class Membership Score

The approaches presented below all use the EP based class membership scoring function of CAEP [126] for the determination of weights. The scoring function is based on the observation that EPs are strong signals for discriminating data of different classes, due to the large differences of their supports in the classes. To determine the membership score of data tuple t in class C, the scoring function uses all EPs of C that match t. It should be noted that the score depends on not only the quality (support growth rate and support in class C), but also the number, of the matching EPs of tuple t in class C.

For each i, let E_{C_i} be the set of (minimal) EPs of C_i for some given thresholds (on minimal support growth rate and minimal home-class support). When $k \geq 3$, E_{C_i} is defined to be the set of EPs with class C_i as the home dataset, and the union of the other classes, namely $\cup_{j=1, j \neq i}^{k} C_j$, as the opposing dataset. The EPs are mined after first discretizing numerical attributes, often using the entropy based method [214]. It should be noted that discretization is only used in the EP mining process; in the classification process the original non-discretized data is used.

A data instance t's *EP based membership score* in a class C_i is defined by

$$\mathsf{MScore}_{ep}(t, C_i) = \sum_{X \subseteq t, X \in E_{C_i}} \frac{\mathsf{gr}(X)}{\mathsf{gr}(X) + 1} * \mathsf{supp}(X, C_i),$$

where $\mathsf{gr}(X)$ is the growth rate (or support ratio) of X (see Chapter 1 for the definition). This class membership score represents the aggregated discriminative power of the EPs of class C_i that match data instance t.

13.3   Emerging Pattern Enhanced Weighted/Fuzzy SVM

Support vector machines (SVMs) [98] are very popular for solving classification problems and have been used in many application fields. Traditional SVM algorithms treat all training data instances as equally important. It can be advantageous if different data instances are given different weights to reflect their importance and relevance. For example, it is desirable to give noise and outlier data instances less weight, and give high quality data instances with unambiguous class membership more weight. In general, it makes sense to assign weights to data instances so that the weights are proportional to our confidence on the membership of the instances in their assigned classes. (It may make sense to refer to this weight as the class membership weight.) From such weighted data one can build weighted/fuzzy[1] SVMs, which extend standard SVMs by considering instance weights in their construction and classification decision. The weighted SVM can be more accurate than plain SVM if we can assign appropriate weights to different data instances.

This section provides three EP based methods to realize that advantage. It presents (1) three EP based methods to determine the weights assigned to data instances, (2) an algorithm to build weighted SVM from weighted data, and (3) a performance evaluation to demonstrate the advantage of the constructed weighted SVMs.

13.3.1   Determining Instance Relevance Weight

The rationale used by the EP-based methods when assigning relevance weights is the following: A high quality training data instance often contains many high quality EPs of its home class and it contains no or few EPs of the opposing classes. On the other hand, a low quality one (e.g. an outlier of the classes) often contains few or no EPs of its home class, or it contains EPs of both its home class and its opposing classes and the EPs of the home class are not significantly stronger than the EPs of the opposing classes.

The **first** EP-based function [140] determines the relevance weights based on the difference of the MScore_{ep} of the home class and the MScore_{ep} of the opposing classes. The function uses a raw difference based score, denoted by MSD_{ep}. For each instance t of a given class C_j, we define the *normalized membership delta weight* as follows:

$$\mathsf{MSD}_{ep}(t) = \mathsf{MScore}_{ep}(t, C_j) - \sum_{i=1, i \neq j}^{k} \mathsf{MScore}_{ep}(t, Ci). \qquad (13.1)$$

The range of the MSD_{ep} values is $(-\infty, \infty)$. It is desirable to normalize MSD_{ep} to get weights whose range is $[0, 1]$. This is done one class at a time. Let C_j be a class, and let $maxS_j$ and $minS_j$ be the maximum and minimum MSD_{ep} values of data instances of C_j.

One may be tempted to normalize $\mathsf{MSD}_{ep}(t)$ (for instance t of class C_j) by directly using the linear mapping given by $\frac{\mathsf{MSD}_{ep}(t) - minS_j}{maxS_j - minS_j}$ or the log-based mapping given by $log(1 + (e-1)\frac{\mathsf{MSD}_{ep}(t) - minS_j}{maxS_j - minS_j})$. There are several problems with these mappings: (1) If $maxS_j$ is much larger than most MSD_{ep} values, we will end up with many small weights (close to 0). (2) If $minS_j$ is much

---

[1]Weighted SVMs are also called fuzzy SVMs in the literature [260].

smaller than most MSD_{ep} values, we will end up with many big weights (close to 1). When problems (1) and (2) actually occur the outcome is clearly not good. (3) The two mappings often assign half of the training instances a weight less than 0.5 and assign the other half a weight more than 0.5. This is very undesirable because too many examples will have small weights and hence will be considered as having little value for the classification task.

One way to solve the problems is to use a mapping that controls the density of instances in various weight intervals. One particular method is the following. The MSD_{ep} values are sorted and divided into three intervals: the top 80%, the next 15%, and the bottom 5%. Then the top 80% of the values are mapped to the range of $(0.8, 1]$, the next 15% are mapped to $(0.5, 0.8]$, and the remaining 5% are mapped to $[0, 0.5]$. These mappings are achieved by using slightly modified versions of the log-based mapping given above. The exact formulas can be obtained by adjusting the *min* and *max* values in the original formula and controlling the ranges of the mapped values.

The method described in the last paragraph was designed based on the following assumptions: (a) Most instances (80%) are good for classification. (b) Some instances (15%) can provide some useful information. (c) A small number (5%) of instances are outliers or noisy data; they are likely to provide misleading information and are likely to be harmful to the classification task.

The normalized MSD_{ep} based function for assigning relevance weights described above may suffer in multi-class classification problems. For example, suppose there are four classes, and the MScore_{ep} values of two particular instances t_1 and t_2, both of class C_1, in the four classes are respectively $(5, 2, 2, 1)$ and $(5, 5, 0, 0)$. Then the MSD_{ep} values of both t_1 and t_1 are equal to 0, and hence these two instances will exert equal influence during training. However, the two instances are quite different and should not be treated as the same. Indeed, we have near 100% that t_2 is in $C_1 \cup C_2$ and it is not in $C_3 \cup C_4$, but we do not have such confidence on any combination of classes for t_1.

The **second** EP-based function [461] for assigning relevance weights is an improvement of the first. The improvement uses a *home-weighted* MSD_{ep}-*difference*, denoted by HWMSD_{ep}. (In [461] HWMSD_{ep} is called *total weight*.) For each instance t of a given class C_j, we define

$$\text{HWMSD}_{ep}(t) =$$

$$\sqrt{\frac{\text{MSD}_{ep}(t, C_j) \times \sum_{p=1}^{k-1} \sum_{q=p+1}^{k} |\text{MSD}_{ep}(t, C_p) - \text{MSD}_{ep}(t, c_q)|}{\binom{k}{2}}} \qquad (13.2)$$

This definition uses the average pairwise MSD_{ep} difference. It also uses the term $\text{MSD}_{ep}(t, C_j)$ for *home class weight*, which is important. Without this term, two instances in a common class (say C_1) with *dms* values of $(9, 1)$ and $(1, 9)$ for two classes respectively will get the same relevance weight.

Using the HWMSD_{ep} function, the two instances t_1 and t_2 with MScore_{ep} values of $(5, 2, 2, 1)$ and $(5, 5, 0, 0)$ will get instance weights of 3.16 and 4.06

respectively. Hence t_2 is more important than t_1. To realize why t_2 is of higher value for classification than t_1, it is instructive to think that many two class classification sub-problems of a given multi-class classification problem can be very useful in making the classifier for the multi-class problem more accurate. As mentioned earlier, t_2 is of high value for the two-class classification problem of $C_1 \cup C_2$ vs $C_3 \cup C_4$, but this is not true with t_1 for any two class sub-problem.

Experiments indicate the second function is usually better than the first function.

The **third** EP-based function for assigning weights to instances is a variant of HWMSD_{ep}, using a standard-deviation like method. Specifically, it replaces the average pairwise difference given by

$$\frac{\sum_{p=1}^{k-1} \sum_{q=p+1}^{k} |\mathrm{MSD}_{ep}(t, C_p) - \mathrm{MSD}_{ep}(t, c_q)|}{\binom{k}{2}} \tag{13.3}$$

by a standard deviation like formula given by

$$\frac{\sum_{p=1}^{k} (\mathrm{MSD}_{ep}(t, C_p) - avg_{q=1}^{k} \mathrm{MSD}_{ep}(t, c_q))^2}{k}. \tag{13.4}$$

Experiments show that, in general, the third function is not as good the second.

In addition to the above three relevance weighting functions, a "distance to class center" based approach was given [260]. Experiments show that that method is not as effective as the EP based methods.

13.3.2 Constructing Weighted SVM

The weighted SVM was first proposed in [260] (where it was called fuzzy support vector machine). This machine treats each individual data instance differently, according to its weight which reflect its importance to the classification problem under consideration. The formulation given below is based on [260].

To construct a weighted SVM (for two classes), we are given a set of labeled training data with weights: (x_1, y_1, s_1), ..., (x_m, y_m, s_m), where, for each i, x_i is a training data instance, $y_i \in \{-1, +1\}$ is the class of x_i, and s_i satisfying $0 < s_i \leq 1$ is the weight of x_i.

Like SVM, we construct a weighted SVM by finding a hyperplane that maximizes the margin of separation and minimizes the classification error, paying attention to the weights on the training data instances. The optimal hyperplane can be given by the solution to the optimization problem that minimizes $\tau(\mathbf{w}, \xi, s)$ subject to the $2m$ constraints given below:

$$\tau(\mathbf{w}, \xi, s) = \frac{1}{2}\mathbf{w} \cdot \mathbf{w} + \alpha \sum_{i=1}^{m} s_i \xi_i$$

$$y_i(\mathbf{w} \cdot x_i + b) \geq 1 - \xi_i, \text{ for } 1 \leq i \leq m$$

$$\xi_i \geq 0, \text{ for } 1 \leq i \leq m$$

Here α is a (complexity) constant to be set, and $\mathbf{w}$ represents the normal vector to the separating hyperplane. Clearly a small s_i reduces the effect of the parameter ξ_i and the importance of the corresponding point (x_i, y_i), in the optimization problem and the corresponding classification problem.

As in the standard SVM case, kernel functions can be used.

13.3.3   Performance Evaluation

Experiments [140, 461] on a large number of datasets from the UCI repository shows that the EP based weighting methods lead to good performance of weighted SVMs, improving the performance of weighted SVMs of [260] and outperforming standard SVMs. In the experiments, the accuracy was obtained by using stratified ten-fold cross-validation (CV-10), the complexity constant α was selected from $\{1, 5, 10, 50, 100, 500\}$, and WEKA's implementation of SVM [176] was used. The polynomial and Radial-Basis Function (RBF) kernels were considered. The discussion below uses relative improvement when we say one method is $x\%$ better than another method.

We first consider the performance of the first weighting function [140]. For the polynomial kernel case, the weighted SVM with normalized MSD_{ep}-based weighting is about 2.3% percent better than the standard SVM on average. For the RBF kernel case, the weighted SVM with normalized MSD_{ep}-based weighting is about 1.7% percent better than the standard SVM on average. So the weighted SVM with normalized MSD_{ep}-based weighting is much better than the standard SVM. Moreover, the weighted SVM using distance-to-class-center based weighting [260] is about 1.6% worse than the weighted SVM with normalized MSD_{ep}-based weighting on average, and the weighted SVM with random weighting is about 2.1% percent worse than the standard SVM on average. Those results show that the normalized MSD_{ep}-based weighting has advantage and can accurately reflect the true relevance of data instances for classification.

We next consider the performance of the second weighting function [461]. For the polynomial kernel case, the weighted SVM with HWMSD_{ep}-based weighting is about 5.7% percent better than the standard SVM on average. For the RBF kernel case, the weighted SVM with HWMSD_{ep}-based weighting is about 3.0% percent better than the standard SVM on average. So the weighted SVM with HWMSD_{ep}-based weighting is much better than the standard SVM. Comparing the relative improvement achieved by the two weighting functions, we can see that HWMSD_{ep} is better. (It should be noted that the two papers

[140, 461] used slightly different sets of datasets from UCI.) Experiments also show that $HWMSD_{ep}$ is better than the third weight function.

Experiments [461] also show that weighted SVM with $HWMSD_{ep}$-based weighting is more resistent to noise than standard SVM. That is, the difference between the SVM with $HWMSD_{ep}$-based weighting built from original datasets and the one built from datasets obtained by adding noise to the original datasets is smaller than that difference for standard SVM.

13.4   Emerging Pattern Based Weighted Decision Trees

Decision trees [344] are one of the most important and popular methods for the classification problem, and have been shown to have excellent performance. However, traditional decision tree algorithms assume that training data instances have crisp class membership. In reality, it is more preferable to assume that training data instances have weighted membership for the classes. Classifier performance may improve if weighted membership can be determined automatically and appropriately.

This section presents (1) an EP based method to determine the class membership weights, (2) an algorithm to build weighted decision trees, and (3) a performance evaluation of the resulting weighted decision trees.

When assigning crisp class membership, domain experts typically use the following general approach: They first give scores to each data instance according to certain perceived relation of the instance with the classes, and then assign the class with the highest score to this instance. In this way, they ignore the relation between this instance and the other classes whose scores are lower than that of the assigned class. This approach may have significant undesirable consequences in some situations, e.g. when the highest and second highest scores are quite close (e.g. those two scores are 51 and 49 respectively).

In the weighted class approach, the class membership weight for each data instance is distributed among all classes, and the weight assigned to a class is proportional to the strength of the relation between the class and the data instance. Specifically, for each instance t and class C, let $w_C(t)$ denote the class membership of t for C. The $w_C()$ functions are required to satisfy these two conditions: $0 \leq w_C(t) \leq 1$ and $\sum_{i=1}^{k} w_{C_i}(t) = 1$.

13.4.1   Determining Class Membership Weight

One might be tempted to directly use the $score(t, C)$ values to assign class membership weights. However, that approach has a problem: Some classes are highly EP-rich and some other classes are highly EP-poor, in the sense that the former classes have many more EPs than latter classes, and this imbalance can cause data instances of EP-poor classes to have smaller *score* value for their home classes than for the opposing EP-rich classes. One solution for this problem is to normalize the *score* values of each class by dividing them using certain *score* values at some fixed percentile (e.g. 85% or median) of the class. This division corrects the EP-rich vs EP-poor imbalance, ensuring that data instances of EP-poor classes have high *score* in their home classes than in EP-rich opposing classes. This normalization idea was first used in [126].

Specifically, the normalization is done as follows. For each class C_j, let $median(C_j)$ be the median of the $score(x, C_j)$ values of all instances x of class C_j. For each instance t (not necessarily of class C_j), let

$$mscore(t, C_j) = \frac{score(t, C_j)}{median(C_j)},$$

and let the *weight* of t for class C_j be defined as

$$w_{C_j}(t) = \frac{mscore(t, C_j)}{\sum_{i=1}^{k} mscore(t, C_i)}.$$

Clearly $0 \leq w_{C_j}(t) \leq 1$, and it is the case that $\sum_{i=1}^{k} w_{C_i}(t) = 1$ if data instance t matches one or more EPs of some classes.

Besides the EP-based class membership weighting method, [8] also considered a nearest neighbor based approach to assigning class membership weights. Specifically, it considers a fixed number ℓ (e.g. 10) of nearest neighbors for each data instance t (including t as a nearest neighbor). The weight of t for class C_i is $\frac{n_i}{\ell}$, where n_i is the number of instances among the ℓ nearest neighbors of t that belongs to class C_i.

13.4.2   Constructing Weighted Decision Trees

The main idea of the approach for building weighted decision trees discussed below is to adapt/generalize the probability, entropy, and information gain concepts for the crisp class case to the weighted class case. Below we present that generalization. Let D be a set of training data instances, each assigned weighted class membership using $w_{C_i}()$ functions for the classes $C_1, ..., C_k$. The probability of class C_j in D for the weighted class case is

$$\hat{p}_j(D) = \frac{\sum_{t \in D} w_{C_j}(t)}{|D|}.$$

Observe that this probability is estimated by considering all instances of D. The information conveyed by the class probabilities, or the entropy, of D, for the weighted class case is defined by

$$Info_w(D) = - \sum_{j=1}^{k} \hat{p}_j(D) * log_2(\hat{p}_j(D)).$$

The information of an attribute A with m values $a_1, ..., a_m$ for the weighted class case is given by

$$Info_w(A, D) = \sum_{i=1}^{m} \frac{|D_i|}{|D|} Info_w(D_i),$$

where $D_i = \{t \in D \mid t[A] = a_i\}$. The information of numerical attributes is defined in terms of split values, similarly to how it is done for the case of standard decision trees. The information gain of A for the weighted class case is then given by

$$Gain_w(A, T) = Info_w(D) - Info_w(A, T).$$

The gain ratio measure is defined similarly as done in the standard decision tree case, to avoid giving preference to attributes with large number of values.

Now, to build a weighted decision tree, one uses the standard decision tree algorithm [344], except that the above weighted version of information gain is used instead of the standard information gain.

13.4.3   Performance Evaluation

An extensive set of experiments [8] on a large number of 34 benchmark datasets from the UCI repository shows that the weighting decision trees often significantly improve the performance of standard decision trees and often outperform SVMs. Indeed, the EP-weight based weighted decision trees are about 4% more accurate (in the absolute sense) than the standard decision trees on average, and are about 0.5% more accurate than SVM on average. Moreover, the EP-weight based weighted decision trees are about 2.7% more accurate than the nearest-neighbor-weight based weighted decision trees. The accuracy is estimated using stratified 10-fold cross validation.

13.4.4   Discussion

The EP-weight based weighted decision trees are usually much faster than typical EP-based classifiers in the classification process, since they use decision trees, instead of using all matching EPs, to classify data instances.

The EP-weight based weighted decision trees are also shown to be more noise tolerant than standard decision trees and SVM. This was confirmed by running the classifiers on datasets injected with varying degrees of noise, and comparing the accuracy loss slopes of the different classifiers. The experiments show that the accuracies of the EP-weight based weighted decision trees decrease much more slowly than those of SVM, and those of SVM decrease more slowly than those of standard decision trees.

Reference [8] also considered the impact of the minimum support threshold and the minimum support ratio threshold used in EP mining on the accuracy of the EP-weight based weighted decision trees. In the experiments of the paper, the minimum support threshold was set to 1%. It was observed that when changing the minimum support ratio from small to large, the classifier's accuracies first increase, then stay flat for a while, and finally decrease. This observation was explained by dividing EPs into two major categories: the noisy EPs (those with very small support ratios) and the sharp EPs (those with very large support ratios). Initially, the increase of the minimum support ratio threshold causes the elimination of some noisy EPs. By using all sharp EPs and using fewer noisy EPs, the assigned weights improve in quality and the classification accuracies increase. Later, the increase in minimum support ratio leads to complete elimination of noisy EPs and the elimination of a small number of sharp EPs. As a result, the accuracy does not change substantially. Finally, the increase in the minimum support ratio threshold causes the elimination of some sharp EPs. The elimination of these important EPs leads to the decrease in accuracy.

13.5   Related Work

Reference [418] considered using emerging patterns to enhance the KNN classifier. Reference [426] considered building emerging pattern random forest for recognition of image data. Reference [304] studied incorporating contrast pattern into decision tree-based classifier.

Chapter 14

CPC: A Contrast Pattern Based Clustering Algorithm

Neil Fore and Guozhu Dong

Department of Computer Science and Engineering, Wright State University

14.1 Introduction

Cluster analysis is concerned with grouping objects according to measured or intrinsic characteristics or similarity [196]. Clustering is often applied for exploratory data analysis, where prior domain knowledge is scarce. This can be problematic for traditional clustering approaches, which often rely on a distance function to define the similarity between objects and evaluate the clustering's quality. The design of a good distance function requires a deep understanding of the dataset under consideration, and standard distance functions (e.g. Euclidean) may be inappropriate for the domain. Moreover, it is well known that distance is not very meaningful in high-dimensional data [51], which includes most cases of categorical data.

This chapter introduces a novel clustering algorithm that relies only on frequent patterns. It focuses on discovering coherence among diverse frequent patterns and does not require a distance function or other prior knowledge of the dataset under consideration.

The algorithm is related to a so-called Contrast Pattern-based Clustering Quality index (CPCQ) introduced in [276]. A *contrast pattern* (CP) of a clustering is a pattern (an itemset) appearing with significantly greater frequency in its home cluster than in any other, similar to the concept of CPs in the context of data with classes (e.g. [118]). The difference in frequency makes a CP a highly discriminative pattern to describe its home cluster and distinguish that cluster from the others. CPCQ was designed to measure the quality, abundance, and diversity of each cluster's CPs. Reference [276] demonstrated that CPCQ consistently prefers expert-given classes to other clusterings.

The algorithm proposed in this chapter, namely the Contrast Pattern-based Clustering algorithm (CPC), constructs clusters on the basis of CPs and uses the same concepts of CP quality, abundance, and diversity. The goals of CPC are 1) to ensure that each cluster has an abundance of high-quality and diverse CPs, and 2) to ensure that no cluster can be further partitioned without significantly decreasing the total number of CPs in the clustering. The rationale for goal 1 is similar to that described in [276]; essentially, there should be many different ways to describe/distinguish a high-quality cluster. Goal 2 is included to ensure intra-cluster coherence. To understand its rationale, consider merging two clusters C_1 and C_2 to form a larger cluster C_3. If the inter-cluster separation between C_1 and C_2 is very high, then they should share very few patterns, making C_3's CP set approximately the union of C_1's and C_2's. That is, few CPs would be gained by merging C_1 with C_2 because they are unrelated, and few would be lost by partitioning C_3 into C_1 and C_2 because its intra-cluster coherence is low.

By achieving the above goals, CPC is able to not only achieve higher CPCQ scores, but also recover expert-given clusterings with significantly greater accuracy than popular clustering algorithms. Experiments show that this is true for categorical datasets as well as numerical and mixed-type datasets.

CPC's main strengths include the following:
(1) By requiring no distance function, CPC is highly useful in exploratory studies and for alternative clustering.
(2) By relying only on frequent patterns, CPC is well suited to high-dimensional data, where distance-based methods often suffer.

(3) Pattern quality, abundance, diversity, and coherence may play an important role in defining ideal distance functions by capturing that "intrinsic similarity" between tuples. CPC-produced clusterings can be used as the basis towards defining such distance functions.

(4) The clusters constructed by CPC can be described succinctly by small sets of CPs. So, CPC can be used as a conceptual clustering algorithm. We note that CPC uses CPs to describe clusters, in contrast with cluster descriptions using (conditional) probabilities [296, 151].

Additionally, CPC provides a useful link between clustering and frequent patterns/contrast patterns, just as CBA [270] and CAEP [126] provide useful links between classification and association rules/contrast patterns.

14.2 Related Work

This section briefly reviews seven other clustering algorithms known to not require distance functions.

RObust **C**lustering using lin**K**s (ROCK) [172], **L**arge**I**tem [423], and **C**lustering with s**LOPE** (CLOPE) [446] are clustering algorithms based primarily on item matching. ROCK measures the similarity between tuples t_1 and t_2 by focusing on the number of tuples sharing items with both t_1 and t_2. LargeItem assigns tuples to clusters based on a cost function that discourages the inter-cluster sharing of frequent items and the presence of infrequent items within clusters. CLOPE attempts to maximize the intra-cluster overlapping of items within clusters, by assigning tuples to clusters to maximize the height-to-width ratio of each cluster's item-frequency histogram.

COOLCAT [39], **s**equential **I**nformation **B**ottleneck (sIB) [371], and sca**L**able **I**nfor**M**ation **BO**ttleneck (LIMBO) [15] are entropy-minimization-based clustering algorithms. COOLCAT samples tuples to find k cluster representatives, and then assigns remaining tuples to clusters, minimizing entropy at each step. sIB begins with a random clustering and repeatedly reassigns tuples to reduce entropy. LIMBO uses a hierarchical approach.

Expectation **M**aximization (EM) [102] uses a mixture model to represent k clusters and performs iterative refinements to fit the model to the data. EM begins with an initial estimate of the model's parameters. Then, it iteratively re-scores tuples against the mixture density produced by those parameters and refines the parameter estimates based on the re-scored tuples.

Each of these algorithms has shortcomings inherent in its premise. Item-matching algorithms tend to treat all attributes/items as equally important, and they ignore discriminative multi-item patterns. Entropy-based algorithms focus on intra-cluster purity, ignoring inter-cluster separation as well as the frequency of multi-item patterns. Mixture-model-based algorithms such as EM represent a cluster by some distribution around a mean/mode.

CPs, which are typically multi-item patterns, naturally provide inter-cluster separation and intra-cluster coherence, and they can represent diverse characteristics within a single cluster. The CPC algorithm carefully assigns such CPs using a coherence measure which considers all frequent patterns in the dataset. Thus, CPC's tuple assignments are ultimately based on a greater amount of information than those of the seven algorithms described above.

14.3   Preliminaries

14.3.1   Equivalence Classes of Frequent Itemsets

Given a frequent itemset I for some support threshold, let $|I|$ denote the number of items in I (i.e. the length of I), and let $\mathsf{mt}(I)$ denote the set of tuples (in the dataset under consideration) that match (i.e. contain) I.

Each frequent itemset I is associated with an equivalence class (EC) of itemsets defined as $EC(I) = \{J \mid \mathsf{mt}(J) = \mathsf{mt}(I)\}$. Each EC can be concisely described by a closed itemset (the longest in the EC) and a set of minimal-generator (MG) itemsets (minimal in the EC with respect to $\subseteq$). An EC contains exactly the itemsets I satisfying "I is a superset of some MG itemset" and "I is a subset of the closed itemset".

Importantly, CPC treats frequent ECs, rather than frequent itemsets, as basic pattern units. This is done both for efficiency and because conceptually, itemsets that always co-occur can be considered to have the same behavior/meaning. **Below, we will use the term "pattern" as a synonym of "EC"**; this also applies to the terms "CP" and "frequent pattern".

Given a pattern (i.e. an EC) P, let $\mathsf{mgLen}(P)$ denote the average length of the MG itemsets in P, and let P_{max} denote P's closed itemset. Given a set PS of patterns, let $\mathsf{mt}(PS)$ denote $\bigcup \{\mathsf{mt}(P) \mid P \in PS\}$. We often say that P *overlaps* a tuple set TS if $\mathsf{mt}(P) \cap TS \neq \emptyset$.

14.3.2   CPCQ: Contrast Pattern Based Clustering Quality Index

The CPCQ index [276] is designed to recognize high-quality clusterings in categorical datasets without the need for a distance function. A high-CPCQ clustering is one having many diverse, high-quality CPs in each cluster. Below, we explain the concepts of CP quality, CP diversity, and CP groups.

CP Quality: An individual CP is considered to have high quality if its MG itemsets are short, its closed itemset is long, and its support in its home cluster is high. A short MG itemset acts as a highly effective discriminator, since few items are needed to distinguish its matching tuple set. If the closed itemset is long, a large portion of each matching tuple is part of the CP, indicating high coherence in the CP's matching tuple set. If a CP's support in its home cluster is high, it describes a large portion of the cluster and increases the usefulness of the two length-based values.

In CPC, given a pattern P, we use the term *length ratio* to denote the ratio of P's closed itemset length to the average length of P's MG itemsets, or $|P_{max}|/\mathsf{mgLen}(P)$. This is a slight departure from [276], which uses the length of a single, representative MG itemset in place of $\mathsf{mgLen}(P)$ to evaluate length ratio in CPCQ. In both CPCQ and CPC, higher length ratios are preferred.

CP Diversity: The diversity requirement of CPCQ is motivated by the fact that natural concepts (captured by clusterings) (e.g. gender: male/female) often can be distinguished/characterized in many highly different ways. CPCQ measures the diversity of two CPs in terms of their matching tuples and the items in their representative MG itemsets. If the MG itemsets share few items, then item overlap is low, and item diversity is high. Similarly, if the CPs share few tuples, then tuple overlap is low, and tuple diversity is high. Given two sets S_1 and S_2 of CPs, item/tuple diversity is measured by averaging the item/tuple diversity of all pairs of CPs in $S_1 \times S_2$.

CP Groups: To measure the abundance and diversity of CPs, CPCQ builds several (some fixed number of) CP groups for each cluster. Ideally, each CP group should be a set of highly diverse, high-quality CPs, and the CPs in each CP group should together cover all tuples in their cluster. Between CP groups, item diversity should also be high (tuple diversity between CP groups is meaningless since each CP group often covers its cluster).

The detailed formulae for CPCQ definitions are given below. We note that these formulae are not necessary to understand or implement CPC. In these formulae, a "pattern" is a representative MG itemset of an EC (rather than the EC itself).

The quality of a CP P of a cluster C is defined as $QC_C(P) = supp_C(P) \times \frac{|P_{max}|}{|P|}$. Item overlap and tuple overlap between two CPs P_1 and P_2 are respectively defined as $ovi(P_1, P_2) = |P_1 \cap P_2|$ and $ovt(P_1, P_2) = |\mathsf{mt}(P_1) \cap \mathsf{mt}(P_2)|$. Item overlap and tuple overlap among CPs in a set G of CPs are defined as $ovi(G) = avg\{ovi(P_1, P_2) \mid P_1, P_2 \in G, P_1 \neq P_2\}$ and $ovt(G) = avg\{ovt(P_1, P_2) \mid P_1, P_2 \in G, P_1 \neq P_2\}$. For a pair of groups G_1 and G_2, $ovi(G_1, G_2) = avg\{ovi(P_1, P_2) \mid P_1 \in G_1, P_2 \in G_2\}$.

The CPCQ quality of a cluster C w.r.t. a CP group G is defined as $QC_G(C) = \frac{\sum_{P \in G} QC_C(P)}{(1+ovt(G)) \times (1+ovi(G))}$. The CPCQ quality of C w.r.t. N CP groups $G_1, ..., G_N$ $(N \geq 1)$ is defined as $QC_{G_{1..N}}(C) = \frac{\sum_{i=1}^{N} QC_{G_i}(C)}{1+avg\{ovi(G_i, G_j)|1 \leq i < j \leq N\}}$.

Finally, the CPCQ of a clustering $\mathcal{C} = (C_1, ..., C_k)$ for a dataset D w.r.t. N groups $G_1^i, ..., G_N^i$ for cluster C_i, $1 \leq i \leq k$, is defined as $CPCQ(\mathcal{C}) = \frac{1}{|D|} \sum_{i=1}^{k} |C_i| \times QC_{G_{1..N}^i}(C_i)$. The CPCQ value of a clustering is determined by the best CP groups that can be found (often determined by greedy search), and N is set to 5 in our experiments.

14.4   CPC Design and Rationale

14.4.1   Overview

The CPC algorithm begins with the frequent patterns mined from a categorical dataset (to be clustered) and constructs a clustering with a high CPCQ value using the concepts of CP diversity, quality, and coherence. CPC does not directly use CPCQ. (Numerical data are first discretized.) The preliminary step, then, is to generate the frequent patterns; in our implementation, that was done using a frequent equivalence class miner [146] based on FP-growth [181].

Once frequent patterns are found, CPC uses a matching-data centric coherence measure to guide the clustering process. This coherence measure, termed *Mutual Pattern Quality* (MPQ), can be viewed as a distance function on a pair of patterns (rather than tuples). MPQ essentially measures the number (richness) and quality of *other* patterns that may become CPs when two tuple-diverse patterns become CPs of the same cluster. (Patterns are *tuple-diverse* if their matching datasets have very small overlap.) A high MPQ value indicates that the two patterns should belong to the same cluster, while a low value indicates they should belong to different clusters.

CPC constructs clusters in four main steps:

(1) Find weakly-related seed patterns (having low pairwise MPQ values) to initially define the clusters.

(2) Iteratively assign patterns to clusters based on high MPQ values between patterns and CPs already assigned to clusters. This builds one diversified CP group per cluster and ensures that many CPs exist for additional CP groups.

(3) Assign remaining patterns as CPs to clusters based on their tuple overlaps with the CP groups created in Step 2.

(4) Assign tuples to clusters based on the CPs they match.

Below, we provide the rationale, formulae, and algorithms.

14.4.2   MPQ

Mutual Patterns and Coherence: A *mutual pattern* of two patterns P_1 and P_2 is a pattern X distinct from P_1 and P_2 such that $\mathsf{mt}(X)$ intersects both $\mathsf{mt}(P_1)$ and $\mathsf{mt}(P_2)$. Below, we often use X to denote a mutual pattern.

Mutual patterns play a key role in determining clusters in CPC by creating *coherence* between diverse CPs. As noted in [276], a highly diverse set of CPs often exists in each cluster of a natural clustering (e.g. expert-defined classes). However, because diverse CPs share few items and tuples, neither the patterns themselves nor their matching datasets indicate coherence. Instead, we postulate that their coherence is reflected indirectly by the gain or loss of other CPs after reassigning one of the two CPs (and its matching dataset) to a different cluster. This important observation is key to our MPQ measure.

Consider a mutual pattern X sharing a significant number of tuples with two tuple-diverse CPs P_1 and P_2. Then, X is very likely to also be a CP if P_1 and P_2 belong to a common cluster. On the other hand, if P_1 and P_2 belong to separate clusters, then X cannot be a CP since it would share a significant number of tuples with two clusters. Figure 14.1 illustrates this; here, each box represents a CP, and the shaded areas represent clusters C_1 and C_2.

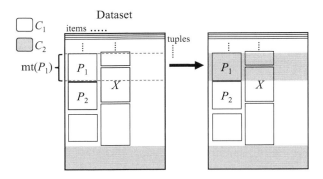

FIGURE 14.1: The mutual pattern X of P_1 and P_2 significantly overlaps $mt(P_1)$ and $mt(P_2)$. Left: P_1 and P_2 are made CPs of C_1, and X becomes a CP of C_1. Right: P_1 and P_2 are made CPs of different clusters, and X is not a high-quality CP of any cluster.

When a mutual pattern X relates to P_1 and P_2 in the manner described by the left panel of Figure 14.1, it is considered as providing significant coherence between P_1 and P_2, and we say that X "connects" P_1 and P_2.

Quality of Individual Mutual Patterns: The *mutual pattern quality* (MPQ) value for tuple-diverse patterns P_1 and P_2, denoted $MPQ(P_1, P_2)$, is defined as a normalized sum of certain weights given to their mutual patterns. The weight, or quality, of each mutual pattern is intended to capture the coherence it provides to P_1 and P_2. More specifically, each weight is intended to reflect the following: A mutual pattern X is strong in connecting P_1 and P_2 if a) assigning P_1 and P_2 to the same cluster causes X to be a CP of that cluster, and if b) assigning P_1 and P_2 to different clusters prevents X from being a CP of any cluster. Similarly, X is weak in connecting P_1 and P_2 if its status as a CP is independent of the cluster assignments of P_1 and P_2. To reflect the certainty of (a), the weight of X is increased if its support count outside of $mt(P_1) \cup mt(P_2)$ is low. To reflect the certainty of (b), the weight of X is increased if $mt(X) \cap mt(P_1)$ and $mt(X) \cap mt(P_2)$ are both large. [If X has high overlap with $mt(P_1)$ but low overlap with $mt(P_2)$, then assigning P_1 and P_2 to different clusters would not necessarily prevent X from being a CP; see Figure 14.2.] Finally, because X is a candidate CP, its weight also increases with its length ratio (a measure of CP quality).

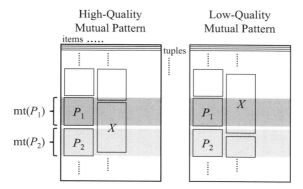

FIGURE 14.2: High-Quality and Low-Quality Mutual Patterns X. Left: X is a CP if, and only if, P_1 and P_2 are CPs belonging to a common cluster. Right: X's status as a CP is independent of P_1 and P_2.

Gross Mutual Pattern Quality: The summation of mutual pattern weights described above is termed *Gross Mutual Pattern Quality* (PQ2). Formally, PQ2 for patterns P_1 and P_2, denoted $PQ2(P_1, P_2)$, is defined as:

$$PQ2(P_1, P_2) = \sum_{X} \left(\frac{|\mathsf{mt}(P_1) \cap \mathsf{mt}(X)| * |\mathsf{mt}(P_2) \cap \mathsf{mt}(X)|}{|\mathsf{mt}(X)|} * \left(\frac{|X_{max}|}{\mathsf{mgLen}(X)|} \right)^2 \right)$$

Here, X is any pattern except P_1 or P_2, and tuple overlap between P_1 and P_2 is assumed to be very small. Notice that X's contribution to PQ2 reflects the properties described above, while X's highest possible contribution is proportional to its total support in the dataset (a factor of its CP quality).

Remark: Length ratio is squared in all CPC formulae only for empirical reasons. Experiments show that this improves results compared to using length ratio linearly or with other powers.

We similarly define PQ2 for a pattern P and pattern set PS, as

$$PQ2(P, PS) = \sum_{X} \left(\frac{|\mathsf{mt}(P) \cap \mathsf{mt}(X)| * |\mathsf{mt}(PS) \cap \mathsf{mt}(X)|}{|\mathsf{mt}(X)|} * \left(\frac{|X_{max}|}{\mathsf{mgLen}(X)} \right)^2 \right)$$

where X ranges over all patterns not in $PS \cup \{P\}$.

PQ2 Normalization: $PQ2(P_1, P_2)$ essentially measures the number and quality of mutual patterns connecting P_1 and P_2. However, the $PQ2(P_1, P_2)$ value alone is not meaningful because it does not reflect exclusivity. That is, $PQ2(P_1, P_2)$ does not consider the number and quality of patterns overlapping $\mathsf{mt}(P_1) \cup \mathsf{mt}(P_2)$ that are *not* mutual patterns of P_1 and P_2. Consider these two situations: *a*) the majority of the patterns overlapping $\mathsf{mt}(P_1) \cup \mathsf{mt}(P_2)$ do not contribute to $PQ2(P_1, P_2)$ and instead create alternate connections (i.e. they are mutual patterns of P_1 or P_2 and another pattern); *b*) most or all patterns overlapping $\mathsf{mt}(P_1) \cup \mathsf{mt}(P_2)$ are high-quality mutual patterns of P_1

and P_2. Clearly, we prefer case (b) if P_1 and P_2 are to belong to a common cluster (even if $PQ2(P_1, P_2)$ is smaller in case (b)). Therefore, PQ2 must be adjusted to distinguish between (a) and (b).

We adjust $PQ2(P_1, P_2)$ by normalizing it. To that end, we measure the number and quality of all patterns overlapping $\mathsf{mt}(P_i)$ for each i. This value, termed *Overlap-Weighted Pattern Quality* (PQ1), is defined for a pattern Q as a weighted sum of its overlapping patterns:

$$PQ1(Q) = \sum_P |\mathsf{mt}(P) \cap \mathsf{mt}(Q)| \left(\frac{|P_{max}|}{\mathsf{mgLen}(P)} \right)^2$$

In this formula, P ranges over all possible patterns; the weight given to P increases with its length ratio and its overlap with $\mathsf{mt}(Q)$, reflecting its potential to contribute to a PQ2 value of Q and another pattern. Now, a strong connection between P_1 and P_2 requires that the patterns contributing to $PQ2(P_1, P_2)$ represent a large portion of $PQ1(P_1)$ or $PQ1(P_2)$. We similarly define PQ1 for a set PS of patterns as

$$PQ1(PS) = \sum_P |\mathsf{mt}(P) \cap \mathsf{mt}(PS)| \left(\frac{|P_{max}|}{\mathsf{mgLen}(P)} \right)^2$$

MPQ Definition: We define the MPQ value for patterns P_1 and P_2 as

$$MPQ(P_1, P_2) = \frac{PQ2(P_1, P_2)}{PQ1(P_1) * PQ1(P_2)}$$

Again, tuple overlap between P_1 and P_2 is assumed to be very small (enforced by CPC). We similarly define MPQ for a pattern P and pattern set PS as

$$MPQ(P, PS) = \frac{PQ2(P, PS)}{PQ1(P) * PQ1(PS)}$$

Remarks: a) Notice that MPQ relies only on the length ratios and matching datasets of candidate CPs; the itemsets themselves are not used. b) PQ1 and PQ2 are defined in terms of support count, but we could equivalently define them in terms of support; this would only affect MPQ by a constant factor.

14.4.3 The CPC Algorithm

The CPC algorithm constructs clusters on the basis of patterns using the four steps outlined in Section 14.4.1 and illustrated in Figure 14.3. The four steps are described in detail below.

1. Find Seeds by MPQ Minimization: To initialize k clusters, we define a set of seed patterns as k patterns where the maximum MPQ value between pairs of patterns in the set is very low. Exhaustively searching each possible set is too expensive, so we use a heuristic. Roughly speaking, M seed sets

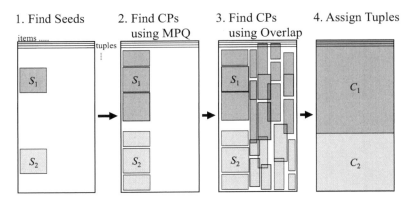

FIGURE 14.3: CPC steps.

are generated at random, the best N are selected for refinement, and the best refined set is returned. (If there is a tie, the set having the highest total support is chosen.) To refine a set, the seed pair responsible for its maximum MPQ value is targeted; a best replacement P is found for each of these two seeds (measured by P's maximum MPQ value with the other $k-1$ seeds), and the seed having the better improvement is replaced by its respective P. This refinement repeats until no improvement is found.

When generating candidate seed sets, we only consider patterns in the set $\{P \in PS \mid |\mathsf{mt}(P)| \geq medSC\}$, where $medSC$ is the median support count in the set PS of all frequent patterns in the dataset. Also, for distinct patterns P and Q of any candidate seed set, the tuple-overlap constraint $|\mathsf{mt}(P) \cap \mathsf{mt}(Q)| \leq threshold * min(|\mathsf{mt}(P)|, |\mathsf{mt}(Q)|)$ must hold.

The $medSC$ restriction balances the number of candidates with their minimum support, since a high value is desired for each. We use $threshold = 0.05/(k-1)$ so that the total overlap between any seed P and the other $k-1$ seeds cannot exceed 5% of $|\mathsf{mt}(P)|$. The values for M and N can be adjusted to compromise between speed and seed quality. We use $M = max\{10^5, 2000/minS\}$, where $minS$ is the minimum support (fraction, not count) in PS, and $N = max\{5, 250 * minS, 5 * 10^5/|PS| - 20\}$.

2. Assign Patterns by MPQ Maximization: Following step 1, each seed pattern is added to the (initially empty) CP group G of a unique cluster C_i, denoted $G(C_i)$. Step 2 adds strongly-related patterns P to CP groups $G(C_1),...,G(C_k)$ by repeatedly searching for the $(P, G(C_i))$ pair that maximizes $MPQ(P, G(C_i))$ and adding P to $G(C_i)$. As said above, only patterns P for which $|\mathsf{mt}(P) \cap \mathsf{mt}(G(C_i))|$ is small (our implementation uses $threshold = 0.05/(k-1)$) are candidates in this step. Patterns are added until no such candidate pattern exists. Pseudocode is shown in Figure 14.4.

3. Assign Patterns by PCM Maximization: After step 2, MPQ can no longer be used to assign patterns to clusters, since no patterns meet the small-

Input: k: the number of clusters; PS: the set of mined patterns;
$P_{S1}, ..., P_{Sk}$: seed patterns for the clusters (returned by step 1)
Output: $G(C_1), ..., G(C_k)$: k CP groups representing k clusters
Method:
1: FOR $i = 1$ to k, let $G(C_i) = \{P_{Si}\}$; // initialize each $G(C)$
2: REPEAT
3:    Let PS_{cand} be the set of patterns P in PS satisfying
        $|\mathsf{mt}(P) \cap \mathsf{mt}(G(C_i))| \le$
            $threshold * min\left(|\mathsf{mt}(P)|, |\mathsf{mt}(G(C_i))|\right)$ for $1 \le i \le k$;
4:    IF $(PS_{cand} = \emptyset)$ THEN BREAK;
5:    Let P_{best} be the pattern in PS maximizing $MPQ(P, G(C))$,
        and let C_{best} be the C for which that maximum occurred;
6:    IF ($MPQ(P_{best}, C_{best}) > 0$ AND C_{best} is unique) THEN
7:        $G(C_{best}) = G(C_{best}) \cup \{P_{best}\}$;
8:    ELSE BREAK;
9: END REPEAT;
10: RETURN $G(C_1), ..., G(C_k)$;

FIGURE 14.4: *CPC* step 2 pseudocode.

tuple-overlap constraint. However, the vast majority of potential CPs have not been assigned. Moreover, the CP groups created in step 2 are unlikely to cover the entire dataset under consideration. Step 3 therefore assigns patterns based on their tuple overlaps with each CP group. Together with the CPs already assigned, these CPs typically cover the entire dataset and allow each tuple's cluster membership to be determined.

Each remaining pattern is assigned to a cluster according to its maximum *Pattern-Cluster Membership* (PCM) value among all clusters. (Although many of these patterns may be poor CPs, their qualities will be quantified in step 4.) The PCM value for a pattern P with respect to a cluster C, denoted $PCM(P, C)$, is defined as the fraction of $PQ1(G(C))$ represented by P:

$$PCM(P, C) = \frac{|\mathsf{mt}(P) \cap \mathsf{mt}(G(C))|}{PQ1(G(C))}$$

(P's length ratio is unnecessary since it is a constant in P's PCM values for all clusters.) Conceptually, $PCM(P, C)$ measures the fraction of C's pattern-based description represented by P, or P's "prevalence" in C. For example, if a cluster C_1 is described by many patterns while a cluster C_2 is described by very few, then a pattern with equal supports in C_1 and C_2 would be assigned to C_2 since it is more prevalent in C_2 (and similarly if C_1 is described by n high-quality patterns while C_2 is described by n low-quality patterns).

This step creates a complete CP set for each cluster C, denoted $PS(C)$. The union of these sets contains all frequent patterns except those whose maximum PCM values occur at two or more clusters. $G(C)$ remains unchanged in this step (i.e. $PS(C) \supset G(C)$), so patterns can be considered in any order.

Note: If PCM values are used outside the CPC algorithm (e.g. for analysis), then $PCM(P, C)$ must be multiplied by $(|P_{max}|/\mathsf{mgLen}(P))^2$ for correctness.

4. Assign Tuples to Clusters: Once frequent patterns are assigned to clusters as CPs, tuples t of the dataset can be assigned to clusters. This is done based on each CP P's *vote* for t's membership in cluster C. The vote, denoted $vote(P)$, reflects P's quality (measured by length ratio), P's prevalence in C (measured by PCM), and P's exclusivity to C. P's exclusivity to C is maximized if it belongs only to C, and minimized if it is nearly equally prevalent in another cluster. These qualities are captured in formula by:

$$vote(P) = \frac{PCM(P, C_{1st}) - PCM(P, C_{2nd})}{\sum_{i=1}^{k} PCM(P, C_i)} * \left(\frac{|P_{max}|}{\mathsf{mgLen}(P)} \right)^2$$

Here, C_{1st} and C_{2nd} denote the two clusters respectively associated with P's highest and second-highest PCM values. By normalizing the PCM difference value, we also take into consideration P's PCM values in other clusters.

Summing votes of all patterns for a single cluster C, we get t's *Tuple-Cluster Membership* (TCM) value for C:

$$TCM(t, C) = \sum_{P} \{ vote(P) \mid P \in PS(C) \wedge t \in \mathsf{mt}(P) \}$$

A tuple t is assigned to the cluster C that maximizes $TCM(t, C)$. [If t's highest TCM value is attained at multiple clusters, it can be assigned later by another method (e.g. a classification algorithm).]

14.4.4   CPC Illustration

The simple dataset SynD below (Table 14.1) is clustered using CPC. Given a minimum support count of 2, there are 15 patterns, each identified by a singleton MG itemset composed of one of the 15 items: {a1}, {a2}, ..., {d3}. We can see that the listed clustering is the best for two clusters since any other clustering $\{C_1, C_2\}$ would significantly increase the number of patterns shared between C_1 and C_2. Notice that 7 CPs exist in each cluster (only {d2} is not a CP), and each CP acts as a mutual pattern connecting other diverse CPs in its cluster (e.g. {b2} connects {a1} and {a2}, etc.).

CPC constructs C_1 and C_2 using the following four steps:

1) Find Seeds by MPQ Minimization: Several candidate seed sets exist which are not connected by mutual patterns, giving each a maximum MPQ value of zero. Of these sets, {{d1},{d3}} has the highest aggregate support in SynD, so {d1} is assigned to $G(C_1)$, and {d3} is assigned to $G(C_2)$.

2) Assign Patterns by MPQ Maximization: Only {d2} meets the small-tuple-overlap constraint with respect to $G(C_1)$ and $G(C_2)$. Since {d2} has equal MPQ values with $G(C_1)$ and $G(C_2)$, it is not assigned to any cluster.

TABLE 14.1: SynD and its CPC Clustering

Tuple ID	A1	A2	A3	A4	Cluster ID
t_1	a1	b1	c1	d1	C_1
t_2	a1	b2	c2	d1	C_1
t_3	a2	b2	c1	d1	C_1
t_4	a2	b1	c2	d2	C_1
t_5	a3	b3	c3	d2	C_2
t_6	a3	b4	c4	d3	C_2
t_7	a4	b4	c3	d3	C_2
t_8	a4	b3	c4	d3	C_2

3) Assign Patterns by PCM Maximization: Patterns {a1}, {a2}, {b1}, {b2}, {c1}, {c2}, and {d1} are added to $PS(C_1)$, since each overlaps $\mathsf{mt}(G(C_1))$ but not $\mathsf{mt}(G(C_2))$ (so their PCM values are positive only for C_1). Similarly, patterns {a3}, {a4}, {b3}, {b4}, {c3}, {c4}, and {d3} are added to $PS(C_2)$. The only remaining pattern, {d2}, overlaps neither CP group, so it is not assigned.

4) Assign Tuples by TCM Maximization: Since tuples t_1-t_4 only match patterns in $PS(C_1)$, $TCM(t_i, C_1) > TCM(t_i, C_2) = 0$ for $1 \leq i \leq 4$, and they are assigned to C_1. Similarly, tuples t_5-t_8 are assigned to C_2.

14.4.5 Optimization and Implementation Details

MPQ Evaluation: Repeatedly evaluating MPQ can be computationally expensive, so we precompute and store $|\mathsf{mt}(P_1) \cap \mathsf{mt}(P_2)|$ for each pattern pair (P_1, P_2), and $PQ1(P)$ for each pattern P. These values can be directly used in $MPQ(P_1, P_2)$. To make use of these precomputed values when evaluating $MPQ(P, PS)$ for a pattern set PS, we note that the following formula is equal to $MPQ(P, PS)$ when $\bigcap \{\mathsf{mt}(P_i) \mid P_i \in PS\} = \emptyset$ (a close approximation when evaluating $MPQ(P, PS)$ in CPC):

$$MPQ(P, PS) \approx \frac{\sum \{MPQ(P, P_i) * PQ1(P_i) \mid P_i \in PS\}}{\sum \{PQ1(P_i) \mid P_i \in PS\}}$$

In our tests, this approximation rarely deviated from $MPQ(P, PS)$ (and never deviated by more than 0.5%) and did not result in different clusterings. Given k clusters $C_1, ..., C_k$, each represented by a CP group $G(C_i)$, this approximation allows $MPQ(P, G(C_i))$ to be stored for each (P, C_i) pair and incrementally updated as necessary by computing only $MPQ(P, P_{last})$, where P_{last} is the pattern last added to $G(C_i)$. Together, these optimizations significantly reduce execution time, often by two orders of magnitude in our tests.

Reducing the Number of Frequent Patterns: By enforcing a minimum length ratio (related to intrinsic pattern qualities), the number of frequent patterns can be reduced, leading to substantially reduced memory use and execution time. This is preferred to increasing the minimum support threshold because the former typically has a much smaller impact on the computed clustering's quality value.

Given a value $maxP$ for the maximum allowable number of patterns, CPC finds the highest length ratio threshold that $maxP$ patterns meet, and all patterns with lower length ratios are deleted. Then, among the remaining patterns, those with the lowest length ratio are randomly deleted until only $maxP$ remain. Experiments show that this method reduces the number of patterns without a significant impact on the clustering's quality value.

Finally, we note that the majority of computations needed by each step of CPC are independent and could be done in parallel.

14.5   Experimental Evaluation

We evaluated CPC based on its CPCQ scores as well as its ability to recover expert-given classes (measured by F-score). Below, we show results for two categorical and one numerical datasets, all from the UCI Repository [23] and chosen to represent a variety of domains. [We also considered Mushroom (categorical), Breast Cancer Wisconsin Diagnostic (numerical), and Statlog Heart (mixed-type), also from UCI; the results are omitted here to save space.] Four other clustering algorithms were used for comparison. Additionally, we show CPC's results for the BlogCatalog dataset [457] to demonstrate CPC's potential for text/document clustering and to show the descriptiveness of its CPs.

To adapt CPC and CPCQ to numerical data, we used equi-density binning with 10 bins per attribute. Other clustering algorithms used the original data, if they were designed for numerical data.

In each results table, clusterings are ranked by their F-scores with respect to the expert-given classes (called the "expert clustering"). In all six datasets from UCI, CPC achieved the highest F-score, while in four of those six datasets, CPC achieved the highest CPCQ score.

14.5.1   Datasets and Clustering Algorithms

The two categorical datasets are SPECT Heart (T=267, A=22, C=2) ('T' for #tuples, 'A' for #attributes, and 'C' for #classes) and Molecular Biology Splice-junction Gene Sequences (T=3190, A=60, C=3). The numerical dataset is Ionosphere (T=351, A=34, C=2).

The four clustering algorithms used for comparison are EM, sIB, CLOPE, and Simple K-means. EM, sIB, and CLOPE (described earlier) require no distance function. Simple K-means, which uses a distance function, is included for its popularity. We used WEKA's implementation of the algorithms [176].

Remark: Although implementations of ROCK, LargeItem, COOLCAT, and LIMBO were unavailable, they are represented by algorithms based on the same principles (ROCK and LargeItem are similar to CLOPE; COOLCAT and LIMBO are similar to sIB).

WEKA's EM implementation initializes its parameters based on the best of 10 runs of Simple K-means, and it handles categorical attributes using a symbol-count based probability estimator. It takes four parameters: number of iterations (default: 100), minimum standard deviation (default: 10^{-6}), number of clusters (k), and a random number seed (s) to initialize centroids.

WEKA's Simple K-means implementation uses the Euclidean distance function by default, which amounts to the Hamming distance for categorical attributes. Cluster centroids are defined by modes for categorical data. It takes four parameters: distance function, maximum number of iterations (default: 500), number of clusters (k), and a random number seed (s).

WEKA's sIB only accepts numerical datasets. It takes six parameters, controlling: maximum number of iterations (default: 100), minimum change in tuple assignments (default: 0), number of clusters (k), number of restarts (default: 5), and a random number seed (s) for an initial clustering.

WEKA's CLOPE implementation only accepts categorical datasets. It takes one parameter: repulsion (r).

14.5.2   CPC Parameters

Our CPC implementation takes three parameters: minimum support threshold ($minS$), number of clusters (k), and maximum number of patterns to consider ($maxP$). Since CPC begins by mining frequent patterns, a $minS$ value must be specified. The $maxP$ parameter is optional (for speed).

Recommended Settings: For categorical datasets, we generally recommend $minS$ values ≤ 0.08 unless the resulting minimum support count is < 15. For numerical and mixed-type datasets (with each attribute discretized to 10 equidensity bins), we recommend $minS$ values ≤ 0.01, regardless of the minimum support count. (Smaller $minS$ values allow smaller clusters to be discovered.)

Typically, CPC's clustering quality is fairly trendless within the $minS$ limits above. However, $minS$- and/or $maxP$-dependent trends may exist (e.g. in the SPECT Heart dataset, discussed later). Therefore, we recommend trying many $minS$ and $maxP$ values and keeping the highest-CPCQ clustering.

14.5.3   Experiment Settings

For all algorithms, k was set to the number of expert-given classes (CLOPE's r parameter was set to produce k clusters). For EM, sIB, and Simple K-Means, we used $s = \{1, 2, 3\}$. For each dataset, only the best F-score for each of the other algorithms is shown. All other parameters were set to WEKA's default values, unless higher F-scores were found using different values. (The default values resulted in the highest F-scores in all cases shown.)

For CPC with categorical datasets, we chose the three lowest $minS$ values (to the nearest 0.01) meeting our recommendations above and such that $\leq$2GB memory was required to precompute tuple overlap. When this was not possible, $maxP$ was used to reduce memory use. For numerical and mixed-type datasets, we used $minS = \{0.01, 0.0075, 0.005\}$, and again used $maxP$ whenever >2GB memory was needed to precompute tuple overlap.

For CPCQ, the minimum support threshold ($minS$) was set to a reasonable value based on the dataset type/size (as above) and on the resulting number of frequent patterns ($\geq$10,000 patterns are desired); the maximum number of CP groups to build was set to 5; the $nDelta$ parameter for a CP's maximum allowable support count outside its home cluster was set as 10% of the minimum support count.

14.5.4   Categorical Datasets

Splice-Junction Gene Sequences Dataset: Results are shown in Table 14.2. CPC achieved significantly higher F-scores than all other algorithms. Although CLOPE ($r = 0.9$) achieved the highest CPCQ score, one of its three clusters was very small (containing <0.5% of the dataset), effectively making it a high-CPCQ clustering for $k = 2$.

TABLE 14.2:   Splice-Junction Sequences: F-scores vs CPCQ scores

Clustering	F-score	CPCQ score $minS = 0.02, nDelta = 6$
Expert	1.000	0.517
CPC: $minS = 0.06$	0.928	0.655
CPC: $minS = 0.05$	0.903	0.634
CPC: $minS = 0.07$	0.887	0.580
EM: $s = 1, 2, 3$	0.735	0.216
CLOPE: $r = 0.9$	0.618	1.470
K-Means: $s = 3$	0.428	0.203

SPECT Heart Dataset: This dataset contains preprocessed SPECT image data. Results are shown in Table 14.3. In this dataset, every $minS$ value meeting our recommendations results in $>5 * 10^5$ patterns, requiring >200GB memory to precompute tuple overlap. We therefore sought an optimal $maxP$ value by gradually increasing $maxP$ from 5,000 to 35,000 for a single $minS$ value (we chose 0.07), and the $maxP$ value resulting in a local maximum in CPCQ scores was chosen: 15,000. All CPC results below used this value. Despite deleting a large number (>97%) of patterns, CPC achieved the highest F-scores and highest two CPCQ scores.

In a previous study on this dataset [224], the CLIP3 supervised learning algorithm generated rules that were 84% accurate. In comparison, CPC's highest accuracy is 83%, which is remarkable since CPC is unsupervised.

TABLE 14.3: SPECT Heart: F-scores vs CPCQ scores

Clustering	F-score	CPCQ score: $minS = 0.06, nDelta = 1$
Expert	1.000	1.52
CPC: $minS = 0.07$	0.831	2.79
CPC: $minS = 0.08$	0.829	2.47
CPC: $minS = 0.06$	0.801	2.80
K-Means: $s = 2$	0.661	2.67
EM: $s = 1, 2, 3$	0.652	2.01
CLOPE: $r = 2$	0.612	2.56

14.5.5 Numerical Dataset

As said above, we used $minS = \{0.01, 0.0075, 0.005\}$ for CPC with numerical/mixed-type datasets. In some cases, precomputing tuple overlap required >2GB memory, so the $maxP$ parameter was used. For all such cases, we found no trend in CPCQ scores for a range of $maxP$ values, so we chose a reasonably high $maxP$ of 35,000 to limit CPC's memory use.

Ionosphere Dataset: Results are shown in Table 14.4. CPC achieved the highest F-scores here by a significant margin, as well as the highest two CPCQ scores.

TABLE 14.4: Ionosphere: F-scores vs CPCQ scores

Clustering	F-score	CPCQ score: $minS = 0.03, nDelta = 1$
Expert	1.000	43.20
CPC: $minS = 0.005, maxP = 35k$	0.898	42.00
CPC: $minS = 0.0075, maxP = 35k$	0.851	8.53
CPC: $minS = 0.01, maxP = 35k$	0.839	42.80
EM: $s = 1, 2, 3$	0.754	8.03
K-Means: $s = 1, 2, 3$	0.709	8.76
sIB: $s = 1, 2, 3$	0.690	10.64

14.5.6 Document Clustering

The results shown in Table 14.5 demonstrate CPC's potential to serve as a document clustering algorithm. We selected four categories (sets of we-blogs), namely health, music, sports, and business, from the BlogCatalog [457] dataset, merged the categories as shown in row 1 of Table 14.5, and clustered the merged data using CPC (with k set to the number of merged categories). Data was preprocessed by removing duplicate weblogs, removing stopwords, and stemming; words were treated as items. CPCQ scores used $minS = 0.01$, 5 CP groups, and $nDelta$ set to 10% of the minimum support count. As with attribute-based datasets, high CPCQ scores tend to coincide with high F-scores, allowing CPCQ to be used in selecting a best CPC-clustering.

TABLE 14.5:   BlogCatalog: F-scores vs CPCQ scores

	health, music		sports, business		health, music sports, business	
$minS =$	F-score	CPCQ	F-score	CPCQ	F-score	CPCQ
0.03	0.890	3.28	0.846	0.625	0.757	0.456
0.02	0.893	11.40	0.830	0.650	0.772	0.411
0.01	0.897	12.00	0.828	0.690	0.710	0.366

CP-based Cluster Descriptions: As said in the introduction, the clusters created by CPC can be described by small sets of CPs. We show these sets in Table 14.6 for the $k = 4, minS = 0.03$ clustering. We used CPCQ to return these sets, and we show the first two CP groups G_1 and G_2.

TABLE 14.6:   Example Cluster Descriptions

	Cluster 1	Cluster 2	Cluster 3	Cluster 4
G_1	{busi, market}	{band, song}	{symptom}	{team, game}
G_2	{monei, internet}	{love, song}	{peopl, disea}	{season, game}

Based only on these cluster descriptions, one can easily estimate the themes of clusters 1-4 to be business, music, health, and sports. Notice that the themes are made clearer by multi-item patterns (e.g. "season" or "game" alone may not indicate a sports theme, but together they do). Such succinct descriptions are useful when the data does not come with category names.

14.5.7   CPC Execution Time and Memory Use

CPC's execution time depends mostly on the numbers of patterns (p) and tuples (n). Since precomputing tuple overlap (the potentially longest-running step) requires an n-size tuple-set intersection for each pair of patterns, CPC has $O(n * p^2)$ time complexity. Figure 14.5 (left scale) shows CPC's actual execution time on the Mushroom dataset (from UCI, with 8124 tuples and 22 attributes) with $minS = 0.01$ and $maxP$ increasing from 5,000 to 35,000. The tests were run using a 2.4GHz Intel Core 2 Duo processor (without multiple threading or SIMD operations). The times shown include frequent pattern mining, precomputing tuple overlap, and clustering.

Memory use also mostly depends on p and n. Storing a precomputed tuple-overlap value for each pattern pair and a bit-set representing each pattern's tuple set, gives CPC a $O(p^2 + p * n)$ space complexity. Actual memory use under the same conditions as above is shown in Figure 14.5 (right scale). For $maxP \leq 15,000$, CPC required less memory than the frequent pattern miner.

If tuple overlap is not precomputed, then CPC has $O(p * n)$ space complexity (typically using less memory than the frequent pattern miner), but this causes execution times to be roughly 50 times higher.

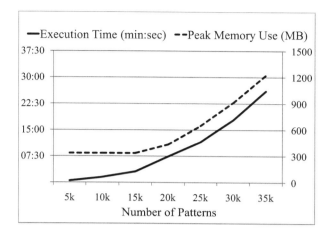

FIGURE 14.5: CPC Execution Time and Peak Memory Use.

14.5.8 Effect of Pattern Limit on Clustering Quality

Here, we use the SPECT Heart and Mushroom datasets to show $maxP$'s effect on F-scores and CPCQ scores (see Figure 14.6). For Mushroom, we used the same tests as above. The trend shows no significant change in either score as $maxP$ is decreased. For SPECT Heart, $minS$ was fixed at 0.07 while $maxP$ was varied. In this case, local maxima in both CPCQ and F-scores occur at $maxP = 15,000$. In both datasets, $maxP$ was reduced to well below the original number of patterns without adversely affecting clustering quality.

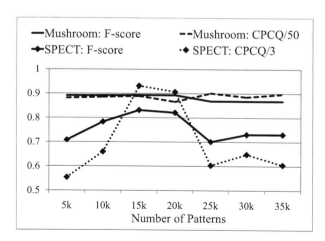

FIGURE 14.6: Effect of $maxP$ on F-score and CPCQ score.

14.6   Discussion and Future Work

14.6.1   Alternate MPQ Definition

Conceptually, an MPQ value is high if the mutual patterns of its arguments are prevalent in each argument's matching dataset and not prevalent elsewhere. Below, we give an alternate MPQ definition to match this description. We first generalize PCM's definition to be in terms of a pattern P and any tuple set TS:

$$PCM(P, TS) = \frac{|\mathsf{mt}(P) \cap TS| \left(\frac{|P_{max}|}{\mathsf{mgLen}(P)} \right)^2}{PQ1(TS)}$$

(The term "Pattern-Cluster Membership" is now a misnomer since TS is not necessarily a cluster.) Here, $PQ1(TS)$ is defined similarly to $PQ1(P)$:

$$PQ1(TS) = \sum_P |\mathsf{mt}(P) \cap TS| \left(\frac{|P_{max}|}{\mathsf{mgLen}(P)} \right)^2$$

Like $PCM(P, C)$, $PCM(P, TS)$ represents the fraction of TS's pattern-based description represented by P (i.e., P's prevalence in TS). We can now give the alternate definition of $MPQ(P_1, P_2)$:

$$MPQ(P_1, P_2) = \sum_X \frac{PCM(X, \mathsf{mt}(P_1)) * PCM(X, \mathsf{mt}(P_2))}{PCM(X, D)}$$

where $X \notin \{P_1, P_2\}$ and D is the set of all tuples in the dataset. This MPQ definition matches our description above and only differs from our original definition by a factor of $PQ1(D)$ (a constant), making them equivalent.

14.6.2   Future Work

Potential for improvements to CPC exists in several directions: (a) CPC relies on a frequent pattern miner, which may be less memory-efficient than the main part of CPC. Therefore, CPC may benefit from a more efficient frequent pattern miner (perhaps tailored for CPC). (b) CPC currently does not consider the item diversity between patterns. Properly doing so may improve results. (c) Step 1 of CPC relies on random sampling to produce an initial seed set. Better seeding algorithms may be possible. (d) Step 2 of CPC continues until no patterns meet the small-tuple-overlap constraint. Since the candidate pool shrinks after each CP is assigned, so does the likelihood that the best candidate is a good CP. A smarter stopping condition could improve results. (e) To adapt CPC to numerical data, we used only equi-density binning. Better methods may be possible. (f) Use CPC to extract useful knowledge from CPC clusterings based on their CPs and MPQ, PCM, vote, and TCM values.

Part V

Contrast Mining for Bioinformatics and Chemoinformatics

Chapter 15

Emerging Pattern Based Rules Characterizing Subtypes of Leukemia

Jinyan Li

Advanced Analytics Institute, University of Technology, Sydney

Limsoon Wong

School of Computing, National University of Singapore

15.1 Introduction

Simple rules are preferable to non-linear distance or kernel functions for classifying gene expression profiles or other types of medical data. This is because rules help us understand more about the application, in addition to performing an accurate classification. In this chapter, we use emerging pattern (EP) mining algorithms to discover some novel rules that describe the gene expression profiles of more than six subtypes of childhood acute lymphoblastic leukemia (ALL) patients. We also describe an EP-based classifier, named PCL, to make effective use of these rules for the subtype classification of leukemia patients. PCL is very accurate in this application, handling multiple parallel classifications as well. This method is evaluated on 327 heterogeneous ALL samples. Its test error rate is competitive to that of support vector machines. It is 71% better than C4.5, 50% better than Naive Bayes, and 43% better than the k-nearest neighbor classifier. Experimental results on another independent dataset are also presented to show the strength of PCL. This chapter is adapted from Ref. [248], ©2003, with permission from Oxford University Press.

15.2   Motivation and Overview of PCL

Childhood ALL is a heterogeneous disease of many subtypes. Since different subtypes of the disease respond differently to the same therapy, it is important to customize treatments for patients using risk-based stratification. The problem of accurate subtype classification and outcome prediction in childhood ALL has been studied previously [449] using microarray gene expression profiling and supervised machine learning algorithms. We use the same dataset from [449], but we report novel rules that describe the expression profiles of more than six subtypes of 327 childhood ALL samples. We also describe a different EP-based classification method that makes use of the discriminating power of the discovered rules for accurate classification.

Classification and rule induction are two closely related but different aspects of supervised learning problems. Classification can be done with high accuracy by high-dimensional non-linear models like neural networks and support vector machines, but it it is hard for these models to provide rules. An ideal learning model should be accurate and, at the same time, can induce valid, novel, and useful rules, because such rules help us gain a deep understanding of the problem at hand.

The classifier presented in this chapter, named PCL (which is short for *Prediction by Collective Likelihoods*), has the desirable attributes discussed above. PCL is accurate, can handle multiple parallel classifications, and can provide valid and useful rules.

PCL is based on the concept of *emerging patterns* [118]. An emerging pattern (EP) is, in the context of this chapter, a conjunction pattern of expression intervals of multiple genes, whose *frequency* increases significantly from one class of data to another class of data. For example, if a pattern has 10% frequency in one class and 0.1% frequency in another class, then it is an emerging pattern with a 100-fold frequency change between the two classes. These emerging patterns are:

(a) *useful* because they can provide reliable rules for predicting classes,

(b) *understandable* because they are conjunction of simple single-attribute conditions, and

(c) *non-obvious* because they involve correlations of multiple features.

Additionally, the validity of these patterns can be conveniently assessed by cross validations and blinded samples. In this chapter, we focus on a special type of emerging patterns: those with *zero* frequency in one class but high frequency in another class. These patterns are naturally more interesting because they have an infinite frequency change rate.

With the discovery of emerging patterns, PCL proceeds to calculate a classification score for every class when a test sample is presented. Then, the class with the highest score is predicted as the class of the test sample. The classification scores are calculated by aggregating the frequencies of multiple top-ranked EPs, as the "committee" of patterns and their collective discriminating power show strong synergistic strength in the classification.

In one of our previous work [253], we have used the concept of emerging patterns to discover diagnostic gene groups from a colon tumor dataset [9] and a leukemia dataset [166]. The colon data set contains 62 samples divided into two classes, and the leukemia data set consists of 38 training and 34 test samples with two classes as well. Here, we would like to see the effectiveness of emerging patterns when applied to large datasets—the data used in this chapter have hundreds of samples with multiple classes.

15.3 Data Used in the Study

The data used is available at http://www.stjuderesearch.org/data/ALL1. The data consist of gene expression profiles of 327 childhood ALL samples [449]. These profiles were obtained by hydridization on the Affymetrix U95A GeneChip containing probes for 12558 genes. The samples cover all of the known childhood ALL subtypes, including T-cell (T-ALL), E2A-PBX1, TEL-AML1, MLL, BCR-ABL, and hyperdiploid (Hyperdip>50). The data were divided into a *training set* of 215 samples and a blind *testing set* of 112 samples [449]. There are 28, 18, 52, 9, 14, and 42 training instances and 15, 9, 27, 6, 6, and 22 test samples respectively for T-ALL, E2A-PBX1, TEL-AML1, BCR-ABL, MLL, and Hyperdip>50. There are also 52 training and 27 test samples of other miscellaneous subtypes named OTHERS here.

15.4   Discovery of Emerging Patterns

In this study the discovery of emerging patterns from the training data takes a two-step process [253]. First, a small number of discriminatory genes are selected from the 12558 genes. Second, emerging patterns are discovered by border-based algorithms [118, 249] from the selected genes' data.

15.4.1   Step 1: Gene Selection and Discretization

An entropy-based discretization method [145] can select important features for accurate classification. This method can be used to automatically remove about 90-95% of the whole feature space as many of the features exhibit random expression distributions. It can also automatically detect "ideal discriminatory genes" that contain clear expression boundaries separating two classes of cells.

Single genes whose expressions have a clear two-ended distribution, where only data from one class appear in each of the two ends, are very useful for classification. We found five such ideal discriminatory genes (Table 15.1) from the training data pair: E2A-PBX1 versus all other subtypes of ALL. As an example, the expression *cut point* of gene 32063_at^1 is 4068.7. This cut point partitions the expression range of this gene over all of the training samples into two intervals $[0, 4068.7)$ and $[4068.7, +\infty)$. Moreover, the expression values of this gene in all of the E2A-PBX1 samples (cells) are ≥ 4068.7, falling into the right interval, while its expression values in samples of any other subtypes are < 4068.7, falling into the left interval. Note that the above rule is valid with respect to the 215 training samples without any exception. This rule is also 100% valid when applied to the reserved 112 testing samples (see Table 15.1).

However, the other genes' expression does not exhibit such a two-ended distribution. In contrast, about 11840 genes (94.28% of all genes) have a random expression distribution without any interval covering a sufficient percentage of E2A-PBX1 or other subtypes of samples. Obviously, these genes are not very relevant for classifying E2A-PBX1 from other subtypes, and they are excluded from our consideration.

The remaining 713 genes are sub-optimal in classification. Their expressions are not randomly distributed, but they are not ideally polarized either (there is no cut point such that each of the resulting two intervals contains only cells of one class). We list 5 of them in Table 15.2.

The entropy-based discretization method [145] can find the "best" cut points for every feature and, it can also identify the ideal discriminatory features, sub-optimal features, and those genes with random expression distributions. Applied to our dataset, this feature selection method ignores most of

---

[1]This is actually the probe id of a gene on the microarray. Here, abusing notation slightly, we use the term gene instead of probe id.

TABLE 15.1: Five ideal discriminatory genes discovered from the training data for differentiating E2A-PBX1 (denoted by C1) from all other subtypes (denoted by C2). The expression cut points can separate C1 and C2 samples clearly. The expression distribution of the test data are shown in parenthesis. Source: Reprinted from Ref. [248], ©2003, with permission from Oxford University Press.

Probes	# of samples in the left interval $[0, x)$ C1 : C2	expression cut point (x)	# of samples in the right interval $[x, : \infty)$ C1 : C2
32063_at	0 : 197 (0 : 103, test)	4068.7	18 : 0 (9 : 0, test)
41146_at	0 : 197 (1 : 102, test)	25842.15	18 : 0 (8 : 1, test)
33355_at	0 : 197 (0 : 103, test)	10966	18 : 0 (9 : 0, test)
1287_at	0 : 197 (1 : 103, test)	34313.9	18 : 0 (8 : 0, test)
430_at	0 : 197 (0 : 101, test)	30246.05	18 : 0 (9 : 2, test)

TABLE 15.2: Five sub-optimal genes which cannot individually differentiate E2A-PBX1 from other subtypes clearly, but their combinations can. C1: E2A-PBX1, C2: other subtypes. Source: Reprinted from Ref. [248], ©2003, with permission from Oxford University Press.

Probes	# of samples in the left interval $[0, x)$ C1 : C2	cut points (x)	# of samples in the right interval $[x, +\infty)$ C1 : C2
40454_at	0 : 187 (0 : 96, test)	8280.25	18 : 10 (9 : 7, test)
41425_at	0 : 183 (0 : 93, test)	6821.75	18 : 14 (9 : 10, test)
753_at	2 : 197 (6 : 102, test)	7106.35	16 : 0 (3 : 1, test)
35974_at	0 : 189 (0 : 99, test)	43730.15	18 : 8 (9 : 4, test)
37493_at	1 : 189 (0 : 95, test)	4543.55	17 : 8 (9 : 8, test)

the 12558 genes. Only about 1000 genes are considered useful in classification. This 10% selection rate provides a much easier basis to derive important classification rules. However, to manually examine 1000 or so genes is still tedious. We then use the *Chi-Squared* ($\mathcal{X}^2$) method [275, 433] to further narrow down to the important genes. Here, if there exist ideal discriminatory genes for a pair of training datasets, then we use those ideal genes for deriving emerging patterns. Otherwise we use 20 top-ranked genes by the $\mathcal{X}^2$ method.

15.4.2　Step 2: Discovering EPs

As discussed, there exist only a small number of genes (e.g., those discussed in Table 15.1) that can each act as an arbitrator by itself alone to clearly distinguish the expression from one subtype to others. However, we found many gene combinations (gene groups) which can be used to separate clearly one subtype from others. For example, an ideal multi-gene discriminator can be obtained if the gene 40454_at and the gene 41425_at (shown in Table 15.2) are combined into a group. The rule is interpreted as:

If the expression of 40454_at is $\geq$ 8280.25 and that of 41425_at is $\geq$ 6821.75, then the sample is an E2A-PBX1. Otherwise it belongs to another subtype.

This rule can be denoted as a *set* with two conditions on the two genes [253]:

$$\{40454\_at@[8280.25, +\infty), 41425\_at@[6821.75, +\infty)\}.$$

Such patterns are real examples of *emerging patterns* [118]. They are also a special type of emerging pattern known as jumping emerging patterns. As 100% of the E2A-PBX1 training samples satisfy these two conditions, we say the pattern's *frequency* in the E2A-PBX1 class is 100%. As an ideal discriminator, the pattern's frequency in the other subtypes is 0%. That is, no samples from any other subtypes satisfy these two conditions.

We use border-based algorithms [118, 249] to discover EPs.

15.5   Deriving Rules from Tree-Structured Leukemia Datasets

A tree-structured decision system was used to classify the childhood ALL samples, as shown in Figure 19 in Supplementary Information of [449] (http://www.stjuderesearch.org/data/ALL1). By using this tree, a sample is first tested to be either a T-ALL or a sample of other subtypes. If it is classified as T-ALL, then the process is terminated. Otherwise, the process is moved to level 2 to see whether the sample can be classified as E2A-PBX1 or the *remaining* other subtypes. Similarly, the system can determine whether the test sample is one of TEL-AML1, BCR-ABL, MLL, Hyperdip>50, or OTHERS.

In correspondence with this hierarchical decision system, six pairs of training and test subsets, one for each level of the tree, were generated from the original training and test data [449]. Below we describe rules discovered from each level's training data; they are then applied to the test data and the error rates of the PCL classifier are computed.

This tree-structured classification scheme was suggested by Drs. Yeoh and Downing, who have extensive domain knowledge. Alternative perspectives are possible, including classifying the 327 samples in a parallel manner (which will be discussed later) instead of hierarchically.

15.5.1 Rules for T-ALL vs OTHERS1

For the first pair of training datasets, T-ALL vs OTHERS1, we found one and only one ideal discriminatory gene, namely 38319_at. Here, OTHERS1 ={E2A-PBX1, TEL-AML1, BCR-ABL, Hyperdip>50, MLL, OTHERS}. The discretization method partitions this gene's expression range into two intervals: $(-\infty, 15975.6)$ and $[15975.6, +\infty)$. EP mining found two EPs:

$$\{gene_{-(38319\_at)}@(-\infty, 15975.6)\}, \qquad \{gene_{-(38319\_at)}@[15975.6, +\infty)\}.$$

The former has a 100% frequency in the T-ALL class but a zero frequency in the OTHERS1 class. The latter has a zero frequency in T-ALL, but a 100% frequency in OTHERS1. Therefore, we have the following rule:

> If the expression of 38319_at is less than 15975.6, then this childhood ALL sample is a T-ALL. Otherwise it is a subtype in OTHERS1.

This simple rule is correct on the 215 (28 T-ALL plus 187 OTHERS1) childhood ALL training samples without any exception.

15.5.2 Rules for E2A-PBX1 vs OTHERS2

We also found a simple rule for contrasting between E2A-PBX1 and OTHERS2. Here, OTHERS2 = {TEL-AML1, BCR-ABL, Hyperdip>50, MLL, OTHERS}. One gene, 33355_at, is identified and, it is then discretized into two intervals: $(-\infty, 10966)$ and $[10966, +\infty)$. Then $\{gene_{-(33355\_at)}@(-\infty, 10966)\}$ and $\{gene_{-(33355\_at)}@[10966, +\infty)\}$ are found to be EPs with 100% frequency in E2A-PBX1 and OTHERS2 respectively. So, the following is a rule for these 187 (18 E2A-PBX1 plus 169 OTHERS2) childhood ALL samples:

> If the expression of 33355_at is less than 10966, then this childhood ALL sample is an E2A-PBX1. Otherwise it is a subtype in OTHERS2.

15.5.3 Rules through Level 3 to Level 6

For the remaining four pairs of datasets, we did not find any ideal discriminatory gene. So, we used the $\mathcal{X}^2$ method to select 20 top-ranked genes for each of those pairs of datasets. After discretizing the selected genes, two groups of EPs are discovered for each of these pairs of datasets. Table 15.3 shows the numbers of discovered emerging patterns. Table 15.4 lists the top 10 EPs (according to their frequency) discovered at Level 3's training data. Observe that some EPs can reach a frequency of 98.94% and most have frequency around 80%. Even though a top-ranked EP may not cover an entire class of samples, it covers a large portion of the whole class.

A rule can be obtained by translating an EP. For example, the first EP of

TABLE 15.3: Total number of EPs discovered from the remaining four pairs of training data sets. Source: Reprinted from Ref. [248], ©2003, with permission from Oxford University Press.

Dataset pair ($\mathcal{D}_1$ vs $\mathcal{D}_2$)	Number of EPs in $\mathcal{D}_1$	Number of EPs in $\mathcal{D}_2$	Total
TEL-AML1 vs OTHERS3	2178	943	3121
BCR-ABL vs OTHERS4	101	230	313
MLL vs OTHERS5	155	597	752
Hyperdip>50 vs OTHERS	2213	2158	4371

the TEL-AML1 class is $\{2, 33\}$. The reference number 2 in this EP represents the right interval of the gene 38652_at, and stands for the condition that: the expression of 38652_at is larger than or equal to 8997.35. Similarly, the reference number 33 represents the left interval of the gene 36937_s_at, and stands for the condition that: the expression of 36937_s_at is less than 13617.05. Thus the pattern $\{2, 33\}$ says that 92.31% of the TEL-AML1 class (48 out of the 52 samples) satisfy the two conditions above, but no sample from OTHERS3 satisfies both of these conditions.

15.6   Classification by PCL on the Tree-Structured Data

Through discovering EPs, many non-obvious novel rules are derived that can well describe the gene expression profiles of more than six subtypes of ALL samples. An important methodology to test the reliability of the rules is to apply them to unseen samples (the so-called blind testing samples). Recall that we have reserved 112 blind testing samples. Our testing results are highlighted as follows: At level 1, all of the 15 T-ALL samples are correctly predicted as T-ALL; all of the 97 OTHERS1 samples are correctly predicted as OTHERS1. At level 2, all of the 9 E2A-PBX1 samples are correctly predicted as E2A-PBX1; all of the 88 OTHERS2 samples are correctly predicted as OTHERS2. For levels 3 to 6, we misclassified only 4-7 samples depending on the number of EPs used. Our method PCL is described below.

15.6.1   PCL: Prediction by Collective Likelihood of Emerging Patterns

For each of level 1 and level 2 of the hierarchical tree-structured datasets, we only have one rule. So, there is no ambiguity on using rules for those two

TABLE 15.4: Ten most frequent EPs in the TEL-AML and OTHERS3 classes. Here, an index number refers to a specific gene combined with a specific expression interval. Source: Reprinted from Ref. [248], ©2003, with permission from Oxford University Press.

EPs {index numbers}	% frequency in TEL-AML1	% frequency in OTHERS3
{2, 33}	92.31	0.00
{16, 22, 33}	90.38	0.00
{20, 22, 33}	88.46	0.00
{5, 33}	86.54	0.00
{22, 28, 33}	84.62	0.00
{16, 33, 43}	82.69	0.00
{22, 30, 33}	82.69	0.00
{2, 36}	82.69	0.00
{20, 43}	82.69	0.00
{22, 36}	82.69	0.00
{1, 23, 40}	0.00	88.89
{17, 29}	0.00	88.89
{1, 17, 40}	0.00	88.03
{1, 9, 40}	0.00	88.03
{15, 17}	0.00	88.03
{1, 23, 29}	0.00	87.18
{17, 25, 40}	0.00	87.18
{17, 23, 40}	0.00	87.18
{9, 17, 40}	0.00	87.18
{1, 9, 29}	0.00	87.18

levels. However, a large number of EPs are discovered for the remaining levels of the tree. A testing sample may contain not only EPs from its own class, but also EPs from its counterpart class. This makes the prediction a bit more complicated. In general, a testing sample should contain many top-ranked EPs from its own class and may contain a few low-ranked EPs—preferably none—from its opposite class. However, according to our observations, a testing sample can sometimes, though rarely, contain 10 to 20 top-ranked EPs from its counterpart class. To make reliable predictions, it is reasonable to use multiple highly frequent EPs of the "home" class to avoid the confusing signals from counterpart EPs.

Given two training datasets $\mathcal{D}_P$ and $\mathcal{D}_N$, and a testing sample T, the first phase of the PCL classifier is to discover EPs from $\mathcal{D}_P$ and $\mathcal{D}_N$. Let's denote the EPs of $\mathcal{D}_P$ in the descending order of their frequency as

$$EP_1^{(P)}, EP_2^{(P)}, \cdots, EP_i^{(P)}.$$

Similarly, denote the EPs of $\mathcal{D}_N$ in the descending order of their frequency as

$$EP_1^{(N)}, EP_2^{(N)}, \cdots, EP_j^{(N)}.$$

Suppose T contains the following EPs of $\mathcal{D}_P$:

$$EP_{i_1}^{(P)}, EP_{i_2}^{(P)}, \cdots, EP_{i_x}^{(P)}, i_1 < i_2 < \cdots < i_x \leq i,$$

and T contains the following EPs of $\mathcal{D}_N$:

$$EP_{j_1}^{(N)}, EP_{j_2}^{(N)}, \cdots, EP_{j_y}^{(N)}, j_1 < j_2 < \cdots < j_y \leq j.$$

The next step is to calculate two scores for predicting the class label of T. Assume that k ($k \ll i$ and $k \ll j$) top-ranked EPs of $\mathcal{D}_P$ and $\mathcal{D}_N$ are used. The score of T in the $\mathcal{D}_P$ class is defined as

$$score(T)\_\mathcal{D}_P = \sum_{m=1}^{k} \frac{frequency(EP_{i_m}^{(P)})}{frequency(EP_m^{(P)})},$$

and, similarly, the score in the $\mathcal{D}_N$ class is defined as

$$score(T)\_\mathcal{D}_N = \sum_{m=1}^{k} \frac{frequency(EP_{j_m}^{(N)})}{frequency(EP_m^{(N)})}.$$

If $score(T)\_\mathcal{D}_P > score(T)\_\mathcal{D}_N$, then T's class is predicted to be the class of $\mathcal{D}_P$. Otherwise T's class is predicted to be the class of $\mathcal{D}_N$. We use the sizes of $\mathcal{D}_P$ and $\mathcal{D}_N$ to break the tie.

The key idea in this classification is to measure how far away the top k EPs contained in T are from the top k EPs of a class. If $k = 1$, then $score(T)\_\mathcal{D}_P$ indicates whether the number one EP contained in T is far or not from the most frequent EP of $\mathcal{D}_P$. If the score is the maximum value 1, then the "distance" is very close, namely the most common property of $\mathcal{D}_P$ is also present in this testing sample. With smaller scores, the distance becomes further. Thus the likelihood of T belonging to the class of $\mathcal{D}_P$ becomes weaker. Using more than one top-ranked EPs, we intend to utilize a "collective" likelihood for more reliable predictions.

With k set at 20, 25, and 30, PCL made only 4 mis-classifications on the samples 94-0359-U95A, 89-0142-U95A, 91-0697-U95A, and 96-0379-U95A.

15.6.2   Strengthening the Prediction Method at Levels 1 & 2

At level 1 or 2, there is only one gene that is used for classification and prediction. In order to be more robust against possible human errors on recording data and noise in microarray gene expression assays, we propose using more than one gene to strengthen our classification method at levels 1 and 2.

The previously selected gene 38319_at at level 1 is an ideal discriminatory gene. There is no other such gene. Besides this gene, we choose also the top 20 genes ranked by the $\mathcal{X}^2$ method to classify the T-ALL and OTHERS1 testing samples. There are 96 EPs in the T-ALL class and 146 EPs in the OTHERS1 class. Using our prediction method, the same perfect accuracy 100% on those blind testing samples is achieved as the one ideal discriminatory gene does.

At level 2 there are a total of five ideal discriminatory genes. These five genes are: 430_at, 1287_at, 33355_at, 41146_at, and 32063_at. Note that 33355_at is already discussed beforehand. All of the five genes are partitioned into two intervals with the following cut points respectively: 30246.05, 34313.9, 10966, 25842.15, and 4068.7. Consequently, there are five EPs in the E2A-PBX1 class and also five EPs in the OTHERS2 class with 100% frequency. Using our prediction method, we correctly classified all the testing samples (at level 2) without any mistake, achieving the perfect 100% accuracy again.

15.6.3 Comparison with Other Methods

There are many notable prediction methods in the machine learning field, including k-nearest neighbor (k-NN) [99], C4.5 [345], Support Vector Machines (SVM) [98, 63], Naive Bayes (NB) [228], etc. C4.5 is a widely used learning algorithm that induces from training data rules that are easy to comprehend. However, it may not have good performance if the real decision boundary underlying the data is not linear. NB uses Bayesian rules to compute a probabilistic summary for each class. Given a testing sample, NB uses the probabilistic summary to estimate the probabilities of the test sample for the classes, and assigns the sample to the highest scoring class. An important assumption used in NB is that the underlying features are mutually independent. However, this is not appropriate for gene expression data analysis as subsets of genes involved in an expression profile are often interacting in a biological pathway and are not independent. The k-NN method assigns a testing sample the class of its nearest training sample in terms of some non-linear distance functions. Even though k-NN is intuitive and has good performance, it is not helpful for understanding complex cases in depth. SVM methods use non-linear kernel functions to construct a complicated mapping between samples and their class labels. SVM has good performance, but it functions as a black box.

We compare PCL's prediction accuracy with the accuracy of k-NN, C4.5, NB, and SVM to demonstrate the competency of PCL. Note that the best accuracy of k-NN and SVM reported in [449] was achieved by using the top 20 χ^2 selected genes. For a fair comparison, the same genes and the same training and testing samples are used by PCL, C4.5, and NB. The classification was conducted by using the WEKA machine learning software package with its standard settings [433]. We found that PCL reduces the misclassifications by 71% from C4.5's 14, by 50% from NB's 8, by 43% from k-NN's 7, and by 33% from SVM's 6. From the medical treatment point of view, this error reduction can benefit patients greatly.

An interesting observation is that the accuracy becomes worse if the original data with the entire set of 12558 genes are applied to the prediction methods. SVM, k-NN, NB, and C4.5 made respectively 23, 23, 63, and 26 mis-classifications on the blind 112 testing samples. These results are much worse than the error rates when the reduced data were applied. So, feature selection has played an important role for the classification models to obtain a high accuracy.

An obvious advantage of PCL over SVM, NB, and k-NN is that meaningful and reliable patterns and rules can be derived. The emerging patterns can provide novel insight into the correlation and interaction of the genes and can help understand the samples beyond a mere classification. Though C4.5 can generate similar rules, it sometimes performs badly (e.g. at level 6) and, its rules are often not very reliable.

15.7 Generalized PCL for Parallel Multi-Class Classification

The hierarchical tree-structured strategy for the subtype classification of ALL samples was initially suggested by the doctors with domain knowledge [449]. Our results above have shown the strength of the structure for classification. However, in the community of machine learning, parallel classification of heterogeneous data is commonly adopted. The parallel classification of multi-class data has the advantage that it does not need any prior knowledge to construct a special classification structure.

Taking the parallel approach, we can discover lists of ranked genes and multi-gene discriminators for differentiating one subtype from all other subtypes. The distinction is global as it is one subtype against *all* others. In contrast, under the hierarchical tree-structured classification strategy, the differentiation is somewhat local since the rules are discovered in terms of one subtype against *the remaining subtypes below it*. Below, we generalize the PCL method to handle data with more than two classes. The generalized PCL is then applied to the data of [449] and to another independent dataset [20].

Suppose we are given c ($c \geq 2$) classes of data, denoted by $\mathcal{D}_1$, $\mathcal{D}_2$, ..., $\mathcal{D}_c$. In the first phase, the generalized PCL discovers c groups of EPs. The nth ($1 \leq n \leq c$) group is for $\mathcal{D}_n$ (versus $\bigcup_{i \neq n} \mathcal{D}_i$). The feature selection and discretization are done in the same way as used in dealing with typical two-class data. Denote the ranked EPs of $\mathcal{D}_n$ as,

$$EP_1^{(n)}, EP_2^{(n)}, \cdots, EP_{i_n}^{(n)},$$

in descending order of their frequency.

Suppose a test sample T contains the following EPs of $\mathcal{D}_n$:

$$EP_{j_1}^{(n)}, EP_{j_2}^{(n)}, \cdots, EP_{j_x}^{(n)}, j_1 < j_2 < \cdots < j_x \leq i_n.$$

Then c scores are computed for predicting the class label of T. Suppose we use k ($k \ll i_n$) top-ranked EPs. Then the score of T in the $\mathcal{D}_n$ class is defined as

$$score(T)\_\mathcal{D}_n = \sum_{m=1}^{k} \frac{frequency(EP_{j_m}^{(n)})}{frequency(EP_m^{(n)})},$$

and similarly for the scores of other classes.

The class with the highest score is predicted as the class of T. We use the sizes of $\mathcal{D}_n$, $1 \leq n \leq c$, to break a tie.

We use an example to illustrate the scores used by the parallel PCL. A BCR-ABL test sample contains almost all of the top-20 BCR-ABL discriminators, and a score of 19.6 is assigned to it. Several top-20 OTHERS discriminators together with some EPs beyond the top-20 list are also contained in this test sample. So, another score of 6.97 is computed. This test sample does not contain any discriminators of E2A-PBX1, Hyperdip>50, or T-ALL. So, the scores are as follows:

subtype	BCR-ABL	E2A-PBX1	Hyperdip>50	
score	19.63	0.00	0.00	
subtype	T-ALL	MLL	TEL-AML1	OTHERS
score	0.00	0.71	2.96	6.97

Therefore, this BCR-ABL sample is correctly predicted as BCR-ABL with a very high confidence.

By this method, we made only 6 to 8 misclassifications for the total 112 testing samples when varying k from 15 to 35. However, C4.5, SVM, NB, and 3-NN made 27, 26, 29, and 11 mistakes respectively.

The data of [20] have only three subtypes (AML, ALL, MLL). There are 57 training samples (20, 17, and 20 resp. for ALL, MLL, and AML) and 15 test samples (4, 3, and 8 resp. for ALL, MLL, and AML). PCL, C4.5, SVM, NB, and k-NN made 0, 3, 1, 0, and 1 mistakes respectively for the 15 test samples.

15.8   Performance Using Randomly Selected Genes

We have shown that the selected top-1 genes or top-20 genes are very useful for classifying the subtypes of childhood leukemia. Experiments show that, if we select genes randomly instead of selecting the top-1 or top-20, then the classifiers' performance will deteriorate significantly. Therefore, feature selection is an important preliminary step before reliable and accurate prediction models are applied.

15.9   Summary

In this chapter, we have reported simple rules discovered from gene expression profiles of childhood leukemia patients. We have compared the performance of different classification methods under the same reduced training and test data. It is known that the performance of a classifier may vary if the number of selected genes is changed. It is also known that there is no theoretical estimation of the optimal number of selected genes even for a specific classifier on a particular application. It will be interesting to see which gene-set size and classification model combination is the best for classifying the subtype of childhood leukemia. Some interesting future work includes a systematic evaluation of gene selection methods and refinements of our method, particularly in techniques for measuring the "interestingness" of individual EPs. Another direction is to consider automatic ways for determining optimal numbers of the most discriminatory genes used for EP discovery.

Chapter 16

Discriminating Gene Transfer and Microarray Concordance Analysis

Shihong Mao

Department of Obstetrics and Gynaecology, Wayne State University

Guozhu Dong

Department of Computer Science and Engineering, Wright State University

16.1 Introduction

Large amounts of microarray gene expression data have been generated/collected using a variety of platforms, from different laboratories, under different conditions. Suitable analysis of such data can lead to better understanding of diseases, and better ways to diagnose and treat diseases. However, during microarray data collection processes, several factors, including platform difference (due to variation of probe sequences targeted by different platforms) and laboratory condition difference, may affect the consistency of the collected data. The consistency of microarray data, with respect to various technology platforms and laboratory conditions, needs to be evaluated before data analysis results from microarray data can be successfully and reliably applied in biological/clinical practices and regulatory decision-making.

The cross platform/laboratory concordance problem has been studied by many research groups using various methods [222, 391, 183, 365, 173, 293].

233

However, most previous studies used the assumption that the expression values of all genes are equally important. That assumption is not appropriate for comparative studies, where the focus is on certain classes of interest. Comparative studies are especially interested in the features that are important to the classes. They aim to discover fundamental patterns of gene regulation related to the classes, and they aim to form/test new class-relevant hypothesis. In order to get reliable concordance results for use in comparative studies, it is desirable to evaluate concordance using appropriate comparative methodologies.

This chapter presents comparative methods for evaluating the concordance of microarray data collected from different platforms and different laboratories. The presented methods evaluate this concordance by measuring the preservation and transferability of discriminating genes and classifiers across platforms and laboratories. These methods give more emphasis to the discriminating genes and ignore the non-discriminating genes; discriminting genes are those that participate in high quality emerging patterns for the classes. If the microarray datasets are concordant with each other with respect to discriminating genes/classifiers, then the knowledge on discriminating genes/classifiers gained from one platform/laboratory can be transferred to another platform/laboratory. This chapter is based on [292].

The discussion in this chapter will often refer to concordance between two datasets. This approach makes the discussion applicable to concordance between platforms or concordance between laboratories.

16.2   Datasets Used in Experiments and Preprocessing

The concordance analysis methodology reported in this chapter was evaluated on the datasets provided by the Microarray Quality Control (MAQC) project [293]. The datasets were generated using more than 10 platforms in more than 30 laboratories. The experiments reported below used the data generated by 12 laboratories using four major commercial platforms (Affymetrix (AFX), Applied Biosystem (ABI), Agilent one color array (AG1), and GE Healthcare (GEH)), leading to a total of 12 datasets. For each platform, there are three repeated datasets, each from one of three laboratories; this design makes both inter/intra platforms comparison possible.

All laboratories used the same 20 samples, which will be denoted by $s_1, ..., s_{20}$, to produce the laboratories' datasets by hybridizing those 20 samples to microarray chips. The 20 samples were obtained from the same four standard mRNA samples (which will be referred to as the sample types), which implies that biological variation has been eliminated. The four mRNAs were named as A, B, C (75%A + 25%B), and D (25%A + 75%B). The 20 samples were generated by having 5 duplicated samples of each of the four mRNA types.

Since C contained more A than B whereas D contained more B than A, mRNAs A and C were grouped into one class, whereas mRNAs B and D were grouped into the other class. This division is used in all datasets.

For each platform, each mRNA sample was measured three times in three different labs, generating three microarray vectors (which will be called repeats). An average dataset for the platform was constructed and used in cross-platform concordance analysis. The average dataset for a given platform was constructed as follows: Let $u_m(g_i, s_j)$ denote the gene expression value of sample s_j on gene g_i in the mth repeat of the given platform, and let $u(g_i, s_j)$ denote the average of the three repeats of s_j on g_i; then $u(g_i, s_j) = (u_1(g_i, s_j) + u_2(g_i, s_j) + u_3(g_i, s_j))/3$. The average dataset for a given platform consists of the average vectors for all samples s_j.

Different platforms may use different gene probes. UniGene IDs are often used to identify common genes shared by different microarray platforms [419]. In this study, 16140 common genes were identified as being present on all four of the analyzed platforms. Gene expression values were averaged in cases where multiple probes for a given UniGene ID were present on the chip.

The gene expression values generated using different platforms cannot be directly compared, because different labeling methods and different probe sequences used by the platforms may give rise to variable signals for the same target (gene). A per-gene baseline adjustment is performed to normalize these datasets. Suppose datasets D_1 and D_2 share m genes $(g_1,...,g_m)$. Let $V_i(g_k, s_j)$ denote gene g_k's expression value for sample s_j in D_i, where $1 \leq i \leq 2$, $1 \leq k \leq m$ and $1 \leq j \leq 20$. Define

$$MaxD_{i,k} = max\{V_i(g_k, s_j) \mid 1 \leq j \leq 20\},$$
$$MinD_{i,k} = min\{V_i(g_k, s_j) \mid 1 \leq j \leq 20\}.$$

The following formula is used to generate the normalized dataset D_1' from D_1.

$$V_1'(g_k, s_j) = \frac{V_1(g_k, s_j) - MinD_{1,k}}{MaxD_{2,k} - MinD_{2,k}} + MinD_{1,k} \qquad (16.1)$$

Here, $V_1'(g_k, s_j)$ denote gene g_k's expression value for sample s_j in D_1'. A similar formula is applied to generate the normalized dataset D_2', where the subscript 1 was exchanged with the subscript 2. The concordance between D_1 and D_2 can be investigated by checking D_1' and D_2 (or equivalently D_1 and D_2') using concordance measures discussed below.

16.3   Discriminating Genes and Associated Classifiers

Before presenting the use of transferability of discriminating genes and of the associated classifiers between datasets to evaluate concordance, in this section we discuss the concepts of discriminating genes and associated classifiers.

For a given dataset, the discriminating genes (DGs) are the genes that are highly correlated with the classes. More specifically, the DGs are the genes that participate in jumping emerging patterns (JEPs) [118, 119]. JEPs are patterns that appear in one class but never appear in other classes. The JEPs are conjunctions of conditions of one of two forms, "$g \leq v_g$" or "$g > v_g$", where g is a gene and v_g is the split value for g determined by the entropy based method [128]. We refer to a JEP with k conditions as a k-gene JEP. JEPs involving multiple genes are important since multiple genes orchestrate physiological functions in the tissues.

In this study, a gene is called a *discriminating gene* (DG) for a given dataset if it occurs in some JEPs for the dataset involving between one and three genes. After determining the discriminative split value [128] for each gene, the so-called "iterative gene club formation algorithm" [291] (see also Chapter 17) was employed to discover the 2-gene and 3-gene JEPs from the two classes of each MAQC microarray dataset. The one-gene JEPs were found by checking the frequencies of $g \leq v_g$ and of $g > v_g$ in the two classes for all genes g and their associated split values v_g. Only the JEPs having 100% frequency in their home class (where the JEPs occur) were selected. Observe that by definition of JEPs, each such JEP has 0% in the non-home class. So the DGs are frequently involved in highly discriminative interactions among genes.

We now turn to defining a simple classifier built using the discriminating genes, which will be used in our concordance analysis methodology. Much has been done on building accurate and noise-tolerant classifiers using emerging patterns (see Chapter 11), for many different data types including microarray data. For classifier-transferability based concordance analysis, it is desirable to use a very simple kind of classifier. To that end, we consider a "vote-by-discriminating-genes" (VBDG) classifier.

The VBDG classifier (for a given dataset D) works as follows: For each discriminating gene g, suppose v_g is g's split value (determined by the entropy based method), and $C_{g,low}$ and $C_{g,high}$ are respectively the majority classes of the $g \leq v_g$ and $g > v_g$ intervals in D. For each case t to be classified, g gives a vote to the class $C_{g,low}$ or $C_{g,high}$, depending on whether $t(g) \leq v_g$ or $t(g) > v_g$ is true. The VBDG classifier classifies t to the class C that has the most of the votes by the DGs.

16.4 Measures for Transferability

16.4.1 Measures for Discriminative Gene Transferability

Generally speaking, we say that the DGs are transferable between two datasets D_1 and D_2, if the DGs of D_1 are highly likely to be DGs of D_2 and vice versa. We present two ways to measure discriminative gene transferability.

The first discriminative gene transferability measure is the so-called *split-value consistency rate*, denoted by SVCR. This ratio measures how class discrimination is transferred between two datasets.

Let D_1 and D_2 be two datasets. Let $V_i(g, s_j)$ denote gene g's expression value for sample s_j in D_i. For each $i \in \{1, 2\}$ and each gene g, let v_{ig} be the split value of g in D_i. For each gene g and sample s_j, define $agree(g, s_j) = 1$ if $(V_1(g, s_j) \leq v_{1g}) \& (V_2(g, s_j) \leq v_{2g})$ is true or $(V_1(g, s_j) > v_{1g}) \& (V_2(g, s_j) > v_{2g})$ is true, and define $agree(g, s_j) = 0$ otherwise. So $agree(g, s_j)$ is 1 iff the tuples for s_j in the two datasets agree with the split values of gene g. The SVCR between D_1 and D_2 with respect to a given set G of genes is defined by

$$\mathsf{SVCR}_G(D_1, D_2) = \frac{\sum_{j=1}^{20} \sum_{g \in G} agree(g, s_j)}{20 * |G|}. \tag{16.2}$$

In the experiments two choices for G were considered: G is the set of all genes or G is the set of all discriminative genes.

The second discriminative gene transferability measure is based on the number of discriminating genes shared by two given datasets D_1 and D_2. A gene is a *shared discriminative gene* if it is a discriminative gene for both D_1 and D_2. While the number of shared discriminative genes can be directly used to evaluate the concordance of D_1 and D_2, a permutation based approach is used to derive the P-value to measure how much evidence we have against the null hypotheses (that there is no difference between two given datasets).

Intuitively, if two given datasets D_1 and D_2 are very similar, then a permutation of sample s_j of D_1 and sample s_j of D_2 will cause a very small change to the set of shared DGs. In other words, the set of shared DGs for the two datasets after the permutation should be very similar to the set for the original two datasets. Thus, by comparing the set of shared DGs from the dataset pair before and after the permutation, we can detect whether the original dataset pair is concordant or not.

We perform a sequence of random permutations, and use the series of shared DG sets of the permutated datasets to derive the P-value. More specifically, let CG_0 be the set of shared discriminating genes of the original dataset pair. For $i \in \{1, ..., m\}$ and $m = 100$, let D_1^i and D_2^i be the respective result of some random number of random permutations of samples between D_1 and D_2, and let CG_i be the set of shared discriminating genes of D_1^i and D_2^i. (In the experiments, m was also set to 300; having $m = 300$ generated results similar to the case of $m = 100$.) Let $F = |CG_0|$ and $F_i = |CG_i \cap CG_0|$. Let μ and σ be the mean and standard deviation of $F_1, ..., F_m$. Then the Chebyshev inequality can be used to estimate (an upper bound of) the P-value.

16.4.2   Measures for Classifier Transferability

In assessing classifier transferability between two datasets D_1 and D_2, the average of the accuracy of the VBDG classifier built from D_1 to classify D_2 and that of the VBDG classifier built from D_2 to classify D_1, is used as the numerical measure for classifier transferability. Below we will call that average accuracy the *cross platform classifier accuracy*.

16.5   Findings on Microarray Concordance

16.5.1   Concordance Test by Classifier Transferability

We used classifier transferability to evaluate both cross-laboratory concordance and cross-platform concordance.

For cross-laboratory concordance, the classifier transferability accuracy is 100% for any given platform.

For cross-platform concordance, the results indicate that the three platforms of AFX, ABI, and GEH are highly concordant with each other, but the AG1 platform is less concordant with the other three platforms. More specifically, the cross platform classifier accuracy is 100% between any pairs of platforms among AFX, ABI, and GEH, and it is $\leq 62.5\%$ when AG1 is one of the platforms.

16.5.2   Split Value Consistency Rate Analysis

Split value consistency rate was examined in two ways. In the first way all genes were considered, and in the other way only the discriminating genes were considered.

For cross-laboratory comparison, the SVCR is around 75% for all platforms if all genes were considered, and it is between 92% and 98.5% if only the discriminating genes were considered.

For cross-platform comparison, the SVCR is around 70% between the ABI, AFX, and GEH platforms, and it is around 50% if AG1 is one of the platform, if all genes were considered; the SVCR is at least 84% between the ABI, AFX, and GEH platforms, and it is around 50% if AG1 is one of the platform, if only the discriminating genes were considered.

In both types of concordance analysis, we see that, for the ABI, AFX, and GEH platforms, SVCR for the case when only discriminating genes are considered is strictly higher than SVCR for the case when all genes are considered. The above is not true when AG1 is one of the platforms.

16.5.3 Shared Discriminating Gene Based P-Value

According to the shared discriminating gene based P-values, there is no statistical significance ($P > 0.05$; the actual P-values are ≥ 0.2) between different laboratories using a common platform, which implies that the laboratories are concordant with each other if they use the same platform. On the other hand, there is no statistical significance between the dataset pairs from platform ABI, AFX, and GEH ($P > 0.05$; the actual P-values are ≥ 0.198), which again implies concordance among those platforms; however, the dataset from AG1 is significantly different from the other three platforms ($P < 0.05$; the actual P-values are ≤ 0.012), which implies non-concordance.

16.6 Discussion

In this chapter we discussed methods that use discriminating gene transferability and discriminating gene based classifier transferability to evaluate cross-laboratory and cross-platform concordance for microarray technology. The experimental results show that different conclusions can be reached if all genes were considered rather than the discriminating genes.

Guo et al. [173] used six gene selection methods to choose and rank genes, reaching different concordance results from their different gene selection methods. Compared with their results, we reached the same conclusion that the datasets within a given platform are highly concordant, and that the datasets from non-AG1 platforms are fairly concordant with each other. However, our discriminating gene based methods conclude that the AG1 platform has low concordance with the three other platforms, whereas [173] concluded that the AG1 platform is also concordant with other platforms.

Guo et al. also noticed the importance of discriminating genes in concordance evaluation, although they used the fold change ranking method to discover discriminating genes. It should be pointed out that their criteria for discriminating gene selection are very different from ours. The fold change method uses the ratio of average of expression values in the two classes to rank genes. Our methods select discriminating genes based on participation in high frequency jumping emerging patterns after entropy based binning.

Chapter 17

Towards Mining Optimal Emerging Patterns Amidst 1000s of Genes

Shihong Mao

Department of Obstetrics and Gynaecology, Wayne State University

Guozhu Dong

Department of Computer Science and Engineering, Wright State University

17.1   Introduction

It is commonly believed that careful analysis of microarray gene expression data can lead to better understanding of, and better ways to diagnose and treat, the associated diseases of the data. It is of interest to discover, from the gene expression data, the gene interaction networks and perhaps even pathways underlying the given diseases. Emerging patterns (EPs), especially the highly discriminative ones, may provide useful insights in such an analysis.

Discovering highly discriminative EPs from microarray datasets is a big challenge because microarray data have extremely high dimensionality[1], because the problem has high computational complexity [427], and because the number of features that can be effectively handled by typical EP mining algorithms is much smaller than the total number of available features. One frequently used approach, which will be referred to as the top-k method, solves the problem by selecting the top k genes ranked in the information gain order or other feature preference order (such as the Chi2-based one of [275]) and performing EP mining on those genes [252]. The top-k approach is not satisfactory since the mined EPs reveal only gene interactions for the underlying disease among the k selected genes. It is desirable to find all EPs that correspond to the most striking gene interactions among all of the genes, or find the optimal EPs containing each of some large subset of the genes.

This chapter presents gene-club based methods to overcome the dimensionality hurdle. After presenting the methods, it reports experimental results to show that those methods can efficiently discover high quality EPs involving *each* of (a large subset of) the genes, and they can discover EPs with much better quality than previous methods, including quite a few signature EPs involving genes that are ranked below the 50th percentile in the information gain based rank. Moreover, it presents an interaction based gene importance index, using the high quality EPs mined using the gene club based methods, to measure the importance of genes based on their participation in important gene groups, for the disease/dataset under consideration.

Important to the methods of this chapter is the following concept. A *gene club* of a gene g consists of a set of genes that are highly interactive with g; g is called the *owner* of the gene club, and the number of genes in the club is the *size* of the club. The owner gene g is always a member of g's gene club.

In general, a gene club based EP mining method works as follows: (1) Form a gene club for each gene g of interest. (2) For each gene club, use an EP mining algorithm to mine the EPs on the genes in the gene club. (3) Select the desired EPs from the mined EPs that result from steps (1) and (2). In steps (1) and (2), for efficiency reasons one may choose to consider a subset of all available genes, instead of all genes, as gene club owners.

In this chapter, by EPs we refer to jumping EPs (EPs whose support is zero in non-home classes). The quality/discriminativeness of such EPs can be indicated by their support in their home class.

This chapter is based on [291].

---

[1] For example, the Illumina human HT12 chip contains over 47,000 gene probes (features).

17.2 Gene Club Formation Methods

This section presents four gene club formation methods, after some general discussion on issues relevant to all those methods.

The size k of gene clubs must be determined when using gene club formation methods. In general, k should be as large as possible to ensure that many genes that are potentially interactive with each other are in the same club, but at the same time k should not be too big to ensure that current EP mining algorithms can effectively handle data with k genes using available computing resources. Gene club formation methods will have k as a parameter.

All gene club formation methods discussed below use some variants of the information gain measure to evaluate class-related interaction among genes. Intuitively, the ability of a group of genes to collectively generate pure partitions with respect to the classes is used as indication of the degree of interaction among the genes.

Before EP mining, microarray gene expression data need to be pre-processed. We use the entropy based method [128] to split/discretize the value range for each gene into two intervals/bins and to rank the genes; one bin will be called "high" and the other "low". The associated ranking of the genes will be referred to as the *information gain based rank*. More details about data pre-processing can be found in Chapter 1.

The discretized microarray data will be used in defining information gain for groups of genes, which generalizes the definition for a single gene. Let S be a given dataset (of data tuples with class labels). Let $\{g_1, g_2, ...g_m\}$ be a set of m genes. For each string $B = b_1 b_2...b_m$, where each b_i is either "low" or "high", of length m, let S_B be the set of tuples in S such that "$g_i = b_i$" is true for each i. Let $Entropy(S_B)$ denote the entropy of S_B. (See Chapter 1.) The *information* for gene group $\{g_1, g_2, ..., g_m\}$ is

$$I(g_1, g_2, ..., g_m) = \sum_B \frac{|S_B|}{|S|} Entropy(S_B),$$

where B ranges over all possible strings over $\{low, high\}$ of length m. The *information gain* for gene group $\{g_1, g_2, ..., g_m\}$ is

$$InfoGain(g_1, g_2, ..., g_m) = Entropy(S) - I(g_1, g_2, ..., g_m).$$

Although the determination of gene clubs share similarities with feature selection methods, it has some unique characteristics: It is centered around the owner gene of a gene club, it is based on the interaction among genes, and it tries to form many gene clubs centered around many given owner genes.

17.2.1   The Independent Gene Club Formation Method

The *independent gene club formation method* (GC_{IN}) forms a gene club for owner gene g by selecting the genes that are independently the most interactive with g. The *condtional information gain* of gene g' with respect to gene g,

$$InfoGain(g' \mid g) = InfoGain(g, g') - InfoGain(g),$$

is used to measure the degree of interaction between g' and g.

The gene club of size k for g formed by GC_{IN} is $\{g, g_1, ..., g_{k-1}\}$, where $g_1, g_2, ..., g_{k-1}$ are the top $k - 1$ genes, ranked by $InfoGain(g' \mid g)$.

Observe that the genes in a gene club are selected based on their interaction with the club owner only; no attention is given to the interaction among the selected non-owner genes.

17.2.2   The Iterative Gene Club Formation Method

The *iterative gene club formation method* (GC_{IT}) forms a gene club by iteratively selecting the genes that are the most interactive with the entire current partial gene club. This is different from the GC_{IN} method, which does not consider the interaction of a new gene with other selected genes.

GC_{IT} is based on the notion of *generalized conditional information gain* for a gene g' with respect to a partial gene club $\{g_1, ..., g_m, g\}$ for owner gene g:

$$InfoGain(g' \mid g_1, g_2, ...g_m, g) = InfoGain(g_1, g_2, ...g_m, g, g')$$
$$-InfoGain(g_1, g_2, ...g_m, g).$$

GC_{IT} finds a gene club of size k for g iteratively as follows: It first selects the gene g_1 having the highest $InfoGain(g' \mid g)$ among all genes $g' \neq g$ and initializes the gene club to $\{g, g_1\}$; then, for $i = 2..k - 1$, it repeatedly selects the next gene g_i having the highest $InfoGain(g' \mid g_1, ..., g_{i-1}, g)$ among all remaining genes g' and adds g_i to the partial gene club.

17.2.3   Two Divisive Gene Club Formation Methods

We now present two divisive methods that are derived from GC_{IN} and GC_{IT}. They are called divisive because they first divide the total dataset under consideration into two partitions and then choose the genes from those selected by GC_{IN} or GC_{IT} from the two partitions.

Given a club owner gene g and a desired gene club size k, we first divide the total dataset D under consideration into two partitions D_1 and D_2 using a split value v (determined using the information gain method), where $D_1 = \{t \in D \mid t(g) \leq v\}$ and $D_2 = \{t \in D \mid t(g) > v\}$. We then use one of GC_{IN} and GC_{IT} to select up to k genes (in a gene club for g) from D_1 and up to k genes from D_2, as candidate members for the gene club for g over D. If GC_{IN} is used for both partitions, the method is called *the divisive independent method* (GC_{DIN}); if GC_{IT} is used, the method is called *the divisive iterative method*

(GC$_{DIT}$). (One can also consider two other combinations, where GC$_{IN}$ is used for one partition and GC$_{IT}$ is used for the other partition.)

The selected genes from D_1 and D_2 are then used to form the overall gene club for g over D, as follows.

GC$_{DIN}$ first selects up to $1/3$ of the k gene club members from each partition having highest conditional information gain, among the genes with non-zero conditional information gain. The last $1/3$ (or more if any partitions did not contribute $1/3$ of k genes in the previous step) is chosen by selecting, from the remaining candidate genes selected from the two partitions, the genes having highest conditional information gain values. (Observe that the conditional information gain used here can come from one or two of the two partitions.)

GC$_{DIT}$ is similar to GC$_{DIN}$ except that, in the final step, it uses a normalized version of generalized conditional information gain to choose the last $1/3$ of the genes. Normalization of a conditional information gain is done by dividing it by the partial gene club size; this is done since it is not very meaningful to compare raw information gain over gene groups with large size differences.

17.3 Interaction Based Importance Index of Genes

Experiments indicate that some genes may not be strongly related with the disease classes individually, but they are very important for the classes when combined with other genes. In other words, they are important for the classes when we consider how they interact with other genes in high quality EPs, but they are not that important when we consider them in isolation.

The commonly used methods for gene ranking, including those based on fold-change and t-statistics [432], together with the entropy based ranking, are all examples where the importance of genes is determined in isolation.

We now present an index for measuring the importance of genes, called *interaction based gene importance*, for a given disease. The index measures the importance of a gene based on how often the gene participates in high quality EPs of the dataset for the given disease and the quality of those EPs. We use IBIG(g) to denote the index value of a gene g in this index.

The method to compute IBIG is as follows. First, for each gene g', use one or more gene club formation methods to find gene clubs for g'. Second, mine the EPs over each of those gene clubs. Third, for each gene g select from the mined EPs the one EP that has the highest support in its home class among the EPs containing g. Let H denote the set of the selected EPs, for all genes.

The IBIG of a gene g is defined as

$$\text{IBIG}(g) = \sum_{g \in P, P \in H} supp(P).$$

The IBIG indexes for different diseases can be different.

17.4   Computing IBIG and Highest Support EPs for Top IBIG Genes

In the above discussion we considered mining EPs for gene clubs of a given set of genes. It will be helpful if we can automatically identify the most important n genes (without asking the user to identify them) and mine the highest support EPs containing those genes, for some fairly large number n.

We now present a method, which we will refer to as Top_IBIG, to achieve the above goal, and computes the IBIG value for each of the top n IBIG ranked genes. It works in iterations as follows. In each iteration, we consider only the top n genes, as gene club owners. In the first iteration, we select the top n genes using the information gain rank. In each subsequent iteration, we select the top n genes ranked by the IBIG computed in the previous iteration. The procedure ends when IBIG converges.

17.5   Experimental Evaluation of Gene Club Methods

The effectiveness of gene club based methods was evaluated in two experiments: (i) the ability to mine the best possible EPs from some 75 genes, and (ii) the ability to mine high quality EPs for all genes by using the gene clubs for some 20 genes. Both experiments indicate that the gene club based methods lead to significant improvement over the top-k mining method. The section also gives an experimental comparison of the four methods.

Below we focus on the colon cancer dataset [9]. Experiments were also conducted on the prostate cancer data [369], breast cancer data [412], and ovarian cancer data [335]; the gene club based methods also produced significant improvement over the top-k method on those datasets.

17.5.1   Ability to Find Top Quality EPs from 75 Genes

Experiments show that the gene club based methods can often find the EPs whose frequencies are very close to the best possible EPs.

To demonstrate the ability claimed above, we conducted experiments on the colon cancer data using the following experiment design (which gives us access to all possible EPs): The top 75 genes ranked by information gain were selected. EPs were exhaustively mined from the 75 genes using one invocation of the border-diff algorithm [118] on all those genes. For each gene g among the 75 genes, let $supEP_{ex}(g)$ be the highest frequency (support) of the discovered EPs containing g. Next, the four gene club based methods, and the top-k method were used to mine EPs from the 75 genes. The gene club size was set to 20 and the top-k method worked on the top 20 genes among the 75 genes.

For each gene g, we checked whether a given method can find an EP containing g with frequency of $supEP_{ex}(g)$ from the 75 genes. We considered how often a method can achieve this. The experiments's results are as follows.

GC_{IT} can find the strongest EPs for about 82.5% of the genes. Moreover, the average frequency (over the 75 genes) of the strongest EPs found by GC_{IT} is more than 98% of the average support of the strongest EPs that exist for the 75 genes. The other three gene club methods also generated similar results.

In contrast, the top-k method can only find the strongest EPs for 32.5% of the genes, and the average frequency of the strongest EPs found by that method is about 77% of the average frequency of the strongest EPs. So the gene club based methods improve over the top-k method by a large margin.

Experiments over randomly selected 75 genes showed similar results.

17.5.2 Ability to Discover High Support EPs and Signature EPs, Possibly Involving Lowly Ranked Genes

Experiments show that the gene club based methods can often find very high quality EPs, even when those high quality EPs involve genes which are ranked very low in the information gain rank. Moreover, the gene club based methods produce significant improvement on the quality of the mined EPs over the top-k method.

Indeed, using the top-k method with $k = 35$, the highest frequency of the mined EPs of the normal tissue class is 77%, and that of the cancer tissue class is 70% [253]. The quality is lower if $k = 20$ is used.

In contrast, using the gene club based methods with gene club size $k = 20$ and considering only gene clubs of the top 20 genes under the information gain rank, the highest frequency of the mined EPs of the normal tissue class is 100%, and that of the cancer tissue class is also 100%. Moreover, using the gene club based methods, 11 EPs of 100% frequency and 19 EPs of 97.5% frequency of the cancer tissue class were mined, and 4 EPs of 100% frequency and 16 EPs of 95.5% frequency of the normal tissue class were mined.

Clearly, all of those 50 high frequency EPs mined by the gene club based methods involve genes whose information gain rank is larger than 35 (since none of them were mined by the top-k method for $k = 35$). In fact, all those EPs involve a gene whose information gain rank is at least 69. Each of those mined EPs with 100% frequency involves at least one gene whose information gain rank is 113 or larger, and such mined EPs involve genes whose information gain rank is as large as 700. The largest information gain rank of genes involved in the 30 mined EPs of the cancer tissue class mentioned above is 1089, and that of the normal tissue class is 1261. Incidentally, a total of 255 out of the 2000 genes of the colon cancer data is a member of at least one of the gene clubs of the top 20 genes.

The most desirable EPs are those so-called signature EPs. We call an EP of a class a *signature EP* of the class if its frequency in the class is 100%. Since signature EPs can completely characterize the diseased tissue class or the normal tissue class respectively, they may be highly useful for understanding gene functions/roles in diseases. The discussion above shows that the gene club based methods can discover signature EPs.

We observe that several signature EPs involve genes ranked as low as 700 in the information gain order, and several EPs whose home class frequency is > 95% involve genes ranked as low as 1089 and 1261. This implies that such genes are very weak for characterizing the cancer individually by themselves, but they can completely characterize the cancer when combined with several other genes. Such genes may not have received enough investigation and deserve attention in future research.

17.5.3   High Support Emerging Patterns Mined

Tables 17.1, 17.2, 17.3, and 17.4 list, respectively, the EPs with highest support mined in diseased tissues and normal tissues for the colon cancer data and for the prostate data. Each number represents a gene, and the number is determined by the gene's rank according to the information gain order. The signs of + and − represent high and low respectively, e.g. 1+ is for gene 1 is high, and 4 − is for gene 4 is low. The accession number and description for some of the genes, together with their split values, can be found in [291].

TABLE 17.1: EPs with Highest Support – Colon Diseased Class. support in normal class is 0 for all listed EPs. Source: Adapted from [291], Copyright 2005, with permission from World Scientific.

EP	support in diseased class	EP	support in diseased class
{1+ 4- 112+ 113+}	100	{1+ 4- 113+ 116+}	100
{1+ 4- 113+ 221+}	100	{1+ 4- 113+ 696+}	100
{1+ 108- 112+ 113+}	100	{1+ 108- 113+ 116+}	100
{4- 108- 112+ 113+}	100	{4- 109+ 113+ 700+}	100
{4- 110+ 112+ 113+}	100	{4- 112+ 113+ 700+}	100
{4- 113+ 117+ 700+}	100	{1+ 6+ 8- 700+}	97.5
{1+ 8- 110+ 112+}	97.5	{1+ 8- 112+ 216+}	97.5
{1+ 8- 112+ 222+}	97.5	{1+ 8- 112+ 700+}	97.5
{1+ 8- 112+ 1089-}	97.5	{1+ 8- 116+ 1089-}	97.5
{1+ 110+ 116+ 263-}	97.5	{1+ 112+ 113+ 263-}	97.5
{1+ 112+ 263- 1089-}	97.5	{1+ 116+ 263- 1089-}	97.5
{4- 8- 112+ 216+}	97.5	{4- 112+ 113+ 263-}	97.5
{4- 112+ 113+ 1089-}	97.5	{6+ 8- 113+ 116+}	97.5
{6+ 8- 113+ 696+}	97.5	{6+ 8- 113+ 700+}	97.5
{8- 38+ 112+ 216+}	97.5	{8- 113+ 114+ 222+ 700+}	97.5

TABLE 17.2: EPs with Highest Support – Colon Normal Class. support in diseased class is 0 for all listed EPs. Source: Adapted from [291], Copyright 2005, with permission from World Scientific.

EP	support in normal class	EP	support in normal class
{12- 21- 35+ 40+ 137+ 254+}	100	{12- 35+ 40+ 71- } 137+ 254+}	100
{20- 21- 35+ 137+ 254+}	100	{20- 35+ 71- 137+ 254+}	100
{5- 35+ 137+ 177+}	95.5	{5- 35+ 137+ 254+}	95.5
{5- 35+ 137+ 419-}	95.5	{5- 137+ 177+ 309+}	95.5
{5- 137+ 254+ 309+}	95.5	{7- 21- 33+ 35+ 69+}	95.5
{7- 21- 33+ 69+ 309+}	95.5	{7- 21- 33+ 69+ 1261+}	95.5
{7- 34- 35+ 69+}	95.5	{7- 34- 69+ 309+}	95.5
{12- 34- 35+ 69+ 136-}	95.5	{12- 35+ 40+ 188- 254+}	95.5
{12- 35+ 69+ 136- 309+}	95.5	{18- 33+ 35+ 40+ 254+}	95.5
{18- 33+ 254+ 309+}	95.5	{21- 35+ 188- 254+}	95.5

TABLE 17.3: EPs with Highest Support – Prostate Diseased Class. support in normal class is 0 for all listed EPs. Source: Adapted from [291], Copyright 2005, with permission from World Scientific.

EP	support in diseased class	EP	support in diseased class
{07- 331- 557+ 5011-}	98.1	{07- 331- 564+ 5011-}	98.1
{07- 331- 708+ 5011-}	98.1	{07- 331- 719- 5011-}	98.1
{07- 557- 657- 5011-}	98.1	{07- 564+ 657- 713+ 5011-}	98.1
{07- 657- 708+ 5011-}	98.1	{07- 657- 719- 5011-}	98.1
{01- 947- 1271-}	96.1	{01- 1271- 2083-}	96.1

17.5.4 Comparison of the Four Gene Club Methods

The four gene club formation methods differ slightly in their ability to identify the high quality EPs and signature EPs.

We first compare the four methods by considering their performance on the top 75 genes. Compared with the exhaustive method (see the second paragraph of Section 17.5.1), the average support of the strongest EPs found by the four gene club based methods are 94.9% of that found by the exhaustive method for GC_{IN}, 94.2% for GC_{DIN}, 98.3% for GC_{IT} and 96.9% for GC_{DIT}. The iterative methods (GC_{IT} and GC_{DIT}) have overall stronger ability to identify high quality EPs than the independent methods (GC_{IN} and GC_{DIN}). (So, if only one gene club method is used for computation time reasons, then one should use GC_{IT}.) This can be attributed to the fact that the gene club members formed by the iterative methods are more strongly correlated than those formed by the independent methods, due to the difference in the corresponding

TABLE 17.4: EPs with Highest Support – Prostate Normal Class. support in diseased class is 0 for all listed EPs. Source: Adapted from [291], Copyright 2005, with permission from World Scientific.

EP	support in normal class	EP	support in normal class
{11- 19- 20+ 41+}	86	{11- 20+ 41+ 3890+}	86
{11- 20+ 41+ 122-}	86	{11- 41+ 78-}	86
{19- 41+ 78- 122-}	86	{01+ 06- 2002+}	84
{04- 11- 19- 41+}	84	{04- 11- 41+ 122-}	84
{04- 11- 41+ 3890+}	84	{04- 18+ 507+ 1937+}	84

conditional information gain definitions. Surprisingly, the average supports of EPs found by the divisive methods are lower than that found by the none-divisive methods. One possible explanation is: the genes deemed useful in one partition may not be very desirable in the other partition.

We next discuss the contribution of the four methods towards finding high frequency EPs based on the gene clubs of the top 20 genes. The discussion below refers to the experiments that were discussed in Section 17.5.2. The majority of the top EPs were mined by GC_{IT} method. For instance, among the 15 signature EPs mined from the colon cancer dataset, 13 were found by the GC_{IT} method and the other two are by the GC_{IN} method. It should also be noted that, experiment results also indicate that GC_{IT} cannot produce all the high quality EPs found by the other methods. Indeed, for the colon dataset, while GC_{DIN} and GC_{DIT} did not contribute any signature EPs, they contributed EPs of support of 97.5% in the diseased class and 95.5% in the normal class, which are in the top 50 EPs list ranked by support.

17.5.5   IBIG vs Information Gain Based Ranking

Table 17.5 compares the IBIG rank against the information gain based rank of some genes for Colon Cancer data. We observe that the gene ranked as the 10th most important by IBIG was ranked at 401 by the information gain rank. (There are a total of 2000 genes.) The genes ranked at 2 and 3 by IBIG are ranked at 114 and 115 by information gain rank.

17.6   Discussion

In many previous gene expression analysis studies, genes are typically grouped by similarity of their expression profiles [166]. We would like to propose a different approach – we group genes using high quality EPs, i.e., genes

TABLE 17.5: IBIG Rank vs IG (information gain based) Rank for Colon Data. Source: Adapted from [291], Copyright 2005, with permission from World Scientific.

IBIG Rank	Gene No.	IG Rank		IBIG Rank	Gene No.	IG Rank
1	1422	8		11	1634	34
2	681	114		12	764	4
3	575	115		13	1559	132
4	1670	1		14	257	12
5	1041	7		15	1885	212
6	1923	242		16	492	3
7	1581	16		17	248	2
8	624	6		18	580	39
9	1632	217		19	1327	66
10	174	401		20	398	14

should be grouped together if they match some high quality EPs. The value of high quality EPs in such grouping is based on the fact that EPs capture the following information: in one of the disease states, some genes are correlated (perhaps because they participate in some common pathway under normal situation) and are fully "in sync", but in the other disease states these genes are no longer "in sync" (perhaps because the pathway is disrupted).

It is also worth noting that EPs mined using gene club based methods can also be used to form EP-based classifiers.

Incidently, we note that the "frequent-item based projection" method will not help significantly regarding the dimensionality challenge for mining high quality EPs in microarray data. Indeed, for the colon cancer data, the average length of projected tuples are still 510 and 820 for the cancer and normal classes respectively, after removing items whose support is < 90% in the class.

Reference [291] reported that many genes in the discovered EPs with high support are known to be related to the studied diseases. However, some genes in such EPs, especially the low-ranked genes, have not received enough investigation. The fact that these genes occur in those high support EPs indicates that these genes are important for the disease under consideration, and they should be studied further in the biology and medicine fields. Finally, the discovered EPs capture high potential gene interactions and can be used to suggest research directions to find gene functions and to discover new pathways.

Interestingly, for some diseases such as leukemia and lung cancer, the gene club methods produced smaller improvement over the top-k approach than for other diseases. This happened because the top-k approach has achieved very high average support (89% in leukemia and 94% in lung cancer data) already, and there is little room for further improvement. Interestingly, this implies that most of the important gene groups for these diseases only involve top ranked genes under the entropy measure. We suggest that this might be used as an indication that these diseases have relatively low disease complexity. On the other hand, colon and prostate cancers may have high disease complexity, since there are important gene groups for these diseases that involve genes that are ranked quite low under the entropy measure.

Chapter 18

Emerging Chemical Patterns – Theory and Applications

Jens Auer, Martin Vogt, and Jürgen Bajorath

Department of Life Science Informatics, Rheinische Friedrich-Wilhelms-Universität, Bonn, Germany.

18.1 Introduction

In chemoinformatics, computational methods are developed and applied to analyze and predict properties of small molecules including their behavior in biological systems. In fact, the prediction of biological activities of chemical compounds is one of the central themes in the chemoinformatics field. Especially during the early stages of pharmaceutical research, chemoinformatics methods are frequently used to help identify novel active compounds, so-called hits, in combination with experimental studies and further optimize their target-specific potency and other drug discovery-relevant parameters (such as, for example, solubility or metabolic stability).

Thus, compound classification techniques play a major role in chemoinformatics and computer-aided medicinal chemistry [36]. For the majority of these compound classification tasks, machine learning methods are applied [165]. Supervised machine learning approaches rely on the use of training sets to derive predictive models. For the classification of active compounds and the search for new hits, this often poses a problem, especially if computational methods should be applied in drug discovery to complement early stages of chemical optimization efforts. In such situations, there are often not enough known active reference compounds available to assemble sufficiently large training sets for conventional machine learning approaches such as decision trees, neural networks, or support vector machines [165]. These potential limitations have motivated us to explore machine learning or pattern recognition concepts that might be capable of deriving high-quality predictive models on the basis of only limited training data. In this context, we have become particularly interested in an approach termed emerging patterns [118, 126], which makes it possible to systematically generate feature patterns for objects with different class labels and identify feature signatures that appear with high frequency in one class, but not other(s). The emerging pattern approach has originated in computer science but has also been applied to biological problems such as the analysis of gene expression profiles [253]. In addition to such bioinformatics applications, we have adapted the emerging pattern methodology for compound classification in chemoinformatics and hence termed our adaptation emerging chemical pattern (ECP) [25]. Our studies have confirmed that ECP is indeed capable of deriving high-quality class label prediction models on the basis of very small training sets, which makes the approach highly attractive for molecular classification and other applications in the area of medicinal chemistry including simulation of lead optimization efforts [25], sequential screening campaigns [26], and bioactive compound conformation analysis [24].

Below, we first provide a brief account of the theory behind the ECP approach. For further details, the reader is referred to original publications of the emerging pattern methodology by Dong and colleagues, some of which are referenced in this chapter. Then, we discuss the application of ECP to compound classification in comparison with other chemoinformatics approaches. Finally, we present additional medicinal chemistry-relevant applications.

18.2   Theory

TABLE 18.1: Classification of molecular descriptors. Depending on the molecular information required for their computation, molecular descriptors can be partitioned into four classes.

Type	Derived from	Examples
I	Global (bulk) molecular properties	Molecular weight, atom counts
II	2D structure (molecular graph)	Structural keys, connectivity indices
III	3D structure	Surface properties, radius of gyration
IV	Biological properties	Biological activity bit strings

The description and prediction of desirable properties shared by chemical compounds such as a specific biological activity are prime topics in chemoinformatics and pharmaceutical research. A simple, yet very popular example is Lipinski's rule of five [268], a heuristic that a bioactive compound should comply with in order to eventually qualify as an orally available bioactive drug candidate. The rule uses four numerical properties derived from the chemical structure of a compound: molecular mass, octanol-water partition coefficient (logP; a measure for hydrophobicity or lipophilicity), and the number of hydrogen bond donors and acceptors. In order to comply with Lipinski's rule of five, a compound should meet at least three of the following four criteria:

1. at most five hydrogen bond donors

2. at most 10 hydrogen bond acceptors

3. molecular mass less than 500 Dalton

4. logP of maximally 5

The four properties are examples of a more general concept, i.e., the "mathematical representation of a molecule resulting from a procedure transforming the structural information encoded within a symbolic representation of a molecule" [395]. Such mathematical representations are called molecular or chemical descriptors that can considerably vary in their complexity and information content. The "Handbook of Molecular Descriptors" [407] provides an extensive reference of literally thousands of descriptors, ranging from simple properties like atom counts over topological descriptors derived from the molecular graph to complex combinations of properties derived from the three-dimensional shape of a molecule. All these descriptors can be classified based on the molecular representation required to compute them (see Table 18.1). Unfortunately, knowledge about experimentally validated three-dimensional bioactive compound conformations is usually rather limited and researchers often need to use descriptors that do not rely on conformational information, but that represent only structural properties of the compounds under investigation. However, the molecular graph often encodes enough information to define meaningful descriptors for the characterization of biological activity.

Given a database of descriptor values, Lipinski's rule of five might be rationalized as an emerging pattern [118], separating orally available from unavailable compounds. Going beyond this simple example, we have further adapted and refined the notion of emerging patterns for processing of chemical compounds and identifying discriminating ECPs.

For the analysis of emerging patterns, input data consist of feature values for sets of objects with different class labels. In the context of ECPs, these are typically values of numerical chemical property descriptors as described above calculated for different types of small molecules such as compounds with ("active") or without ("inactive") a specific biological activity. For the derivation of attribute-value pairs that constitute patterns, observed descriptor values ranges must be discretized into meaningful intervals. For ECP, a (compound) class information entropy-dependent discretization method relying on training data was applied [145, 433]. Alternatively, an unsupervised method discretizing values into three ranges based upon the mean and standard deviation of descriptor values also has been applied [26].

Chemical patterns are defined as class-specific combinations of chemical descriptor value ranges. A descriptor value range is denoted as a designated pair D : [low; upp), where D is the descriptor name while low and upp define the lower and upper bound of the value range, respectively. Round parentheses and square brackets are used to distinguish between open and closed intervals, respectively. A compound matches a descriptor value range if the corresponding descriptor value for that compound lies between the lower and upper boundaries of the interval. A *chemical pattern* p can then be interpreted as a combination of descriptor value ranges, i.e. $p = \{A_1 : [\text{low}_1, \text{upp}_1), \ldots, A_n : [\text{low}_n, \text{upp}_n)\}$ where all A_i are distinct. The *support* $\text{supp}_p(A)$ of a pattern p in a data set S is the percentage of compounds in S matching all descriptor value ranges. Patterns with strong support in one dataset D_1 of objects and weak support in another dataset D_2 are called *emerging patterns* [118, 126, 253]. If we study two compound classes (i.e., "active" vs. "inactive") represented by two data sets, ECPs can be searched for. The significance of an ECP can be quantified using the *growth rate*, defined as the ratio of the support a pattern has in two datasets:

$$\text{growth}_{D_1, D_2}(p) = \frac{\text{supp}_p(D_1)}{\text{supp}_p(D_2)}$$

If the support of a pattern is non-zero in D_1 but zero in D_2, the pattern is termed a *jumping emerging pattern* (JEP) [243] for which the growth is not defined and informally said to be *infinite*. JEPs are expected to be highly discriminatory. Chemical patterns can be partially ordered by a subset relationship, where a pattern s is considered to be a subset of pattern p if it is less restrictive than p. This means it consists of a subset of the descriptors present in p and each of the values ranges for descriptors in s contains the corresponding value range in p. Thus, any set that contains a JEP as a subset is also a JEP. This gives rise to the notion of *most expressive* JEPs. Most expressive JEPs are JEPs that are minimal with respect to the subset relationship, i.e., they do no contain any pattern that is itself a JEP [243]. Accordingly, most expressive JEPs represent highly discriminatory features for classification. Given the computational complexity of JEP mining (which represents an NP-hard problem) [427], a hypergraph-based algorithm [35] has been applied to identify most expressive JEPs for binary classification tasks. For classification and prediction of active compounds, we focus on most expressive JEPs. Specifically, we define *ECPs as the most expressive JEPs identified by numerical chemical descriptor analysis* [25].

18.3   Compound Classification

TABLE 18.2: Compound datasets for ECP classification. N is the number of compounds per set and compound potencies are reported as IC50 values (μM). The table has been generated using data taken from reference [25].

Class	N	< 1μM	≥ 1μM
BZR	321	283	38
DHR	586	249	337
GSK	464	281	183
HIV	967	821	146

For classification, ECPs are determined for an active and an inactive compound class used for training. Then, class labels are predicted for test compounds as follows: For each compound with unknown activity state, all pre-computed ECPs from each class are determined. For these ECPs, the cumulative support in the positive (active) and negative (inactive) training data is calculated, yielding two scores. The higher of the two scores determines whether the compound is classified as active or inactive. A normalization procedure is applied to account for the possibility that unevenly sized training sets generate significantly different numbers of ECPs for classification. Therefore, for each test compound, the cumulative support of ECPs is divided by the sum of all ECPs computed for the training data. The calculation of the cumulative score follows the CAEP (Classification by Aggregating Emerging Patterns) [126, 243] method except for the normalization step, which in our case will yield scores in the range 0 to 1. Classification is of course not limited to two classes of compounds (active and inactive). For example, compounds belonging to different activity classes might be classified or, alternatively, classification of compounds (belonging to an individual class) according to different activity (potency) levels might be attempted. In an exemplary application, ECP-based classification was performed on four datasets of active compounds [6] including benzodiazepines (BZR), dihydrofolate reductase inhibitors (DHR), glycogen synthase kinase-3 inhibitors (GSK3), and HIV protease inhibitors (HIV). These compound sets are summarized in Table 18.2.

The datasets were separated into two subsets (classes) of compounds with potency above or below 1 μM to obtain compound classes with higher (nanomolar) and lower (micromolar) potency. For different classification trials, initially, training sets of increasing size comprising 10%–50% of all micromolar or nanomolar compounds were selected. Then, much smaller training sets consisting of only three to 10 compounds were assembled. ECP-based classification was compared to two other classification approaches that are popular in the chemoinformatics field including binary QSAR [225] and decision trees [358]. For all three approaches, classification models were derived for series of 500 randomly selected training sets that were then applied to predict the micromolar or nanomolar class label of the remaining test compounds. As features, a set of 61 conformation-independent numerical molecular property descriptors with limited pair-wise correlation was evaluated [25]. Value ranges of these descriptors for each dataset were binned using information entropy-based discretization. For ECP classification, individual descriptors whose values only mapped to a single interval were omitted.

TABLE 18.3: Classification results for small training sets. Average prediction accuracies are reported for very small training sets of $N = 3$, 5, or 10 nanomolar and micromolar compounds using ECP, binary QSAR (BIN), and decision tree (DT) calculations. The table has been generated using data taken from reference [25].

	Nanomolar compounds								
Training	N=3			N=5			N=10		
	ECP	BIN	DT	ECP	BIN	DT	ECP	BIN	DT
BZR	0.62	0.72	1.00	0.75	0.58	0.57	0.74	0.57	0.59
DHR	0.54	0.68	1.00	0.72	0.54	0.58	0.73	0.71	0.59
GSK	0.57	0.74	1.00	0.80	0.64	0.68	0.82	0.51	0.69
HIV	0.79	0.73	1.00	0.78	0.65	0.63	0.81	0.57	0.66
	Micromolar compounds								
Training	N=3			N=5			N=10		
	ECP	BIN	DT	ECP	BIN	DT	ECP	BIN	DT
BZR	0.88	0.45	0.0	0.75	0.55	0.64	0.79	0.58	0.63
DHR	0.75	0.39	0.0	0.55	0.55	0.50	0.59	0.44	0.50
GSK	0.86	0.44	0.0	0.68	0.52	0.65	0.72	0.70	0.62
HIV	0.57	0.45	0.0	0.61	0.52	0.59	0.65	0.62	0.63

For training sets consisting of 10%–50% of all micro- or nanomolar compounds, the three classification methods yielded similarly high performance, achieving an overall classification accuracy of ca. 80%. Thus, under these training conditions, ECP classification reached the performance level of standard chemoinformatics approaches. Then, classification performance was evaluated for unusually small training sets of three, five, or 10 compounds, which would usually not be considered for machine learning applications in chemoinformatics. Under these conditions, the ECP approach clearly showed higher prediction accuracy than binary QSAR or decision trees. The results are summarized in Table 18.3. For the smallest ($N = 3$) learning sets, decision trees had no predictive ability because they classified all test compounds as nanomolar (yielding an artificial prediction accuracy of 100% for this class). In three instances, binary QSAR produced slightly better predictions than ECP for nanomolar compounds. However, for training sets of three micromolar compounds, binary QSAR prediction accuracy was worse than random (50%). For training sets of five compounds, prediction accuracy of ECP calculations was consistently and significantly higher than for binary QSAR or decision trees. Taken together, the results revealed that only ECP calculations produced meaningful classification results for very small training sets.

These findings confirmed that ECP analysis was capable of extracting highly discriminatory feature patterns from only a few training examples, which set the approach apart from standard machine learning methods for compound classification. We considered the ability of ECP to successfully operate on the basis of very small training sets a cardinal feature of this approach, which opened the door to address a number of special applications, for which other methods were difficult to apply.

18.4   Computational Medicinal Chemistry Applications

For several types of applications that are particularly relevant for medicinal chemistry projects, only a limited number of compounds are usually available for knowledge extraction and learning. Exemplary applications are discussed in the following.

18.4.1   Simulated Lead Optimization

In medicinal chemistry, the lead optimization process aims at converting newly identified active compounds into highly potent molecules with favorable molecular properties that ultimately qualify these leads for pre-clinical and clinical evaluation. Leads are typically optimized by subjecting them to a series of chemical modifications that cause desired potency progression. Thus, during the early stages of such medicinal chemistry projects, only a few active compounds (analogs) are available to guide optimization efforts.

To simulate lead optimization, we applied an iterative ECP classification protocol on the basis of small training sets ($N = 5$ or 10) [6]. The goal of these calculations was to gradually increase the potency of selected compounds. This corresponds to the ability to progressively predict more potent compounds on the basis of only few known actives, consistent with the goals of chemical optimization.

The analysis was carried out for the compound sets reported in Table 18.2. After an initial ECP classifier was derived, 10 iterations were carried out per compound set, representing an optimization trial. A total of 500 independent trials were carried out for each of the four compound datasets (and the results were averaged). During each iteration of a trial, training sets of five or 10 nano- and micromolar compounds were randomly selected from the current compound pool. This compound set was used to train the ECP classifier for this iteration, and the class label of all remaining test compounds was predicted. Then, all predicted micromolar (weakly active) compounds were removed from the test set and only compounds predicted to have nanomolar potency were retained for the next iteration. Over all iterations of a trial, the enrichment of nanomolar compounds in test sets of decreasing size was monitored and average potency values of these compounds were calculated. Thus, it was attempted to continuously refine ECP classification during search trials. Representative results are shown in Figure 18.1. All calculations with $N = 5$ or $N = 10$ training sets reached convergence during the first eight iterations producing final selection sets of fewer than 10 compounds with average nanomolar potency. Dependent on the compound class, average potency increases ranged from one to three orders of magnitude. In the course of the optimization, a sharp decline in compound numbers was generally accompanied by large increases in potency. Thus, for small training sets that were then further divided into subsets based on a simple potency ranking, ECP analysis was capable of identifying test compounds with significantly increased average potency within only a few iterations. These findings also revealed the successful identification of highly discriminatory patterns on the basis of only very few training examples, which then predicted increasingly potent compounds at a high rate. Hence, on the basis of these results, ECP classification should have significant potential to support early chemical optimization efforts through the prediction of new active compounds on the basis of alternative candidate compounds and/or small series of analogs.

18.4.2   Simulated Sequential Screening

Biological compound screening is the major source of new active compounds for medicinal chemistry [37]. Experimental and computational screening approaches can be applied in a synergistic manner, giving rise to sequential (or iterative) screening schemes [37]. In sequential screening, computational methods are applied to pre-select subsets of large compound libraries for experimental evaluation based on the likelihood of database compounds to display a desired biological activity. The computational pre-selection typically requires known active compounds as input (reference molecules). The selected database subset is then experimentally tested and newly identified active compounds are used as additional reference molecules for the next round of computational selection from the remaining non-tested compounds. The new candidates are again experimentally screened and this iterative process is continued until a sufficient number of new and chemically interesting active compounds is identified. The basic idea of this combined computational and experimental screening process is to substantially reduce the number of screening experiments required for hit identification [37]. However, for sequential screening, only very small numbers of active reference molecules are usually available compared to the size of screening libraries. Hence, it has also been attractive to investigate the ECP approach for the simulation of sequential screening trials. For this purpose, a publicly available dihydrofolate reductase inhibitor screening dataset was used in a pilot study [26]. This screening set consisted of 50,000 compounds, only 32 of which were experimentally confirmed to inhibit dihydrofolate reductase. ECP classifiers were trained using sets of five randomly selected inhibitors and 20 inactive screening set compounds. The same descriptor set and discretization procedure as described above were applied. Using these ECP classifiers, test compounds were ranked on the basis of matching patterns derived from active training sets. Hence, instead of binary classification (active vs. inactive), pattern-based ranking was carried out in this case according to the likelihood of activity. To simulate sequential screening, the highest ranked 10, 100, or 500 compounds were selected from the screening set and active compounds were identified (hence mimicking the experimental testing phase). In each case, the top-ranked 10 compounds were added to the training set for the next round (regardless of whether they were active or inactive) and all remaining newly identified hits. This procedure was applied to further refine the classifier for the subsequent iteration. For each selection set size (10, 100, or 500 molecules), 100 individual search trials were carried out. Each trial consisted of nine screening iterations such that the total number of evaluated screening dataset compounds was smaller than 10% (for the largest selection set size). Because five inhibitors were used for training, the screening set of nearly 50,000 molecules contained only 27 active test compounds. Thus, this simulated screening scenario was akin to a search for "needles in haystacks". During training, we monitored the distribution of patterns derived for classification. For active training compounds, on average ca. 10,700 patterns consisting of ca. 7.5 descriptor value pairs per pattern were generated. However, for inactive compounds, on average only ca. 170 patterns with ca. 3.3 descriptor value pairs were obtained. The likely reason for this observation was that an active training compound needed to be distinguished from many more inactive ones than vice versa. Accordingly, the large difference in the number of patterns between active and inactive compounds was due to the fact that the number of possible patterns exponentially grows in descriptor spaces of increasing dimensionality.

Table 18.4 reports average cumulative recovery rates of active compounds. For selection sets of 10, 100, and 500 database compounds, rates of ca. 19%, 26%, and 39% were observed, respectively. For selection sets of 10 compounds, the rate corresponded to the identification of approx. five new active compounds among only 115 evaluated database molecules. For the largest selection set, 10–11 active compounds were detected among 4525 database molecules. A steady increase in average recovery rates over different iterations was observed. Particularly noteworthy was the detection of proportionally large numbers of active compounds within the smallest selection sets (using only five active compounds for training). On average, evaluating 50 times more database molecules only doubled the number identified active compounds compared to the smallest selection sets.

Taken together, the results of this study [26] further confirmed that ECP classification could be successfully carried out on the basis of small training sets. Moreover, ECP calculations in the context of sequential screening tri-

TABLE 18.4: Average cumulative ECP recovery rates of active compounds. Average results are reported for 100 independent search trials and selection sets of 10, 100, and 500 database molecules. The total number of evaluated database compounds ("tested") and the average cumulative recovery rates ("RR") are listed for subsequent iterations ("It."). "TR" gives the size of the training sets and "ACT" the total number of active compounds that were detected. Newly identified hits were included in the training for the next iteration. The table has been generated using data taken from reference [26].

	10				100			
It.	**Tested**	**TR**	**ACT**	**RR**	**Tested**	**TR**	**ACT**	**RR**
1	35	35	1.32	4.9%	125	36.00	2.41	8.9%
2	45	45	1.78	6.6%	225	46.84	3.78	14.0%
3	55	55	2.73	10.1%	325	57.26	4.69	17.4%
4	65	65	3.53	13.1%	425	67.74	5.41	20.0%
5	75	75	4.00	14.8%	525	78.00	5.80	21.3%
6	85	85	4.50	16.6%	625	89.00	6.40	23.7%
7	95	95	4.90	18.2%	725	99.00	6.60	24.6%
8	105	105	5.10	18.9%	825	109.00	6.90	25.6%
9	115	115	5.20	19.4%	925	119.00	7.10	26.3%

	500			
It.	**Tested**	**TR**	**ACT**	**RR**
1	525	37.40	3.94	14.6%
2	1025	49.09	6.29	23.3%
3	1525	60.01	7.47	27.7%
4	2025	70.61	8.26	30.6%
5	2525	81.24	8.94	33.1%
6	3025	91.80	9.52	35.3%
7	3525	102.15	9.95	36.9%
8	4025	112.40	10.20	37.8%
9	4525	122.71	10.60	39.1%

als were characterized by a high level of sensitivity and specificity for small compound selection sets. ECP analysis detected ca. 20% of available active compounds in only ca. 100 of 50,000 screening set compounds that were evaluated, providing considerable theoretical support for the sequential screening paradigm.

18.4.3   Bioactive Conformation Analysis

A major problem in medicinal chemistry and drug design is the correct prediction of bioactive compound conformations (i.e., the 3D structures that active compounds adopt upon specific binding to their biological targets) [107, 334]. To this date, consistently successful predictions are not feasible. We were interested in exploring the question whether it might be possible to

systematically distinguish between experimentally observed binding conformations and modeled low-energy conformations of active compounds. Typically, only small numbers of observed bioactive conformations are available
for a compound activity class, which makes ECP classification an attractive
approach to address this question. Thus, the major goal of our analysis was
the search for specific descriptor patterns that might effectively distinguish
between bioactive and modeled conformations. However, different from the
lead optimization and sequential screening tasks, this objective required the
exploration of three-dimensional descriptors.

Bioactive and modeled conformations were systematically compared for
sets of compounds active against 18 different target proteins [24]. Bioactive
conformations of compounds available in X-ray structures of their targets were
extracted from these complexes. For each compound, one or more low energy
conformations were modeled using a stochastic conformational search protocol
that iteratively sampled local energy minima, as illustrated in Figure 18.2. Low
energy conformations were retained if the root mean square (RMS) gradient of
the chosen force field function met the pre-defined threshold value for relaxed
structures of $0.001 \, \mathrm{kcal \, mol^{-1} Å^{-1}}$ and if the conformations differed from each
other in their all heavy-atom RMS deviation (RMSD) by at least 0.1 Å. For
the 18 target protein sets, between five and 30 compounds with experimental
binding conformations were collected and for these compounds, between 16
and 247 low-energy conformers were sampled. On average, experimental binding and theoretical low-energy conformations displayed heavy atom RMSDs
between 2 and 3 Å. Thus, these conformations typically departed from each
other. These sets of experimental vs. modeled conformations were then uti-
lized for pattern analysis and ECP classification. As descriptors, a set of 67
conformation-dependent (3D) descriptors was used that represented charge
distributions, molecular surface-, or volume-derived properties [24].

ECP analysis was then carried out in order to identify patterns that discriminated between bioactive and modeled conformations. Encouragingly, for
each of the 18 target sets such patterns could be identified [24]. In most instances between 10 and 30 discriminatory ECPs were obtained and the descriptor composition of these patterns often varied in a target set-specific
manner. The majority of strongly discriminatory ECPs had infinite growth,
i.e., these patterns only appeared in bioactive, but not modeled conformations. Despite target set variations among discriminatory patterns, there were
common trends. For example, it is well known that binding to target proteins generally induces energetic strain in ligands [334]. Accordingly, many
discriminatory patterns that were highly specific for bioactive conformations
contained various energy descriptors including, for example, potential, torsional, or out-of-plane energy terms. Occasionally, patterns containing a single
energy descriptor value range combination were identified. Nevertheless, discriminatory patterns without energy descriptors were also found in a number
of instances. Importantly, in many cases, it was possible to interpret discriminatory patterns on the basis of ligand conformations and/or protein-ligand

TABLE 18.5: Most discriminatory ECPs for adenosine deaminase inhibitors. Reported are the 10 ECPs ("Patterns") that best discriminated between bioactive and modeled inhibitor conformations. The growth of these patterns is reported. "B" stands for bioactive/binding, "M" for modeled conformations, and "E" for energy descriptors (accounting for various bonded and non-bonded energy terms). For the purpose of our discussion, detailed definition of individual descriptors is not required. The table has been generated using data taken from reference [24].

Growth	B [%]	B	M [%]	M	Pattern
∞	93	14	0	0	$E_{\text{strain}} = (24.46 : \infty]$
∞	80	12	0	0	$E_{\text{str}} = (14.90 : \infty]$
∞	53	8	0	0	$\{E_{\text{tor}} = (1.88 : \infty],$ std.dim.2 $= (1.81 : \infty]\}$
∞	53	8	0	0	$\{E_{\text{tor}} = (1.88 : \infty],$ pmiY $= (1141.06 : \infty]\}$
∞	53	8	0	0	$E_{\text{oop}} = (1.64 : \infty]$
∞	53	8	0	0	$E_{\text{ang}} = (17.54 : \infty]$
∞	100	15	0	0	$E_{\text{strain}} = (15.69 : \infty]$
∞	87	13	0	0	$E_{\text{str}} = (10.26 : \infty]$
∞	73	11	0	0	$E_{\text{ang}} = (13.51 : \infty]$
∞	53	8	0	0	$E_{\text{stb}} = (0.96 : \infty]$

interactions seen in x-ray structures and thus rationalize why these patterns discriminated between experimental and theoretical conformations [24]. The frequent interpretability of discriminatory ECPs very well complemented their predictive power in data mining and compound classification. In the following, two exemplary cases are discussed to illustrate major findings of ECP-based conformation analysis.

The adenosine deaminase set contained five inhibitors with known bioactive conformations and 139 theoretical conformers of these inhibitors, with an average RMSD of 2.45 Å. Table 18.5 reports the top 10 most discriminatory patterns for this set (all of which have infinite growth). All of these patterns are formed by a single or maximally two descriptor-value range pairs. In each pattern, an energy descriptor is found that accounts for strain, torsional, out-of-plane, or angular energy terms. These findings can be rationalized by comparing experimental and theoretical conformations, as illustrated in Figure 18.3. In the bioactive conformation of the inhibitor, all rings are to a more or lesser extent twisted, which maximizes van der Waals interactions between these rings and the binding pocket of the enzyme. This induced fit compensates for the unfavorable ring geometry. In the modeled low-energy conformations, these rings adopt energetically preferred planar geometry. This is the major discrepancy between experimental and theoretical conformations, which is well reflected by the various associated energy terms that occur in the most discriminatory ECPs.

TABLE 18.6: Most discriminatory ECPs for trypsin inhibitors. Reported are the top three most discriminatory ECPs ("Patterns") for experimental and modeled trypsin inhibitor conformers. "B" stands for bioactive/binding, "M" for modeled conformations, and "E" for energy descriptors. For the purpose of our discussion, detailed definition of individual descriptors is not required. The table has been generated using data taken from reference [24].

Growth	B [%]	B	M [%]	M	Pattern
∞	100	30	0	0	$E_{\text{strain}} = (5.11 : \infty]$
∞	63	19	0	0	$E_{\text{str}} = (10.03 : \infty]$
∞	63	19	0	0	$E_{\text{stb}} = (0.53 : \infty]$

As a second example, trypsin inhibitors are presented. This set contained 30 inhibitors with known bioactive conformations and 195 modeled conformers. In this case, the average RMSD between experimental and theoretical conformers was only 1.74 Å (i.e., smaller than in most other cases). Hence, structural differences between many bioactive and modeled conformations were relatively subtle here. However, compared to modeled low-energy conformers, nearly 80% of all bioactive conformations showed increased, strain, bond stretching, angle bending, and potential energy, which was again well reflected by the top three discriminatory ECPs in Table 18.6.

In Figure 18.4, a major structural difference between bioactive conformations and modeled conformers of trypsin inhibitors is highlighted. In the experimental conformation, the diaminomethyl group is in axial position (because it is constrained by strong hydrogen bonding interactions within its binding pocket), whereas this group is in the lower-energy equatorial position in modeled conformers. Thus, energetic effects associated with relatively small yet well-defined structural differences between experimental binding conformations and theoretical low-energy conformers of these trypsin inhibitors were captured by most discriminatory ECPs.

18.5   Chemoinformatics Glossary

Compound Classification: A process that divides compound datasets into different subsets or classes having different properties. In chemoinformatics, typical class labels include "active" and "inactive" with respect to a given biological activity or "activity 1", "activity 2", "activity 3" . . . for classification according to different specific biological activities.

Conformational Sampling: Computational search for preferred conformations of molecules on the basis of randomly or systematically introduced structural changes followed by potential energy evaluation.

Emerging Chemical Patterns: The most expressive jumping emerging patterns identified by numerical chemical descriptor analysis.

Hit: A new active compound identified through biological screening or computational analysis followed by experimental confirmation.

Lead Optimization: A central task in medicinal chemistry where the potency of specifically active compounds and other molecular properties are optimized through a series of chemical modifications to ultimately generate candidates for pre-clinical and clinical evaluation.

QSAR: Quantitative structure-activity relationship analysis.

Sequential Screening: A compound screening strategy that involves iterative cycles of computational candidate selection and experimental testing, taking information from newly identified active compounds into account during subsequent rounds.

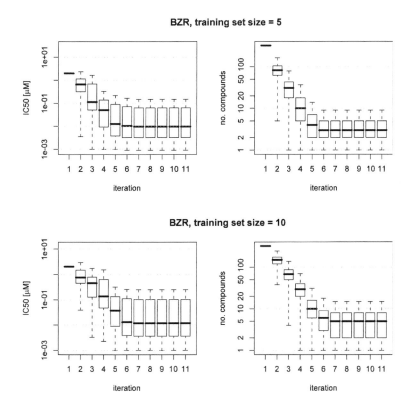

FIGURE 18.1: Simulated Lead Optimization. Representative search results are shown for compound activity class BZR and training sets of $N = 5$ and 10 compounds. Box plot representations report the average potency values and numbers of test compounds for 500 independent search trials. The box shows the 0.75 (top) and 0.25 quartile (bottom) separated by the median (horizontal bar). The lines indicate the largest and smallest values within a distance of maximal 1.5 times of the box size (relative to the nearest boundary).

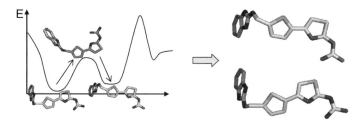

FIGURE 18.2: Illustration of conformer generation. For ligands with experimentally determined binding conformations (bioactive conformations), theoretical low-energy conformations were generated by stochastic conformational sampling in combination with energy minimization to screen local energy minima on a theoretical potential energy surface.

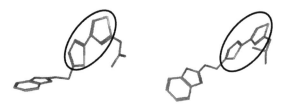

FIGURE 18.3: Conformational analysis of an adenosine deaminase inhibitor. Most distorted ring systems in the bioactive conformation that are regularized in energy-minimized conformers are encircled. On the left, the experimental binding conformation is shown and on the right, a modeled low-energy conformation.

FIGURE 18.4: Conformational analysis of a trypsin inhibitor. Different positions of the diaminomethyl group in the bioactive and modeled conformations are encircled. On the left, the experimental binding conformation is shown and on the right, a modeled low-energy conformation.

Chapter 19

Emerging Patterns as Structural Alerts for Computational Toxicology

Bertrand Cuissart, Guillaume Poezevara, Bruno Crémilleux

Groupe de Recherche en Informatique, Image, Automatique et Instrumentation de Caen, University of Caen Basse-Normandie, CNRS UMR 6072

Alban Lepailleur

Centre d'Etudes et de Recherche sur le Médicament de Normandie, University of Caen Basse-Normandie, UPRES EA 4258 - FR CNRS 3038

Ronan Bureau

Centre d'Etudes et de Recherche sur le Médicament de Normandie, University of Caen Basse-Normandie, UPRES EA 4258 - FR CNRS 3038

19.1   Introduction

Thanks to significant advances on both the algorithmic and the practical sides, mining graph data has turned into a key domain of data mining. Various domains use graphs to model their data and graph patterns have widely demonstrated their potential, especially in the field of chemoinformatics where chemical structures are commonly modeled as graphs. Computational toxicology, which aims at studying toxicity by using computer tools, is a typical example of an important field for developing graph mining methods. Even though there already exist useful tools such as Derek [353] that rely on fragments for assessing the toxic behavior of molecules, these methods suffer from two limitations [411]: (i) there is a lack of objectivity when a human expert assesses the level of toxicity caused by a molecular fragment and (ii) there is no decision rule based on the conjunction of two or more molecular fragments. Thus, there is a strong need of methods that can extract conjunctions of molecular fragments whose occurrences demonstrate relationships with a toxic behavior.

The chapter meets this need by designing a method, based on the notion of *emerging pattern* [118], called the *Frequent Emerging Molecular Pattern (FEMP)* [339, 340]. Given a chemical dataset partitioned into two classes (e.g. toxic molecules and non-toxic ones), a FEMP is a conjunction of molecular fragments such that: (i) its frequencies between the classes are sufficiently different and (ii) its frequency in the target class is high enough to be significant to support further use. In chemoinformatics, this notion positively answers the need of an automatic and understandable method for extracting the conjunctions of fragments related to a given behavior: FEMPs have already demonstrated their usefulness in computational ecotoxicology [288].

Section 19.2 explains our methodological contributions, i.e. (i) the FEMPs, their computation, and (ii) a condensed representation summarizing the extracted information. Section 19.3 gives the key results of an experimental study, where we quantitatively assess the effectiveness of the FEMPs as structural alerts in computational toxicology. Section 19.4 provides a thorough chemical analysis of the information brought by the extracted FEMPs. That chemical analysis represents a solid qualitative reasoning that advocates and demonstrates the advantages of the use of the FEMPs in computational toxicology.

19.2 Frequent Emerging Molecular Patterns as Potential Structural Alerts

This section introduces the notion of a *Frequent Emerging Molecular Pattern (FEMP)*. Here, we stress on the intuitions and the key ideas, and illustrate them by the example in Figure 19.1. Formal definitions and proofs of the results are given in [340]. Sections 19.3 and 19.4 will show that FEMPs are at the core of the chemical information discovered by data mining processes.

19.2.1 Definition of Frequent Emerging Molecular Pattern

The left side of Figure 19.1 displays molecular structures in the usual manner: *2D molecular graphs*. *Graphs* are frequently used to model elements having relationships – the edges of the graphs represent relationships. Then, a molecular structure is depicted as a set of elements, the atoms, that interact by means of edges, the chemical bonds. An element of a molecular graph is *labeled* with the atomic number it represents, while the label of an edge indicates the type of the chemical bond. In Figure 19.1, the chemical dataset is partitioned in two parts: toxic molecules and non-toxic ones.

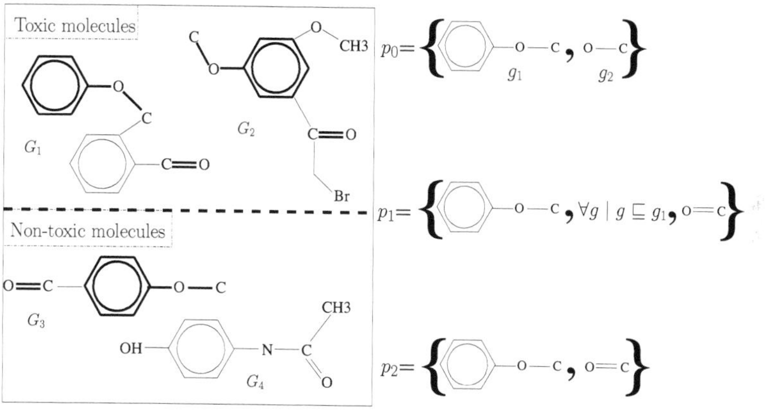

FIGURE 19.1: An illustrative chemical dataset.

The right side of Figure 19.1 displays *molecular fragments*; a molecular fragment represents a part of a molecule. A fragment is said to *occur* within a molecule if there is an embedding of the fragment in the molecule that satisfies both the relational structure of the fragment (the presence and the absence of every edge) and the labeling scheme of the edges. As an example, the embedding of the fragment g_1 is shown in bold on the molecular graphs. The *frequency of a fragment* in a chemical dataset quantifies the portion of molecules of the dataset where the fragment occurs. For instance, g_1 occurs in

100% of the toxic molecules and 50% in the non-toxic ones (cf. Figure 19.1). A *molecular pattern* is defined to be a set of molecular fragments. The *length* of a molecular pattern corresponds to the number of fragments it contains. A molecular pattern *occurs* in a molecule if each one of its fragments occurs in the molecule. The *frequency of a pattern* in a chemical dataset quantifies the portion of molecules of the dataset where the pattern occurs. In Figure 19.1, the pattern p_0 has a frequency of 50% in the non-toxic molecules.

In order to automatically discover structural alerts, it appears to be highly appropriate to look for contrasts between toxic and non-toxic molecules. When a molecular pattern sufficiently occurs within the toxic molecules and has a frequency which significantly increases from the non-toxic molecules to the toxic ones, then it stands as a potential structural alert related to the toxicity.

The notion of a Frequent Emerging Molecular Pattern embodies this natural idea by using the growth-rate measure. When a dataset is partitioned between targeted examples and non-targeted ones (also called "classes"), the *growth-rate of a pattern* p is defined to be the ratio between the frequency of p in the target class over its frequency outside the target class. Following our example, the growth-rate of a molecular pattern is obtained by dividing its frequency in the toxic molecules by its frequency in the non-toxic ones. As usual when the denominator is equal to zero (and the numerator is different of zero), the value of the growth-rate is denoted with the infinity symbol, ∞. An *emerging pattern* [118] is a pattern whose growth-rate value exceeds a threshold given by the user. For example, in Figure 19.1, the growth-rate value of the molecular pattern p_0 is equal to 2. Thus, as soon as the minimum threshold is set to less than 2, p_0 is an emerging pattern, from the non-toxic molecules to the toxic molecules. We can now state the definition of a FEMP:

Definition 19.1 (Frequent Emerging Molecular Pattern (FEMP)) *Let $\mathcal{G}$ be a chemical dataset whose molecules are partitioned into two classes. Given a frequency threshold f_{min} and a growth-rate threshold ρ_{min}, a molecular pattern p is a* frequent emerging molecular pattern *if its frequency in the target class is greater or equal than f_{min} and its growth-rate from the non-target class molecules to the target class is greater or equal than ρ_{min}.*

To simplify, henceforth the property "being a FEMP in the chemical dataset $\mathcal{G}$ partitioned according to a classification and given a frequency threshold f_{min} and a growth-rate threshold ρ_{min}" will be abbreviated as "being a FEMP".

19.2.2   Using RPMPs as Condensed Representation of FEMPs

In practice, FEMPs are often numerous and include redundant information. This section deals with this issue by proposing a condensed representation of the FEMPs – the Representative Pruned Molecular Patterns (RPMP).

The growth-rate of a molecular pattern is computed from its frequencies in the classes in the chemical dataset. It implies that the property of being a FEMP only relies on its *extent*, the set of molecules of the input dataset in which the molecular pattern occurs. Patterns can be condensed by using specific forms of patterns such as the closed patterns [326, 375]; by condensation we mean that all FEMPs can be regenerated (from the condensed patterns) with their exact values of growth-rate and frequency. A *closed pattern* is a pattern from which no element can be added without decreasing its extent. Given any extent of the input dataset, there is at most one closed graph pattern corresponding to this extent. Relying on this property, one can condense a set of FEMPs by retaining only the related *closed* FEMPs. This significantly reduces the number of patterns without losing information.

A molecular fragment may occur in another fragment, in the same way as a molecular fragment occurs in a molecule. As a consequence, the relationship "occurs in" induces a partial order between the molecular structures, depicting either a molecule or a fragment. The fact that g_1 occurs in g_2 is denoted $g_1 \sqsubseteq g_2$. As it is a partial order, the relation $\sqsubseteq$ is transitive and it follows that the extent of a fragment is included in the extent of any of its "subfragments". For example, the benzene ring ($\bigcirc$) is a subfragment of the fragment g_1 of Figure 19.1, and its extent in the chemical dataset $\mathcal{G}$, namely $\{G_1, G_2, G_3, G_4\}$, contains the extent of g_1, namely $\{G_1, G_2, G_3\}$. Thus, one can add a new fragment to a molecular pattern without decreasing its extent, as long as the added fragment is a subfragment of an element of the pattern. For example, adding the benzene ring to the molecular pattern p_o in Figure 19.1 will not change the extent of p_0 because the benzene is a subfragment of g_1, which is an element of p_0. As a consequence, a closed molecular pattern always contains all the subfragments of any of its fragments.

In practice, closed patterns tend to be long patterns and a large portion of their fragments are subfragments of another bigger fragment. These subfragments have no meaning and can be removed without loss of information. By pruning any fragment of a closed pattern p which is a subfragment of another fragment of p, we get a shorter representation of the closed pattern. We call the resulting patterns *Representative Pruned Molecular Patterns (RPMPs)*. There is a one-to-one correspondence between the RPMPs and the closed molecular patterns, and this correspondence preserves the extent [340]. For example, in Figure 19.1, the pattern p_1 is the closed pattern sharing the same extent as the pattern p_0. Not only p_1 contains g_1, but also all its subfragments. p_2 is the RPMP associated to the closed pattern p_1; p_2 has been built by removing any fragment of p_1 that is a subfragment of another fragment of p_1. p_2 enables us to provide a meaningful and understandable representation of p_1.

Definition 19.2 (Representative Pruned Molecular Pattern (RPMP))
Let $\mathcal{G}$ be a chemical dataset. A molecular pattern p is a representative pruned molecular pattern if the molecular pattern obtained by adding all the subfragments of the elements of p is a closed molecular pattern in $\mathcal{G}$.

Given a chemical dataset partitioned between targeted and non-targeted molecules, a minimum frequency threshold and a minimum growth-rate threshold, we have designed a method to mine the set of the Representative Pruned Molecular Patterns that are Frequent Emerging Molecular Patterns. This is discussed next.

19.2.3   Notes on the Computation

This section gives a sketch of our method for computing RPMPs. Let $\mathcal{G}$ be a given dataset partitioned into targeted molecules and non-targeted ones. Recall that a FEMP is a molecular pattern whose frequency amongst the targeted molecules exceeds a given frequency threshold f_{min}. Since the relation "occurs in" is transitive, the frequencies, in the target class of molecules, of all molecular fragments in a FEMP must also exceed f_{min}. Our method uses this property by firstly extracting these frequent fragments. Second, it describes each molecule of the dataset by indicating for each of the frequent fragments whether it occurs or not in the molecule. Third, relying on this new description, one extracts the FEMPs by using an existing method dedicated to discover the emerging patterns.

The FEMPs and their associated RPMPs are computed by integrating three existing tools: GASTON [317], MICMAC [375], and VFLIB [96]. First, frequent fragments amongst the targeted molecules are extracted using the graph mining tool GASTON. GASTON computes the extent of a frequent fragment amongst the targeted molecules. We have updated it in order to simultaneously provide the extent of a frequent fragment in the whole input $\mathcal{G}$. The result of the step is a dataset $\mathcal{D}$ which is a description of $\mathcal{G}$ based on the occurrences of the frequent fragments amongst the targeted molecules. Then, MICMAC mines from $\mathcal{D}$ the closed patterns that also are frequent emerging patterns. Finally, the RPMPs are obtained by pruning these closed patterns: a fragment is removed from a closed pattern p as soon as it is a subfragment of another fragment of p. This step requires to perform subgraph isomorphism tests; they are done using an implementation based on the functionalities provided by the graph matching library VFLIB.

19.2.4   Related Work

Several methods have been designed for discovering graphs that are correlated to a given class. All these algorithms operate on a graph dataset partitioned into two classes, targeted examples and non-targeted ones.

Molfea [218] relies on a level-wise algorithm. It extracts the *linear subgraphs(chains)* which are frequent amongst the targeted examples and infrequent amongst the non-targeted ones. However, the restriction to linear subgraphs disables a direct extraction of the fragments containing a branching point or a ring, as the benzene.

Moss [54] is a program dedicated to discovering frequent fragments by mining molecular graphs; it can be extended to find the *discriminative fragments*. Given two frequency thresholds f_M and f_m, a discriminative fragment corresponds to a connected fragment whose frequency is above f_M amongst the targeted molecules and below f_m amongst the non-targeted ones. This definition differs from the usual notion of emergence which is based on the growth-rate measure as introduced in the previous section. Note that the set of the discriminative fragments according to the thresholds f_M and f_m does not contain the whole set of the FEMPs having a growth rate higher than f_M/f_m or any other given growth rate threshold. Moreover, such fragments only correspond to patterns of length 1.

Another work has been dedicated to the discovery of the *contrast fragments* [406]. A contrast fragment is a fragment that occurs in the targeted examples and never occurs in the non-targeted ones. Although this notion is very interesting, it requires a lot of computation. To the best of our knowledge, the calculus is limited to graph datasets containing one targeted example and the mining of a molecule exceeding 20 atoms brings up a significant challenge.

19.3   Experiments in Predictive Toxicology

This section aims to experimentally assess the utility of the Frequent Emerging Molecular Patterns (FEMPs) for predictive toxicology. Following the results shown in the previous section, we use Representative Pruned Molecular Patterns (RPMPs) as a condensed representation of the FEMPs. For the sake of simplicity, in the following by a RPMP we mean a RPMP which is also a FEMP. In this section, first, the chemical dataset and the experimental setup are detailed, then the potential of the FEMPs is assessed by examining whether they retain their properties outside a learning set. Finally, quantitative results about the RPMPs in predictive toxicology are provided.

19.3.1   Materials and Experimental Setup

Chemical Dataset

Data were obtained from the *EPA Fathead Minnow Acute Toxicity Database* (EPAFHM) [134]. The data were collected by the Environment Protection Agency of the United States. EPAFHM has already been used for expert systems in computational toxicology [414]. The chemical dataset used here include molecules selected from EPAFHM based on the LC50 value as-

Growth-rate	Category (%)				
threshold	i	ii	iii	iv	v
2	25.2	13.1	30.0	16.7	14.6
5	24.4	12.0	32.1	11.1	20.1
10	27.6	8.7	34.1	6.6	22.8
25	33.7	1.2	31.3	3.0	30.5
∞	34.8	0.0	29.3	2.6	33.1

TABLE 19.1: The RPMPs outside the learning set.

sociated to the molecules[1] – we selected the molecules known as very toxic or non-toxic. The dataset includs 297 molecules, partitioned according to their level of toxicity: 74 molecules are very toxic and 172 are non-toxic.

Experimental Setup

Results given in this section are obtained from averaging over a five-folds cross-validation scheme: The dataset was randomly shuffled and then divided into five folds, such that each fold preserves the initial ratio between very toxic molecules and non-toxic ones. Each fold is successively the *test set*, with the union of the four other folds forming the *learning set*. A learning set averages 196.8 molecules (59.2 very toxic and 137.6 non-toxic) whereas a test set averages 49.2 molecules (14.8 very toxic and 34.4 non-toxic).

By definition, the property of "being a RPMP" relies on two thresholds: a minimum frequency value and a minimum growth-rate value. Throughout this experiment, the minimum frequency threshold is set to 8% (i.e., a pattern has to appear in 5 very toxic molecules to be extracted) and the minimum growth-rate threshold varies. With this minimum frequency threshold, 104.2 frequent fragments are extracted on average from a learning set (consisting of the very toxic molecules), and these frequent fragments contain on average 5.7 atoms. The number of RPMPs decreases from 318 (when the growth-rate value is 2) to 43.3 (when the growth-rate value is set to ∞). The RPMPs are mostly conjunctions of several molecular fragments and their average length is between 2 and 3 fragments, whatever the growth-rate threshold value is.

19.3.2 Generalization of the RPMPs

Generalization of the Properties of the RPMPs

As previously seen, "being a RPMP" relies on two key properties: (i) a RPMP is frequent enough to be representative and to ensure further uses and (ii) its growth-rate value conveys a relation between the RPMP and the toxicity. This section assesses whether these key properties can be general-

---

[1] The Lethal Concentration 50 (LC50) of a molecule indicates the concentration that kills half of a population of fish; for the sake of simplicity, the term "toxicity" is used even if the LC50 indicates the ecotoxicity of a molecule.

Growth-rate threshold	Length (l)	Coverage		Success (%)		
		rate (%)	contrast	TP	TN	OV
2	l≥1	71.1	1.54	94.5	38.9	55.69
	l=1	64.2	1.84	94.5	48.8	62.6
5	l≥1	44.7	3.0	83.7	72.0	75.6
	l=1	37.8	4.03	79.7	80.2	80.08
10	l≥1	34.1	4.9	77.0	84.3	82.11
	l=1	26.4	6.06	63.5	89.5	81.7
25	l≥1	23.1	6.5	56.7	91.2	80.89
	l=1	13.0	6.97	32.4	95.3	76.42
∞	l≥1	20.3	5.97	48.6	91.8	78.86
	l=1	9.3	8.36	24.3	97.0	75.2

TABLE 19.2: Prediction of the toxicity of a molecule thanks to the RPMPs.

ized outside the learning set. For that purpose, we follow the cross-validation scheme and examine the behavior of every RPMP in the test set related to the learning set it has been extracted from. By examining its extent in the test set, each RPMP is classified into one of the following five exclusive categories: (i) the RPMP meets both the frequency threshold and the growth-rate threshold, (ii) it only meets the frequency threshold, (iii) it only meets the growth-rate threshold, (iv) it meets neither the frequency threshold nor the growth-rate one, (v) it does not occur in the test set.

Table 19.1 gives the portions of the RPMPs in each category for several growth-rate thresholds. The sum of the portions of the first three categories shows that two-thirds of the RPMPs still meet the frequency threshold or the growth-rate one in a test set. By comparing results in categories (ii) and (iii), one note that a RPMP more often meets the growth-rate threshold than the frequency one (a half of the RPMP meets the growth-rate threshold whereas only a third still meets the frequency one). Taken together, these results indicate that the key properties associated to a RPMP are satisfied outside the learning set.

The RPMPs for Predicting Toxicity of Molecules

In order to quantitatively assess the RPMPs in predictive toxicology, the following decision rule has been implemented: *a molecule is classified as very toxic if it contains at least one RPMP*. Table 19.2 displays the results by using such a classification rule on the related test set. The first column gives the value of the growth-rate that has been used for extracting the RPMPs. The *coverage rate* indicates the portion of the molecules of a test set that contains at least one RPMP. The *coverage contrast* corresponds to the ratio of the coverage rate amongst the very toxic molecules over the coverage rate amongst the non-toxic ones. *TP* (i.e., True Positive) displays the portion of very toxic molecules that are correctly processed by the decision rule and *TN* (i.e. True Negative) is the ratio of non-toxic molecules correctly processed. *OV* indicates the overall success rate of the decision rule.

Results show that such a decision rule is able to reach fair overall success rates, greater than 80%. Moreover the contrast values indicate that the decision rule is more often triggered in the very toxic molecules than in the non-toxic ones; such a result indicates the reliability of the process. Table 19.2 also provides the results obtained by using only the RPMPs of length 1. We see that the portions of very toxic molecules that are correctly classified (i.e. *TP*) are significantly higher by using the whole set of RPMPs instead of RPMPs of length 1. Thus, one concludes that there exist conjunctions of non-emerging molecular fragments that have an influence on the toxic behavior of a molecule. Relationships between the chemical composition of some RPMPs and their effect on toxicity are discussed in the following section.

19.4   A Chemical Analysis of RPMPs

RPMPs have the advantage to support a chemical analysis. This section describes such an analysis that gives valuable new information for structure-toxicity relationships. The analysis is carried out according to two chemical functions or groups, the alkyl chains and the aromatic groups.

Alkyl Chains

Growth rate	Molecular fragment
2.7	
6.9	
11.5	
13.8	
∞	

TABLE 19.3: Growth-rate values of the alkyl chains according to their order

A first illustration deals with the impact of the order associated to the alkyl chains (the fragments are ordered by their number of atoms). The corresponding discovered patterns (cf. Table 19.3) show a clear relation between the growth-rate values and their orders of the fragments. The meaningful order of the alkyl chains begins for C6 (6 carbons, growth-rate of 2.7), it increases strongly for C7 (growth-rate of 6.9) to reach a maximum value for C11 (a growth-rate of ∞). It is well known that the hydrophobicity of an alkyl chain correlates with its order and that hydrophobicity of a fragment favors a toxic behavior. The above analysis shows that the growth-rate values match the chemical knowledge on toxicity.

Aromatic Groups

The second illustration is related to the aromatic groups. These groups have a strong impact on the toxicity of chemicals. Our analysis shows that the nature of the substituents on the aromatic ring plays a major role on toxicity.

Growth rate	Molecular fragments
3.01	
3.06	
10.7	
20.7	

TABLE 19.4: Association between alkyl chains and aromatic groups

The first example is the combination between an aromatic group and an alkyl chain. An aromatic group alone has a growth-rate value of 3. Associated with a C2 alkyl chain, we do not observe a modification of the growth-rate value but the growth-rate increases strongly for C3 and C4 alkyl chains (cf. Table 19.4).

The second example corresponds to the chlorinated benzenes or chlorinated phenols (cf. Table 19.5, the dotted lines depict a flexibility for the nature of the last atom associated to the aromatic feature). Chlorine atoms on aromatic groups lead to an increase of toxicity. This point clearly appears in our study. The addition of one chlorine increases the growth-rate by a factor of around 4. The addition of two chlorines increases the growth-rate by a factor of 8, reaching a maximum value with two chlorines in ortho positions on the aromatic group. We observe the same evolution for the phenol functions.

The third example concerns the combination between an alkene function and an aromatic group (cf. Table 19.6-A). The growth-rate is maximum (i.e.

Chlorines in the benzene function		Chlorines in the phenol function	
Growth rate	**Molecular fragments**	**Growth rate**	**Molecular fragments**
2.08	(benzene ring)	3.64	(benzene ring)—O
7.66	(benzene ring with Cl)	13.8	Cl—(benzene ring)—O
16.1	(benzene ring with 2 Cl)	∞	Cl—(benzene ring)—O, with Cl
∞	(benzene ring with Cl, —Cl)		

TABLE 19.5: Addition of chlorines

∞), showing the potentially high toxicity of the association. One can note that the alkene function alone has a high growth-rate value (10.73).

The last example deals with the association between a carbonyl function and an aromatic group (cf. Table 19.6-B). In this case, we observe no significant evolution of the growth-rate values compared to the patterns without this function (see the alkyl chains and the aromatic group in Table 19.4). So, the impact of the carbonyl function on the toxicity is not characterized.

19.5   Conclusion

In this chapter, we have defined the notion of frequent emerging molecular patterns, and have shown that such patterns are useful in chemoinformatics. We have shown that the whole set of frequent emerging molecular patterns can be condensed by means of their related representative pruned molecular patterns. An experimental study has been carried out on a chemical dataset. This study has indicated the effectiveness of using the information provided by the occurrences of frequent emerging molecular patterns in predictive toxicology: a decision rule based on such patterns can distinguish between a very toxic molecule and non-toxic one in 80% of the cases. Besides, it has been shown in Section 19.4 that the evolution of the growth-rate values associated to each Representative Pruned Molecular Patterns gives new keys to understand the impact of an atom, a group of atoms, or a chemical function on the

A- Alkene and aromatic group			B- Carbonyl function and aromatic group		
Growth rate	Molecular fragments		Growth rate	Molecular fragments	
10.73	c══c		3.06	c══o	
∞	c══c		10.35	c══o	
			16.01	c══o	

TABLE 19.6: Combination with an aromatic group

toxicity of a chemical derivative. These results strongly advocate the potential of this new approach for computational toxicology.

Part VI

Contrast Mining for Special Domains

Chapter 20

Emerging Patterns and Classification for Spatial and Image Data

Łukasz Kobyliński and Krzysztof Walczak

Institute of Computer Science, Warsaw University of Technology

20.1 Introduction

One of the most burning issues in computing currently is to develop methods, which will allow us to cope with the stream of multimedia data that is being generated and disseminated through the Internet every day. This must be done by providing a way to intelligently filter the incoming information, classify and present it to the users in a comprehensible manner. Much work has been done already in the field of processing large quantities of numeric and textual data and also in the field of multimedia data processing. Providing efficient algorithms for processing the amount of multimedia data we have available today remains to be a major challenge.

There are several specific problems associated with the domain of image and, more generally, multimedia data that need to be tackled in order to provide a successful solution to any of the tasks most commonly considered in the case of data mining. The diversity of multimedia requires that such data undergoes a preliminary transformation step, which is tightly connected with the particular type of data being analyzed. Multimedia data is unstructured and as such needs to be preprocessed to enable any type of further analysis. This data is also of a spatial (image) or spatio-temporal (video) character and only methods taking into account this multi-dimensionality may be applied to it. Finally, multimedia data seems to convey information in a relative way, much more than in absolute values, as in regular databases. Differences between objects and background, contrast, movement are the characteristics that need to be taken into account in the analysis of such data.

A number of new techniques for data analysis have been developed in the course of the fruitful research in the area of contrast pattern mining. Following their success in many areas of application, we propose a supervised learning approach to classifying multimedia data, which uses classifiers created on the basis of Jumping Emerging Patterns mined from training data. In this chapter we address the problem of efficiently discovering JEPs and using them directly for classifying multimedia data. We propose an enhancement of the traditional transactional database representation to include important information about spatial (and possibly temporal) relationships between features, which may be discovered in data. We also introduce new types of patterns to tackle such data – the jumping emerging patterns with occurrence counts (occJEPs) and spatial emerging patterns (SEPs). On the basis of the proposed image representation method, we also show a possible application of jumping emerging substrings (JESs) to the problem of multimedia data mining.

20.2   Previous Work

Many applications of emerging patterns (EPs) have been proposed to date, with a particularly fruitful research in the area of bioinformatics, specifically classification and finding relationships in gene data. The first EP-based algorithms concerning analysis of such data have been proposed in [252, 253].

The concept of recurrent items in transactional data has been presented in the area of multimedia data analysis in [458] in the context of association rules, and general and efficient algorithms for discovering rules with recurrent items have been studied in [320] and [347]. The extension of jumping emerging patterns to include recurrent items and using them for building classifiers has been proposed in [210]. The idea of mining emerging substrings as means of capturing interesting relationships in textual data has been proposed in [74].

20.3   Image Representation

The ability to reason in a multimedia database on the basis of image content relies in a great manner on the method of representing the visual information in a structured way. This is most commonly done by creating constant-size feature vectors, which should correspond to human perception of an image as closely as possible. Many approaches to spatial and image data representation have been proposed, namely approaches using low-level visual features, an intermediate semantic representation, or local image representation. Here, we propose a straightforward tile-based approach to image representation, which allows us to capture important characteristics of the underlying data and use it in pattern-based classification methods.

The images are uniformly divided into a grid of $x \times y$ tiles, where x and y are the numbers of rows and columns respectively, and for each of the tiles image features are calculated. In our experiments we have selected to use color and texture features of the images. Color features are represented by a histogram calculated in the HSV color space, with the hue channel quantized to h discrete ranges, while saturation and value channels to s and v ranges respectively. In effect, the representation takes the form of a $h \times s \times v$ element vector of real values between 0 and 1. For the representation of texture we use a feature vector consisting of mean and standard deviation values calculated from the result of filtering an original image with a bank of Gabor functions. These filters are scaled and rotated versions of the base function, which is a product of a Gaussian and a sine function. By using m orientations and n scales we get a feature vector consisting of mean (μ) and standard deviation (σ) values, and thus having a size of $2 \times m \times n$ values for each filtered image.

In the next step we aggregate all calculated image features and employ a clustering algorithm to reduce the number of values into a chosen number of groups. In this way, we create a dictionary that consists of the most representative color and texture features of the images in the learning set. The clustering is performed using the k-Means algorithm with a histogram intersection measure for comparing color feature vectors f_c and Gabor feature distance for comparing texture feature vectors f_t. Centroids resulting from the clustering operation become the elements of the dictionary and are labeled $B_1, \ldots, B_k$ in case of color and $T_1, \ldots, T_k$ in case of texture features, where k is the feature dictionary size. These identifiers are then used to describe the images in the database by associating an appropriate label with every tile of each image. This is performed by finding the closest centroid to a feature vector calculated for a given image tile, using appropriate distance measures for each of the features. The dictionary created for the learning set is reused during the classification phase.

Figure 20.1 presents an example of such a symbolic image representation,

DB	Representation
$\mathcal{D}$	$B_1,\ B_2,\ B_3,\ B_4,$ $B_6,\ B_7,\ B_8$ $T_1,\ T_2,\ T_3,\ T_4,$ $T_7,\ T_8$
$\mathcal{D}^r$	$1\cdot B_1,\ 2\cdot B_2,\ 8\cdot B_3,\ 3\cdot B_4,$ $41\cdot B_6,\ 3\cdot B_7,\ 6\cdot B_8$ $1\cdot T_1,\ 5\cdot T_2,\ 4\cdot T_3,\ 11\cdot T_4,$ $5\cdot T_7,\ 38\cdot T_8$

FIGURE 20.1: A symbolic representation of an image from the *food* dataset. $\mathcal{D}$ – binary transaction system, $\mathcal{D}^r$ – transaction system with recurrent items. Source: Adapted from Ref. [213], with kind permission from Springer Science+Business Media.

showing labels of its individual tiles and the representation of the whole image as a binary transaction and a transaction with recurrent items.

20.4 Jumping Emerging Patterns with Occurrence Counts

20.4.1 Formal Definition

Let a transaction system with recurrent items be a pair $(\mathcal{D}^r, \mathcal{I})$, where $\mathcal{D}^r$ is a database and $\mathcal{I}$ is an itemspace (namely a set of standard items). We define database $\mathcal{D}^r$ as a finite set of transactions $\{T_1^r, \ldots, T_n^r\}$. We define a *recurrent itemset* (a multiset of items) X^r as a set of pairs: $X^r = \{(x_1, p_1), \ldots, (x_m, p_m)\}$, where $x_1, \ldots, x_m$ are distinct items in $\mathcal{I}$, each $p_i \in \mathbb{N}$, and m is a natural number. For convenience we represent the p_i's using a function p on the items such that $p(x_i) = p_i$. We will also write $X^r = (X, p)$. We say that $x \in X^r \iff p(x) \geq 1$ and define $X = \{x \mid x \in X^r\}$. Each transaction T^r in database $\mathcal{D}^r$ is a recurrent itemset.

Given two recurrent itemsets $X^r = (X, p)$, $Y^r = (Y, q)$ and an occurrence threshold $\theta \geq 1$ we define an inclusion relation between the itemsets as follows:

$$X^r \overset{\theta}{\subseteq} Y^r \iff \forall_{x \in \mathcal{I}}\ q(x) \geq \theta \cdot p(x). \tag{20.1}$$

Based on the above definition we may say that for the given occurrence threshold the *matching data* of a recurrent itemset X^r in a dataset D^r is given by $\mathsf{mt}(X^r, D^r, \theta) = \{T^r \mid T^r \in D^r, T^r \overset{\theta}{\supseteq} X^r\}$. The *count* and *support* are modified accordingly: $\mathsf{count}(X^r, D^r, \theta) = |\mathsf{mt}(X^r, D^r, \theta)|$ and $\mathsf{supp}(X^r, D^r, \theta) =$

$\frac{\mathsf{count}(X^r,D^r,\theta)}{|D^r|}$. We will assume that the relation $\subseteq$ is equivalent to $\overset{1}{\subseteq}$ in the context of two recurrent itemsets.

Example 20.1 *The support of a recurrent itemset $X^r = \{1\cdot white,\ 2\cdot yellow\}$ for threshold $\theta = 1$ in transaction dataset $D_1^r = (T_{1,2,3}^r)$ given by Table 20.1 is $\mathsf{supp}(X^r, D_1^r, 1) = 0$. Similarly, for $D_2^r = (T_{4,5}^r)$, $\mathsf{supp}(X^r, D_2^r, 1) = 1$. Given the threshold $\theta = 2$, $\mathsf{supp}(X^r, D_1^r, 2) = 0$ and $\mathsf{supp}(X^r, D_2^r, 2) = 0$.*

TABLE 20.1: Transaction database example. T_i – transactions with binary items, T_i^r – transactions with recurrent items. Source: Adapted from Ref. [213], with kind permission from Springer Science+Business Media.

	i	T_i	T_i^r
D_1^r	1	blue, green, white, yellow	$8\cdot blue,\ 4\cdot green,\ 3\cdot white,\ 1\cdot yellow$
	2	beige, red, yellow	$10\cdot beige,\ 3\cdot red,\ 3\cdot yellow$
	3	white, magenta	$12\cdot white,\ 4\cdot magenta$
D_2^r	4	blue, brown, white	$6\cdot blue,\ 2\cdot brown,\ 8\cdot white$
	5	black, white, red, yellow	$9\cdot black,\ 2\cdot white,\ 3\cdot red,\ 2\cdot yellow$

We now extend the definition of a transaction system to differentiate items, which represent class labels and call them "decision items". The definition will be used in Section 20.4.3 to formally describe the classification algorithm.

Let a decision transaction system be a tuple $(\mathcal{D}^r, \mathcal{I}, \mathcal{I}_d)$, where $(\mathcal{D}^r, \mathcal{I} \cup \mathcal{I}_d)$ is a transaction system with recurrent items and $\forall_{T^r \in \mathcal{D}^r} |T \cap \mathcal{I}_d| = 1$. Elements of $\mathcal{I}$ and $\mathcal{I}_d$ are called condition and decision items, respectively. A support for a decision transaction system $(\mathcal{D}^r, \mathcal{I}, \mathcal{I}_d)$ is understood as a support in the transaction system $(\mathcal{D}^r, \mathcal{I} \cup \mathcal{I}_d)$. For each decision item $c \in \mathcal{I}_d$ we may distinguish a dataset of class c as $C_c^r = \{T^r \mid T^r \in D^r, c \in T^r\}$. In addition, for a dataset $D^r \subseteq \mathcal{D}^r$ we define a complementary dataset $D^{r\prime} = \mathcal{D}^r - D^r$.

Given two databases $D_1^r, D_2^r \subseteq \mathcal{D}^r$ we call a recurrent itemset X^r a *jumping emerging pattern with occurrence counts* (occJEP) from D_1^r to D_2^r, if $\mathsf{supp}(X^r, D_1^r, 1) = 0 \wedge \mathsf{supp}(X^r, D_2^r, \theta) > 0$, where θ is the occurrence threshold. A set of all occJEPs with a threshold θ from D_1^r to D_2^r is called an occJEP space and denoted by $occJEP(D_1^r, D_2^r, \theta)$. We distinguish the set of all minimal occJEPs as $occJEP_m$, $occJEP_m(D_1^r, D_2^r, \theta) \subseteq occJEP(D_1^r, D_2^r, \theta)$. Notice also that $occJEP(D_1^r, D_2^r, \theta) \subseteq occJEP(D_1^r, D_2^r, \theta - 1)$ for $\theta \geq 2$. In the rest of the paper we will refer to recurrent itemsets as itemsets and use the symbol X^r to avoid confusion.

Example 20.2 *For $D_1^r = (T_{1,2,3}^r)$ and $D_2^r = (T_{4,5}^r)$ from Table 20.1, the set of minimal occJEPs from D_1^r to D_2^r with threshold $\theta = 1$ is equal to: $\{\{1 \cdot black\},$ $\{1 \cdot brown\}, \{1 \cdot blue, 4 \cdot white\}, \{1 \cdot red, 1 \cdot white\}, \{1 \cdot white, 2 \cdot yellow\}\}$. Changing the threshold to $\theta = 2$ results in reducing the set of patterns to: $\{\{1\cdot black\}, \{1\cdot brown\}, \{1\cdot blue, 4\cdot white\}, \{1\cdot red, 1\cdot white\}\}$. This is because*

$\mathsf{supp}(\{1 \cdot white, 2 \cdot yellow\}, D_1^r, 1) = 0$ *and* $\mathsf{supp}(\{1 \cdot white, 2 \cdot yellow\}, D_2^r, 1) > 1$, *but* $\mathsf{supp}(\{1 \cdot white, 2 \cdot yellow\}, D_2^r, 2) = 0$.

The introduction of an occurrence threshold θ allows for differentiating transactions containing the same sets of items with a specified tolerance margin of occurrence counts. It is thus possible to define a difference in the number of occurrences, which is necessary to consider such a pair of transactions as distinct sets of items.

For the example image database given by Table 20.1 we can see that the differences between counts of such items as *white* and *yellow* may be too small to assume they represent a general pattern present in the database that would allow building a classifier. Setting the threshold to a higher value results in a smaller number of patterns, but the discovered ones have a greater confidence.

20.4.2   Mining Algorithm

The border-based occJEP discovery algorithm is an extension of the EP-mining method described in [119]. Similarly, as proved in [250] for regular emerging patterns, we can use the concept of borders to represent a collection of occJEPs. This is because the occJEP space S^r is convex, that is, it satisfies: $\forall X^r, Z^r \in S^r \; \forall Y^r (X^r \subseteq Y^r \subseteq Z^r \Rightarrow Y^r \in S^r)$. For the sake of readability we will now onward denote particular items with consecutive alphabet letters, with an index indicating the occurrence count, and skip individual brackets, e.g. $\{a_1 b_2, c_3\}$ instead of $\{\{1 \cdot i_1, 2 \cdot i_2\}, \{3 \cdot i_3\}\}$.

Example 20.3 $S^r = \{a_1, a_1 b_1, a_1 b_2, a_1 c_1, a_1 b_1 c_1, a_1 b_2 c_1\}$ *is a convex collection of sets, but* $S^{r\prime} = \{a_1, a_1 b_1, a_1 c_1, a_1 b_1 c_1, a_1 b_2 c_1\}$ *is not convex. We can partition it into two convex collections* $S^{r\prime}_1 = \{a_1, a_1 b_1\}$ *and* $S^{r\prime}_2 = \{a_1 c_1, a_1 b_1 c_1, a_1 b_2 c_1\}$.

A border is an ordered pair $< \mathcal{L}, \mathcal{R} >$ such that $\mathcal{L}$ and $\mathcal{R}$ are antichains, $\forall X^r \in \mathcal{L} \; \exists Y^r \in \mathcal{R}$ such that $X^r \subseteq Y^r$ and $\forall X^r \in \mathcal{R} \; \exists Y^r \in \mathcal{L}$ such that $Y^r \subseteq X^r$. The collection of sets represented by a border $< \mathcal{L}, \mathcal{R} >$ is equal to:

$$[\mathcal{L}, \mathcal{R}] = \{Y^r \mid \exists X^r \in \mathcal{L}, \exists Z^r \in \mathcal{R} \text{ such that } X^r \subseteq Y^r \subseteq Z^r\}. \qquad (20.2)$$

Example 20.4 *The border of collection* S^r, *introduced in earlier example, is equal to* $[\mathcal{L}, \mathcal{R}] = [\{a_1\}, \{a_1 b_2 c_1\}]$.

The most basic operation involving borders is a border differential, defined as:

$$< \mathcal{L}, \mathcal{R} > = < \{\emptyset\}, \mathcal{R}_1 > - < \{\emptyset\}, \mathcal{R}_2 > . \qquad (20.3)$$

As proven in [250] this operation may be reduced to a series of simpler operations. For $\mathcal{R}_1 = \{U_1^r, \ldots, U_m^r\}$:

$$< \mathcal{L}_i, \mathcal{R}_i > = < \{\emptyset\}, \{U_i^r\} > - < \{\emptyset\}, \mathcal{R}_2 > . \qquad (20.4)$$

$$< \mathcal{L}, \mathcal{R} > = < \bigcup_{i=1}^m \mathcal{L}_i, \bigcup_{i=1}^m \mathcal{R}_i > . \qquad (20.5)$$

A direct approach to calculating the border differential would be to expand the borders and compute set differences.

Example 20.5 *The border differential between* $[\{\emptyset\}, \{a_1 b_2 c_1\}]$ *and* $[\{\emptyset\}, \{a_1 c_1\}]$ *is equal to* $[\{b_1\}, \{a_1 b_2 c_1\}]$. *This is because:*

$$[\{\emptyset\}, \{a_1 b_2 c_1\}] = \{\emptyset, a_1, b_1, b_2, c_1, a_1 b_1, a_1 b_2, a_1 c_1, b_1 c_1, b_2 c_1, a_1 b_1 c_1, a_1 b_2 c_1\}$$
$$[\{\emptyset\}, \{a_1 c_1\}] = \{\emptyset, a_1, c_1, a_1 c_1\}$$
$$[\{\emptyset\}, \{a_1 b_2 c_1\}] - [\{\emptyset\}, \{a_1 c_1\}] = \{b_1, b_2, a_1 b_1, a_1 b_2, b_1 c_1, b_2 c_1, a_1 b_1 c_1, a_1 b_2 c_1\}$$

On the basis of optimizations proposed in [119], we now show the extensions necessary for discovering emerging patterns with occurrence counts. All of the ideas presented there for reducing the number of operations described in the context of regular EPs are also applicable for recurrent patterns. The first idea allows avoiding the expansion of borders when calculating the collection of minimal itemsets $\text{Min}(\mathcal{S}^r)$ in a border differential $\mathcal{S}^r = [\{\emptyset\}, \{U^r\}] - [\{\emptyset\}, \{S_1^r, \ldots, S_k^r\}]$. It has been proven in [119] that $\text{Min}(\mathcal{S})$ is equivalent to:

$$\text{Min}(\mathcal{S}) = \text{Min}(\{\bigcup\{s_1, \ldots, s_k\} \mid s_i \in U - S_i, 1 \leq i \leq k\}). \qquad (20.6)$$

In the case of emerging patterns with occurrence counts we need to define the left-bound union and set theoretic difference operations between recurrent itemsets $X^r = (X, p)$ and $Y^r = (Y, q)$. These operations guarantee that the resulting patterns are still minimal.

Definition 20.1 *The left-bound union of recurrent itemsets* $X^r \cup Y^r = Z^r = (Z, r)$, *where* $Z = \{z \mid z \in X \vee z \in Y\}$ *and* $r(z) = max(p(z), q(z))\ \forall z \in Z$.

Definition 20.2 *The left-bound set theoretic difference of recurrent itemsets* $X^r - Y^r = Z^r = (Z, r)$, *where* $Z = \{z \mid z \in X \wedge p(z) > q(z)\}$ *and* $r(z) = q(z) + 1$ $\forall z \in Z$.

Observe that $r(z) = q(z) + 1$ is the smallest number i such that z_i occurs in X^r and z_i does not occur in Y^r.

Example 20.6 *For the differential:* $[\{\emptyset\}, \{a_1 b_3 c_1 d_1\}] - [\{\emptyset\}, \{b_1 c_1\}, \{b_3 d_1\}, \{c_1 d_1\}]$. $U^r = \{a_1 b_3 c_1 d_1\}$, $S_1^r = \{b_1 c_1\}$, $S_2^r = \{b_3 d_1\}$, $S_3^r = \{c_1 d_1\}$. $U^r - S_1^r = \{a_1 b_2 d_1\}$, $U^r - S_2^r = \{a_1 c_1\}$, $U^r - S_3^r = \{a_1 b_1\}$. *Calculating the Min function:*

$$\text{Min}([\{\emptyset\}, \{a_1 b_3 c_1 d_1\}] - [\{\emptyset\}, \{b_1 c_1\}, \{b_3 d_1\}, \{c_1 d_1\}]) =$$
$$= \text{Min}(\{a_1 a_1 a_1, a_1 a_1 b_1, a_1 c_1 a_1, a_1 c_1 b_1, b_2 a_1 a_1,$$
$$b_2 a_1 b_1, b_2 c_1 b_1, d_1 a_1 a_1, d_1 a_1 b_1, d_1 c_1 a_1, d_1 c_1 b_1\}) =$$
$$= \text{Min}(\{a_1, a_1 b_1, a_1 c_1, a_1 b_1 c_1, a_1 b_2, a_1 b_2, b_2 c_1, a_1 d_1, a_1 b_1 d_1, a_1 c_1 d_1, b_1 c_1 d_1\}) =$$
$$= \{a_1, b_2 c_1, b_1 c_1 d_1\}.$$

Similar changes are necessary when performing the border expansion in an incremental manner, which has been proposed as the second possible algorithm optimization. The union and difference operations in the following steps need to be conducted according to Definitions 20.1 and 20.2 above, see Algorithm 4.

Algorithm 4 Incremental Expansion

Input: U^{r}, S_i^{r}
Output: $\mathcal{L}$
1: $\mathcal{L} \longleftarrow \{\{x\} \mid x \in U^{\mathrm{r}} - S_1^{\mathrm{r}}\}$;
2: **for** $i = 2$ **to** k **do**
3:      $\mathcal{L} \longleftarrow \mathrm{Min}\{X^{\mathrm{r}} \cup \{x\} \mid X^{\mathrm{r}} \in \mathcal{L},\ x \in U^{\mathrm{r}} - S_i^{\mathrm{r}}\}$
4: **end**

Lastly, a few points need to be considered when performing the third optimization (avoiding generating nonminimal itemsets). Originally, the idea was to avoid expanding such itemsets during incremental processing, which are known to be minimal beforehand. This is the case when the same item is present both in an itemset in the old $\mathcal{L}$ and in the set difference $U^{\mathrm{r}} - S_i^{\mathrm{r}}$ (line 3 of Algorithm 4). In case of recurrent patterns this condition is too weak to guarantee that all patterns are still going to be generated, as we have to deal with differences in the number of item occurrences. The modified conditions of itemset removal are thus as follows:

1. If an itemset X^{r} in the old $\mathcal{L}$ contains an item x from $T_i^{\mathrm{r}} = U^{\mathrm{r}} - S_i^{\mathrm{r}}$ and its occurrence count is equal or greater than the one in T_i^{r}, then move X^{r} from $\mathcal{L}$ to $NewL$.

2. If the moved X^{r} is a singleton set $\{(x, p(x))\}$ and its occurrence count is the same in $\mathcal{L}$ and T_i^{r}, then remove x from T_i^{r}.

Example 20.7 *Let* $U^{\mathrm{r}} = \{a_1 b_2\}$, $S_1^{\mathrm{r}} = \{a_1\}$, $S_2^{\mathrm{r}} = \{b_1\}$. *Then* $T_1^{\mathrm{r}} = U^{\mathrm{r}} - S_1^{\mathrm{r}} = \{b_1\}$ *and* $T_2^{\mathrm{r}} = U^{\mathrm{r}} - S_2^{\mathrm{r}} = \{a_1 b_2\}$. *We initialize* $\mathcal{L} = \{b_1\}$ *and check it against* T_2^{r}. *While* T_2^{r} *contains* $\{b_2\}$, $\{b_1\}$ *may not be moved directly to* $NewL$, *as this would falsely result in returning* $\{b_1\}$ *as the only minimal itemset, instead of* $\{a_1 b_1, b_2\}$. *Suppose* $S_1^{\mathrm{r}} = \{a_1 b_1\}$, *then initial* $\mathcal{L} = \{b_2\}$ *and this time we can see that* $\{b_2\}$ *does not have to be expanded, as the same item with at least equal occurrence count is present in* T_2^{r}. *Thus,* $\{b_2\}$ *is moved directly to* $NewL$, *removed from* T_2^{r} *and returned as a minimal itemset.*

The final algorithm, consisting of all proposed modifications, is presented below as Algorithm 5.

Algorithm 5 Border Differential

Input: $< \{\emptyset\}, \{U^{\mathrm{r}}\} >, < \{\emptyset\}, \{S_1^{\mathrm{r}}, \ldots, S_k^{\mathrm{r}}\} >$

Output: $\mathcal{L}$

1: $T_i^{\mathrm{r}} \longleftarrow U^{\mathrm{r}} - S_i^{\mathrm{r}}$ **for** $1 \leq i \leq k$;
2: **if** $\exists T_i^{\mathrm{r}} = \{\emptyset\}$ **then**
3:      **return** $< \{\}, \{\} >$
4: **end**;
5: $\mathcal{L} \longleftarrow \{\{x\} \mid x \in T_1^{\mathrm{r}}\}$;
6: **for** $i = 2$ **to** k **do**
7:      $NewL \longleftarrow \{X^{\mathrm{r}} = (X, p) \in \mathcal{L} \mid X \cap T_i \neq \emptyset \wedge \forall x \in (X \cap T_i)\ p(x) \geq t(x)\}$;
8:      $\mathcal{L} \longleftarrow \mathcal{L} - NewL$;
9:      $T_i^{\mathrm{r}} \longleftarrow T_i^{\mathrm{r}} - \{x \mid \{(x, p(x))\} \in NewL\}$;
10:      **for each** $X^{\mathrm{r}} \in \mathcal{L}$ sorted according to increasing cardinality **do**
11:          **for each** $x \in T_i$ **do**
12:              **if** $\forall Z^{\mathrm{r}} \in NewL\ \mathsf{supp}(X^{\mathrm{r}} \cup \{x\}, Z^{\mathrm{r}}, 1) = 0$ **then**
13:                  $NewL \longleftarrow NewL \cup (X^{\mathrm{r}} \cup \{x\})$
14:              **end**
15:          **end**
16:      **end**;
17: $\mathcal{L} \longleftarrow NewL$;
18: **end**

20.4.3 Use in Classification

Creating an occJEP-based classifier involves discovering all minimal occ-JEPs to each of the classes present in a particular decision system. We can formally define the set of patterns in a classifier $occJEP_C^\theta$ for a given occurrence threshold θ as: $occJEP_C^\theta = \bigcup_{c \in \mathcal{I}_d} occJEP_{\mathrm{m}}(C_c^{\mathrm{r}\prime}, C_c^{\mathrm{r}}, \theta)$, where $C_c^{\mathrm{r}} \subseteq \mathcal{D}_L^{\mathrm{r}}$ is a dataset of class c and $C_c^{\mathrm{r}\prime}$ is a complementary dataset in a learning database $\mathcal{D}_L^{\mathrm{r}}$.

To discover patterns between two dataset pairs, we first need to remove non-maximal itemsets from each of them. Next, we multiply the occurrence counts of itemsets in the background dataset by the user-specified threshold. Finally, we need to iteratively call the Border-differential function and create a union of the results to find the set of all minimal jumping emerging patterns with occurrence counts from $C_c^{\mathrm{r}\prime}$ to C_c^{r} (see Algorithm 6).

Example 20.8 *Consider a learning database $\mathcal{D}_L^{\mathrm{r}}$ containing transactions of three distinct classes: $C_1^{\mathrm{r}}, C_2^{\mathrm{r}}, C_3^{\mathrm{r}} \subset \mathcal{D}_L^{\mathrm{r}}$. $C_1^{\mathrm{r}} = \{b_2, a_1 c_1\}$, $C_2^{\mathrm{r}} = \{a_1 b_1, c_3 d_1\}$ and $C_3^{\mathrm{r}} = \{a_3, b_1 c_1 d_1\}$. We need to discover occJEPs to each of these classes: $occJEP_{\mathrm{m}}(C_2^{\mathrm{r}} \cup C_3^{\mathrm{r}}, C_1^{\mathrm{r}}, \theta)$, $occJEP_{\mathrm{m}}(C_1^{\mathrm{r}} \cup C_3^{\mathrm{r}}, C_2^{\mathrm{r}}, \theta)$, and $occJEP_{\mathrm{m}}(C_1^{\mathrm{r}} \cup C_2^{\mathrm{r}}, C_3^{\mathrm{r}}, \theta)$. Suppose $\theta = 2$. Calculating the set of all minimal patterns involves invoking the Discover-minimal-occJEPs function three times, in which the base Border-differential function is called twice each time and the resulting occJEPs*

Algorithm 6 Discover Minimal occJEPs

Input: $C_c^{r'}$, C_c^r, θ
Output: $\mathcal{J}$
1: $\mathcal{L} ='$ Remove-non-maximal-itemsets(C_c^r);
2: $\mathcal{R} =$ Remove-non-maximal-itemsets($C_c^{r'}$);
3: **for** $S_i^r \in \mathcal{R}$ **do**
4:     $S_i^r \longleftarrow (S_i, s(x) \cdot \theta)$
5: **end**;
6: $\mathcal{J} \longleftarrow \{\emptyset\}$;
7: **for** $L_i^r \in \mathcal{L}$ **do**
8:     $\mathcal{J} \longleftarrow \mathcal{J} \cup$ Border-differential($< \{\emptyset\}, \{L_i^r\} >, < \{\emptyset\}, \{S_1^r, \ldots, S_k^r\} >$);
9: **end**

---

are as follows: $\{a_1c_1\}$ to class 1, $\{c_3, a_1b_1\}$ to class 2 and $\{a_3, b_1c_1, b_1d_1\}$ to class 3.

Classification of a particular transaction in the testing database $\mathcal{D}_T^r$ is performed by aggregating all minimal occJEPs, which are supported by it [141]. A scoring function is calculated and a category label is chosen by finding the class with the maximum score:

$$\text{score}(T^r, c) = \sum_{X^r} \text{supp}_{C_c^r}(X^r), \qquad (20.7)$$

where $C_c^r \subseteq \mathcal{D}_T^r$ and $X^r \in occJEP_m(C_c^{r'}, C_c^r)$, such that $X^r \subseteq T^r$. It is possible to normalize the score to reduce the bias induced by unequal sizes of datasets of particular classes. This is performed by dividing the calculated score by a normalization factor: norm-score(T^r, c) = score(T^r, c)/base-score(c), where base-score is the median of scores of all transactions with decision item c in the learning database: base-score(c) = median$\{$score(T^r, c) $| T^r \in C_c^r \subseteq \mathcal{D}_L^r\}$.

20.5   Spatial Emerging Patterns

The method of mining jumping emerging patterns described in the previous section helps to capture information about recurrent features present on images of a particular class and allows to contrast it with images of different categories. An equally important source of information is the spatial arrangement of features or objects on an image. One approach is to include the information about spatial context into the symbolic representation itself. In the 9DLT representation [76] the relationships between objects are denoted

by associating directional codes with pairs of items, which provide information about the angle between two image features. The 9DLT representation
defines nine directional codes, $\mathcal{R} = \{0, 1, \ldots, 8\}$, which are an equivalent of a
range of angles between two objects in a scene. Figure 20.2(a) depicts the use
of codes: "0" means "the same spatial location as", "1" means "the north of",
"2" means "the north-west of", and so on.

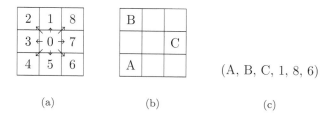

<table>
<tr><td>2</td><td>1</td><td>8</td></tr>
<tr><td>3</td><td>0</td><td>7</td></tr>
<tr><td>4</td><td>5</td><td>6</td></tr>
</table>

(A, B, C, 1, 8, 6)

(a)   (b)   (c)

FIGURE 20.2: The 9DLT representation: (a) directional codes, (b) example
scene, (c) its symbolic representation. Source: Adapted from Ref. [212], with
kind permission from Springer Science+Business Media.

We use the definition of a spatial pattern, presented in [232], to extend
the definition of our transactional system. A spatial pattern X^s is defined as
a pattern of a form $X^s = (i_1, i_2, \ldots, i_n, r_1, r_2, \ldots, r_m)$, where $i_j \in \mathcal{I}$ are items
and $r_k \in \mathcal{R}$ are directional codes. Here, $m = C_2^n = n(n-1)/2$, $1 \le j \le n$ and
$n \ge 2$. Each of the directional codes, $1 \le k \le m$, denotes a spatial relationship
between two corresponding items, taken from left to right, e.g. the relationship
between i_1 and i_2 is r_1, while between i_1 and i_3 is r_2.

Example 20.9 *Consider the image presented on Fig. 20.2(b). Its symbolic
representation as a spatial pattern takes the form shown on Fig. 20.2(c).*

We say that spatial pattern $Y^s = (i'_1, i'_2, \ldots, i'_k, r'_1, r'_2, \ldots, r'_l)$ is a sub-
pattern of a pattern $X^s = (i_1, i_2, \ldots, i_n, r_1, r_2, \ldots, r_m)$, denoted as $Y^s \sqsubseteq X^s$,
when $\{i'_1, i'_2, \ldots, i'_k\} \subseteq \{i_1, i_2, \ldots, i_n\}$ and each spatial relationship between
every two items is exactly the same in both patterns. Furthermore, we say
that two spatial relationships $r_i, r_j \ne 0$ are complementary, when $r_i = (r_j +
4)$ mod 8.

Example 20.10 *Consider the following 4-element spatial pattern:* $X^s =
(A, B, C, D, 8, 7, 8, 6, 1, 2)$. *There are four 3-element sub-patterns of pattern*
X^s: $Y_1^s = (A, B, C, 8, 7, 6)$, $Y_2^s = (A, B, D, 8, 8, 1)$, $Y_3^s = (A, C, D, 7, 8, 2)$ *and*
$Y_4^s = (B, C, D, 6, 1, 2)$.

A spatial transactional system is a pair $(\mathcal{D}^s, \mathcal{I})$, where $\mathcal{D}^s$ is a finite set of transactions $\{T_1^s, \ldots, T_n^s\}$. Each transaction is a pattern
$(i_1, i_2, \ldots, i_n, r_1, r_2, \ldots, r_m)$, where $i_j \in \mathcal{I}$ are items and $r_k \in \mathcal{R}$ are directional codes. The *matching data* of a spatial pattern X^s in a dataset $\mathcal{D}^s$

is thus defined as: $\mathsf{mt}(X^s, D^s) = \{T^s \mid T^s \in D^s, T^s \sqsupseteq X^s\}$. Consequently, $\mathsf{count}(X^s, D^s) = |\mathsf{mt}(X^s, D^s)|$ and the support of a spatial pattern X^s in a dataset D^s is defined as: $\mathsf{supp}(X^s, D^s) = \frac{\mathsf{count}(X^s, D^s)}{|D^s|}$.

Based on the earlier definitions, we now define a new kind of pattern, namely a Spatial Emerging Pattern (SEP), which is able to capture interesting differences between sets of spatial data. Given two spatial databases D_1^s and D_2^s, we define the support ratio of a pattern X^s in the same way as stated in Chapter 1, but using the definition of support presented above. Having a ratio threshold σ_r, we define a pattern X^s to be a σ_r-spatial emerging pattern (σ_r-SEP) from D_1^s to D_2^s if $\mathsf{gr}(X^s, D_2^s) > \sigma_r$. The definition of a Jumping Spatial Emerging Pattern (JSEP) is analogous to the one proposed for regular EPs.

We may introduce another way of representing spatial emerging patterns, which shows the connection between SEPs and regular emerging patterns. By enumerating all encoded relationships and creating unique item for each of them, we get a new space of items, defined by $\mathcal{I}' = \mathcal{I} \times \mathcal{R} \times \mathcal{I}$. Then, each pattern of a form $X^s = (i_1, i_2, \ldots, i_n, r_1, r_2, \ldots, r_m)$ may be represented as:

$$X^s = (i_1 i_2 r_1, i_1 i_3 r_2, \ldots, i_1 i_n r_k, \ldots, i_{n-1} i_n r_m). \qquad (20.8)$$

Example 20.11 *A pattern* $X^s = (A, B, C, 1, 8, 6)$ *may also be represented as* $X^s = (AB1, AC8, BC6)$, *written for convenience as* $X^s = (A_1 B, A_8 C, B_6 C)$.

Remark: While all patterns may be represented in the second manner, not all patterns may be described in the original, shortened form.

Example 20.12 *Consider two sets of spatial data, represented by 9DLT patterns:* $D_1^s = ((A, B, C, 1, 8, 6)) = ((A_1 B, A_8 C, B_6 C))$ *and* $D_2^s = ((A, B, 1), (A, C, 8), (B, C, 7)) = ((A_1 B), (A_8 C), (B_7 C))$. *We mine strong JSEPs between these sets by looking for minimal patterns, which occur in one set and never in the other. In the case of JSEPs from* D_1^s *to* D_2^s *we have* $JSEP_1 = (B, C, 6) = (B_6 C)$ *and* $JSEP_2 = (A, B, C, 1, 8, ?) = (A_1 B, A_8 C)$. *Similarly, in the direction of* D_2^s *to* D_1^s *we have* $JSEP_3 = (B, C, 7) = (B_7 C)$.

Here, we are only interested in mining patterns for the use in building classifiers. For that reason we may limit ourselves to mining only strong jumping spatial emerging patterns, that is JSEPs, which are minimal and have a specified minimum support in one of the databases. For this purpose, the border-based algorithm proposed by [119] may be used. Classification is performed using the same methodology as for regular JEPs and occJEPs (see Section 20.4.3).

20.6 Jumping Emerging Substrings

In this section we describe an alternative approach of spatial data representation, in which sequences of symbols are taken into consideration when discovering contrast patterns. We use a substring mining algorithm, proposed by [74] to discover strings, which characterize particular classes of images and then use them for classification of unknown data. The strings are formed by concatenating the horizontal, vertical, and diagonal sequences of symbols, taken from the tile-based representation of a particular image, as described in Section 20.3 (see Fig. 20.3).

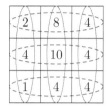 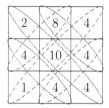

FIGURE 20.3: Representation used to mine JESs between classes of images. Strings are formed from horizontal, vertical, and diagonal sequences of symbols.

Formally, a sequence is a non-empty string with finite length over an alphabet $\Sigma = \{a_1, a_2, \ldots, a_m\}$. Having a string $s = s_1 s_2 \ldots s_k$ of length k and a sequence $T^t = t_1 t_2 \ldots t_l$ of length l, we say that s is a substring of T^t, denoted as $s \sqsubseteq T^t$ if $\exists i \in 1 \ldots (l - k + 1)$ such that $s_1 s_2 \ldots s_k = t_i t_{i+1} \ldots t_{i+k-1}$. If $s \neq T^t$, s is a proper substring of T^t, denoted as $s \sqsubset T^t$.

A database $\mathcal{D}^t$ is a set of sequences T_i^t, each associated with a class label $c_{T_i} \in C = \{c_1, c_2, \ldots, c_n\}$. The support of a string s in a dataset D^t is the fraction of sequences in D^t that s is a substring of: $\mathsf{supp}(s, D^t) = \frac{\mathsf{count}(s, D^t)}{|D^t|}$, where $\mathsf{count}(s, D^t) = |\mathsf{mt}(s, D^t)|$ and $\mathsf{mt}(s, D^t) = \{T^t \mid T^t \in D^t, T^t \sqsupseteq s\}$. Given two databases $D_1^t, D_2^t \subseteq \mathcal{D}^t$ we say that a string s is a jumping emerging substring (JES) from D_1^t to D_2^t if $\mathsf{supp}(s, D_1^t) = 0 \wedge \mathsf{supp}(s, D_2^t) > 0$. The task of JES mining is to find all strings having a given minimum support θ in D_2^t, being a JES from D_1^t to D_2^t. We will denote this set of strings as $JES(D_1^t, D_2^t, \theta)$. Furthermore, we can distinguish the set of only minimal JESs, that is sequences, for which no frequent substrings exist: $JES_m(D_1^t, D_2^t, \theta) = \{T \in JES(D_1^t, D_2^t, \theta) \mid \neg \exists s \in JES(D_1^t, D_2^t, \theta) \ s \sqsubset T\}$.

Example 20.13 *Table 20.2 shows a simple two-class database and its jumping emerging substrings. Based on the definition presented above, we look at all possible substrings of strings in class A and find these, which are not present in class B. Similarly, we check for JESs from class B to A. The string "ac" would* *be the only JES, if we were to find only jumping emerging substrings with minimum support of 1. Finally, we reduce the set of discovered patterns to only minimal JESs:* $JES_\mathrm{m}(D_A^\mathrm{t}, D_B^\mathrm{t}, 1/2) = \{b, e\}$, $JES_\mathrm{m}(D_B^\mathrm{t}, D_A^\mathrm{t}, 1/2) = \{ac\}$.

TABLE 20.2: Example database and its jumping emerging substrings. Source: Adapted from Ref. [211], with kind permission from Springer Science+Business Media.

class A	class B
acd	cde
ac	ab

JES	support class A	support class B	direction
b	0	1/2	A → B
e	0	1/2	A → B
ab	0	1/2	A → B
ac	1	0	B → A
de	0	1/2	A → B
acd	1/2	0	B → A
cde	0	1/2	A → B

The classifier is created on the basis of the substrings mined for each of the classes. We then use the classifier to assign previously unseen images to respective categories. This is done by aggregating all minimal JESs that match the representation of a particular image and determining the majority class of the patterns. The winning category is then assigned to the example, similarly as described in Section 20.4.3.

20.7   Experimental Results

Here we provide the results of experiments and accuracy comparison of the most commonly used classification methods with a classifier based on regular JEPs, the proposed JEPs with occurrence counts and jumping emerging substrings. We are not directly comparing these methods to the spatial emerging pattern-based classifier, as it is using a different image representation model. The experiments have been conducted on the dataset, which is a collection of images made available by the authors of the SIMPLIcity CBIR system [420]. It consists of 1000 photographs, which are JPEG color image files, having a resolution of 384×256 pixels. The images used in the experiments have been classified into four categories: *flower*, *food*, *mountain*, and *elephant*. The data contains ca. 400 instances and 16 recurrent attributes, where each instance is an image represented by 8 types of texture and 8 types of color features, possibly occurring multiple times on a single image; here a type corresponds to a cluster. An example selection of photographs is presented on Figure 20.4.

We have used the following parameter values for the experiments: images

FIGURE 20.4: Example images from the SIMPLIcity test database.

partitioned into 8×8 tiles ($x = y = 8$), the sizes of feature vectors $|f_c| = 162$ ($h = 18$, $s = 3$, $v = 3$), and $|f_t| = 48$ ($m = 6$, $n = 4$) values. The dictionary size was set at $k = 8$ values. The parameters are dataset dependent: the number of tiles should be chosen based on the resolution of analyzed images and the dictionary size reflects the diversity of the dataset.

The accuracy achieved by applying the classifier based on regular JEPs and occJEPs, along with a comparison with other frequently used classification methods is presented in Table 20.3. All experiments have been conducted as a ten-fold cross-validation using the WEKA package [433], having discretized the data into 10 equal-frequency bins for all algorithms, except the occJEP method. The parameters of all used classifiers have been left at their default values. The results of experiments using the JES method on the same data is presented in Table 20.4.

TABLE 20.3: Classification accuracy of the SIMPLIcity dataset with the classifier based on jumping emerging patterns (JEPs and occJEPs) and comparison with other state of the art methods.

method	accuracy (%)					
	flower/ food	*flower/ elephant*	*flower/ mountain*	*food/ elephant*	*food/ mountain*	*elephant/ mountain*
JEP	95.83	91.67	96.35	88.50	93.50	83.50
occJEP	97.92	**98.96**	**97.92**	88.00	91.00	88.50
C4.5	93.23	89.58	85.94	87.50	92.50	82.00
SVM	90.63	91.15	93.75	87.50	84.50	84.50

In case of the spatial emerging pattern-based classifier we have performed experiments using synthetic data. We have verified the influence of the relation between pattern and image sizes on classification accuracy and the time needed to mine spatial patterns. The results are presented in Table 20.5 and show an increase of accuracy when pattern size approaches the size of the image. (Here the meaning of "image size" and "pattern size" is as follows: With "image size" of 7, an image is divided into 7×7 tiles; and with "pattern size"

TABLE 20.4: Classification accuracy of the SIMPLIcity dataset with a classifier based on the jumping emerging substrings (JESs).

minimum support	accuracy (%)					
	flower/ food	*flower/ elephant*	*flower/ mountain*	*food/ elephant*	*food/ mountain*	*elephant/ mountain*
0.250	92.26	93.68	96.37	30.50	83.50	58.00
0.200	94.79	95.26	96.89	41.00	89.50	66.00
0.150	96.37	97.89	96.89	63.50	93.00	74.50
0.100	97.94	98.95	96.89	85.00	94.00	89.00
0.050	**98.47**	98.95	96.89	**93.00**	95.50	92.00
0.025	98.47	98.95	96.89	93.00	**96.00**	**93.50**
0.005	98.47	98.95	96.89	93.00	95.50	93.50

TABLE 20.5: Classification accuracy of the synthetic dataset with relation to image and pattern sizes. Source: Adapted from Ref. [212], with kind permission from Springer Science+Business Media.

Image size (*n*)	Accuracy (%)	Time (ms)
4	95,50	1738
5	92,20	2790
6	94,30	3218
7	92,70	3607
8	95,00	3752
9	93,10	3934
10	92,90	3653

Pattern size (*m*)	Accuracy (%)	Time (ms)
2	82,00	2397
3	95,00	3545
4	98,00	5840
5	98,50	8109

of 3, a pattern has 3×3 tiles (overlayed on images).) This is because there is relatively less random noise in the generated data in comparison to the differentiating pattern. The image size alone, however, does not directly influence the classification accuracy or pattern mining time, as it has no relation to the size of 9DLT representation and number of discovered JSEPs.

20.8   Conclusions

We have proposed new types of patterns that may be used to build accurate classifiers for multimedia data. The presented results show that the proposed methods may achieve equal or better performance than well-known tree-based C4.5 algorithm and support vector machines (SVMs). The main advantage of using a pattern-based classifier over other algorithms is the high accuracy and interpretability of the classifier, which may be analyzed by a human expert.

The biggest drawback of the method lies in the number of discovered patterns, which is however less than in the case of regular JEPs found in discretized data.

Chapter 21

Geospatial Contrast Mining with Applications on Labeled Spatial Data

Wei Ding

Department of Computer Science, University of Massachusetts Boston

Tomasz F. Stepinski

Department of Geography, University of Cincinnati

Josue Salazar

Department of Computer Science, Rice University

21.1 Introduction

Geospatial data identifies the geographic location and characteristics of natural, constructed, or socially-based features. A set of geographically co-registered geospatial datasets captures various aspects of an environmental process, involving variables that are highly coupled through a complex chain of mutual interactions and feedback loops. The analysis of relationships among different variables is challenging due to inherent nonlinearity and spatial variability of such systems. Recent advances in data collecting techniques (for example, satellite-based remote sensing) result in the "data rich" setting and provide an opportunity for more thorough analysis. However, the full benefit of these enormous quantities of data can only be realized by automating the process of extracting relevant information and summarizing it in a fashion that is comprehensible and meaningful to a domain expert. In this chapter, we introduce a framework of discovery and summarization of empirical knowledge contained in spatial patterns observed in geospatial data using a fusion of techniques, including association analysis, reinforcement learning, and similarity measurement.

Given a geospatial dataset classified into two binary (yes/no) classes, our goal is to discover patterns in terms of (explanatory) variables that are capable of distinguishing between the two classes. Emerging patterns proposed and studied in [118, 247, 255, 141] can be used towards achieving that goal. However, not much work has been done to understand the contrasts between spatially extended classes. Generalizing the methods of standard emerging patterns to spatial domain is a non-trivial task. Geospatial data often contain continuous variables that need to be categorized in order to be subjected to association analysis. Categorization inevitably leads to information loss as it introduces sharp artificial boundaries between different regions. Furthermore, in contrast to the assumption that data instances are independent in traditional data mining, spatial data often exhibit spatial continuity and exhibit high autocorrelation among geographically nearby features.

Our proposed methodology aims at addressing these problems (Fig. 21.1). Specifically, we focus on the following three challenges: (1) identifying representative patterns in terms of explanatory variables that capture statistical difference between geospatial classes, (2) seeking the optimal spatial boundary between classes to help us discover high quality class-discriminating patterns, and (3) summarizing the identified patterns and presenting domain experts with a relevant and concise report. To address challenges (1) and (2), we introduce the concept of *geospatial discriminating patterns* and propose a new value-iteration method designed to find the optimal geospatial boundary between classes using a reinforcement-learning model. To address challenge (3), we define a similarity measure using information theory and use the proposed similarity metric to summarize identified patterns by clustering them into a small number of "super-patterns". We design and implement a set of algorithms to efficiently mine class-discriminating patterns.

This chapter also presents results obtained by applying our algorithm and approach in several important applications, including vegetation analysis, presidential election analysis, and biodiversity analysis.

21.2   Related Work

Firstly introduced by Dong *et al.* in [118], emerging patterns are those patterns whose supports increase significantly from one dataset to another. Li *et al.* [247, 255] have systematically studied various statistical measures of "emergence", including relative risk ratio, odds ratio, risk difference, and

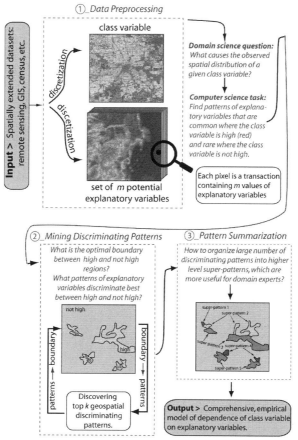

FIGURE 21.1: Overall design of the proposed method for auto-generating an empirical model of class variable dependence on explanatory variables.

delta-discriminative emerging patterns. In our work, we adopt the relative risk ratio as the measure of pattern emergence. Emerging patterns have been applied to many scientific applications, including medical science [57, 255], network traffic control [97], and data credibility analysis [338], etc. However, little work has been done with respect to analyzing emerging patterns in spatial datasets.

Identifying emerging patterns in spatial datasets has its own challenges. Geospatial variables are highly coupled through a complex chain of interactions resulting in their mutual inter-dependence. Ceci *et al.* [70] applied emerging patterns to spatial databases, although that paper did not consider spatial neighboring relationship in spatial data. We propose a different solution by first seeking the optimal spatial boundary between the classes, from which geospatial discriminating patterns are identified. One of our ultimate goals is to discover a set of controlling factors that provides knowledge for building empirical models of the classes of given applications.

Other studies indirectly related with our present work are spatial association and co-location mining [364, 441, 191, 451]. These methods have studied the discovery of spatial associations. Our work is to find patterns that capture statically important differences between two classes.

21.3   Problem Formulation

The proposed method is organized around a raster data format; a raster, $\mathcal{R}(x, y)$, $x = 1, \ldots, N_x$, $y = 1, \ldots, N_y$, is a 2-D array of constituent grid cells (hereafter referred to as pixels). Each pixel holds an object $o = \{x, y; f_1, f_2, \ldots, f_m; c\}$, where x and y are pixel's spatial coordinates, f_i, $i = 1, \ldots, m$, are values of m explanatory variables as measured at (x, y), and c is the value (label) of class variable. Without a loss of generality we will consider a binary class variable with the pixels belonging to an "interesting" class labeled $c = 1$ and the remaining pixels labeled $c = 0$. From the data mining point of view, each pixel (after disregarding its spatial coordinates and its class label) is a transaction containing a set of exactly m items $\{f_1, f_2, \ldots, f_m\}$. The entire raster can be viewed as a set of $N_x \times N_y$ fixed-length transactions. An itemset (hereafter also referred to as a pattern) is a set of items. A transaction *supports* an itemset if the itemset is a subset of this transaction; the number of all transactions supporting a pattern is referred to as a *support* of this pattern. Because transactions have spatial locations, there is also a spatial manifestation of support which we call a *footprint* of a pattern.

21.4   Identification of Geospatial Discriminative Patterns and Discovery of Optimal Boundary

A discriminating pattern X is an itemset representing a condition on explanatory variables that has much larger support in $\mathcal{O}_p$ than in $\mathcal{O}_n$, where $\mathcal{O}_p$ is the set of transactions stemming from pixels with $c = 1$ and $\mathcal{O}_n$ is the set stemming from pixels with $c = 0$. For a pattern X to be accepted as a discriminating pattern, its growth rate, $\frac{\sup(X, \mathcal{O}_p)}{\sup(X, \mathcal{O}_n)}$, must exceed a predefined threshold δ, where $sup()$ is the support of X in a dataset. The difference between a discriminating pattern and a better known notion of emerging pattern is that we require a discriminating pattern to be a *closed* [326] and frequent pattern. We opt for closed patterns to increase computational efficiency of our method. Closed patterns represent a minimal representation of a set of non-closed itemsets, yet they preserve the information about support of corresponding non-closed itemsets. Furthermore, we have proved in [109] that footprints of closed frequent patterns supersede the footprints of corresponding non-closed itemsets. This property allows us to determine a boundary between $\mathcal{O}_p$ and $\mathcal{O}_n$ regions without mining for all non-closed frequent patterns. We opt for patterns that are frequent in $\mathcal{O}_p$ because only such patterns can sufficiently reflect a phenomenon we want to model. Infrequent patterns are just not interesting enough from the point of view of building an empirical model of a given phenomenon.

Mining for discriminating patterns requires a prior existence of binary classification of class variable. In most problems stemming from natural phenomena, such division does not occur automatically; this is in contrast to a situation in say, medicine, where clear distinction exists between sick and healthy subjects. Instead, in natural phenomena, a division into $\mathcal{O}_p$ and $\mathcal{O}_n$ is introduced be means of arbitrarily defined threshold value. However, we have noticed that threshold-based division of class variable may lead to spurious results as the natural boundaries are rarely as sharp as those introduced by a threshold. Another way of defining an extent of the phenomenon is by tracking the presence of its controlling factors instead of the values of its magnitude. We propose to find the controlling factors (discriminating patterns) *and* the optimal boundary between $\mathcal{O}_p$ and $\mathcal{O}_n$ simultaneously using an iterative procedure. In our context, the boundary is optimal when it provides a best compromise between the threshold-based and controlling factor-based definitions of $\mathcal{O}_p$. The optimal region is as close as possible to the union of the footprints of all discriminating patterns (making a discrimination between $\mathcal{O}_p$ and $\mathcal{O}_n$ strong), but, at the same time, the values inside $\mathcal{O}_p$ drop below the threshold in as few places as possible.

To achieve this goal, we propose an interactive approach based on the reinforcement learning model [49]. In this model, an algorithm learns how to achieve its goal by trial-and-error interactions with its environment. The three steps of the proposed procedure are as follows:

(1) **Initialization.** We first define the initial $\mathcal{O}_p^0$ and $\mathcal{O}_n^0$ using an arbitrary threshold on the value of the class variable. Using this initial division of the scene, our algorithm mines for discriminating patterns. We calculate a footprint of each pattern and the union of all footprints. The union of the footprints intersects, but is not identical to $\mathcal{O}_p^0$.

(2) **Modification of $\mathcal{O}_p$.** In this step we calculate the next iteration of the region of interest, $\mathcal{O}_p^1$, and the new set of discriminating patterns. The pixels that are initially in $\mathcal{O}_n^0$ are added to $\mathcal{O}_p^1$ if they are in the union of footprints of the patterns calculated in step 1, their class variable values are "high enough," and they touch $\mathcal{O}_p^0$. Because of this last requirement, step 2 is in itself an iterative procedure implemented in the form of cellular automata [174] in order to allow the expansion of $\mathcal{O}_p^0$ beyond its immediate neighbors. (The cellular automata will iteratively evaluate a pixel's Moore neighborhood

of eight neighbors.) The requirement that values of incorporated pixels have "high enough" values of class variable is fulfilled by defining a buffer zone. The buffer zone is easily defined in a raster of ordinal values; it consists of pixels having a value one-scale less than the minimum value allowed in $\mathcal{O}_p^0$. Once $\mathcal{O}_p^1$ is established, a new (iteration 1) set of discriminating patterns is calculated.

(3) Iteration until convergence. Finally, we repeat step 2 calculating $\mathcal{O}_p^i$ and its corresponding set of discriminating patterns from the results of iteration $i - 1$ until the iteration process converges. Note that convergence is assured by the design of the process which utilizes the Bellman update [49] in the reinforcement learning model. The result is the optimal division of the scene and the optimal set of discriminating patterns.

We now give some highlights of the reinforcement learning model. A partitioning of $\mathcal{O}$ into $\mathcal{O}_p$ and $\mathcal{O}_n$ is called a state. Let $reward(s)$ denote some quality measure (we use the average growth rate) of the top k discriminating patterns for a state s. We transform one state s to another one s' using some action a, denoted as $transit(s, a, s')$. The desirability of a state is defined by its utility $utility(s)$. The utilities of the states can be solved by Bellman update [49]:

$$utility_{i+1}(s) \leftarrow reward(s) + max_a \sum_{s'} transit(s, a, s') \times utility_i(s').$$

We use this equation to update the utility of each state from the utilities of its neighbors. The fixed point of the algorithm is the optimal boundary solution.

21.5   Pattern Summarization

In the iterative method discussed above, a relatively large k needs to be selected to give near-complete coverage on the footprint of $\mathcal{O}_p$. In our case study experiments we use $1,500$ to $2,000$ best geospatial discriminating patterns. Once the optimal boundary between $\mathcal{O}_p$ and $\mathcal{O}_n$ is identified, it is desirable to summarize the top k patterns derived from classes $\mathcal{O}_p$ and $\mathcal{O}_n$ so the results are usable to a domain scientist. Such summarization is achieved by clustering the k patterns into a small number of "super-patterns". A distance function is needed in order to use the clustering algorithm we selected to use. One typical way to measure the distance is using similarity measure between the patterns and then convert it into a distance measure with $distance = \frac{1}{similarity} - 1$.

We define a new similarity measure between patterns, based on information theory and inspired by the method proposed by Lin in [261]. Our similarity measure takes advantage of the fact that discretization of explanatory variables results in a set of ordinal variables, since the original features values are numerical and the order between feature values is meaningful.

We define the similarity between two geospatial discriminating patterns X and Y as the average similarity of the two patterns on all attributes:

$$s(X,Y) = \frac{\sum_{i=1}^{m} s(X_i, Y_i)}{m} \qquad (21.1)$$

where X_i, Y_i are the value of ith feature, f_i, of patterns X and Y, respectively.

Lin in [261] defines a similarity metric in information theoretic terms, which has been proven to be effective for measuring the similarity between ordinal values. Specifically, the similarity between two ordinal values X_i and Y_i is measured by the ratio between the amount of information on the commonality of X_i and Y_i and the information needed to describe both X_i and Y_i. However, in the context of geospatial discriminating patterns, a feature f_i is not always present in both patterns, and there are four possible cases regarding the presence and absence. Using "−" to denote the absence of f_i in a pattern, we need to consider four cases to define $s(X_i, Y_i)$.

Let $Z_1, ..., Z_n$ be all of the ordinal values of f_i listed in decreasing order.
Case 1: None of the two ordinal values X_i and Y_i is "−" (i.e. feature f_i is present in both X and Y). Then the similarity between X_i and Y_i is

$$s(X_i, Y_i) = \frac{2 \times log\ P(Z_\ell \vee Z_{\ell+1} \ldots \vee Z_h)}{log\ P(X_i) + log\ P(Y_i)} = \frac{2 \times log\ (\sum_{j=\ell}^{h} P(Z_j))}{log\ P(X_i) + log\ P(Y_i)} \qquad (21.2)$$

where $P(Z_j)$ is the probability of Z_j in $\mathcal{O}$ (which is estimated using frequency), and $Z_\ell, Z_{\ell+1}, \ldots, Z_h$ are the intervals delimited by X_i and Y_i (i.e. $X_i = Z_\ell$ and $Y_i = Z_h$, or $Y_i = Z_\ell$ and $X_i = Z_h$). The commonality between two ordinal values is the interval of ordinal values delimited by them.
Case 2: The ordinal value X_i is "−" and Y_i is not (i.e. feature f_i is absent in X and present in Y). Intuitively, we want to define $s(-, Y_i)$ as a weighted average between Y_i and the ordinal values Z_j present in the footprint of pattern X. We choose to use the probability of value Z_j in transactions that support X, $P_X(Z_j)$, as the weight. Formally, we define the similarity as

$$s(-, Y_i) = \sum_{j=1}^{n} P_X(Z_j) s(Z_j, Y_i). \qquad (21.3)$$

Observe that $Y_i \in \{Z_1, Z_2, \ldots, Z_n\}$ and $\sum_{j=1}^{n} P_X(Z_j) = 1$.
Case 3: The ordinal value Y_i is "−" and X_i is not. Similarly, we define

$$s(X_i, -) = \sum_{j=1}^{n} P_Y(Z_j) s(X_i, Z_j) \qquad (21.4)$$

where $P_Y(Z_j)$ is the probability of value Z_j in transactions that support Y.
Case 4: Both X_i and Y_i are "−". Again we use a weighted average and define

$$s(-, -) = \sum_{j=1}^{n} \sum_{l=1}^{n} P_X(Z_j) P_Y(Z_l) s(Z_j, Z_l). \qquad (21.5)$$

21.6   Application on Vegetation Analysis

In this section, we present the results of applying our methods to a case study featuring real geospatial data. We have constructed a fusion of several datasets that pertain to the distribution of topography, climate, and soil properties across the continental United States. Our purpose is to identify dominant factors responsible for spatial distribution of the region of high vegetation density. The spatial distribution of vegetation density is approximated by the distribution of the Normalized Difference Vegetation Index (NDVI). The NDVI is an index calculated from visible and near-infrared channels of satellite observations, and it serves as a standard proxy for vegetation density. The 8 explanatory variables can be divided into climate-related (average annual precipitation rate, average minimum annual temperature, average maximum annual temperature, and average dew point temperature), soil-related (available water capacity, permeability, and soil pH), and topography-related (elevation). The available water capacity is the volume of water that soil can store for plants. The pH measures the degree to which water in soil is acid or alkaline. Bulk permeability relates to the physical form of the soil. The dew temperature is an indicator of relative humidity. These datasets are from different sources and are available in different spatial resolutions. We have fused all the datasets to 9 co-registered latitude-longitude grids with a resolution of $0.5° \times 0.5°$. Each grid has 618×982 pixels, of which 361,882 pixels ($59.6\% = \frac{361882}{618 \times 982}$) have values for all the 9 variables.

The optimal boundary between $\mathcal{O}_p$ and $\mathcal{O}_n$ is depicted in Figure 21.2(b). Figure 21.2(c) overlays the footprints of the new $\mathcal{O}_p$ with the original $\mathcal{O}_p$ and $\mathcal{O}_p^-$. Here, $\mathcal{O}_p^-$ is the subset of transactions t in $\mathcal{O}_n$ such that t corresponds to a pixel whose class attribute value is highest in $\mathcal{O}_n$. As illustrated in the figure, the boundary is expanded in the buffer zone of $\mathcal{O}_p^-$, but it does not exactly overlay the buffer zone. The top geospatial discriminating patterns, derived from the optimized split between $\mathcal{O}_p$ and $\mathcal{O}_n$, have a significantly higher growth ratio than the top patterns derived from an initial, arbitrary boundary. This is exactly what we have expected because the boundary is optimized using those top patterns.

We classify the top $2,000$ emerging patterns into 5 groups of super-patterns using the K-means clustering algorithm. Figures 21.2(d-h) depict the footprints of the 5 super-patterns. The super-patterns represent five different major combinations of controlling factors that lead to high vegetation density; high vegetation density is associated with different factors in different spatial locations. Each super-pattern can be succinctly described on the basis of its constituent patterns. For example, the super-pattern depicted on Figure 21.2(g) represents high values of temperature and humidity and low values of elevation, whereas the super-pattern depicted on Figure 21.2(d) represents only average values of temperature and humidity, but higher values of ele-

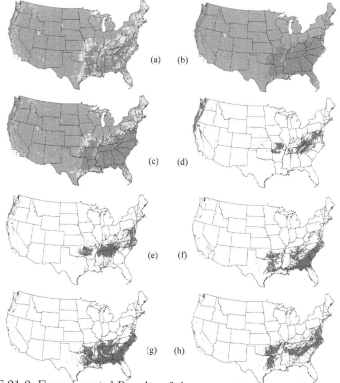

FIGURE 21.2: Experimental Results of the vegetation-cover dataset. (a) Original boundary between high vegetation cover and not-high vegetation cover. (b) Optimal boundary of high vegetation cover. (c) Optimal boundary vs. original high vegetation cover and the buffer zone. (d)-(h) Footprints of 5 groups of geospatial discriminating patterns. Color: orange - footprints of $\mathcal{O}_p$, yellow - footprints of $\mathcal{O}_P^-$, blue - footprints of $\mathcal{O}_n$, green - footprints of identified 5 super-patterns. Source: Reprinted from Ref.[109], Copyright 2009, with permission from Society for Industrial and Applied Mathematics.

vation. Both combinations are apparently compatible with high vegetation density, but they occur in different geographical locations. The results conform to the domain knowledge of the climate and soil conditions that support high density of vegetation. Overall, our case study shows that the range of patterns supporting high vegetation density is not completely separated in the spatial domain as is made clear from overlaps of footprints shown on Figures 21.2(d-h).

The results indicate that there does not exist highly nonlinear dependency of vegetation density on its controlling factors. Examination of patterns related to the high vegetation cover provides a summary of data dependencies that help to develop a better empirical model of vegetation growth.

21.7   Application on Presidential Election Data Analysis

We use the county-level 2008 presidential election data for 3,108 counties within the contiguous United States as an expository example to apply our method to the area of political analysis [380]. For these counties we have selected 13 socio-economics indicators using the Census Bureau data. These indicators are: (1) population density, (2) % of urban population, (3) % of female population, (4) % of foreign-born population, (5) per capita income, (6) median household income, (7) % of population with high school or higher education, (8) % of population with bachelor degree or higher education, (9) % of population that is white, (10) % of population living in poverty, (11) % of houses occupied by owners, (12) percentage of population receiving Social Security benefits, (13) average Social Security monthly benefit. The socio-economic indicators are transformed into ordinal-valued attributes using K-means to identify natural break points in order to fulfill association analysis requirement for categorical variables. We use five categories (bins) denoted as "lowest", "low", "average", "high", and "highest", respectively.

We conducted two different experiments: (1) using a single transaction for each county (all counties contribute equally regardless of their population) (2) using a number of (identical) transactions for each county in proportion to the its population. The results of the two experiments differ; due to space limitations we report here only on the results of experiment (1). Discriminative patterns were found using a growth rate threshold $\delta = 15$. With such threshold 3,097 patterns were found ranging in support from as little as 9 counties to as much as 103.

In-depth analysis of the 3,097 patterns of different levels of specificities and supports is not practical. We use our pattern similarity measure to cluster the patterns into a small number of clusters of patterns (called super-patterns). Fig.21.3 shows the result of such clustering. Panel A is the Sammon map that visualizes in 2-D the "distances" between the patterns - similar patterns are close to each other on the Sammon map. The map reveals that all patterns could be naturally divided into just two large clusters. The four different colors of points corresponding to patterns on the map represents four clusters found using the agglomerative clustering (see panel B). The hierarchy of clustering is terminated (arbitrarily) at four clusters; three of these (closely related) clusters correspond to the agglomeration seen in the left-upper corner of the Sammon map. Panel C shows geographical distribution of footprints corresponding to the four super-patterns. Each supper-pattern agglomerates a large number (from as little as 550 to as much as 1185) individual patterns. Panel D gives a brief socio-economic interpretation to each super-pattern. Note that super-patterns, just like individual patterns, are not described in terms of all potential indicators. Super-pattern 1 is found in sparsely populated, low income counties with large minority populations. The other three super-patterns are found in counties dominated by urban populations. In addition, super-patterns 2 and 3 are associated with counties with disproportionately large female populations, and super-patterns 2 and 3 are associated with low percentage of home ownership. The footprints of different super-patterns overlap; however, there are only six counties where all four patterns are found. There is little geographical overlap between the footprint of super-pattern 1 and the other super-patterns. There are 125 counties (mostly associated with major cities) where footprints of all three urban super-patterns overlap.

21.8 Application on Biodiversity Analysis of Bird Species

We aim to discover associations between environmental factors and the spatial distribution of biodiversity across the contiguous United States. Roughly, biodiversity measures a number of different species (of plants and/or animals) within a spatial region. A pressing problem in biodiversity studies is to find the optimal strategy for protecting the species given limited resources. In order to design such a strategy it is necessary to understand associations between environmental factors and the spatial distribution of biodiversity. In this context we aim to discover existence of different environments (patterns or motifs of environmental factors) which associate with the high levels of biodiversity [381].

The database is composed of spatial accounting units resulting from tessellation of the US territory into equal area hexagons with center-to-center spacing of approximately 27 km. For each unit the measure of biodiversity (class variable) and the values of environmental variables (attributes) are given. The biodiversity measure is provided by the number of species of birds exceeding a specific threshold of probability of occurrence in a given unit. The environmental attributes include terrain, climatic, landscape metric, land cover, and environmental stress variables that are hypothesized to influence biodiversity; we consider $m=32$ such attributes. The class variable and the attributes are discretized into up to seven ordinal categories (lowest, low, medium-low, medium, medium-high, high, highest) using the "natural brakes" method.

First we have transformed the hexagon-based dataset into the square-based dataset. Each square unit (pixel) has a size of 22 × 22 km and there are $N=21,039$ data-carrying pixels in the transformed dataset. The dataset does not have explicit labels. Because we are interested in contrasting the region characterized by high biodiversity with the region characterized by not-high biodiversity we have partitioned the dataset into $\mathcal{O}_p$ corresponding to $c = 1$ class and consisting initially of the objects having high and highest categories of biodiversity and $\mathcal{O}_n$ corresponding to $c = 0$ class and consisting initially of

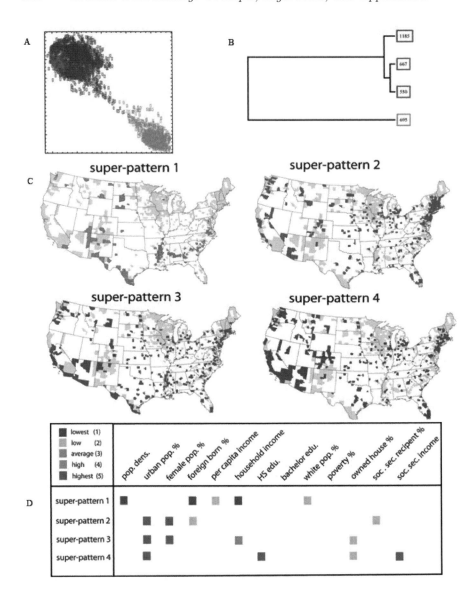

FIGURE 21.3: (A) Sammon's map showing topological relations between 3,907 discriminative patterns. (B) Dendrogram showing results of agglomerative clustering of 3,097 discriminative patterns into 4 super-patterns; the four clusters contain 1185, 667, 550 and 695 discriminative patterns respectively (top to bottom). (C) Geographical distribution of footprints of the 4 identified super-patterns. (D) Meaning of 4 super-patterns in terms of socio-economic indicators. Source: Reprinted from Ref. [380], copyright 2010, with permission from ACM.

the objects having lowest to medium-high categories of biodiversity. The label disambiguation module modifies the initial partition during the consecutive rounds of discriminative data mining.

We identify frequent closed patterns discriminating between $\mathcal{O}_p$ and $\mathcal{O}_n$ using an efficient depth-first search method [62]. We mine for patterns having growth rate ≥ 50 and are fulfilled by at least 2% of transactions (pixels) in $\mathcal{O}_p$. We also keep only the patterns that consist of eight or more attributes; shorter patterns are not specific enough to be of interest to us. We have found 1,503 such patterns. The patterns have lengths between 8 and 20 attributes; the pattern length is broadly distributed with the maximum occurring at 12 attributes. Pattern size (support) varies from 31 to 91 pixels; the distribution of pattern size is skewed toward the high values and the maximum occurs at 40 pixels.

We report 5 super-pattern clusters that discriminate high-biodiversity from from-biodiversity. Fig. 21.4(A) illustrates the footprints of the 5 super-pattern clusters, and Fig. 21.4(B) shows the bar-coded description for the 5 clusters corresponding to different biodiversity regimes. If a given category is absent within a cluster the bar is gray; black bars with increasing thickness denote categories with increasingly large presence in a cluster. Five clusters indicate 5 distinct motifs of environmental attributes associated with high levels of biodiversity. The results can help develop optimal strategies for protecting bird species given limited resources.

21.9 Conclusion

In this chapter, we have formulated the problem of mining geospatial discriminating patterns in the domain of geoscience. This domain uses remote sensing datasets that are mostly in the form of spatially co-registered rasters, which exhibits complex interactions among multiple attributes. We proposed a value-iteration method gearing to identify the optimal boundary between geospatial classes, thus maximizing the (growth rate of the) patterns to be identified. We introduced a new similarity metric that is specially designed for ordinal variables. We applied our methods to three important real spatial datasets, US vegetation data, presidential election data, and biodiversity of bird species. Discovered patterns conform to existing knowledge, and they deliver this knowledge in a quantitative, as well as comprehensive and systematic manner.

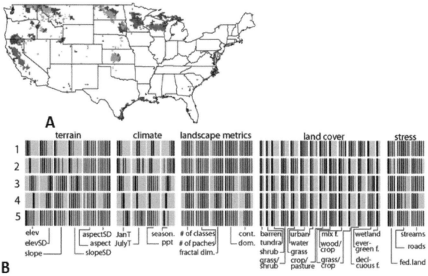

FIGURE 21.4: (A) Spatial footprints of five pattern clusters. White – not high biodiversity region; gray – high biodiversity region; purple (cluster #1), light green (cluster #2), yellow (cluster #3), blue (cluster #4), and red (cluster #5) – footprints of the five clusters. (B) Bar-code representation of the five regimes (clusters) of high biodiversity. Source: Reprinted from Ref. [381], copyright 2010, with kind permission from Springer Science+Business Media.

Chapter 22

Mining Emerging Patterns for Activity Recognition

Tao Gu

Department of Mathematics and Computer Science, University of Southern Denmark

Zhanqing Wu, XianPing Tao

State Key Laboratory for Novel Software Technology, Department of Computer Science and Technology, Nanjing University

Hung Keng Pung

School of Computing, National University of Singapore, Singapore

Jian Lu

State Key Laboratory for Novel Software Technology, Department of Computer Science and Technology, Nanjing University

22.1   Introduction

With the rapid advances of sensors and wireless networks, recognizing human activity based on sensor readings has been recently attracting much research interest in the pervasive computing community. A typical application is monitoring activities for the elderly and cognitively impaired people, and providing them with proactive assistance.

In real life, people perform activities in not only a sequential manner (i.e., performing one activity after another), but also an interleaved (i.e., switching between the steps of two or more activities) or concurrent manner (i.e., performing two or more activities simultaneously). Recognizing activities in such a complex situation is important not only for meeting real life needs but also for advancing the field of pervasive computing.

In this chapter, we formulate activity recognition [394, 336] as a pattern based classification problem, and propose a novel Emerging Patterns based approach to recognize sequential, interleaved, and concurrent activities. We build our activity models based on Emerging Patterns (EPs) [118]. We mine a set of EPs for each sequential activity from the training dataset, and use the sets of EPs obtained to recognize not only simple (i.e., sequential), but also complex (i.e., interleaved and concurrent) activities. This approach does not require training for complex activities; and hence it has great flexibility and applicability for real-life pervasive computing applications. Evaluation results on a real-world activity trace collection on four volunteers in a smart home environment demonstrate both the effectiveness and flexibility of our solution.

22.2   Data Preprocessing

We built a wireless sensor platform [170] from off-the-shelf sensors to collect sensor information. Our sensor platform measures a user's movement (i.e., left hand, right hand, and body movements), user location, the living environment (i.e., temperature, humidity and light), and the human-object interaction (i.e., the objects that a user touches). To process the data, we first convert the sensor readings to a series of *observation vectors* where each *observation vector* consists of 15 features as shown below.

$$o = [accel\_body\_x, accel\_body\_y, accel\_body\_z, accel\_right\_x, accel\_right\_y,$$
$$accel\_right\_z, accel\_left\_x, accel\_left\_y, accel\_left\_z, temperature,$$
$$humidity, light, location, left\_object, right\_object]$$

Here, *accel, temperature, humidity, light* refer to acceleration, temperature, humidity, and light data obtained by wearable sensors; *location* refers to user location detected by RFID readers; *body, left, right* refer to sensors located on user's body, left hand, and right hand, respectively; x, y, z refer to acceleration directed on the x, y, and $z-$axes, respectively.

We compute each *observation vector* in a fixed time interval which is set to one second in our experiments. We then transform these *observation vectors* into *feature vectors*. A *feature vector* consists of *feature items*, where a *feature item* refers to a feature-value pair in which a feature can be numeric or nominal. A numeric feature is denoted as $numfeature_i$. We call $numfeature_i@[a,b]$ a *numeric feature item*, meaning that the value of $numfeature_i$ is limited inclusively between a and b (e.g., $accel\_body\_x@(-737.5, -614.5])$. The entropy-based discretization method [145] is used to discretize numeric features. We denote a nominal attribute as $nomfeature_j$. We call $nomfeature_j@n$ a *nominal feature item*, meaning that the value of $nomfeature_j$ is n (e.g. $object@cup$). These *feature items* are indexed by a simple encoding scheme and will be used as inputs to the EPs mining process described in the next section.

22.3 Mining Emerging Patterns For Activity Recognition

22.3.1 Problem Statement

We formulate the problem of sequential, interleaved, and concurrent activity recognition as follows. Given a training dataset that consists of a sequence of observations for sequential activities only (i.e., formally, a training trace O consists of T observations, $O = \{o_1, o_2, ..., o_T\}$, associated with sequential activity labels $\{SA_1, SA_2, ..., SA_m\}$, where there are m sequential activities), our objective is to train a model that can assign each new observation with the correct activity label(s) and segment the new activity trace.

22.3.2 Mining Emerging Patterns from Sequential Activity Instances

We use sequential activity instances for training. Note that the instances of interleaved and concurrent activities are not used in our mining process. An instance here refers to the union of all the observations that belong to a sequential activity during a continuous period of time. For each sequential activity class SA_i, we mine a set of EPs to contrast its instances, D_{SA_i}, against all other activity instances D'_{SA_i}, where $D'_{SA_i} = D - D_{SA_i}$ and D is the entire sequential activity dataset. We refer EP_{SA_i} as the EPs of sequential activity SA_i. We discover the EPs by an efficient algorithm described in [247].

TABLE 22.1:   A subset of EPs for activity *Cleaning a Dining Table.*
Source: Adapted from Ref. [170], with permission from IEEE.

EPs	Support(%)	Growth rate
location@kichen, object@plate	100	∞
object@cleanser, object@plate, object@wash_cloth, *location@kichen*	95.24	∞
object@bowl, accel_body_x@$(-155.25, -52.25]$, *light@*$(24.5, 28.5]$, *object@plate*	66.67	256
object@bowl, accel_left_z@$(-684.5, -453.5]$, *object@plate, location@kichen, light@*$(24.5, 28.5]$	66.67	∞

The algorithm mines closed patterns and generators simultaneously under one depth-first search scheme.

After computation, we get n sets of EPs, one set per sequential activity class. TABLE 22.1 presents an example of the EPs of the *cleaning a dining table* activity. For example, the EP {*object@cleanser, object@plate, object@wash_cloth, location@kichen*} has a support of 95.24% and a growth rate of ∞. It has an intuitive meaning that cleanser, plate, and wash_cloth are the common objects involved in this activity, and this activity usually occurs in the kitchen. In fact, one of the advantages of EPs is that they are easy to understand.

22.4   The *epSICAR* Algorithm

22.4.1   Score Function for Sequential Activity

22.4.1.1   EP Score

Given a test instance $S_{t \sim t + L_{SA_i}}$ for a possible activity SA_i with average duration L_{SA_i}, the EP score measures the likelihood of a set of SA_i's EPs contained in this instance. It provides a probabilistic measurement on the fraction of EP_{SA_i} (i.e., the discriminating features of SA_i) contained in $S_{t \sim t + L_{SA_i}}$. To make use of each EP set, we combine the strength of each set of EPs based on the aggregation method described in [126].

Suppose an instance $S_{t \sim t + L_{SA_i}}$ contains an EP, X, where $X \in EP_{SA_i}$, then the odds that $S_{t \sim t + L_{SA_i}}$ belongs to SA_i is defined as $\frac{growth\_rate(X)}{growth\_rate(X)+1}$. The differentiating power of a single EP is then defined by the odds and the fraction of the population of class that contain the EP. More specifically, the differentiating power of X is given by $\frac{growth\_rate(X)}{growth\_rate(X)+1} * supp_{SA_i}(X)$. The aggregated EP score of $S_{t \sim t+L_{SA_i}}$ for SA_i is defined as

$$aggregated\_score(SA_i, S_{t \sim t+L_{SA_i}}) =$$
$$\sum_{X \subseteq S_{t \sim t+L_{SA_i}}, X \in EP_{SA_i}} \frac{growth\_rate(X)}{growth\_rate(X) + 1} * supp_{SA_i}(X) \qquad (22.1)$$

where $supp_{SA_i}(X)$ is the support of X in class SA_i, and $growth\_rate(X)$ is $supp_{SA_i}(X)$ divided by the X's support in non-SA_i class. The EP score of each activity is then normalized using a baseline score; we define the EP score as

$$ep\_score(SA_i, S_{t \sim t+L_{SA_i}}) = \frac{aggregated\_score(SA_i, S_{t \sim t+L_{SA_i}})}{base\_score(SA_i)} \qquad (22.2)$$

where $base\_score(SA_i)$ is the median value of the $aggregated\_score(SA_i, S_{t \sim t+L_{SA_i}})$ values of all the training instances of SA_i.

22.4.1.2   Coverage Score

Given a test instance $S_{t \sim t+L_{SA_i}}$ for a possible activity SA_i, the Sliding-Window Coverage score (coverage score for short) measures a fraction of irrelevant observations contained in this instance with respect to SA_i. The lower the percentage of irrelevant observations covered, the larger the coverage score is obtained. We denote $coverage\_score(SA_i, S_{t \sim t+L_{SA_i}})$ as the coverage score of instance $S_{t \sim t+L_{SA_i}}$ for SA_i. This score is computed based on a function, $relevance(SA_i, f_p)$, where f_p is a feature vector contained in L_{SA_i}. We first compute $relevance(SA_i, item_h)$ for each $item_h \in f_p$, and then aggregate their scores for computing $relevance(SA_i, f_p)$.

$$relevance(SA_i, item_h) = P(item_h | SA_i) + \sum_{item_h \in X, X \in EP_{SA_i}} supp_{SA_i}(X) \qquad (22.3)$$

where the probability $P(item_h | SA_i)$ is obtained from the training data, and $\sum_{item_h \in X, X \in EP_{SA_i}} supp_{SA_i}(X)$ indicates that more weights are given to an item which appears in EP_{SA_i}.

We now aggregate the values of $relevance(SA_i, item_h)$ for all $item_h \in f_p$. The aggregation can be simply done using $\sum_{item_h \in f_p} relevance(SA_i, item_h)$. However, if EP_{SA_i} has many more items than EP_{SA_j}, then a feature vector usually gets higher scores for SA_i than SA_j even for the feature vectors of SA_j. Hence, we need a normalized scheme. The normalized $relevance(SA_i, f_p)$ is computed as follows:

$$relevance(SA_i, f_p) = \frac{unnorm\_relevance(SA_i, f_p)}{base\_relevance(SA_i)} \qquad (22.4)$$

where $unnorm\_relevance(SA_i, f_p) = \sum_{item_h \in f_p} relevance(SA_i, item_h)$, and

$base\_relevance(SA_i)$ be the median of the values of $unnorm\_relevance(SA_i, f_p)$ in the training data.

We now can compute $coverage\_score(SA_i, S_{t\sim t+L_{SA_i}})$. A simply way is to sum up all the $relevance(SA_i, f_p)$ in L_{SA_i}. However, it may bias towards longer activities. Hence, we compute $coverage\_score(SA_i, S_{t\sim t+L_{SA_i}})$ by averaging all the $relevance(SA_i, f_p)$ as follows:

$$coverage\_score(SA_i, S_{t\sim t+L_{SA_i}}) = \frac{1}{L_{SA_i}} \sum_{f_p \in L_{SA_i}} relevance(SA_i, f_p) \qquad (22.5)$$

22.4.1.3 Correlation Score

Human activities are usually performed in a non-deterministic fashion. However, there exist some correlations between them, i.e., when an activity SA_j has been performed, there is some likelihood that another activity SA_i is performed. We use conditional probability to model such correlations between activities, i.e., $P(SA_i|SA_j)$ which is the conditional probability of SA_i given SA_j. We can easily obtain such probabilities from training dataset. Note that the initial value is set to zero, i.e., $P(SA_i|NULL) = 0$.

22.4.2 Score Function for Interleaved and Concurrent Activities

We denote CA_i as both interleaved activities (i.e., in this case, we denote CA_i as $SA_a\&SA_b$) and concurrent activities (i.e., in this case, we denote CA_i as $SA_a + SA_b$), where two single activities SA_a and SA_b are involved[1]. We define the sliding-window length of CA_i as $L_{CA_i} = L_{SA_a} + L_{SA_b}$, and use L_{CA_i} to get the test instance $S_{t\sim t+L_{CA_i}}$. Since an instance of CA_i containing both EP_{SA_a} and EP_{SA_b} (i.e., some of the steps that belong to SA_a and SA_b respectively are interleaved or overlapped), we compute the EP score of CA_i as follows:

$$\begin{aligned} &ep\_score(CA_i, S_{t\sim t+L_{CA_i}}) \\ &= max[ep\_score(SA_a, S_{t\sim t+L_{CA_i}}), ep\_score(SA_b, S_{t\sim t+L_{CA_i}})] \end{aligned} \qquad (22.6)$$

When computing the coverage score of CA_i, we choose the higher score from $relevance(SA_a, f_p)$ and $relevance(SA_b, f_p)$ since CA_i contains both the observations of SA_a and SA_b in $S_{t\sim t+L_{CA_i}}$, i.e., $relevance(CA_i, f_p) = max(relevance(SA_a, f_p), relevance(SA_b, f_p))$. Then the coverage score of CA_i can be computed as follows:

$$coverage\_score(CA_i, S_{t\sim t+L_{CA_i}}) = \frac{1}{L_{CA_i}} \sum_{f_p \in L_{CA_i}} relevance(CA_i, f_p) \qquad (22.7)$$

---

[1]We set the number of single activities involved in interleaved or concurrent activities to two for illustrations although in theory it can be more than two.

There are three situations when computing the correlation score: a sequential activity followed by an interleaved or a concurrent activity, an interleaved or a concurrent activity followed by a sequential activity, and an interleaved or a concurrent activity followed by another interleaved or concurrent activity. We choose the maximum value of all possible conditional probabilities for all these cases. To illustrate, given an interleaved or concurrent activity CA_j involving SA_c and SA_d, such probability for CA_i involving SA_a and SA_b can be computed as follows.

$$P(CA_i|CA_j) = max(P(SA_a|SA_c), P(SA_a|SA_d), P(SA_b|SA_c), P(SA_b|SA_d))$$
$$(22.8)$$

The computation of $P(SA_i|CA_j)$ and $P(CA_i|SA_j)$ follows a similar method, and we use $P(A_i|A_j)$ to denote all the three cases. In addition, we apply correlation analysis to measure the likelihood of SA_a and SA_b appeared in an interleaved ($SA_a\&SA_b$) or concurrent (SA_a+SA_b) activity. This probability can be computed as $P(SA_aSA_b)$. Finally, we define the correlation score as follows.

$$correlation(A_i) = P(A_i|A_j)P(SA_aSA_b) \qquad (22.9)$$

where A_i can be CA_i or SA_i, A_j can be CA_j or SA_j, SA_a and SA_b are two single activities involved in CA_i. When A_i is SA_i, $P(SA_aSA_b)$ is defined as $P(A_i)$.

In summary, the score function for sequential, interleaved, and concurrent activities is defined as follows.

Definition 3 Given a time t, and an activity A_j which ends at t, for each activity A_i, a test instance $S_{t\sim t+L_{A_i}}$ is obtained from t to $t + L_{A_i}$, the likelihood of A_i is computed as follows:

$$score(A_i, A_j, S_{t\sim t+L_{A_i}}) = c_1 * ep\_score(A_i, S_{t\sim t+L_{A_i}}) +$$
$$c_2 * coverage\_score(A_i, S_{t\sim t+L_{A_i}}) + c_3 * correlation(A_i) \qquad (22.10)$$

Here, c_1, c_2, and c_3 are coefficients, representing the weight of each individual score. These coefficients have different implications. For example, a higher c_1 implies that the subject always performs his activities in a consistent manner. A higher c_2 implies that all the instances of the activity are performed in a constant duration whereas a lower c_2 implies that the variance of the instances can be large. A higher c_3 implies that the subject usually performs his activities in certain order. These weights reflect a subject's habit in his daily routine.

22.4.3 The *epSICAR* Algorithm

We now can apply the score function to recognize the activity label in the test instance obtained using a slide window method. Given m sequential

Algorithm: slidingWinRecog
Input: feature vector of length L_{max}: $F = \{f_t, f_{t+1}, f_{t+2}, ..., f_{t+L_{max}}\}$,
    where prediction starts at time t,
    predicted activity A_j in the previous sliding window;
Output: An ordered pair $< A_i, A'_i >$, where A_i is the activity label
with the highest score and A'_i is the activity label with the second
highest score;
Method:
1: **for each** activity $A_i, i = 1, 2, ..., m^2$ **do**
2:      get instance $S_{t \sim t+L_{A_i}} = \bigcup\limits_{p=t}^{t+L_{A_i}} f_p$;
3:      compute $score(A_i, A_j, S_{t \sim t+L_{A_i}})$;
4: **end for**
5: **return** $< A_i, A'_i >$;

FIGURE 22.1: Sliding-window based Recognition Algorithm.

activities, the number of interleaved and concurrent activities can be computed by $m(m-1)$. Then the total number of activities is m^2. We define L_{max} as $max\{L_{A_k} \mid k = 1, 2, ..., m^2\}$. A straightforward method is to test each activity label using its corresponding slide window and the one with the highest score wins out. Figure 22.1 describes this approach. Then the entire process in the *epSICAR* algorithm is as shown in Figure 22.2 [2].

22.5 Empirical Studies

To evaluate our proposed algorithm, we conducted our own trace collection in a complex, real-world situation. In this section, we first describe our experimental setup and metric, then present and discuss the results obtained from a series of experiments.

22.5.1 Trace Collection and Evaluation Methodology

Trace collection was done in StarHome - a real smart home built by us. We deployed our sensor platform and tagged over 100 objects. We randomly selected 26 activities out of common activities. We then chose 15 interleaved activities and 16 concurrent activities. The data were collected over a period of two weeks. We collected a total number of 532 activity instances in which the numbers of sequential, interleaved, and concurrent activities are 422, 44,

---

[2]The adjustBoundary algorithm is for accurate activity trace segmentation; please refer to [170] for more details.

Algorithm: epSICAR
Input: an observation sequence $O = \{o_1, o_2, ..., o_T\}$ with a length of T;
m sequential activities $\{SA_1, SA_2, ..., SA_m\}$;
Output: assign the activity label to each observation;
Method:
1: pre-process O to obtain feature vectors $F = \{f_1, f_2, ..., f_T\}$;
2: $t = 1$;
3: $A_{previous} = null$; $A_{current} = null$; $A_{candidate} = null$;
4: **while** $t \leqslant T$
5: $< A_{current}, A'_{current} >$=slidingWinRecog($F_{t,t+L_{max}}, A_{previous}$);
6: $L_{A_{current}} = adjustBoundary(F_{t,t+L_{max}}, A_{current}, A'_{current}) - t$;
7: **if** $t = 1$ or $A_{current} = A_{candidate}$
8: Assign label $A_{current}$ to $o_t \sim o_{t+L_{A_{current}}}$;
9: $t = t + L_{A_{current}}$;
10: $A_{previous} = A_{current}$;
11: $A_{candidate} = null$;
12: **else if** $A_{candidate} \neq A_{current}$
13: $t = adjustBoundary(F_{t-L_{A_{previous}}, t+L_{A_{current}}}, A_{previous}, A_{current})$;
14: $A_{candidate} = A_{current}$;
15: **end if**
16: **end while**

FIGURE 22.2: *epSICAR* Activity Recognition Algorithm.

---

and 66, respectively [3]. We use ten-fold cross-validation and time-slice accuracy defined as follows to evaluate the performance of our algorithm:

$$Slice\_Accuracy = \frac{\sum\limits_{SA_i \in LB_G \cap LB_R} L_{SA_i}}{\sum\limits_{SA_i \in LB_G \cup LB_R} L_{SA_i}} \quad (22.11)$$

Here LB_G are the ground-truth label(s), and LB_R are the predicted label(s).

22.5.2 Experiment 1: Accuracy Performance

In this experiment, we evaluate time-slice accuracy for different activity cases. The average accuracies of sequential, interleaved, and concurrent activities are 90.96%, 88.10%, and 82.53% respectively, and the overall accuracy is 88.67%. The accuracy of sequential activity is the highest among all the three cases, while the accuracies of interleaved and concurrent activities are lower. The result probably can be explained as follows. Firstly, each of the four volunteers may perform his interleaved or concurrent activities in a different manner. This difference does not influence the sequential activity recognition much but some of the specific characteristics of interleaved and concurrent

---

[3]More details about this trace collection could be found in [170].

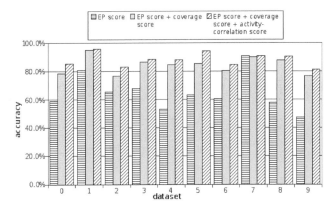

FIGURE 22.3: Analysis of the score function. Source: Adapted from Ref. [170], with permission from IEEE.

activities performed by different individuals may not be captured. Nevertheless, the result is reasonably good, and we achieve our objective of building a unified activity model to recognize all the three activity cases based on sequential activity training data only. Second, the accuracy of concurrent activity is 5.57% lower than that of interleaved activity while the accuracy of interleaved activity is close to that of sequential activity. It is probably due to the sliding-window length. We apply $L_{CA_i} = L_{SA_a} + L_{SA_b}$ to calculate the sliding-window length of CA_i. This estimation seems to work well in the case of interleaved activity as the observations of SA_a and SA_b do not overlap each other. However, for concurrent activity, there exists some overlapped steps between SA_a and SA_b, hence L_{CA_i} should be much shorter than $L_{SA_a} + L_{SA_b}$.

22.5.3   Experiment 2: Model Analysis

In this experiment, we evaluate and analyze the *epSICAR* algorithm with respect to our score function. Figure 22.3 shows that the accuracies of the *epSICAR* algorithm with *EP score*, *EP score + coverage score*, and *EP score + coverage score + activity-correlation score*, respectively. The figure suggests that *epSICAR* achieves an accuracy of 65% on average with the *EP score* only, demonstrating that the concept of *EPs* works effectively. However, the effectiveness of the *EP score* is not as high as expected and there exists some variations. More sensor features can be developed to improve the result. Figure 22.3 also suggests that, by introducing the *coverage score*, the accuracy is improved significantly by about 15% and the variance also decreases. We also observe that the accuracy is further improved by about 2% when adding in the *activity-correlation score*.

22.6   Conclusion

In this chapter, we studied the problem of human activity recognition based on sensor readings in a smart home. We investigated a challenging problem of how we can apply a model, which can be learnt from sequential activity instances only, in recognizing both simple (i.e., sequential) and complex (i.e., interleaved and concurrent) activities. We exploited EPs as powerful discriminators to differentiate activities and proposed the *epSICAR* algorithm. We conducted comprehensive evaluation studies using our data set and analyze our algorithm in detail. The results demonstrated both the effectiveness and flexibility of our algorithm.

Chapter 23

Emerging Pattern Based Prediction of Heart Diseases and Powerline Safety*

Keun Ho Ryu, Dong Gyu Lee, and Minghao Piao

Department of Computer Science, Chungbuk National University

23.1   Introduction

Emerging patterns (EPs) are itemsets whose supports increase significantly from one dataset to another. EPs can capture emerging trends in timestamped databases, or useful contrasts between data classes. In this chapter, we introduce three applications of EPs: prediction of myocardial ischemia (MI), coronary artery disease (CAD) diagnosis, and classification of powerline safety. We present the background of these three applications, the classification problems, the important features, and how to prepare the data for mining EPs. We also give some EPs examples for these applications.

For the prediction of MI, diagnostic features are extracted from ST segments and used for building the EP based prediction model. For the diagnosis of CAD, linear and non-linear features are created after Heart Rate Variability (HRV) analysis and used to perform the disease diagnosis. For the classification of powerline safety, load factors are extracted from daily load consumption data and used to predict non-safe powerlines (those more likely to result in dangerous situations like power failure, fire, etc.). This chapter uses classification by aggregating emerging pattern (CAEP) [126] to perform prediction in these applications. CAEP uses the following scoring function to make classification decisions.

---

*This work was supported by the National Research Foundation of Korea(NRF) grant funded by the Korea government(MEST)(No. 2011-0001044).

Definition 23.1 *(SC: score) Given a test T and a set $E(C_i)$ of EPs for class C_i, the aggregate score of T for C_i is,*

$$SC(T, C_i) = \sum Str(X) = \sum \frac{GR(X)}{GR(X) + 1} \times sup(X),$$

where the summation ranges over all EPs of $E(C_i)$ that match T, and $GR(X)$ denotes the growth rate of X (defined as the support ratio of the support X in C_i and in the complement of C_i). The class with the highest (normalized) score is the predicted class of T.

The aggregate score, especially when normalized by the median score of training instances of each class, have been used in CAEP to achieve high predictive accuracy.

23.2   Prediction of Myocardial Ischemia

Ischemia is an absolute or relative lack of blood supply to an organ. Ischemia could result in tissue damage due to the lack of oxygen and nutrients. Ultimately, this causes great damage because of a buildup of metabolic wastes. Electrocardiogram (ECG), which records the electrical activity of the heart over time is widely used for the diagnosis of heart disease like Myocardial Ischemia (MI). A schematic representation of ECG is shown in Figure 23.1.

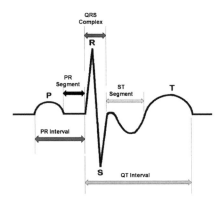

FIGURE 23.1: Schematic representation of ECG. Source: Reprinted from Ref. [337], Copyright 2009, with permission from IEEE Press.

Statistical and data mining approaches to analyzing the ECG data are often used to find effective ways of the diagnosis and treatment of heart diseases. From previous data mining based studies, we can see that the approaches have achieved good results, but there are still several weaknesses that have to be addressed, i.e., neural-network based approaches do not provide explanations for the classification decisions even though they achieve high performance. In contrast, rule-based approaches give more explainable results, but their accuracy is lower.

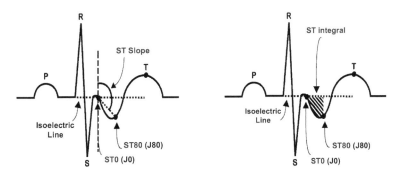

FIGURE 23.2: ECG features extracted from recordings. Source: Reprinted from Ref. [337], Copyright 2009, with permission from IEEE Press.

In [337], a dataset that consists of 99 patients with MI and 94 control subjects is used to test the EP based prediction methodology. For each sample subject, four features are extracted from recorded ECG signals [135]: *ST0* (*J0*), *ST80* (*J80*), *ST Slope*, and *ST integral*. *ST80* is the value of *ST* 80ms after *ST0* point (*heart rate 120 beats/min*). The *ST slope* is the slope of the line connecting the *ST0* point and *ST80*, *ST integral* is the area between the *isoelectric line* and the points *ST0* and *ST80* as shown in Figure 23.2. Moreover, each subject's clinical information is also collected, concerning *Blood Pressure, Glucose Content* and presence of lipids in the blood, etc. Details of used clinical information are:

- HBP (hbp/normal): Hyper Blood Pressure
- DM (dm/normal): Diabetes Mellitus
- OLDMI (Experience/normal): Old Myocardial Infraction
- EF (continuous): Ejection Fraction
- Glucose (continuous): Blood Glucose
- Uricacid (continuous): Uric acid
- TC (continuous): Total Cholesterol
- TP (continuous): Triglyceride
- Hyperlip (hyperlipid/normal): Hyperlipidemia
- SBP (continuous): Systolic Blood Pressure
- DBP (continuous): Diastolic Blood Pressure
- Smoking (smoker/nonsmoker): Smoking habit

Since several features are continuous variables, entropy-based discretization method has been used. Each continuous variable is discretized into a number of intervals.

The performance of the methodology is compared with several algorithms using the same dataset as shown in Figure 23.3. This figure shows that different accuracy is achieved when different numbers of bins are used. With 9 bins, subjects with MI are all predicted as MI, although there are misclassified subjects in the Control group - 28 subjects in Control group are predicted as MI (the used dataset has 99 MI and 94 Control). Since the MI group is the focus of this application, the error rate in the control group is acceptable to a certain degree. Table 23.1 shows the sample of derived emerging patterns for the MI class.

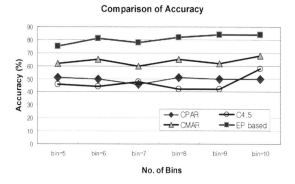

FIGURE 23.3: Comparison of classification accuracy. Source: Reprinted from Ref. [337], Copyright 2009, with permission from IEEE Press.

TABLE 23.1: Example emerging patterns of the myocardial ischemia class. Source: Reprinted from [337], Copyright 2009, with permission from IEEE.

Emerging Patterns	Sup.(MI)	GR
EF=(66.2-72.1], DBP=(66.7-70], OLDMI=nomi	0.26	2.06
ST80=(0.0343-0.190367], EF=(66.2-72.1], DBP=(66.7-70], OLDMI=nomi	0.07	2.21
EF=(66.2-72.1], DBP=(66.7-70], DM=normal, OLDMI=nomi	0.23	2.18
SBP=(113.3-120], EF=(66.2-72.1], OLDMI=nomi	0.15	2.03
HBP=normal, HYPERLIP=hyperlipidemia, SMOKING=nonsmoker, OLDMI=nomi	0.09	2.14
DBP= (76.7-80], HBP=normal, OLDMI=nomi	0.13	2.47
ST0=(0.041656-0.198167], HBP=normal, HYPERLIP=hyperlipidemia	0.05	2.37
EF=(66.2-72.1], DBP=(66.7-70], HYPERLIP=hyperlipidemia	0.16	2.53
INTEGRAL=(-inf-4.816611], HBP=hbp, DM=normal, SMOKING=nonsmoker	0.17	2.02
CLUCOSE=(-inf-113.6], DBP=(76.7-80], EF=(66.2-72.1]	0.03	∞

23.3 Coronary Artery Disease Diagnosis

Coronary artery disease (CAD; also known as atherosclerotic heart disease, coronary heart disease) is a narrowing of the small blood vessels that supply blood and oxygen to the heart: producing blockages in the vessels which nourish the heart itself. ECG is a diagnostic tool that is routinely used to assess the electrical and muscular functions of the heart. HRV is considered by scientists and physicians to be an excellent non-invasive measurement of nervous system activity and heart health. HRV can be calculated from basic pulse rate data.

In [234], the ECG signals are retrieved to measure consecutive RR intervals by using the MATLAB based R wave detection software. For HRV analysis, last 512 stationary RR intervals are obtained from each signal of recumbent position. The power spectra of the 512 RR intervals are obtained by means of fast Fourier Transformation. The direct current component is excluded in the calculation of power spectrum to remove the non-harmonic components in the very low-frequency region (< 0.004Hz). The area of spectral peaks within the whole range of 0 to 0.4Hz was defined as *Total Power (TP)*, the area of spectral peaks within the ranges of 0 to 0.15Hz as *Low Frequency Power (LF)*, and the area of spectral peaks within the range of 0.15 to 0.4Hz as *High Frequency Power (HF)*, respectively. The *Normalized Low Frequency* Power ($nLF=100 \cdot LF/TP$) is used as an index of sympathetic modulation; the *Normalized High Frequency* Power ($nHF=100 \cdot HF/TP$) as the index of sympathovagal balance.

- TP: The variance of normal RR intervals in HRV over 5 min (≤ 0.40Hz)
- VLF: Power in very low frequency range (<0.04Hz)
- LF: Power in low frequency range ($0.04 \sim 0.15$Hz)
- HF: Power in high frequency range ($0.15 \sim 0.40$Hz)
- LF/HF: LF/HF
- nLF: Normalized Low Frequency Power (LF/TP$\times$100)
- nHF: Normalized High Frequency Power (HF/TP$\times$100)
- SDNN: The standard deviation of NN intervals

Clinical information is also useful in diagnosis and treatment of heart disease because it is the first type of medical examination on the patients. Relevant clinical features include: *age, hyper blood pressure, diabetes mellitus, smoking, old myocardial infarction, ejection fraction, blood glucose, total cholesterol, triglyceride, hyperlipidemia, systolic blood pressure*, and *diastolic blood pressure*. The multi-interval discretization method [145] is used to discretize continuous features.

After EP mining, a set of EPs is selected for classification. Patients with stenosis of the luminal narrowing greater than 0.5 were recruited as the CAD group, the others were classified as the normal group. The accuracy was obtained by using stratified 10 fold cross validation method. The result was compared with Naïve Bayesian, C4.5 [345], CBA [270], and CMAR [258] as shown in Figure 23.4. The EP based classifier has achieved higher precision in CAD group; thus it misclassifies fewer CAD cases as Control and it successfully detects many patients with CAD.

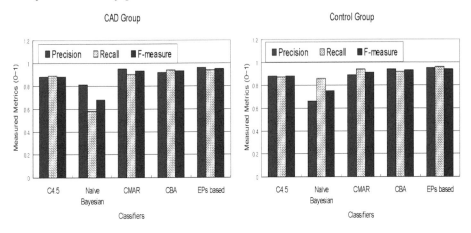

FIGURE 23.4: Comparison with other classifiers on CAD diagnosis.

23.4   Classification of Powerline Safety

The use of data mining techniques on power load management can help electricity related industries to make more accurate decisions based on information obtained from the classification models. Classification models are used for predicting power load to find relationships between input and output variables. Classification methods are used in customer classification or pattern recognition to discover new unseen rules. Application of clustering methods could help the identification and analysis of load profiles. Also, using temporal and spatial analysis techniques enables examination of the current situation and problems, facilitates demand analysis and load management and the analysis of the relationship and impact between customers, facilities, load and outages [366].

In [236], power consumption data of customers obtained from Korea Electric Power Research Institute (KEPRI) is used to evaluate an EP based approach for powerline safety analysis. Selected power load patterns are restructured as daily representative vectors in Eqn 23.1:

$$V^{(c)} = \{V_0^{(c)}, \ldots, V_h^{(c)}, \ldots, V_H^{(c)}\} \tag{23.1}$$

where c=customer, $0 < h < H$, and H=2345. For each customer c, $V^{(c)}$ denotes the total daily power usage of c for 24 hours. The power usage is measured once every 15 minutes, hence each total daily power usages vector has 96 dimensions. Dimension names are noted as 0000, 0015, 0030, ..., 1415, 1430, ..., 2345. A value such as 1415 means the measured time 14:15 PM.

TABLE 23.2: Extracted load factors. Source: Reprinted from Ref. [324], Copyright 2009, with permission from IEEE Press.

The Load Factors	Formula
F_1: Load Factor (24h)	$F_1 = \frac{Avg.for\_day}{Max.for\_day}$
F_2: Night Impact (8h: 23pm~07am)	$F_2 = \frac{1}{3} \times \frac{Avg.for\_night}{Avg.for\_day}$
F_3: Lunch Impact (3h: 12am~03pm)	$F_3 = \frac{1}{8} \times \frac{Avg.for\_lunch}{Avg.for\_day}$
F_4: Midnight Impact (7h: 00am~07am)	$F_4 = \frac{7}{24} \times \frac{Avg.for\_night}{Avg.for\_day}$
F_5: Morning Impact (3h: 09pm~12pm)	$F_5 = \frac{1}{8} \times \frac{Avg.for\_morning}{Avg.for\_day}$
F_6: Afternoon Impact (3h: 13pm~17pm)	$F_6 = \frac{1}{8} \times \frac{Avg.for\_afternoon}{Avg.for\_day}$
F_7: Evening Impact (4h: 19pm~23pm)	$F_7 = \frac{1}{6} \times \frac{Avg.for\_evening}{Avg.for\_day}$

For dimensionality reduction, seven load factors are extracted (see Table 23.2): F_1 measures the usage for the full 24 hours, night impact F_2 measures the usage from 23:00 to 07:00 (8h), lunch impact F_3 measures the usage from 12:00 to 15:00 (3h), midnight impact F_4 measures the usage from 00:00 to 07:00 (7h), morning impact F_5 measures the usage from 09:00 to 12:00 (3h), afternoon impact F_6 measures the usage from 13:00 to 17:00 (3h), evening impact F_7 measures the usage from 19:00 to 23:00 (4h). Definition of these time intervals depends on characteristics of the datasets, and they were determined after discussion with power related experts for the accurate extraction of load factors. *Avg.* and *Max.* values, which are used in the Table 23.2, are the average and maximum values of the measured power usages during corresponding time intervals. For example, for load factor F_1, the *Avg.for_day* is the average value of the total daily power usage $V^{(c)}$ during 24 hours.

Since these factors have different relative importance some weights have been applied. Maximizing the utility of load factors is the most challenging task in this application. After that, information entropy minimization heuristic is used to discretize the continuous-valued attributes into nominal forms.

As shown in Table 23.3, EP based classifier resulted in higher accuracy than other classifiers on non-safe power lines, while other classifiers resulted in higher accuracy on the safe power lines. Lower accuracy at safe lines may decrease the total accuracy of EPs based classifier; however, the performance of EP based classifier is more desirable since the main purpose of this application is to find the non-safe lines.

TABLE 23.3: Comparison with other algorithms.

Algorithms		Predicted class(%)	
		Safe	Non-safe
EPs based	Safe	92.95	7.05
	Non-safe	4.63	95.37
CMAR	Safe	83.87	16.13
	Non-safe	20.50	79.50
Bayesian Network	Safe	97.08	2.92
	Non-safe	11.44	88.56
Naïve Bayesian	Safe	97.06	2.94
	Non-safe	11.44	88.56
SVM	Safe	98.97	1.03
	Non-safe	11.30	88.70
C4.5	Safe	94.86	5.14
	Non-safe	7.27	92.73

23.5   Conclusion

Applications often raise new research issues and bring deep insight on the strength and weakness of an existing solution. This is also true for EP mining. We feel the bottleneck of EP mining is not on whether we can derive the *complete* set of EPs under certain constraints efficiently but on whether we can derive a *compact but high quality* set of patterns that are most useful in applications. The set of EPs derived by most of the current pattern mining methods is too huge for effective usage [118, 249, 33]. There are proposals on reduction of a huge set of frequent patterns and we can apply these methods on mining of EPs to reduce the size of EPs. However, it is important to analyze the theoretical properties of different solutions. Furthermore, it is still not clear what kind of EPs (such as Jumping EPs and Strong EPs) will give us satisfactory pattern sets in both compactness and representative quality for a particular application. Much research is still needed to substantially reduce the size of derived pattern sets and enhance the quality of retained EPs [178].

From the examples given in this chapter, we can see that it is important to select powerful features to build high quality EP based classifiers. To improve the performance of the EP based classification and to improve the usability of EP based classification, it will be nice to have some easy-to-use tools to help make it easier to carry out this feature selection and feature discretization for EP mining and for building accurate EP based classifiers.

Chapter 24

Emerging Pattern Based Crime Spots Analysis and Rental Price Prediction

Naoki Katoh and Atsushi Takizawa

Department of Architecture and Architectural Engineering, Kyoto University

24.1 Introduction

This chapters presents two applications of emerging patterns (EPs). The first is an analysis of crime occurrences [387] and the second is a prediction of apartment rental price [390]. For each application, we will explain details of data used, how EPs are extracted, and how the EPs help to obtain accurate prediction models.

24.2 Street Crime Analysis

Since street crimes have a big impact on the quality of life and can even be life-threatening, reduction of them is an important issue for urban police. It has been empirically known that street crime tends to occur not randomly but in particular places of urban areas. That is, incidents of street crime seems to relate very much to the spatial configuration of locations on the streets. Based on this premise the idea called Crime Prevention Through Environmental Design (CPTED) was proposed in the United States in the 1970s [315], and it has now come to be implemented throughout the world. CPTED performs environmental design based on the concepts of natural surveillance, natural territorial control, and natural access control. Since these concepts are given empirically, the quantitative validation on the relation between spatial attributes and crime has started in recent years after the development of geographic information systems [360]. Previous studies have mainly analyzed only crime places but have not considered intensively crime-free areas. Therefore, understanding the difference of criminal tendency among locations has not been achieved yet. Moreover, since it can be thought that crime incidents depend on multiple factors such as population distribution, number of pedestrians, building type, etc., the analysis by a simple model such as a linear regression model is not sufficient. From those backgrounds, we apply CAEP [126] to the data of bag-snatching in Kyoto City and reveal the difference between crime places and other areas [387]. In addition to this study, we have performed crime analysis by applying emerging patterns in [388] and [389]. Meanwhile, criminal analysis and crime prevention are classified into an accident analysis [346] in a broad sense. Accident analysis tries to identify the causality of an accident and ties the cause to its prevention. The idea and methodology are mainly applied to traffic accident analysis, plant breakdown analysis, and so on. We can expect that the technology of data mining will serve as a knowledge discovery tool of the preliminary step of causality analysis.

24.2.1   Studied Area and Databases

The studied area is located in the center of Fushimi-ku, a suburb of Kyoto City in Japan. The area is a rectangle of about 0.8 km by 1 km and the total length of the streets studied is about 20 km. This area includes three train stations. We also consider four other stations when estimating the number of pedestrians by a random walk approach in the next section.

We use seven databases in this study. Database 1 (DB1) includes the data on snatching incidents. From January 2004 to December 2005, 343 incidents of bag-snatching were recorded in the Fushimi-ku area, 52 of which took place in the area studied. The other databases are a Digital Map 2500 (Spatial Data Framework) (DB2), a land-use map (DB3), a map of detailed building-footprints (DB4), population census data (DB5), enterprise census data (DB6), and all-around image data by Asia Air Survey Co. Ltd. (DB7). In addition, we measured the illuminance on the streets during the night.

24.2.2   Attributes on Visibility

Wall Visibility: Space visibility is a central concept in natural surveillance. The visibility analysis proposed here investigates the openness of a plane and can be executed at any point outside building polygons. We also consider the effect of wall components. So we need a method that precisely detects the building walls (see Figure 24.1(a)). This is a simple visibility-graph-based method that detects both endpoints of a line segment w that indicates the surface of a wall within a radius of vr meters from a viewpoint v. W_v represents the set of line segments visible from v, and the radius vr limits the visible range. v is selected as a sampling point along a road side (see Section 24.2.3). We set $vr = 40$ meters. For each detected visible line segment w, we calculate the Euclidean distance between v and the line segment $d(v, w)$, the angle of spread of the line segment $\theta(v, w)$, and the length of the visible line segment $l(v, w)$ as basic geometric information on the visible wall associated with w; see Figure 24.1(b). Then, the amount of base wall visibility of a wall w from a viewpoint v is given by the product of normalized visible angle and normalized distance to the wall:

$$bwv(v, w) = \frac{\theta(v, w)}{\pi} \frac{vr - d(v, w)}{vr}. \tag{24.1}$$

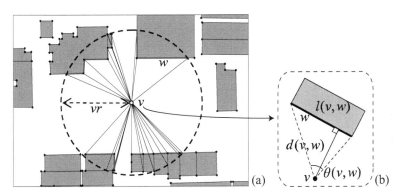

FIGURE 24.1: Visibility analysis. Source: Modified from Ref.[387], Copyright 2011, with permission from Elsevier.

We also consider the area of various types of wall components, namely $wc \in \{\text{door(dr)}, \text{normal window(wn)}, \text{grilled window(wg)}, \text{Kyoto-style grilled window(wk)}, \text{window with a shutter(ws)}, \text{piloti or non-wall facade(pn)}, \text{shutter(sh)}\}$. The total area of each wc in wall w is denoted as $ac(w, wc)$. In this study, the effect of a wall component wc on natural surveillance is the ratio of the total area of wc to the area of the first-floor portion of the wall. The height of the first floor for all walls is wh, which we set to $wh = 3.5$ meters.

The amount of base wall visibility $bwvc(v, w, wc)$ that w gives to v for wc is

$$bwvc(v, w, wc) = bwv(v, w) \frac{ac(w, wc)}{l(v, w)wh}. \tag{24.2}$$

The second term is the ratio of the area of wc to the area of w. In addition, we consider the effect of two different building categories Btype1 and Btype2 defined in DB4: Btype1={general building(gb), landmark building(tb), non-wall building(nw)}, and Btype2 = {public building(pb), apartment building(ab), individual house(ih), business institutions(bi), other building(ob)}.

For each $bt \in$ Btype1 $\cup$ Btype2, let $W_v(bt) \subset W_v$ denote the subset of line segments in W_v that belong to a building of the building type bt. Then, for a point v the amount of wall visibility with respect to all walls that belong to buildings of building type bt is defined as follows.

$$awvb(v, bt) = \sum_{w \in W_v(bt)} bwv(v, w). \tag{24.3}$$

Its feature name is denoted as $awvb\_bt$; an example is $amvb\_nw$.

In addition, for a wall component wc belonging in the wall w at a point v the amount of wall visibility for the building type bt is defined as follows.

$$awvbc(v, bt, wc) = \sum_{w \in W_v(bt)} bwvc(v, w, wc). \tag{24.4}$$

Its feature name is denoted as $awvbc\_bt\_wc$; an example is $awvbc\_nw\_pn$.

Although four other indices on visibility were defined in [387], here we focus on the ones used in the top EPs in Tables 24.1 and 24.2 to save space.

Number of Pedestrians on the Street: Since most incidents of bag-snatching occur on the street, it is important to know the pedestrian flow. However, it is difficult to know it because several complicated factors affect it. In this study, the pedestrian movement in the area surrounding each station is approximated by random walks.

Initially, a pedestrian agent is placed at one of the stations. Then, the agent is moved randomly to a new vertex connected to the current vertex. The random walk is repeated until the agent moves beyond the movement range which is set to 1.2 km from the station where the agent started from. The estimated number of pedestrians at a point on the street who started from station st is denoted rw_st where $st \in$ {Keihan Kangetsukyo (KKG), Keihan Tambabashi (KTB), Keihan Chushojima (KCJ), Keihan Fushimimomoyama (KFM), Kintetsu Tambabashi (CTB), Kintetsu Momoyamagoryomae (CMG), JR Momoyama (MY)}. We also define the expected sum of pedestrians that pass a node from the seven stations by considering the number of passengers using each station per day. It is denoted rw_TTL.

Other Attributes: In addition to those indices, we define many other attributes; the number of restaurants and stores along the roadside, the number of clerks along the roadside, the shortest network distance from the nearest station, the population density of the small area surrounding a point, the average illuminance of the street, and the nearest land-use excluding roads.

24.2.3 Preparation of the Analysis

The unit of analysis is a point. Since pedestrians tend to walk on the edge of the road, the sampling points are placed 1 meter inward from the boundary of the road. The interval of sampling points on the road is set to 10 meter. In this way, 2,769 sampling points are generated. A class label of P or N representing occurrence or non-occurrence of bag-snatching, respectively, is assigned to each sampling point and to the 52 crime points.

It is said that a criminal of bag-snatching selects a victim from a distance, shadows the victim, and conducts the crime when the opportunity comes. Therefore, it is reasonable to assume that not only actual crime points but also their neighboring points which are visible from each crime point should be labeled with P. In order to define the neighboring area, we use the semi-supervised point clustering method [387] (the details are omitted). As a result, 505 points labeled as P and 2,380 points are labeled as N.

To apply CAEP to the datasets, we discretize the values of the original numeric attributes using the equi-density method with three subintervals. The discretized attribute is expressed as $attributename = (-inf, value1], (value1, value2], (value3, inf)$, where inf represents infinity.

We apply an apriori algorithm [3] to extract item sets, with minimum support set to 0.01. The CAEP parameter values are as follows: minimum growth rate $= 3$, and maximum dimension of itemset $= 2$ (a higher maximum dimension improves the classification accuracy, but the computation time increases significantly).

24.2.4 Result

The classification accuracy by CAEP through 10-fold cross validation is evaluated by TPrate, TNrate, and Precision, and they are all 0.857. Considering the uncertainty of criminal occurrence, it can be said that this accuracy is satisfactory.

CAEP found 1,452 EPs in class P and 2,015 EPs in class N. The EPs with the ten highest contributions are listed in Tables 24.1 and 24.2. The definition of contribution on our analysis is as follows. Suppose an attribute A has two distinct class labels C and $\overline{C}$, and consider datasets D_C and $D_{\overline{C}}$ obtained by partitioning the original dataset D. In our application, D corresponds to the entire dataset for all sampled points, and it is partitioned into two datasets depending on its class label clustered as P or N. Let t denote a record that belongs to C, $e \subseteq t$ denote an itemset (spatial pattern) of t, $sup_C(e)$ denote the support of e containing t in D_C, and $growth\_rate_C(e)$ denote the growth

TABLE 24.1: Class P: EPs with the five highest contributions. Source: Modified from Ref.[387], Copyright 2011, with permission from Elsevier.

Item 1	Item 2	Contribution
rw_MY=(-inf, 0.050]	$awvb\_nw$=(0.014, inf)	0.158
rw_MY=(0.581, inf)	$awvbc\_bi\_pn$=(-inf, 0.000]	0.155
rw_KTB=(-inf, 0.101]	$awvb\_nw$=(0.014, inf)	0.154
rw_KKG=(0.818, inf)	rw_TTL=(36820, inf)	0.152
rw_CTB=(-inf, 0.147]	$awvb\_nw$=(0.014, inf)	0.152

TABLE 24.2: Class N: EPs with the five highest contributions. Source: Modified from Ref.[387], Copyright 2011, with permission from Elsevier.

Item 1	Item 2	Contribution
rw_KFM=(-inf, 0.711]	$awvbc\_nw\_sh$=(-inf, 0.000]	0.316
rw_KFM=(-inf, 0.711]	$awvbc\_nw\_dr$=(-inf, 0.000]	0.315
rw_KFM=(-inf, 0.711]	rw_CMG=(-inf, 0.199]	0.311
rw_KFM=(-inf, 0.711]		0.310
rw_KTB=(-inf, 0.101]	rw_KFM=(-inf, 0.711]	0.309

rate of e from $D_{\overline{C}}$ to D_C. Then, the contribution of itemset e to class C is

$$contribution(e) = \frac{growth\_rate_C(e)}{growth\_rate_C(e) + 1} sup_C(e). \qquad (24.5)$$

For class P, we see a combination of itemsets such as rw***=(some value other than infinity, inf), which indicates a relatively large number of pedestrians, and $awvb$*** which indicates that the natural surveillance level from walls with various building types and components is important. For class N, we see the itemset rw_KFM=(-inf, 0.711] in all the EPs. In the case of class N, the influence of the number of pedestrians from a specific station is strong, whereas in the case of class P, both this number and the existence of certain wall components in the neighborhood seem to affect the criminal activity.

Figure 24.2 shows the classification result for each point. The circles of various sizes represent the area of the sampling points labeled with P for each crime point by the clustering method [387]. It can be said that the classification by CAEP works well as a whole. Figure 24.3 shows two panoramic images at points A and B indicated in Figure 24.2, where the sum of the contribution of the EPs is the highest. At point A (for Class P), we can see a concrete block wall; there are no residential buildings nearby. We can also see a multilevel parking tower, which is the type of non-wall building. Thus, many class-P patterns revealed by CAEP are included at point A. Point B (for Class N) is located at a riverside point far from the stations. It is not crowded with buildings, and single-family houses face the roadside. At point B, many patterns that correspond to class N can be observed, e.g., a large distance from Keihan Fushimimomoyama Station.

We draw the following conclusion from the above results. Criminal activity

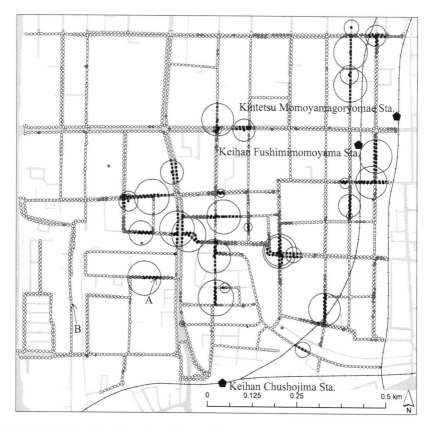

FIGURE 24.2: Classification of sampling points and actual crime points by CAEP. A circle indicates an area of sampling points clustered as P; we call it as a P-area. A sampling point or an actual crime point painted in black represents that it is correctly classified as P, a point painted in white represents that it is correctly classified as N, a point painted in gray and included in a P-area represents that is is misclassified as N, and a point painted in gray and not included in any P-area represents that it is misclassified as P. Source: Modified from Ref.[387], Copyright 2011, with permission from Elsevier.

Class P: at point A   Class N: at point B

FIGURE 24.3: Panoramic images from DB7 with the highest contribution of EPs. Source: Reprinted from LOCATION VIEW, Copyright 2010, with permission from Asia Air Survey Co., Ltd.

is more likely near non-wall buildings, where there are few people during the day, and near office buildings, where there are few people at night. Criminal activity is less likely when there are fewer pedestrians from stations and more residential houses or apartments with certain wall components. By using CAEP, we obtained both good classification result leading to crime prediction and a lot of spatial patterns for enhancing the understanding of the relationship between street crimes and spatial configuration.

24.3   Prediction of Apartment Rental Price

24.3.1   Background and Motivation

In this section, we will present the price analysis of rental residences of apartment buildings. In a general hedonic approach for dwellings, the value (i.e. price or rent) of a residence is estimated based on attributes such as the occupied area, the distance from the nearest station, the building age, facilities and so on [267, 132]. However the information of the room layout has not been fully used in the conventional approach although it seems to be crucial to evaluate usability and fineness of space.

The room layout can be represented by a graph, but a graph itself cannot be directly handled by a fundamental method such as multiple regression analysis since conventional statistical analysis usually can deal with only numerical or categorical data. However, the room layout has often been used for spatial analysis in the field of architecture and urban planning [188]. When focusing on the effect of a room layout to rent price, it is not plausible that the whole room layout influences the rent price, but there may be a certain key substructure that greatly affects the rent price.

In order to extract such substructures, we will apply a graph mining method [223] to those subgraph structures that frequently appear in room layouts of targeted apartments. Among those extracted, we will further select those that are highly related to rent price by examining emerging patterns. We will then construct a prediction model with high accuracy by incorporating those substructures into explanatory variables.

24.3.2   Data

We use the data of CHINTAI Web (http://www.chintai.net/) which is one of the most popular websites on real estate especially rental apartments in Japan. We limit the target of our research to the family-oriented residences of apartments classified as "3LDK", "3DK", or "3K". In Japan, dwelling-types are distinguished by the term such as 3LDK where "3" means the number of bed rooms, "L" a family room, "D" a dining room and "K" a kitchen. In fact,

3LDK, 3DK or 3K dwelling-types are most popular among condominiums in Japan.

We choose the target area as that along the railways of Hankyu Kyoto Line and JR Tokaido Line located in the south west of Kyoto City. These areas have common features as dormitory suburb of Kyoto or Osaka. Among them 15 areas are selected and classified according to the nearest station of these railways. We obtained 996 records by downloading html files from CHINTAI Webpage. The attributes of each record include the area and the nearest railway station, and image data of the room layout.

Tables 24.3, 24.4, and 24.5 show numerical and categorical attributes respectively. Rent does not include utility fee.

TABLE 24.3: List of numerical attributes (part I). Source: Reprinted from Ref.[390], Copyright 2007, with permission from IEEE.

attribute	mean	standard deviation
rent price	81,770 yen	14,866
building age	16.5 years	7
occupied area	60.4 m^2	7.4
area of the largest Japanese room	6.0 jou	0.7
area of the middle Japanese room	3.2 jou	2.7
area of the smallest Japanese room	0.1 jou	0.7
area of the largest western room	5.7 jou	1.2
area of the middle western room	2.2 jou	2.7
area of the smallest western room	0.1 jou	0.5
area of dining room	9.6 jou	2.7

TABLE 24.4: List of numerical attributes (part II). Source: Reprinted from Ref.[390], Copyright 2007, with permission from IEEE.

attribute	mean	standard deviation
number of stories	4.8	2.2
distance to the nearest station	13.1 minutes	6.9
distance to a super market	418m	254
distance to a convenience store	501m	286
distance to a hospital	258m	216
distance to a police	657m	288
distance to a kindergarten	417m	205
distance to an elementary school	504m	255
distance to a junior high school	753m	377
distance to a high school	1,242m	608

As shown in Figure 24.4, a room layout image is converted manually to a graph structure (called room layout graph data), where a vertex represents a room and edges represent adjacency relationship. We now explain the details of vertex and edge types.

a. Vertex types: We define the following eight vertex types.

(e): an entrance vertex. It can be found in all floor plans. For example, an entrance vertex is defined even if an entrance is directly connected to a dining room. The detail will be explained next.

TABLE 24.5: List of categorical attributes. Source: Reprinted from Ref.[390], Copyright 2007, with permission from IEEE.

attribute	value (no. of records)
room layout type	3LDK(707), 3DK(285), 3K(4)
residence type	apartment(914), cooperative(5), tenement(4), others(73)
structure type	reinforced concrete (821), steel framed reinforced concrete (28), steel-framed (68), light gauge steel (59), timber structure(17), others (3)
orientation of main opening	east (361), west (84), south (450), north (9), south east (31), south west (47), north east (13), north west (1)
nearest station	8 stations of Hankyu Kyoto line, 2 stations of Hankyu Arashiyama line, 4 stations of JR Tokaido line, one station of Keifuku Arashiyama line
Facility	parking lot (813), city gas (745), air conditioner (498), pets allowed (61), piano allowed (34), internet (24), card key entry (7), and etc (total 45 attributes)

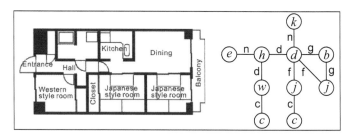

FIGURE 24.4: Conversion from room layout image to a room layout graph. Source: Reprinted from Ref.[390], Copyright 2007, with permission from IEEE.

(h): a hall vertex which is defined as the space which is between an entrance and a dining room. A hall vertex is defined if it is partitioned by a door or a fusuma (fusuma is a Japanese sliding door).

(d): a dining room vertex. In modern Japanese residences, a dining room usually contains a kitchen and a living room. They are usually distinguished by the term such as 3K, 3DK, or 3LDK. However in this paper we do not distinguish them.

(j): a Japanese room vertex which is a traditional room with tatami, fusuma, oshiire, and other traditional Japanese fittings as shown in Figure 24.5. Tatami is a Japanese floor mat which is made of rush. Fusuma is a sliding door. Oshiire is a Japanese closet whose opening is fusuma.

(w): a western room vertex. The term "western" is contrasted with "Japanese". A western room has flooring or carpet, door, and curtain.

(b): a balcony vertex. Balcony is not usually large in Japan. The main function of the balcony is to hang out the laundry. If the room is on the first floor and has its own garden outside, we regard the garden as a balcony.

(c): any kind of closet, including oshiire, is represented by this vertex. If there is more than one closet in a room, they are combined into a single closet vertex.

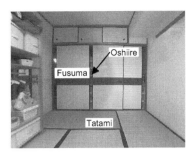

FIGURE 24.5: Japanese style room. Source: Reprinted from Ref.[390], Copyright 2007, with permission from IEEE.

(k): a kitchen vertex which is defined only if the kitchen is separated from the dining room as shown in Figure 24.6. This is an important distinction.

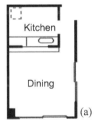 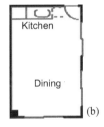

FIGURE 24.6: Distinction of kitchen vertices; (a) has a kitchen vertex and (b) does not. Source: Reprinted from Ref.[390], Copyright 2007, with permission from IEEE.

b. Edge types: We classify adjacency relationship between rooms into the following five types: door (**d**), closet (**s**), glass (**g**), fusuma (**f**), non-partition (**n**). Glass edge is only used to denote glass door between a dining room (or a living room) and a balcony.

24.3.3 Extracting Frequent Subgraphs

Frequent subgraphs are extracted by using a graph mining tool, and those "subgraph data" is constructed and analyzed. Subgraph data is then transformed to a 0-1 categorical one which indicates the absence presence of the subgraph in the room layout. We used the graph mining algorithm gSPAN [445] to do frequent subgraph mining. The minimum support of a subgraph is set to be 0.5%. This corresponds to 5 transactions in our dataset consisting of 996 residences. This seems to be very small. However, considering the diversity of floor plans, general patterns with large frequency do not seem to be enough for evaluating room layouts. Rarer patterns with small frequency should be considered. As a result of graph mining, 8,556 subgraphs were extracted.

24.3.4   Discovering Primary Subgraphs by Emerging Patterns

This subsection examines the influence of subgraphs on rent. For this, we will use Emerging Patterns (EPs) [118]. Many subgraphs for which in parent-child relationship holds tend to have the same growth-rate (gr for short).

We divide the whole data into two classes H and L such that class H (resp. L) is the subset of data whose rent price falls into the upper (resp. lower) half among those whose nearest railway station is the same. The sizes of classes H and L are 490 and 506, respectively.

1) The top three EPs on classes H and L are shown in Figure 24.7. We select EPs having at least 10 residences (about 1% of the whole data) in order to keep the minimum amount of generality. Consider the top EPs for class H in Figure 24.7 (left figure). The three one-edge subgraphs, 1-22, 1-16 and 1-12, respectively indicate "a separate kitchen", "a dining room facing a balcony", and "the existence of a closet in the western style room". The three two-edge subgraphs, 2-71, 2-66 and 2-57, respectively indicate "two western style rooms connected to a balcony", "a dining room with a separate kitchen that faces a balcony", and "a dining room with a separate kitchen connected to a western style room". Notice that the last two graphs, 2-66 and 2-57, contain as their subgraphs the one-edge EPs shown in the upper part of the figure. In addition, we observe that as the number of edges increases, gr tends to become larger.

Figure 24.7 (right figure) shows EPs for the lower half (class L). The single-edge graphs 1-21, 1-23, and 1-0 respectively indicate "a dining room directly connected to a hall without any partition", "a dining room connected to an entrance", and "a dining room connected to a Japanese style room through a door". The two-edge graphs 2-37, 2-48, and 2-103 respectively indicate "a dining room connected to a hall through a fusuma and to a Japanese style room through a door", "a dining room connected to an entrance without any partition and to a western style room through a door", and "a dining room connected to a hall without any partition and to a Japanese style room through a fusuma". Each of these two-edge EPs contains at least one of the three one-edge EPs as subgraphs. Grs of EPs for the lower half (class L) are larger than those for class H, implying that the existence of a small portion of room layout has a crucial negative influence on the rent price.

2) Residences whose rent is close to the average may obscure the influence of subgraphs on rent price in the analysis given above. In order to see more clearly the influence of subgraphs, we select the upper half of the class H (denoted by class HH) and the lower half of the class L (denoted by class LL). The numbers of residences in HH and LL are 206 and 187, respectively. Since the sizes of classes HH and LL are small and simple subgraphs with one or two edges have small gr, EPs are sought without limiting the number of edges.

Figure 24.8 (left) shows the top two EPs for class HH. These two graphs, 4-502 and 6-989, respectively indicate "a dining room facing a balcony", and "a dining room connected to a western style room and a hall through doors".

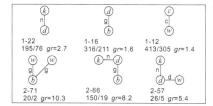 

FIGURE 24.7: EPs for the class H (on the left) and L (on the right). Numbers such as 1-22 are ids for subgraphs. Fractions such as 195/76 represent the frequency ratios of numbers of residences in classes H and L (left figure), and in classes L and H (right figure), respectively. Source: Reprinted from Ref.[390], Copyright 2007, with permission from IEEE.

Both EPs have common characteristics such as a separate kitchen and a dining room connected to a Japanese style room through a fusuma.

Figure 24.8 (right) shows the top three EPs for the class LL. The graphs 2-49, 4-935, and 8-778 in the figure respectively indicate "a dining room directly connected to a hall", "a dining room directly connected to an entrance without any partition and to a western style room through a fusuma", and "two Japanese style rooms facing a balcony". From these observations we obtain the conclusion that the segregation level of a dining from an entrance and a hall, the presence or the absence of a separate kitchen, and the position of a Japanese style room seem to greatly influence the rent.

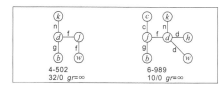 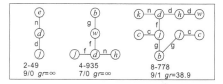

FIGURE 24.8: Top EPs for the class HH (left) and LL (right). Meaning of fractions c/d is similar to Figure 24.7. Source: Reprinted from Ref.[390], Copyright 2007, with permission from IEEE.

24.3.5 Rent Price Prediction Model

We created three rent price prediction models based on multiple regression. Model 1 uses only numerical and categorical data as explanatory attributes while Model 2 uses only subgraph data. Model 3 uses numerical and categorical data as well as subgraph data. Since 8,556 subgraphs are extracted as mentioned in Section 24.3.3, we first reduced the size of such subgraph data to 54 by applying correlation-based feature subset selection (CFS) [177].

Table 24.6 presents prediction accuracy of these three models. Model 3 exhibits the highest decision coefficient which is higher than Model 2 by 0.09, and the lowest absolute error which is 700 yen smaller than Model 2. Decision coefficient 0.552 obtained by Model 2 shows that we can predict rent price to a certain degree even if we use only room layouts.

Table 24.7 shows the attributes having ten highest/lowest coefficients, respectively. Six of the ten attributes of Table 24.7.a are subgraphs. Each subgraph in Table 24.7.a is an emerging pattern of class P and each subgraph except 5-360 in Table 24.7.b is an EP of class N. Each attribute representing a subgraph is binary, taking the value 1 if the subgraph appears in the room layout. Other binary attributes such as "For company only" are assigned value in the natural manner.

In Table 24.7.b coefficients of some subgraphs take large values while attributes concerning distance, building age are large as can be expected. From these results, we can confirm the significant influence of room layout. Moreover, subgraphs in Table 24.7.a all contain more than five edges, while those subgraphs which appear in Table 24.7.b have fewer edges. This result implies that house renters evaluate a residence by demerit system such that they put a low value on the entire residence if it has a little fault in the room layout.

TABLE 24.6: Prediction accuracy of three models. Source: Reprinted from Ref.[390], Copyright 2007, with permission from IEEE.

	Model 1	Model 2	Model 3
multiple correlation coefficient	0.823	0.743	0.876
mean absolute error (yen)	5,985	7,421	5,298

TABLE 24.7: 10 attributes of most positive partial regression coefficients (a) and 10 attributes of most negative coefficients (b) in Model 3. Source: Reprinted from Ref.[390], Copyright 2007, with permission from IEEE.

(a)

attribute	coefficient
Occupied area	27100.7
For company only	16288.1
8-780	11716.5
5-397	11593.8
5-1042	8961.4
6-748	8961.4
Area of a family room	8817.4
5-879	7190.4
Area of the smallest western style room	6865.8
5-1436	6721.1

(b)

attribute	coefficient
Walking time to the nearest station	-15752.6
Building age	-14373.2
4-893	-12951.4
Tenement	-12686.6
Card key system	-10787.4
Distance to a hospital	-10101.7
Piano allowed	-8128.6
5-360	-6574.2
2-49	-6048.7
5-440	-5825.0

Part VII

Survey of Other Papers

Chapter 25

Overview of Results on Contrast Mining and Applications

Guozhu Dong

Department of Computer Science and Engineering, Wright State University

This chapter provides a structured outline of, and pointers to, *representative* publications on contrast data mining and applications, for various major topic areas, with a focus on papers not already cited in previous chapters. To prevent the book from becoming too long, we have not tried to be complete, and we apologize if some related papers are not included here. References are given to chapters, but papers cited in those chapters will normally not be repeated here. Combined with references to earlier chapters, this chapter serves as a topic based outline of results on contrast data mining and applications.

25.1   General Papers, Events, PhD Dissertations

Several related survey/overview papers have been published, including a survey [114] on the main results of contrast data mining and applications, a survey [129] on emerging pattern based contrast mining and applications (in Chinese), a survey [319] on contrast set, emerging pattern and subgroup mining, and a review [55] on contrast and change mining. References [427][175] gave complexity results on the emerging pattern mining problem and certain related algorithms.

Two special events on contrast data mining and applications took place in the last few years, including a tutorial [31] at ICDM 2007 presented by Bailey and Dong and a workshop [113] at ICDM 2011 organized by Dong and Bailey. The name "contrast data mining" was coined during James Bailey's sabbatical visit with Guozhu Dong at Wright State University in 2004; other names such as "comparative data mining" were also discussed.

Historically, reference [64] was an earlier work on mining patterns for characterizing and differentiating classes, although it focused on high support patterns obtained using the attribute-oriented-induction approach.

Contrast data mining is related to "comparative data analysis," which is focused on finding commonalities and uniqueness of several datasets, or classes. For example, comparative data analysis can aim to organize two Web search result sets into clusters with common/unique descriptive themes [226], to help users quickly get a sense of the relationship between the two sets.

Contrast data mining can be especially useful in "domain driven data mining" [65], when domain specifics are captured by the classes or conditions to be contrasted. It can also be used in multi-dataset mining [201].

While feature selection [274] and general classification (see e.g., [179]) can both be considered as belonging to contrast data mining, they are excluded in this book, since our focus is mining and utilizing contrasting patterns.

The following are PhD dissertations (known to us) on topics closely related to contrast data mining and applications: [241], [463], [136], [4], [290], [197], [27], [208], [307], [396], [86], [282], [164], [161]. There are also a number of highly related MS theses, some of them cited elsewhere in the book.

25.2   Analysis and Measures on Contrasts and Similarity

Chapter 2 discusses various measures on contrasts, including some traditional ones from statistics. Reference [460] considered measuring the uncertainty of differences for contrasting groups. Reference [343] studied the estimation of confidence intervals for structural differences between contrast groups with missing data. Reference [30] used the Fisher test to select significant contrast patterns. Reference [1] considered evaluation measures for multi-class subgroup discovery.

Comprehension and utility of contrast patterns for domain experts is dependent on the relationship among the constituent items present in the patterns. Reference [144] provided an analysis of the types of interactions that may occur among items in contrast patterns, and proposed to categorize contrast patterns according to four types of item interaction, namely, driverpassenger, coherent, independent additive, and synergistic beyond independent additive.

Reference [202] gave a tree-based framework for difference summarization. Reference [159] gave a framework for measuring changes in data characteristics.

Reference [416] considered using cross dataset minimum coding length difference to define similarity between datasets. Reference [325] studied exploiting dataset similarity for distributed mining. Reference [101] considered context-based similarity measures between attributes and sub-relations in categorical databases.

25.3   Contrast Mining Algorithms

The following chapters are concerned with mining algorithms for various kinds of contrasts in various types of data: Chapter 3 is on tree-based contrast mining algorithms, Chapter 4 is on the ZBDD-based contrast mining algorithm, Chapter 5 is on efficient direct mining of selective discriminative patterns for classification, Chapter 6 is on contrast mining for more structured data, Chapter 17 is on mining optimal emerging patterns when there are thousands of genes, Chapter 7 is on incremental maintenance of emerging patterns, Chapter 8 is on more general contrast patterns, such as disjunctive emerging patterns and fuzzy emerging patterns and contrast inequalities, and their mining, Chapter 20 is on mining emerging patterns with occurrence counts (and other variants) for image data, Chapter 9 is on emerging data cube representations for OLAP database mining, Chapter 10 is on mining algorithms based on relationship between emerging patterns and rough set theory, and Chapter 21 is on geospatial contrast mining on labeled spatial data.

25.3.1   Mining Contrasts and Changes in General Data

Reference [271] considered discovering fundamental rule changes. Reference [269] considered mining changes for real-life applications. Reference [424] considered mining changes of classification by correspondence tracing. Reference [256] linked emerging pattern mining with mining high confidence association rules without support threshold. Reference [115] studied niche pattern mining based on emerging patterns, and reference [237] studied the exceptional model mining problem, both concerned with mining local patterns that contradict some global patterns/models. Reference [285] studied mining influential attributes that capture class and group contrast behavior, and reference [17] considered the problem of discovering attributes/properties that account for the abnormality of a given group of anomalous individuals (the outliers) with respect to an overall given population (the inliers). Reference [254] examined the structural issues of the space of emerging patterns. Reference [143] considered mining low-support discriminative patterns from dense and high-dimensional data. Reference [431] studied the problem of mining group differences. Reference [462] studied detecting differences between contrast groups. Reference [318] studied mining contrast set through subgroup discovery. Reference [305] gave a framework to mine high-level emerging patterns by attribute-oriented induction. Reference [193] gave a method for finding emerging large itemsets. Reference [137] gave an efficient single-scan algorithm for mining "essential" jumping emerging patterns for classification. Reference [194] studied discovering emerging patterns from nearest neighbors. Reference [14] considered constrained logistic regression for discriminating pattern mining. Reference [368] studied exploratory quantitative contrast set mining using a discretization approach. Reference [361] considered a new approach concerning contrasting the contrast sets. Reference [187] considered statistical methodologies for mining potentially interesting contrast sets. Reference [434] studied the mining of negative contrasts. Reference [13] studied mining diverging patterns with significant frequency change dissimilarities. Reference [19] studied discovering relational emerging patterns. Reference [40] considered mining flipping correlations from large datasets with taxonomies. Reference [377] studied condensed representation of emerging patterns. Reference [66] considered visual representations to visually contrast two collections of frequent itemsets. Reference [84] studied mining emerging patterns shared by two datasets. Reference [376] studied summarizing contrasts by recursive pattern mining. Reference [272] considered discovering holes in data, and reference [153] studied bump hunting in data.

Reference [238] studied the mining of contrasting correlations among items by an efficient double-clique condition. Reference [393] considered a kind of hidden conditional correlation patterns. A conditional correlation is a pair of itemsets whose degrees of correlations are higher in a given local dataset than in the global dataset. Reference [52] considered the mining of "stimulating patterns," namely patterns X for which there exist many closed patterns Y, such that adding X to Y reduces the support in the negative class much more than in the positive class. These two kinds of patterns are related to conditional contrasts [122] discussed below.

25.3.2 Mining Contrasts in Stream, Temporal, Sequence Data

On streaming data, reference [7] studied mining emerging patterns and classification in data streams. Reference [12] studied instance-based classification of streaming data using emerging patterns. Reference [69] studied novelty detection from evolving complex data streams. Reference [264] considered mining discriminative items in multiple data streams. Reference [447] studied mining in anticipation for concept change and proactive-reactive prediction in data streams. Reference [206] studied detecting change in data streams. Reference [278] studied mining distribution change in stock order streams. Reference [262] extended the notion of contrast sets to time series and multimedia data. Reference [93] considered efficient mining of temporal emerging itemsets from data streams.

On temporal data, reference [22] studied relational temporal difference mining. Reference [205] gave a sliding-window dual-support framework for mining emerging trends.

On sequence data, references [198, 199] (also see Chapter 6) studied mining minimal distinguishing subsequence patterns with gap constraints. Reference [468] considered finding novel diagnostic gene patterns based on interesting non-redundant contrast sequence rules. Reference [281] considered mining closed discriminative dyadic sequential patterns (from input sequence pairs both coming from the same class). Reference [408] gave a change detection method for sequential patterns. Reference [105] gave an occurrence based approach to mine emerging sequences. Reference [104] studied contrasting sequence groups by emerging sequences. Reference [124] contains chapters on contrast mining and feature selection/construction for sequences.

25.3.3 Mining Contrasts in Spatial, Image, and Graph Data

Reference [72] studied "sustained" emerging spatio-temporal co-occurrence pattern mining. Reference [380] studied discovering spatio-social discriminative pattern mining on electoral data, reference [109] considered discovery of geospatial discriminating patterns from remote sensing data, and reference [379] studied discovering controlling factors of geospatial variables (also see Chapter 21). Reference [70] studied discovering emerging patterns in spatial databases using a multi-relational approach.

Chapter 20 studied mining emerging patterns with occurrence counts (and other variants) and using those EPs for classification in image data. Reference [108] gave a visual word weighting scheme based on emerging itemsets for video annotation.

Reference [279] gave a graph classification approach based on frequent closed emerging patterns. Reference [340] considered extracting and summarizing the frequent emerging graph patterns from a dataset of graphs. Reference [339] studied discovering emerging graph patterns from chemicals. Reference [73] studied discovering and summarizing regions of correlated spatio-temporal change in evolving graphs. Reference [321] studied mining correlation and contrast link formation patterns in a time evolving graph. Reference [158] studied the mining of top-k "breaker" emerging subgraph patterns from graph data.

25.3.4   Unusual Subgroup Discovery and Description

Subgroup discovery [435, 229] is concerned with finding subgroups of an underling population that are statistically "most interesting", e.g. they are large and have unusual statistical (distributional) characteristics with respect to a target variable. Subgroup discovery produces a relatively small set of subgroup descriptions of the matching populations of the subgroups. Reference [319] gave a survey on contrast set, emerging pattern and subgroup mining. An overview on subgroup discovery was given in [186].

25.3.5   Mining Conditional Contrasts and Gradients

Reference [122] introduced the problem of mining conditional contrasts, which capture situations where a small change in patterns is associated with a big change in the matching data of the patterns. More precisely, a conditional contrast is a triple (B, F_1, F_2), where B is the condition/context pattern, and F_1 and F_2 are the contrasting factor patterns. It can offer insights on discriminating patterns given condition B, and it is of interest if the item difference, $|(F_1 - F_2) \cup (F_2 - F_1)|$, is relatively small, and the matching data difference between the matching datasets $\mathsf{mt}(B \cup F_1)$ and $\mathsf{mt}(B \cup F_2)$ is relatively large. All three of B, F_1, and F_2 are dynamically mined from one given dataset. Conditional contrasts are related to gradients [117] in data cubes; a gradient is a pair of patterns (data cube cells) that are very similar to each other in dimension values but very different in measure values. They are also related to stimulating patterns and contrasting correlation patterns discussed earlier.

25.4   Contrast Pattern Based Classification

The following chapters are related to contrast-pattern based or enhanced classification: Chapter 11 is an overview and analysis of contrast pattern based classification, Chapter 12 is on using length statistics of emerging patterns (EPs) in outlier detection and rare-class prediction, Chapter 13 is on using EPs to enhance traditional classifiers, Chapter 15 is on using EP-based rules for classifying/characterizing subtypes of leukemia in the field of bioinformatics, Chapter 18 is on emerging chemical pattern based classification of chemical compounds in the field of chemoinformatics, Chapter 19 is on emerging molecular pattern based analysis of toxicity of chemical molecules in the field of chemoinformatics, Chapter 20 is on EP-based classification for spatial/image data, Chapter 24 is on EP-based crime spots analysis and rental price prediction, Chapter 23 is on EP-based diagnosis of heart diseases and prediction of powerline safety, and Chapter 22 is on EP-based activity recognition.

There are many papers on contrast pattern based classification. Reference [242] studied instance-based classification by emerging patterns. References [243, 251] considered emerging pattern based classification. Reference [466] studied using emerging-pattern based behavior knowledge in classification. Reference [138] considered a Bayesian approach to use emerging patterns for classification. References [34, 350] studied classification using (constrained) emerging patterns. Reference [156] considered classification based on the highest impact jumping emerging patterns. Reference [359] considered using emerging subsequence in classifying protein structural classes. Reference [163] gave an algorithm for mining discriminative regularities and its application in classification. Reference [467] considered CAEP-based prediction of translation initiation sites, and Reference [85] considered emerging patterns and classification algorithms, for DNA sequences. Reference [75] considered using emerging substrings for sequence classification. Reference [440] studied mining sequence classifiers for early prediction. References [410][409] considered emerging pattern based prediction of polyadenylation sites. Reference [392] used CAEP and JEPC for music melody classification. Reference [279] gave a graph classification approach based on frequent closed emerging patterns. Reference [280] studied classification of software behaviors for failure detection using discriminative patterns. Reference [286] examined using highly expressive contrast patterns for classification. Reference [316] considered efficiently finding the best parameter for the emerging pattern-based classifier PCL. Reference [304] considered decision tree-based classifier incorporating contrast patterns. Ramamohanarao gave several invited talks on contrast pattern mining and application for building robust classifiers [348, 349]. Reference [404] gave a review of associative classification.

25.5 Contrast Pattern Based Clustering

Chapter 14 presents CPC, a contrast pattern based clustering algorithm, and CPCQ, a contrast pattern based clustering quality measure. On given datasets, CPC forms clusters and describes the clusters using small sets of high quality contrast patterns. No distance function is needed.

Reference [116] studied discovering and describing dynamic logical blog communities based on their contrast patterns (also called distinct interest profiles), using CPC. Reference [125] considered describing contrasting blog collections using small sets of discriminating words, which make a highly accurate naive Bayes classifier for the clusters; the NBC was chosen to "simulate" how humans get a sense of what the clusters contain by looking at those discriminating words only. Reference [203] studied selecting minimal discriminative patterns to probabilistically characterize clusters. Reference [209] considered emerging pattern based subspace clustering of microarray gene expression data using mixture models. Reference [10] studied detecting significant distinguishing sets among bi-clusters.

25.6   Contrast Mining and Bioinformatics and Chemoinformatics

Three chapters are related to bionformatics: Chapter 15 is on using EP-based rules for classifying/characterizing subtypes of leukemia, Chapter 17 is on mining optimal emerging patterns when there are thousands of genes, Chapter 16 is on discriminating-gene transferability based microarray concordance analysis. A very notable feature of Chapter 17 is the interaction-based importance index (IBIG) of genes, for the analysis of complex diseases.

Two chapters are related to chemoinformatics: Chapter 18 is on emerging chemical pattern (ECP) based classification of chemical compounds. It reported that studies have confirmed that ECP can derive high-quality class prediction models on the basis of very small training sets, which makes the approach highly attractive for molecular classification and other applications in medicinal chemistry including simulation of (drug) lead optimization [25], sequential screening campaigns [26], and bioactive compound conformation analysis [24]. Chapter 19 is on emerging molecular pattern based analysis of toxicity of chemical molecules, using emerging graph patterns.

Reference [56] considered mining interaction structures of the emerging pattern type from microarray data. Reference [209] studied emerging pattern based subspace clustering of microarray gene expression data using mixture models. Reference [452] considered application of emerging patterns for multi-source bio-data classification and analysis. Reference [112] considered classifying chemical compounds using contrast and common patterns. Reference [120] gave an overview of applications of emerging patterns for microarray gene expression data analysis. Reference [123] examined the use of emerging patterns in the analysis of gene expression profiles for the diagnosis and understanding of diseases. Reference [10] studied detecting significant distinguishing sets among bi-clusters. Reference [157] considered a classification method using array comparative genome hybridization data, based on the concept of limited jumping emerging patterns.

25.7   Contrast Mining Applications in Various Domains

25.7.1   Medicine, Environment, Security, Privacy, Activity Recognition

For medicine and environment protection, reference [217] considered contrast set mining for distinguishing between similar diseases. Reference [190] studied adverse drug reaction patterns in sub-population groups using contrast pattern mining approach. Reference [327] considered mining discriminative mutation chains in virus sequences. Reference [372] studied the mining of trends from noisy longitudinal data with application on a study in diabetic retinopathy. Reference [454] studied using emerging pattern based projected clustering and gene expression data for cancer detection. Reference [436] studied emerging pattern based birth defect detection. Reference [378] considered using emerging patterns from clusters to characterize social subgroups of patients affected by atherosclerosis. Reference [273] studied mining the change of event trends for decision support in environmental scanning.

For security, references [442][68] considered discovering and using emerging patterns in intrusion detection and anomaly detection in network connection data. Reference [443] studied metamorphic malware detection technology based on aggregating emerging patterns. Chapter 12 presents the use of length statistics of emerging patterns in outlier and rare-class prediction, with special application on masquerader detection using command sequences as input. Reference [259] considered emerging pattern based e-mail categorization and filtering.

For privacy, reference [90] considered hiding emerging patterns with local recoding generalization for privacy presentation, and reference [16] considered lazy DeEPs-based approach to privacy preserving classification with emerging patterns.

For crime analysis, references [388][389][387] considered using emerging patterns and CAEP on urban spatial data for risk discovery of car-related crimes, snatch theft crimes, and crime occurrence locations.

Chapter 22 studied emerging pattern based activity recognition. Reference [171] studied mining emerging patterns for recognizing activities of multiple users.

25.7.2   Business, Customer Behavior, Music, Video, Blog

For business and customer behavior mining, reference [373] studied mining changes (including emerging patterns) of customer behavior in an Internet shopping mall. Reference [83] considered mining changes in customer behavior in retail marketing. Reference [306] reported a contrast pattern based study on the impact of media contact on the purchase process. Reference [230] studied identifying changes and trends in tourism. Reference [386] gave an analysis of Kansei evaluation on entrance halls of rental office buildings using CAEP.

For music analysis, reference [240] studied mining emerging melody structures from music query data to show new trends in music. Reference [392] used CAEP and JEPC for music melody classification.

For video and image analysis, Chapter 20 studied mining emerging patterns with occurrence counts (and other variants) and using those EPs for classification in image data. Reference [108] gave a visual word weighting scheme based on emerging itemsets for video annotation. Reference [425] gave an emerging pattern based method to instantly tell what happens in a video sequence. For blog analysis, reference [116] studied discovering and describing dynamic logical blog communities based on their distinct interest profiles, and reference [125] considered describing contrasting blog collections using small sets of discriminating words, which make a highly accurate naive Bayes classifier of the clusters.

25.7.3   Model Error Analysis, and Genetic Algorithm Improvement

References [43, 45] considered using contrast sets to characterize model errors and differences. Reference [204] considered preserving frequent patterns contained in good solutions during genetic mutations of genetic algorithms, and included "preserving emerging patterns" as a future research direction.

Bibliography

[1] Tarek Abudawood and Peter A. Flach. Evaluation measures for multi-class subgroup discovery. In *Proc. of European Conf. on Machine Learning and Principles and Practice of Knowledge Discovery in Databases (ECML/PKDD)*, pages 35–50, 2009.

[2] Charu C. Aggarwal and Philip S. Yu. Outlier detection for high dimensional data. In *Proc. of ACM Int'l Conf. on Management of Data (SIGMOD)*, pages 37–46, 2001.

[3] Rakesh Agrawal, Tomasz Imielinski, and Arun N. Swami. Mining association rules between sets of items in large databases. In *Proc. of ACM Int'l Conf. on Management of Data (SIGMOD)*, pages 207–216, 1993.

[4] Hamad Alhammady. *The Application of Emerging Patterns in Solving Classification Problems*. PhD Thesis, University of Melbourne, 2005.

[5] Hamad Alhammady and Kotagiri Ramamohanarao. Using emerging patterns and decision trees in rare-class classification. In *Proc. of IEEE Int'l Conf. on Data Mining (ICDM)*, pages 315–318, 2004.

[6] Hamad Alhammady and Kotagiri Ramamohanarao. Expanding the training data space using emerging patterns and genetic methods. In *Proc. of SIAM Int'l Conf. on Data Mining (SDM)*, 2005.

[7] Hamad Alhammady and Kotagiri Ramamohanarao. Mining emerging patterns and classification in data streams. In *Proc. of IEEE/WIC/ACM Int'l Conf. on Web Intelligence*, pages 272–275, 2005.

[8] Hamad Alhammady and Kotagiri Ramamohanarao. Using emerging patterns to construct weighted decision trees. *IEEE Trans. Knowl. Data Eng.*, 18(7):865–876, 2006.

[9] U. Alon, N. Barkai, et al. Broad patterns of gene expression revealed by clustering analysis of tumor and normal colon tissues probed by oligonucleotide arrays. *Proc. Natl. Acad. Sci.*, 96:6745–6750, 1999.

[10] Faris Alqadah and Raj Bhatnagar. Detecting significant distinguishing sets among bi-clusters. In *Proc. of 17th ACM Conf. on Information and Knowledge Management (CIKM)*, pages 1455–1456, 2008.

[11] AMEinfo. Website: http://www.ameinfo.com/231603.html.

[12] Mohd Amir and Durga Toshniwal. Instance-based classification of streaming data using emerging patterns. In *Proc. of Int'l Conf. on Information and Communication Technologies (ICT)*, pages 228–236, 2010.

[13] Aijun An, Qian Wan, Jiashu Zhao, and Xiangji Huang. Diverging patterns: discovering significant frequency change dissimilarities in large databases. In *Proc. of Int'l Conf. on Information and Knowledge Management (CIKM)*, pages 1473–1476, 2009.

[14] Rajul Anand and Chandan K. Reddy. Constrained logistic regression for discriminative pattern mining. In *Proc. of European Conf. on Machine Learning and Principles and Practice of Knowledge Discovery in Databases (ECML/PKDD)*, 2011.

[15] Periklis Andritsos, Panayiotis Tsaparas, Renée J. Miller, and Kenneth C. Sevcik. LIMBO: Scalable clustering of categorical data. In *Proc. of Int'l Conf. on Extending Database Technology (EDBT)*, pages 123–146, 2004.

[16] Piotr Andruszkiewicz. Lazy approach to privacy preserving classification with emerging patterns. In *Proc. of 19th Int'l Symp. Emerging Intelligent Technologies in Industry (ISMIS)*, pages 253–268, 2011.

[17] Fabrizio Angiulli, Fabio Fassetti, and Luigi Palopoli. Discovering characterizations of the behavior of anomalous sub-populations. *IEEE Trans. on Knowledge and Data Engineering (TKDE)*, 2012.

[18] Maria-Luiza Antonie and Osmar R. Zaïane. Mining positive and negative association rules: An approach for confined rules. In *Proc. of European Conf. on Principles and Practice of Knowledge Discovery in Databases (PKDD)*, pages 27–38, 2004.

[19] Annalisa Appice, Michelangelo Ceci, Carlo Malgieri, and Donato Malerba. Discovering relational emerging patterns. In *Proc. of 10th Congress of the Italian Association for Artificial Intelligence (AI*IA)*, pages 206–217, 2007.

[20] S. A. Armstrong and J. E. Staunton et al. MLL translocations specify a distinct gene expression profile that distinguishes a unique leukemia. *Nat Genet*, pages 41–47, 2002.

[21] Bavani Arunasalam and Sanjay Chawla. CCCS: A top-down associative classifier for imbalanced class distribution. In *Proc. of ACM Int'l Conf. on Knowledge Discovery and Data Mining (KDD)*, 2006.

[22] Nima Asgharbeygi, David J. Stracuzzi, and Pat Langley. Relational temporal difference learning. In *Proc. of Int'l Conf. on Machine Learning (ICML)*, pages 49–56, 2006.

[23] Arthur Asuncion and David Newman. UCI machine learning repository, 2007.

[24] Jens Auer and Jürgen Bajorath. Distinguishing between bioactive and modeled compound conformations through mining of emerging chemical patterns. *Journal of Chemical Information and Modeling*, 46:2502–2514, 2006.

[25] Jens Auer and Jürgen Bajorath. Emerging chemical patterns: a new methodology for molecular classification and compound selection. *Journal of Chemical Information and Modeling*, 46:2502–2514, 2006.

[26] Jens Auer and Jürgen Bajorath. Simulation of sequential screening experiments using emerging chemical patterns. *Medicinal Chemistry*, 4:80–90, 2008.

[27] Jens Horst Auer. *Emerging Chemical Patterns for Virtual Screening and Knowledge Discovery*. PhD Thesis, Rheinische Friedrich-Wilhelms-Universität, Bonn, 2008.

[28] Stefan Axelsson. Intrusion detection systems: A survey and taxonomy. Technical Report 99-15, Chalmers Univ., March 2000.

[29] Jay Ayres, Jason Flannick, Johannes Gehrke, and Tomi Yiu. Sequential pattern mining using a bitmap representation. In *Proc. of ACM Int'l Conf. on Knowledge Discovery and Data Mining (SIGKDD)*, pages 429–435, 2002.

[30] Paulo J. Azevedo. Rules for contrast sets. *Intell. Data Anal.*, 14(6):623–640, 2010.

[31] James Bailey and Guozhu Dong. Contrast data mining: methods and applications. Tutorial at the IEEE Int'l Conf. on Data Mining (ICDM), 2007.

[32] James Bailey and Elsa Loekito. Efficient incremental mining of contrast patterns in changing data. *Inf. Process. Lett.*, 110(3):88–92, 2010.

[33] James Bailey, Thomas Manoukian, and Kotagiri Ramamohanarao. Fast algorithms for mining emerging patterns. In *Proc. of European Conf. on Principles and Practice of Knowledge Discovery in Databases (PKDD)*, pages 39–50, 2002.

[34] James Bailey, Thomas Manoukian, and Kotagiri Ramamohanarao. Classification using constrained emerging patterns. In *Proc. of Int'l Conf. on Web-Age Information Management (WAIM)*, pages 226–237, 2003.

[35] James Bailey, Thomas Manoukian, and Kotagiri Ramamohanarao. A fast algorithm for computing hypergraph transversals and its application in mining emerging patterns. In *Proc. of IEEE Int'l Conf. on Data Mining (ICDM)*, pages 485–488, 2003.

[36] Jürgen Bajorath. Selected concepts and investigations in compound classification, molecular descriptor analysis, and virtual screening. *Journal of Chemical Information and Computer Sciences*, 41:233–245, 2001.

[37] Jürgen Bajorath. Integration of virtual and high-throughput screening. *Nature Reviews Drug Discovery*, 1:882–894, 2002.

[38] Elena Baralis and Silvia Chiusano. Essential classification rule sets. *ACM Trans. Database Syst.*, 29(4):635–674, 2004.

[39] Daniel Barbará, Yi Li, and Julia Couto. COOLCAT: an entropy-based algorithm for categorical clustering. In *Proc. of ACM Int'l Conf. on Information and Knowledge Management (CIKM)*, pages 582–589, 2002.

[40] Marina Barsky, Sangkyum Kim, Tim Weninger, and Jiawei Han. Mining flipping correlations from large datasets with taxonomies. In *Proc. of Int'l. Conf. on Very Large Data Bases (VLDB)*, pages 370–381, 2011.

[41] Eric Bauer and Ron Kohavi. An empirical comparison of voting classification algorithms: Bagging, boosting, and variants. *Machine Learning*, 36(1):105–139, 1999.

[42] Stephen D. Bay and Michael J. Pazzani. Detecting change in categorical data: Mining contrast sets. In *Proc. of ACM Conf. on Knowledge Discovery and Data Mining (KDD)*, pages 302–306, 1999.

[43] Stephen D. Bay and Michael J. Pazzani. Characterizing model errors and differences. In *Proc. of Int'l Conf. on Machine Learning (ICML)*, pages 49–56, 2000.

[44] Stephen D. Bay and Michael J. Pazzani. Detecting group differences: Mining contrast sets. *Data Min. Knowl. Discov.*, 5(3):213–246, 2001.

[45] Stephen D. Bay, Daniel G. Shapiro, and Pat Langley. Revising engineering models: Combining computational discovery with knowledge. In *Proc. of European Conf. on Machine Learning (ECML)*, pages 10–22, 2002.

[46] Roberto J. Bayardo. Efficiently mining long patterns from databases. In *Proc. of ACM Int'l Conf. on Management of Data (SIGMOD)*, pages 85–93, 1998.

[47] Jan G. Bazan, Hung Son Nguyen, Sinh Hoa Nguyen, Piotr Synak, and Jakub Wroblewski. Rough set algorithms in classification problem.

Rough set methods and applications: new developments in knowledge discovery in information systems, pages 49–88, 2000. Physica-Verlag GmbH Heidelberg, Germany.

[48] Jan G. Bazan, Andrzej Skowron, and Piotr Synak. Dynamic reducts as a tool for extracting laws from decisions tables. In *Proc. of 8th Int'l Symp. on Methodologies for Intelligent Systems (ISMIS)*, pages 346–355, 1994.

[49] Richard Bellman. *Dynamic Programming*. Princeton University Press, 1957.

[50] BeyeNetwork. Website: http://www.b-eye-network.com/view/7188.

[51] Kevin S. Beyer, Jonathan Goldstein, Raghu Ramakrishnan, and Uri Shaft. When is "nearest neighbor" meaningful? In *Proc. of Int'l Conf. on Database Theory*, pages 217–235, 1999.

[52] Ryan Bissell-Siders, Bertrand Cuissart, and Bruno Crémilleux. On the stimulation of patterns - definitions, calculation method and first usages. In *Proc. of 18th Int'l Conf. on Conceptual Structures (ICCS)*, pages 56–69, 2010.

[53] Francesco Bonchi and Claudio Lucchese. On closed constrained frequent pattern mining. In *Proc. of IEEE Int'l Conf. on Data Mining (ICDM)*, pages 35–42, 2004.

[54] Christian Borgelt and Michael R. Berthold. Mining molecular fragments: Finding relevant substructures of molecules. In *Proc. of IEEE Int'l Conf. on Data Mining (ICDM)*, pages 51–58, 2002.

[55] Mirko Böttcher. Contrast and change mining. *Wiley Interdisc. Review: Data Mining and Knowledge Discovery*, 1(3):215–230, 2011.

[56] Anne-Laure Boulesteix and Gerhard Tutz. Identification of interaction patterns and classification with applications to microarray data. *Computational Statistics & Data Analysis*, 50(3):783–802, 2006.

[57] Anne Laure Boulesteix, Gerhard Tutz, and Korbinian Strimmer. A CART-based approach to discover emerging patterns in microarray data. *Bioinformatics*, 19(18):2465–72, 2003.

[58] Leo Breiman. Bagging predictors. *Machine Learning*, 24(2):123–140, 1996.

[59] Sergey Brin, Rajeev Motwani, and Craig Silverstein. Beyond market baskets: Generalizing association rules to correlations. In *Proc. of ACM Int'l Conf. on Management of Data (SIGMOD)*, pages 265–276, 1997.

[60] Bjorn Bringmann, Siegfried Nijssen, and Albrecht Zimmermann. Pattern-based classification: A unifying perspective. In *Proc. of ECML/PKDD Workshop on From Local Patterns to Global Models*, 2009.

[61] Randal E. Bryant. Graph-based algorithms for boolean function manipulation. *IEEE Transactions on Computers*, 35(8):677–691, 1986.

[62] Doug Burdick, Manuel Calimlim, and Johannes Gehrke. MAFIA: A maximal frequent itemset algorithm for transactional databases. In *Proc. of IEEE Int'l Conf. on Data Engineering (ICDE)*, 2001.

[63] Christopher J. C. Burges. A tutorial on support vector machines for pattern recognition. *Data Min. Knowl. Discov.*, 2(2):121–167, 1998.

[64] Yandong Cai, Nick Cercone, and Jiawei Han. Attribute-oriented induction in relational databases. In *Knowledge Discovery in Databases*, pages 213–228. AAAI/MIT Press, 1991.

[65] Longbing Cao, Chengqi Zhang, Yanchang Zhao, Philip S. Yu, and Graham Williams. DDDM2007: Domain driven data mining. *SIGKDD Explorations*, 9(2):84–86, 2007.

[66] Christopher L. Carmichael, Yaroslav Hayduk, and Carson Kai-Sang Leung. Visually contrast two collections of frequent patterns. In *Proc. of IEEE ICDM Workshops: Workshop on Contrast Data Mining and Applications*, pages 1128–1135, 2011.

[67] Alain Casali, Rosine Cicchetti, and Lotfi Lakhal. Extracting semantics from data cubes using cube transversals and closures. In *Proc. of ACM Int'l Conf. on Knowledge Discovery and Data Mining (KDD)*, pages 69–78, 2003.

[68] Michelangelo Ceci, Annalisa Appice, Costantina Caruso, and Donato Malerba. Discovering emerging patterns for anomaly detection in network connection data. In *Proc. of 17th Int'l Symp. Foundations of Intelligent Systems (ISMIS)*, pages 179–188, 2008.

[69] Michelangelo Ceci, Annalisa Appice, Corrado Loglisci, Costantina Caruso, Fabio Fumarola, and Donato Malerba. Novelty detection from evolving complex data streams with time windows. In *Proc. of Int'l Symp. on Foundations of Intelligent Systems (ISMIS)*, pages 563–572, 2009.

[70] Michelangelo Ceci, Annalisa Appice, and Donato Malerba. Discovering emerging patterns in spatial databases: A multi-relational approach. In *Proc. of European Conf. on Principles and Practice of Knowledge Discovery in Databases (PKDD)*, pages 390–397, 2007.

[71] Michelangelo Ceci, Annalisa Appice, and Donato Malerba. Emerging pattern based classification in relational data mining. In *Proc. of Int'l Conf. on Database and Expert Systems Applications (DEXA)*, pages 283–296, 2008.

[72] Mete Celik, Shashi Shekhar, James P. Rogers, and James A. Shine. Sustained emerging spatio-temporal co-occurrence pattern mining: A summary of results. In *Proc. of IEEE Int'l Conf. on Tools with Artificial Intelligence (ICTAI)*, pages 106–115, 2006.

[73] Jeffrey Chan, James Bailey, and Christopher Leckie. Discovering and summarising regions of correlated spatio-temporal change in evolving graphs. In *Proc. of ICDM Workshops*, pages 361–365, 2006.

[74] Sarah Chan, Ben Kao, Chi Lap Yip, and Michael Tang. Mining emerging substrings. In *Proc. of Int'l Symp. on Database Systems for Advanced Applications (DASFAA)*, pages 119–126, 2003.

[75] Wing-yan Sarah Chan. *Emerging substrings for sequence classification.* Master of Philosophy Thesis, University of Hong Kong, 2003.

[76] Yung-Kuan Chan and Chin-Chen Chang. Spatial similarity retrieval in video databases. *Journal of Visual Communication and Image Representation*, 12:107–122, 2001.

[77] Chih-Chung Chang and Chih-Jen Lin. *LIBSVM: a library for support vector machines*, 2001. Software available at http://www.csie.ntu.edu.tw/~cjlin/libsvm.

[78] Philippe Chatalic and Laurent Simon. Multi-Resolution on Compressed Sets of Clauses. In *Proc. of IEEE Int'l Conf. on Tools with Artificial Intelligence*, pages 2–10, 2000.

[79] Nitesh V. Chawla, Kevin W. Bowyer, Lawrence O. Hall, and W. Philip Kegelmeyer. SMOTE: Synthetic minority oversampling technique. *Journal of Artificial Intelligence Research*, 16:321–357, 2002.

[80] Nitesh V. Chawla, Nathalie Japkowicz, and Aleksander Kotcz. Editorial: Learning from imbalanced datasets. *SIGKDD Explorations*, 6(1), 2004.

[81] Chen Chen, Xifeng Yan, Philip S. Yu, Jiawei Han, Dong-Qing Zhang, and Xiaohui Gu. Towards graph containment search and indexing. In *Proc. of the Very Large Databases Conf. (VLDB)*, pages 926–937, 2007.

[82] Lijun Chen and Guozhu Dong. Masquerader detection using OCLEP: One class classification using length statistics of emerging patterns. In *Int'l Workshop on Information Processing over Evolving Networks (WINPEN)*, 2006.

[83] Mu-Chen Chen, Ai-Lun Chiu, and Hsu-Hwa Chang. Mining changes in customer behavior in retail marketing. *Expert Syst. Appl.*, 28(4):773–781, 2005.

[84] Xiangtao Chen and Lijuan Lu. A new algorithm based on shared pattern-tree to mine shared emerging patterns. In *Proc. of IEEE ICDM Workshops: Workshop on Contrast Data Mining and Applications*, pages 1136–1140, 2011.

[85] Xiaoyun Chen and Jinhua Chen. Emerging patterns and classification algorithms for DNA sequence. *Journal of Software*, 6(6):985–992, 2011.

[86] Hong Cheng. *Towards Accurate and Efficient Classification: A Discriminative and Frequent Pattern-Based Approach*. PhD Thesis, University of Illinios at Urbana-Champion (UIUC), 2009. Recipient of finalist for 2009 ACM SIGKDD Doctoral Dissertation Award Competition.

[87] Hong Cheng, David Lo, Yang Zhou, Xiaoyin Wang, and Xifeng Yan. Identifying bug signatures using discriminative graph mining. In *18th Int'l Symp. on Software Testing and Analysis*, pages 141–151, 2009.

[88] Hong Cheng, Xifeng Yan, Jiawei Han, and Chih-Wei Hsu. Discriminative frequent pattern analysis for effective classification. In *Proc. of IEEE Int'l Conf. on Data Engineering*, pages 716–725, 2007.

[89] Hong Cheng, Xifeng Yan, Jiawei Han, and Philip S. Yu. Direct discriminative pattern mining for effective classification. In *Proc. of IEEE Int'l Conf. on Data Engineering*, pages 169–178, 2008.

[90] Michael W. K. Cheng, Byron Choi, and William Kwok-Wai Cheung. Hiding emerging patterns with local recoding generalization. In *Proc. of Advances in Knowledge Discovery and Data Mining (PAKDD)*, pages 158–170, 2010.

[91] David Wai-Lok Cheung, Jiawei Han, Vincent T. Y. Ng, and C. Y. Wong. Maintenance of discovered association rules in large databases: an incremental updating technique. In *Proc. of Int'l Conf. On Data Engineering (ICDE)*, pages 106–114, 1996.

[92] Yun Chi, Haixun Wang, Philip S. Yu, and Richard R. Muntz. Catch the moment: maintaining closed frequent itemsets over a data stream sliding window. *Knowledge and Information Systems*, 10(3):265–294, 2006.

[93] Chun-Jung Chu, Vincent S. Tseng, and Tyne Liang. Efficient mining of temporal emerging itemsets from data streams. *Expert Syst. Appl.*, 36(1):885–893, 2009.

[94] Frans Coenen, Paul H. Leng, and Shakil Ahmed. Data structure for association rule mining: T-trees and P-trees. *IEEE Transaction on Knowledge and Data Engineering*, 16(6):774–778, 2004.

[95] Gao Cong, Kian-Lee Tan, Anthony K.H. Tung, and Xin Xu. Mining top-k covering rule groups for gene expression data. In *Proc. of ACM Int'l Conf. on Management of Data (SIGMOD)*, pages 670–681, 2005.

[96] Luigi P. Cordella, Pasquale Foggia, Carlo Sansone, and Mario Vento. A (sub)graph isomorphism algorithm for matching large graphs. *IEEE Trans. Pattern Anal. Mach. Intell.*, 26:1367–1372, 2004.

[97] Graham Cormode and S. Muthukrishnan. What's new: Finding significant differences in network data streams. In *Proc. of IEEE INFOCOM*, 2004.

[98] Corinna Cortes and Vladimir Vapnik. Support-vector networks. *Machine Learning*, 20(3):273–297, 1995.

[99] T. M. Cover and O. E. Hart. Nearest neighbor pattern classification. *IEEE Transaction on Information Theory*, pages 21–27, 1967.

[100] CSI/FBI. CSI/FBI Computer Crime and Security Survey, 2003.

[101] Gautam Das and Heikki Mannila. Context-based similarity measures for categorical databases. In *Proc. of European Conf. on Principles and Practice of Knowledge Discovery in Databases (PKDD)*, pages 201–210, 2000.

[102] A. P. Dempster, N. M. Laird, and D. B. Rubin. Maximum likelihood from incomplete data via the EM algorithm. *Journal of the Royal Statistical Society, Series B*, 39(1):1–38, 1977.

[103] Stephane P. Demri and Ewa S. Orlowska. *Incomplete Information: Structure, Inference, Complexity.* Springer-Verlag, 2002.

[104] Kang Deng and Osmar R. Zaïane. Contrasting sequence groups by emerging sequences. In *Proc. of Discovery Science*, pages 377–384, 2009.

[105] Kang Deng and Osmar R. Zaïane. An occurrence based approach to mine emerging sequences. In *Proc. of Int'l Conf. on Data Warehousing and Knowledge Discovery*, pages 275–284, 2010.

[106] Mukund Deshpande, Michihiro Kuramochi, Nikil Wale, and George Karypis. Frequent substructure-based approaches for classifying chemical compounds. *IEEE Trans. on Knowledge and Data Engineering*, 17(8):1036–1050, 2005.

[107] David J. Diller and Kenneth M. Merz. Can we separate active from inactive conformations? *Journal of Computer-Aided Molecular Design*, 16:105–112, 2002.

[108] Guiguang Ding, Jianmin Wang, and Kai Qin. A visual word weighting scheme based on emerging itemsets for video annotation. *Inf. Process. Lett.*, 110(16):692–696, 2010.

[109] Wei Ding, Tomasz F. Stepinski, and Josue Salazar. Discovery of geospatial discriminating patterns from remote sensing datasets. In *Proc. of SIAM Int'l Conf. on Data Mining (SDM)*, pages 425–436, 2009.

[110] Pedro Domingos. MetaCost: A general method for making classifiers cost-sensitive. In *Proc. of ACM Int'l Conf. on Knowledge Discovery and Data Mining (KDD)*, pages 155–164, 1999.

[111] Pedro Domingos. A unified bias-variance decomposition and its applications. In *Proc. of Int'l Conf. on Machine Learning*, pages 231–238, 2000.

[112] Andrzej Dominik, Zbigniew Walczak, and Jacek Wojciechowski. Classifying chemical compounds using contrast and common patterns. In *Proc. of 8th Int'l Conf. on Adaptive and Natural Computing Algorithms (ICANNGA)*, pages 772–781, 2007.

[113] Guozhu Dong and James Bailey. IEEE ICDM Workshops: Workshop on Contrast Data Mining and Applications, 2011.

[114] Guozhu Dong and James Bailey. Overview of contrast data mining as a field and preview of an upcoming book. In *Proc. of IEEE ICDM Workshops: Workshop on Contrast Data Mining and Applications*, pages 1141–1146, 2011.

[115] Guozhu Dong and Kaustubh Deshpande. Efficient mining of niches and set routines. In *Proc. of Pacific-Asia Conf. on Knowledge Discovery and Data Mining (PAKDD)*, pages 234–246, 2001.

[116] Guozhu Dong and Neil Fore. Discovering dynamic logical blog communities based on their distinct interest profiles. In *Proc. of Int'l Conf. on Social Eco-Informatics (SOTICS)*, 2011.

[117] Guozhu Dong, Jiawei Han, Joyce M. W. Lam, Jian Pei, Ke Wang, and Wei Zou. Mining constrained gradients in large databases. *IEEE Trans. Knowl. Data Eng.*, 16(8):922–938, 2004.

[118] Guozhu Dong and Jinyan Li. Efficient mining of emerging patterns: Discovering trends and differences. In *Proc. of ACM Conf. on Knowledge Discovery and Data Mining (KDD)*, pages 43–52, 1999.

[119] Guozhu Dong and Jinyan Li. Mining border descriptions of emerging patterns from dataset pairs. *Knowl. Inf. Syst.*, 8(2):178–202, 2005.

[120] Guozhu Dong and Jinyan Li. Applications of emerging patterns for microarray gene expression data analysis. In *Encyclopedia of Database Systems*, page 107. 2009.

[121] Guozhu Dong and Jinyan Li. Emerging pattern based classification. In *Encyclopedia of Database Systems*, page 985. 2009.

[122] Guozhu Dong, Jinyan Li, Guimei Liu, and Limsoon Wong. *Mining Conditional Contrast Patterns. Chapter in Post-Mining of Association Rules: Techniques for Effective Knowledge Extraction.* Yanchang Zhao and Chengqi Zhang and Longbing Cao eds. IGI Global, 2009.

[123] Guozhu Dong, Jinyan Li, and Limsoon Wong. The Use of Emerging Patterns in the Analysis of Gene Expression Profiles for the Diagnosis and Understanding of Diseases. In New Generation of Data Mining Applications, Mehmed Kantardzic and Jozef Zurada Eds, IEEE Press., 2005.

[124] Guozhu Dong and Jian Pei. *Sequence Data Mining.* Springer, 2007.

[125] Guozhu Dong and Ting Sa. Analyzing and tracking weblog communities using discriminative collection representatives. In *Proc. of Advances in Social Computing, Third Int'l Conf. on Social Computing, Behavioral Modeling, and Prediction (SBP)*, pages 256–264, 2010.

[126] Guozhu Dong, Xiuzhen Zhang, Limsoon Wong, and Jinyan Li. CAEP: Classification by aggregating emerging patterns. In *Proc. of Discovery Science*, pages 30–42, 1999.

[127] Ming Dong and Ravi Kothari. Look-ahead based fuzzy decision tree induction. *IEEE Trans. on Fuzzy Systems*, 9(3):461–468, 2001.

[128] James Dougherty, Ron Kohavi, and Mehran Sahami. Supervised and unsupervised discretization of continuous features. In *Proc. of Int'l Conf. on Machine Learning (ICML)*, pages 194–202, 1995.

[129] Lei Duan, Changjie Tang, Guozhu Dong, Ning Yang, and Chi Gou. Survey on emerging pattern based contrast mining and applications. *Journal of Computer Applications*, 32(2):304–308, 2012.

[130] Lei Duan, Changjie Tang, Liang Tang, Tianqing Zhang, and Jie Zuo. Mining class contrast functions by gene expression programming. In *Proc. of Int'l Conf. on Advanced Data Mining and Applications (ADMA)*, pages 116–127, 2009.

[131] Lei Duan, Jie Zuo, Tianqing Zhang, Jing Peng, and Jie Gong. Mining contrast inequalities in numeric dataset. In *Proc. of Int'l Conf. on Web-Age Information Management (WAIM)*, pages 194–205, 2010.

[132] R. A. Dubin. Predicting house prices using multiple listings data. *Journal of Real Estate Finance and Economics*, 17:35–59(1), 1998.

[133] William DuMouchel, Wen-Hua Ju, Alan F. Karr, Matthias Schonlau, Martin Theusan, and Yehuda Vardi. Computer intrusion: Detecting masquerades. *Statistical Science*, 16(1):1–17, 2001.

[134] EPAFHM. *Environement Protection Agency Fathead Minnow Acute Toxicity*, 2008. http://www.epa.gov/med/Prods_Pubs/fathead_minnow.htm.

[135] Themis P. Exarchos, Costas Papaloukas, Dimitrios I. Fotiadis, and Lampros K. Michalis. An association rule mining-based methodology for automated detection of ischemic ECG beats. *IEEE Trans. on Biomedical Engineering*, 53(8):1531–1540, 2006.

[136] Hongjian Fan. *Efficient Mining of Interesting Emerging Patterns and Their Effective Use in Classification*. PhD Thesis, University of Melbourne, May 2004.

[137] Hongjian Fan and Kotagiri Ramamohanarao. An efficient single-scan algorithm for mining essential jumping emerging patterns for classification. In *Proc. of Pacific-Asia Conf. on Knowledge Discovery and Data Mining (PAKDD)*, pages 456–462, 2002.

[138] Hongjian Fan and Kotagiri Ramamohanarao. A Bayesian approach to use emerging patterns for classification. In *Proc. of Australasian Database Conf.*, pages 39–48, 2003.

[139] Hongjian Fan and Kotagiri Ramamohanarao. Noise tolerant classification by chi emerging patterns. In *Proc. of Pacific-Asia Conf. on Knowledge Discovery and Data Mining (PAKDD)*, pages 201–206, 2004.

[140] Hongjian Fan and Kotagiri Ramamohanarao. A weighting scheme based on emerging patterns for weighted support vector machines. In *Proc. of IEEE Int'l Conf. on Granular Computing*, pages 435–440, 2005.

[141] Hongjian Fan and Kotagiri Ramamohanarao. Fast discovery and the generalization of strong jumping emerging patterns for building compact and accurate classifiers. *IEEE Trans. Knowl. Data Eng.*, 18(6):721–737, 2006.

[142] Wei Fan, Kun Zhang, Hong Cheng, Jing Gao, Xifeng Yan, Jiawei Han, Philip S. Yu, and Olivier Verscheure. Direct mining of discriminative and essential frequent patterns via model-based search tree. In *Proc. of ACM Conf. on Knowledge Discovery and Data Mining (KDD)*, pages 230–238, 2008.

[143] Gang Fang, Gaurav Pandey, Wen Wang, Manish Gupta, Michael Steinbach, and Vipin Kumar. Mining low-support discriminative patterns from dense and high-dimensional data. CSE-TR 09-011, University of Minnesota, 2009.

[144] Gang Fang, Wen Wang, Benjamin Oatley, Brian Van Ness, Michael Steinbach, and Vipin Kumar. Characterizing discriminative patterns. *Computing Research Repository*, abs/1102.4, 2011.

[145] Usama M. Fayyad and Keki B. Irani. Multi-interval discretization of continuous-valued attributes for classification learning. In *Proc. of Int'l Joint Conf. on Artificial Intelligence (IJCAI)*, pages 1022–1029, 1993.

[146] Mengling Feng, Guozhu Dong, Jinyan Li, Yap-Peng Tan, and Limsoon Wong. Pattern space maintenance for data updates and interactive mining. *Computational Intelligence*, 26(3):282–317, 2010.

[147] Mengling Feng, Jinyan Li, Guozhu Dong, and Limsoon Wong. *Maintenance of Frequent Patterns: A Survey. Chapter in Post-Mining of Association Rules: Techniques for Effective Knowledge Extraction.* Yanchang Zhao and Chengqi Zhang and Longbing Cao eds. IGI Global, 2009.

[148] Cândida Ferreira. Gene expression programming: A new adaptive algorithm for solving problems. *Complex Systems*, 13:87–129, 2001.

[149] Johannes Fischer, Volker Heun, and Stefan Kramer. Fast frequent string mining using suffix arrays. *Proc. of IEEE Int'l Conf. on Data Mining (ICDM)*, pages 609–612, 2005.

[150] Johannes Fischer, Volker Heun, and Stefan Kramer. Optimal string mining under frequency constraints. In *Proc. of 10th European Conference on Principles and Practice of Knowledge Discovery in Databases (PKDD)*, pages 139–150, 2006.

[151] Douglas H. Fisher and Pat Langley. Approaches to conceptual clustering. In *Proc. of Int'l Joint Conf. on Artificial Intelligence (IJCAI)*, pages 691–697, 1985.

[152] Neil Fore and Guozhu Dong. CPC: A contrast pattern based clustering algorithm requiring no distance function. Technical report, Department of Computer Science and Engineering, Wright State University, 2011.

[153] Jerome H. Friedman and Nicholas I. Fisher. Bump hunting in high-dimensional data. *Statistics and Computing*, 9(2):123143, 1999.

[154] Hiroshige Fujii, Goichi Ootomo, and Chikahiro Hori. Interleaving based variable ordering methods for ordered binary decision diagrams. In *Proc. of IEEE/ACM Int'l Conf. on Computer-Aided Design*, pages 38–41, 1993.

[155] Dragan Gamberger and Nada Lavrac. Expert-guided subgroup discovery: Methodology and application. *Journal of Artificial Intelligence Research*, 17:501–527, 2002.

[156] Tomasz Gambin and Krzysztof Walczak. Classification based on the highest impact jumping emerging patterns. In *Proc. of Int'l Multiconference on Computer Science and Information Technology*, pages 37–42, 2009.

[157] Tomasz Gambin and Krzysztof Walczak. A new classification method using array comparative genome hybridization data, based on the concept of limited jumping emerging patterns. *BMC Bioinformatics*, 10(S-1), 2009.

[158] Min Gan and Honghua Dai. Efficient mining of top-k breaker emerging subgraph patterns from graph datasets. In *Proc. of Australasian Data Mining Conference (AusDM)*, 2009.

[159] Venkatesh Ganti, Johannes Gehrke, and Raghu Ramakrishnan. A framework for measuring changes in data characteristics. In *Proc. of ACM Symp. on Principles of Database Systems (PODS)*, pages 126–137, 1999.

[160] Chuancong Gao and Jianyong Wang. Direct mining of discriminative patterns for classifying uncertain data. In *Proc. of ACM Int'l Conf. on Knowledge Discovery and Data Mining (KDD)*, pages 861–870, 2010.

[161] Milton Garcia-Borroto. *Searching Extended Emerging Patterns for Supervised Classification*. PhD Thesis, National Institute for Astrophysics Optics and Electronics, Puebla, Mexico, 2010.

[162] Milton García-Borroto, José Fco. Martínez-Trinidad, and Jesús Ariel Carrasco-Ochoa. Fuzzy emerging patterns for classifying hard domains. *Knowledge and Information Systems*, 28(2):473–489, 2011.

[163] Milton García-Borroto, José Francisco Martínez Trinidad, Jesús Ariel Carrasco-Ochoa, Miguel Angel Medina-Pérez, and José Ruiz-Shulcloper. LCMine: An efficient algorithm for mining discriminative regularities and its application in supervised classification. *Pattern Recognition*, 43(9):3025–3034, 2010.

[164] Dominique Gay. *Constraint-based pattern mining for classification purpose*. PhD Thesis, Universit de Nouvelle Caldonie INSA de Lyon, 2009.

[165] Hanna Geppert, Martin Vogt, and Jürgen Bajorath. Current trends in ligand-based virtual screening: molecular representations, data mining methods, new application areas, and performance evaluation. *Journal of Chemical Information and Modeling*, 50:205–216, 2010.

[166] T. R. Golub and D. K. Slonim et al. Molecular classification of cancer: class discovery and class prediction by gene expression monitoring. *Science*, 286(5439):531–537, 1999.

[167] Gosta Grahne and Jianfei Zhu. Fast algorithms for frequent itemset mining using FP-trees. *IEEE Transactions on Knowledge and Data Engineering*, 17(10):1347–1362, 2005.

[168] Jim Gray, Surajit Chaudhuri, Adam Bosworth, Andrew Layman, Don Reichart, Murali Venkatrao, Frank Pellow, and Hamid Pirahesh. Data

cube: A relational aggregation operator generalizing group-by, cross-tab, and sub totals. *Data Min. Knowl. Discov.*, 1(1):29–53, 1997.

[169] Jerzy W. Grzymala-Busse and Wojciech Ziarko. Data mining based on rough sets. *Data mining: opportunities and challenges*, pages 142–173, 2003.

[170] Tao Gu, Zhanqing Wu, XianPing Tao, Hung Keng Pung, and Jian Lu. epSICAR: An emerging patterns based approach to sequential, inter-leaved and concurrent activity recognition. In *Proc. of IEEE Int'l Conf. on Pervasive Computing and Communications (PerCom)*, pages 1–9, 2009.

[171] Tao Gu, Zhanqing Wu, Liang Wang, Xianping Tao, and Jian Lu. Mining emerging patterns for recognizing activities of multiple users in pervasive computing. In *Proc. of Mobile and Ubiquitous Systems*, 2009.

[172] Sudipto Guha, Rajeev Rastogi, and Kyuseok Shim. ROCK: A robust clustering algorithm for categorical attributes. *Inf. Syst.*, 25(5):345–366, 2000.

[173] Lei Guo, Edward K Lobenhofer, and Charles Wang et al. Rat toxicoge-nomic study reveals analytical consistency across microarray platforms. *Nature Biotechnology*, 24:1162–1169, 2006.

[174] Howard Gutowitz. *Cellular Automata: Theory and Experiment*. Brad-ford Books, 1991.

[175] Matthias Hagen. Lower bounds for three algorithms for the transver-sal hypergraph generation. In *Proc. of Workshop on Graph-Theoretic Concepts in Computer Science*, pages 316–327, 2007.

[176] Mark Hall, Eibe Frank, Geoffrey Holmes, Bernhard Pfahringer, Pe-ter Reutemann, and Ian H. Witten. The WEKA data mining software: an update. *SIGKDD Explor. Newsl.*, 11(1):10–18, 2009. http://www.cs.waikato.ac.nz/ml/weka/.

[177] Mark A. Hall. *Correlation-based Feature Subset Selection for Machine Learning*. PhD thesis, The University of Waikato, New Zealand, 1999.

[178] Jiawei Han, Hong Cheng, Dong Xin, and Xifeng Yan. Frequent pattern mining: current status and future directions. *Data Mining and Knowl-edge Discovery*, 15(1):55–86, 2007.

[179] Jiawei Han, Micheline Kamber, and Jian Pei. *Data Mining: Concepts and Techniques (3rd edition)*. Morgan Kaufmann, 2011.

[180] Jiawei Han, Jian Pei, and Yiwen Yin. Mining frequent patterns without candidate generation. In *Proc. of ACM Int'l Conf. on Management of Data (SIGMOD)*, pages 1–12, 2000.

[181] Jiawei Han, Jian Pei, Yiwen Yin, and Runying Mao. Mining frequent patterns without candidate generation: A frequent-pattern tree approach. *Data Min. Knowl. Discov.*, 8(1):53–87, 2004.

[182] Shuli Han, Bo Yuan, and Wenhuang Liu. Rare class mining: Progress and prospect. In *Proc. of Chinese Conf. on Pattern Recognition (CCPR)*, pages 1–5, 2009.

[183] Gary Hardiman. Microarray platforms — comparisons and contrasts. *Pharmacogenomics*, 5(5):487–502, 2004.

[184] D. M. Hawkins. *Identification of outliers.* Monographs on applied probability and statistics. Chapman and Hall, 1980.

[185] He He and Ali Ghodsi. Rare class classification by support vector machine. In *Proc. of Int'l Conf. on Pattern Recognition (ICPR)*, pages 548–551, 2010.

[186] Francisco Herrera, Cristóbal J. Carmona, Pedro González, and María José del Jesús. An overview on subgroup discovery: foundations and applications. *Knowl. Inf. Syst.*, 29(3):495–525, 2011.

[187] Robert J. Hilderman and Terry Peckham. Statistical methodologies for mining potentially interesting contrast sets. In *Proc. of Quality Measures in Data Mining*, pages 153–177. 2007.

[188] B. Hilier and J. Hanson. *The Social Logic of Space.* Cambridge University Press, 1984.

[189] Victoria J. Hodge and Jim Austin. A survey of outlier detection methodologies. *Artif. Intell. Rev.*, 22(2):85–126, 2004.

[190] Johan Hopstadius and G. Niklas Norén. Robust discovery of local patterns: subsets and stratification in adverse drug reaction surveillance. In *Proc. of ACM SIGHIT Int'l Health Informatics Symp.*, pages 265–274, 2012.

[191] Yan Huang, Jian Pei, and Hui Xiong. Mining co-location patterns with rare events from spatial data sets. *Geoinformatica*, 10(3):239–260, 2006.

[192] Farhad Hussain, Huan Liu, Einoshin Suzuki, and Hongjun Lu. Exception rule mining with a relative interestingness measure. In *Proc. of Pacific-Asia Conf. on Knowledge Discovery and Data Mining (PAKDD)*, pages 86–97, 2000.

[193] Susan P. Imberman, Abdullah Uz Tansel, and Eric Pacuit. NUWEP – an efficient method for finding emerging large itemsets. In *Proc. of Workshop on Mining Temporal and Sequential Data at SIGKDD.* 2004.

[194] H. Inakoshi, T. Ando, A. Sato, and S. Okamoto. Discovery of emerging patterns from nearest neighbors. In *Proc. of Int'l Conf. on Machine Learning and Cybernetics*, 2002.

[195] Akihiro Inokuchi, Takashi Washio, and Hiroshi Motoda. An apriori-based algorithm for mining frequent substructures from graph data. In *Proc. of European Conf. on Principles and Practice of Knowledge Discovery in Databases (PKDD)*, pages 13–23, 2000.

[196] Anil K. Jain. Data clustering: 50 years beyond K-means. *Pattern Recognition Letters*, 31(8):651–666, 2010.

[197] Xiaonan Ji. *Constraint Based Sequential Pattern Mining and its Applications*. PhD Thesis, University of Melbourne, 2008.

[198] Xiaonan Ji, James Bailey, and Guozhu Dong. Mining minimal distinguishing subsequence patterns with gap constraints. Recipient of ICDM 2005 Best Research Paper Award. In *Proc. of IEEE Int'l Conf. on Data Mining (ICDM)*, pages 194–201, 2005.

[199] Xiaonan Ji, James Bailey, and Guozhu Dong. Mining minimal distinguishing subsequence patterns with gap constraints. *Knowl. Inf. Syst.*, 11(3):259–286, 2007.

[200] Ning Jin, Calvin Young, and Wei Wang. GAIA: Graph classification using evolutionary computation. In *Proc. of ACM Int'l Conf. on Management of Data (SIGMOD)*, pages 879–890, 2010.

[201] Ruoming Jin and Gagan Agrawal. Systematic approach for optimizing complex mining tasks on multiple databases. In *Proc. of Int'l Conf. on Data Engineering*, page 17, 2006.

[202] Ruoming Jin, Yuri Breitbart, and Rong Li. A tree-based framework for difference summarization. In *Proc. of IEEE Int'l Conf. on Data Mining (ICDM)*, pages 209–218, 2009.

[203] Yoshitaka Kameya, Satoru Nakamura, Tatsuya Iwasaki, and Taisuke Sato. Verbal characterization of probabilistic clusters using minimal discriminative propositions. In *Proc. of Int'l Conf. on Tools with Artificial Intelligence (ICTAI)*, pages 873–875, 2011.

[204] Yoshitaka Kameya and Chativit Prayoonsri. Pattern-based preservation of building blocks in genetic algorithms. In *Proc. of IEEE Congress on Evolutionary Computation*, pages 2578–2585, 2011.

[205] M. Sulaiman Khan, Frans Coenen, David Reid, R. Patel, and L. Archer. A sliding windows based dual support framework for discovering emerging trends from temporal data. *Knowl.-Based Syst.*, 23(4):316–322, 2010.

[206] Daniel Kifer, Shai Ben-David, and Johannes Gehrke. Detecting change in data streams. In *Proc. of Int'l Conf. on Very Large Data Bases (VLDB)*, pages 180–191, 2004.

[207] Hyungsul Kim, Sangkyum Kim, Tim Weninger, Jiawei Han, and Tarek F. Abdelzaher. NDPMine: Efficiently mining discriminative numerical features for pattern-based classification. In *Proc. of European Conf. on Machine Learning and Principles and Practice of Knowledge Discovery in Databases (ECML/PKDD)*, pages 35–50, 2010.

[208] Young Bun Kim. *Comprehensive Data Analysis for Biomarker Pattern Discovery Using DNA/Protein Microarrays*. PhD Thesis, University of Texas at Arlington, 2008.

[209] Young Bun Kim, Jung Hun Oh, and Jean Gao. Emerging pattern based subspace clustering of microarray gene expression data using mixture models. In *Proc. of Int'l Conf. on Advances in Bioinformatics and its Applications*, 2004.

[210] Łukasz Kobyliński and Krzysztof Walczak. Jumping emerging patterns with occurrence count in image classification. In *Proc. of Pacific-Asia Conf. on Knowledge Discovery and Data Mining (PAKDD)*, pages 904–909, 2008.

[211] Łukasz Kobyliński and Krzysztof Walczak. Jumping emerging substrings in image classification. In *Proc. of Int'l Conf. on Computer Analysis of Images and Patterns (CAIP)*, pages 732–739, 2009.

[212] Łukasz Kobyliński and Krzysztof Walczak. Spatial emerging patterns for scene classification. In *Proc. of Int'l Conf. on Artificial Intelligence and Soft Computing (ICAISC)*, pages 515–522, 2010.

[213] Łukasz Kobyliński and Krzysztof Walczak. Efficient mining of jumping emerging patterns with occurrence counts for classification. *Trans. on Rough Sets*, 13:73–88, 2011.

[214] Ron Kohavi, George H. John, Richard Long, David Manley, and Karl Pfleger. MLC++: A machine learning library in C++. In *Proc. of IEEE Int'l Conf. on Tools with Artificial Intelligence (ICTAI)*, pages 740–743, 1994.

[215] George Kollios, Dimitrios Gunopulos, Nick Koudas, and Stefan Berchtold. Efficient biased sampling for approximate clustering and outlier detection in large data sets. *IEEE Trans. Knowl. Data Eng.*, 15(5):1170–1187, 2003.

[216] Eun Bae Kong and Thomas G. Dietterich. Error-correcting output coding corrects bias and variance. In *Proc. of Int'l Conf. on Machine Learning (ICML)*, pages 313–321, 1995.

[217] Petra Kralj, Nada Lavrac, Dragan Gamberger, and Antonija Krstacic. Contrast set mining for distinguishing between similar diseases. In *Proc. of Artificial Intelligence in Medicine*, pages 109–118, 2007.

[218] Stefan Kramer, Luc De Raedt, and Christoph Helma. Molecular feature mining in HIV data. In *Proc. of ACM Int'l Conf. on Knowledge Discovery and Data Mining (KDD)*, pages 136–143, 2001.

[219] Marzena Kryszkiewicz and Katarzyna Cichon. Towards scalable algorithms for discovering rough set reducts. *Trans. Rough Sets*, pages 120–143, 2004.

[220] Marzena Kryszkiewicz and Katarzyna Cichon. Support oriented discovery of generalized disjunction-free representation of frequent patterns with negation. In *Proc. of Pacific-Asia Conf. on Knowledge Discovery and Data Mining (PAKDD)*, pages 672–682, 2005.

[221] Taku Kudo, Eisaku Maeda, and Yuji Matsumoto. An application of boosting to graph classification. In *Advances in Neural Information Processing Systems 17*, pages 729–736, 2004.

[222] Winston Patrick Kuo, Tor-Kristian Jenssen, Atul J. Butte, Lucila Ohno-Machado, and Isaac S. Kohane. Analysis of matched mRNA measurements from two different microarray technologies. *Bioinformatics*, 18(3):405–412, 2002.

[223] Michihiro Kuramochi and George Karypis. Frequent subgraph discovery. In *Proc. of IEEE Int'l Conf. on Data Mining (ICDM)*, pages 313–320, 2001.

[224] Lukasz A. Kurgan, Krzysztof J. Cios, Ryszard Tadeusiewicz, Marek R. Ogiela, and Lucy S. Goodenday. Knowledge discovery approach to automated cardiac spect diagnosis. *Artificial Intelligence in Medicine*, 23(2):149–169, 2001.

[225] Paul Labute. Binary QSAR: a new method for the determination of quantitative structure activity relationships. In *Proc. of Pacific Symp. on Biocomputing*, volume 4, pages 444–455, 1999.

[226] Hardik Lagad and Guozhu Dong. Comparative web search system and method. United States Patent 7,912,847, March 2011.

[227] Laks V. S. Lakshmanan, Jian Pei, and Jiawei Han. Quotient cube: How to summarize the semantics of a data cube. In *Proc. of Int'l Conf. on Very Large Data Bases (VLDB)*, pages 778–789, 2002.

[228] Pat Langley, Wayne Iba, and Kevin Thompson. An analysis of Bayesian classifiers. In *Proc. of National Conf. on Artificial Intelligence (AAAI)*, pages 223–228, 1992.

[229] Nada Lavrac, Branko Kavsek, Peter A. Flach, and Ljupco Todorovski. Subgroup discovery with CN2-SD. *Journal of Machine Learning Research*, 5:153–188, 2004.

[230] Rob Law, Jia Rong, Huy Quan Vu, Gang Li, and Hee Andy Lee. Identifying changes and trends in Hong Kong outbound tourism. *Tourism Management*, 32(5):1106–1114, 2011.

[231] Aleksandar Lazarevic, Levent Ertöz, Vipin Kumar, Aysel Ozgur, and Jaideep Srivastava. A comparative study of anomaly detection schemes in network intrusion detection. In *Proc. of SIAM Int'l Conf. on Data Mining (SDM)*, 2003.

[232] Anthony J. T. Lee, Ruey-Wen Hong, Wei-Min Ko, Wen-Kwang Tsao, and Hsiu-Hui Lin. Mining spatial association rules in image databases. *Information Sciences*, 177(7):1593–1608, 2007.

[233] Chang-Hung Lee, Cheng-Ru Lin, and Ming-Syan Chen. Sliding window filtering: an efficient method for incremental mining on a time-variant database. *Information Systems*, 30(3):227–244, 2005.

[234] Heon Gyu Lee, Kiyong Noh, Bum Ju Lee, Ho-Sun Shon, and Keun Ho Ryu. Cardiovascular disease diagnosis method by emerging patterns. In *Proc. of Second Int'l Conf. on Advanced Data Mining and Applications (ADMA)*, pages 819–826, 2006.

[235] Jae-Gil Lee, Jiawei Han, Xiao Li, and Hong Cheng. Mining discriminative patterns for classifying trajectories on road networks. *IEEE Trans. on Knowledge and Data Engineering*, 23(5):713–726, 2011.

[236] Jong Bum Lee, Minghao Piao, and Keun Ho Ryu. Incremental emerging patterns mining for identifying safe and non-safe power load lines. In *Proc. of IEEE Int'l Conf. on Computer and Information Technology*, pages 1424–1429, 2010.

[237] Dennis Leman, Ad Feelders, and Arno J. Knobbe. Exceptional model mining. In *Proc. of European Conference on Machine Learning and Knowledge Discovery in Databases (ECML/PKDD)*, pages 1–16, 2008.

[238] Aixiang Li, Makoto Haraguchi, and Yoshiaki Okubo. Contrasting correlations by an efficient double-clique condition. In *Proc. of 7th Int'l Conf. on Machine Learning and Data Mining in Pattern Recognition (MLDM)*, pages 469–483, 2011.

[239] Haiquan Li, Jinyan Li, Limsoon Wong, Mengling Feng, and Yap-Peng Tan. Relative risk and odds ratio: a data mining perspective. In *Proc. of ACM Symp. on Principles of Database Systems (PODS)*, pages 368–377, 2005.

[240] Hua-Fu Li. MEMSA: mining emerging melody structures from music query data. *Multimedia Syst.*, 17(3):237–245, 2011.

[241] Jinyan Li. *Mining Emerging Patterns to Construct Accurate and Efficient Classifiers*. PhD Thesis, University of Melbourne, 2001.

[242] Jinyan Li, Guozhu Dong, and Kotagiri Ramamohanarao. Instance-based classification by emerging patterns. In *Proc. of European Conf. on Principles and Practice of Knowledge Discovery in Databases (PKDD)*, pages 191–200, 2000.

[243] Jinyan Li, Guozhu Dong, and Kotagiri Ramamohanarao. Making use of the most expressive jumping emerging patterns for classification. In *Proc. of Pacific-Asia Conf. on Knowledge Discovery and Data Mining (PAKDD)*, pages 220–232, 2000.

[244] Jinyan Li, Guozhu Dong, and Kotagiri Ramamohanarao. Making use of the most expressive jumping emerging patterns for classification. *Knowl. Inf. Syst.*, 3(2):131–145, 2001.

[245] Jinyan Li, Guozhu Dong, Kotagiri Ramamohanarao, and Limsoon Wong. DeEPs: A new instance-based lazy discovery and classification system. *Machine Learning*, 54(2):99–124, 2004.

[246] Jinyan Li, Haiquan Li, Limsoon Wong, Jian Pei, and Guozhu Dong. Minimum description length principle: Generators are preferable to closed patterns. In *Proc. of 21st National Conf. on Artificial Intelligence and 18th Innovative Applications of Artificial Intelligence Conf.*, pages 409–414, 2006.

[247] Jinyan Li, Guimei Liu, and Limsoon Wong. Mining statistically important equivalence classes and delta-discriminative emerging patterns. In *Proc. of ACM Conf. on Knowledge Discovery and Data Mining (KDD)*, pages 430–439, 2007.

[248] Jinyan Li, Huiqing Liu, James R. Downing, Allen Eng-Juh Yeoh, and Limsoon Wong. Simple rules underlying gene expression profiles of more than six subtypes of acute lymphoblastic leukemia (ALL) patients. *Bioinformatics*, 19(1):71–78, 2003.

[249] Jinyan Li, Thomas Manoukian, Guozhu Dong, and Kotagiri Ramamohanarao. Incremental maintenance on the border of the space of emerging patterns. *Data Min. Knowl. Discov.*, 9(1):89–116, 2004.

[250] Jinyan Li, Kotagiri Ramamohanarao, and Guozhu Dong. The space of jumping emerging patterns and its incremental maintenance algorithms. In *Proc. of 17th Int'l Conf. on Machine Learning (ICML)*, pages 551–558, 2000.

[251] Jinyan Li, Kotagiri Ramamohanarao, and Guozhu Dong. Combining the strength of pattern frequency and distance for classification. In *Proc. of Pacific-Asia Conf. on Knowledge Discovery and Data Mining (PAKDD)*, pages 455–466, 2001.

[252] Jinyan Li and Limsoon Wong. Emerging patterns and gene expression data. *Genome Informatics*, 12:3–13, 2001.

[253] Jinyan Li and Limsoon Wong. Identifying good diagnostic gene groups from gene expression profiles using the concept of emerging patterns. *Bioinformatics*, 18(10):1406–1407, 2002.

[254] Jinyan Li and Limsoon Wong. Structural geography of the space of emerging patterns. *Intell. Data Anal.*, 9(6):567–588, 2005.

[255] Jinyan Li and Qiang Yang. Strong compound-risk factors: Efficient discovery through emerging patterns and contrast sets. *IEEE Trans. on Information Technology in Biomedicine*, 11(5):544–552, 2007.

[256] Jinyan Li, Xiuzhen Zhang, Guozhu Dong, Kotagiri Ramamohanarao, and Qun Sun. Efficient mining of high confidence association rules without support thresholds. In *Proc. of European Conf. on Principles and Practice of Knowledge Discovery in Databases (PKDD)*, pages 406–411, 1999.

[257] Jiuyong Li, Rodney Topor, and Hong Shen. Construct robust rule sets for classification. In *Proc. of ACM Conf. on Knowledge Discovery and Data Mining (KDD)*, pages 564–569, 2002.

[258] Wenmin Li, Jiawei Han, and Jian Pei. CMAR: Accurate and efficient classification based on multiple class-association rules. In *Proc. of IEEE Int'l Conf. on Data Mining (ICDM)*, pages 369–376, 2001.

[259] Yan Li and Xiguang Dong. The e-mail categorization and filtering technology based on eEP. In *Proc. of Int'l Symp. on Computer Science and Computational Technology (ISCSCT)*, pages 259–262. 2010.

[260] Chun-Fu Lin and Sheng-De Wang. Fuzzy support vector machines. *IEEE Trans. on Neural Networks*, 13(2):464–471, March 2002.

[261] Dekang Lin. An information-theoretic definition of similarity. In *Proc. of Int'l Conference on Machine Learning*, 1998.

[262] Jessica Lin and Eamonn J. Keogh. Group SAX: Extending the notion of contrast sets to time series and multimedia data. In *Proc. of European Conf. on Principles and Practice of Knowledge Discovery in Databases (PKDD)*, pages 284–296, 2006.

[263] Tsau Young Lin, Yiyu Y. Yao, and Lotfi A. Zadeh, editors. *Data mining, rough sets and granular computing*. Physica-Verlag, Heidelberg, Germany, 2002.

[264] Zhenhua Lin, Bin Jiang, Jian Pei, and Daxin Jiang. Mining discriminative items in multiple data streams. *World Wide Web*, 13:497–522, December 2010.

[265] Charles X. Ling and Chenghui Li. Data mining for direct marketing: Problems and solutions. In *Proc. of Int'l Conf. on Knowledge Discovery and Data Mining (KDD)*, pages 73–79, 1998.

[266] Pawan Lingras. Comparison of neofuzzy and rough neural networks. *Information Sciences*, 110(3-4):207–215, 1998.

[267] P. Linneman. Some empirical results on the nature of the hedonic price function for the urban housing market. *Journal of Urban Economics*, 8:47–68(1), 1980.

[268] Christopher A. Lipinski, Franco Lombardo, Beryl W. Dominy, and Paul J. Feeney. Experimental and computational approaches to estimate solubility and permeability in drug discovery and development settings. *Advanced Drug Delivery Reviews*, 46:3–26, 2001.

[269] Bing Liu, Wynne Hsu, Heng-Siew Han, and Yiyuan Xia. Mining changes for real-life applications. In *Proc. of Int'l Conf. on Data Warehousing and Knowledge Discovery (DaWaK)*, pages 337–346, 2000.

[270] Bing Liu, Wynne Hsu, and Yiming Ma. Integrating classification and association rule mining. In *Proc. of ACM Conf. on Knowledge Discovery and Data Mining (KDD)*, pages 80–86, 1998.

[271] Bing Liu, Wynne Hsu, and Yiming Ma. Discovering the set of fundamental rule changes. In *Proc. of ACM Conf. on Knowledge Discovery and Data Mining (KDD)*, pages 335–340, 2001.

[272] Bing Liu, Ke Wang, Lai-Fun Mun, and Xin-Zhi Qi. Using decision tree induction for discovering holes in data. In *Proc. of Pacific Rim Int'l Conf. on Artificial Intelligence*, pages 182–193, 1998.

[273] Duen-Ren Liu, Meng-Jung Shih, Churn-Jung Liau, and Chin-Hui Lai. Mining the change of event trends for decision support in environmental scanning. *Expert Syst. Appl.*, 36(2):972–984, 2009.

[274] Huan Liu and Hiroshi Motoda. *Feature selection for knowledge discovery and data mining*. Springer, 1998.

[275] Huan Liu and Rudy Setiono. Chi2: Feature selection and discretization of numeric attributes. In *Proc. of IEEE 7th Int'l Conf. on Tools with Artificial Intelligence*, pages 338–391, 1995.

[276] Qingbao Liu and Guozhu Dong. A contrast pattern based clustering quality index for categorical data. In *Proc. of IEEE Int'l Conf. on Data Mining (ICDM)*, pages 860–865, 2009.

[277] Qingbao Liu and Guozhu Dong. CPCQ: Contrast pattern based clustering quality index for categorical data. *Pattern Recognition*, 45(4):1739–1748, 2012.

[278] Xiaoyan Liu, Xindong Wu, Huaiqing Wang, Rui Zhang, James Bailey, and Kotagiri Ramamohanarao. Mining distribution change in stock order streams. In *Proc. of IEEE Int'l Conf. on Data Engineering (ICDE)*, pages 105–108, 2010.

[279] Yong Liu, Jianzhong Li, and Jinghua Zhu. A novel graph classification approach based on frequent closed emerging patterns. *Journal of Computer Research and Development*, 44(7):1169–1176, 2007.

[280] David Lo, Hong Cheng, Jiawei Han, Siau-Cheng Khoo, and Chengnian Sun. Classification of software behaviors for failure detection: a discriminative pattern mining approach. In *Proc. of ACM Conf. on Knowledge Discovery and Data Mining (KDD)*, pages 557–566, 2009.

[281] David Lo, Hong Cheng, and Lucia. Mining closed discriminative dyadic sequential patterns. In *Proc. of Int'l Conf. on Extending Database Technology (EDBT)*, pages 21–32, 2011.

[282] Elsa Loekito. *Mining Simple and Complex Patterns Efficiently Using Binary Decision Diagrams*. PhD Thesis, University of Melbourne, 2009.

[283] Elsa Loekito and James Bailey. Fast mining of high dimensional expressive contrast patterns using zero-suppressed binary decision diagrams. In *Proc. of ACM Conf. on Knowledge Discovery and Data Mining (KDD)*, pages 307–316, 2006.

[284] Elsa Loekito and James Bailey. Are zero-suppressed binary decision diagrams good for mining frequent patterns in high dimensional datasets? In *Proc. of 6th Australasian Data Mining Conference (AusDM)*, pages 139–150, 2007.

[285] Elsa Loekito and James Bailey. Mining influential attributes that capture class and group contrast behaviour. In *Proc. of ACM Conf. on Information and Knowledge Management (CIKM)*, pages 971–980, 2008.

[286] Elsa Loekito and James Bailey. Using highly expressive contrast patterns for classification - is it worthwhile? In *Proc. of Pacific-Asia Conf. on Knowledge Discovery and Data Mining (PAKDD)*, pages 483–490, 2009.

[287] Elsa Loekito, James Bailey, and Jian Pei. A binary decision diagram based approach for mining frequent subsequences. *Knowledge and Information Systems*, 24(2):235–268, 2010.

[288] Sylvain Lozano, Guillaume Poezevara, Marie-Pierre Halm-Lemeille, Elodie Lescot-Fontaine, Alban Lepailleur, Ryan Bissell-Siders, Bruno Cremilleux, Sylvain Rault, Bertrand Cuissart, and Ronan Bureau. Introduction of jumping fragments in combination with QSARs for the assessment of classification in ecotoxicology. *Journal of Chemical Information and Modeling*, 50(8):1330–1339, 2010.

[289] Larry M. Manevitz and Malik Yousef. One-class SVMs for document classification. *Journal of Mach. Learn. Res.*, 2:139–154, 2002.

[290] Shihong Mao. *Comparative Microarray Data Mining*. PhD Thesis, Wright State University, 2007.

[291] Shihong Mao and Guozhu Dong. Discovery of highly differentiative gene groups from microarray gene expression data using the gene club approach. *Journal of Bioinformatics and Computational Biology*, 3(6):1263–1280, 2005.

[292] Shihong Mao, Charles Wang, and Guozhu Dong. Evaluation of inter-laboratory and cross-platform concordance of DNA microarrays through discriminating genes and classifier transferability. *Journal of Bioinformatics and Computational Biology*, 7(1):157–173, 2009.

[293] MAQC Consortium and Leming Shi et al. The microarray quality control (maqc) project shows inter- and intraplatform reproducibility of gene expression measurements. *Nature Biotechnology*, 24:1151–1161, 2006.

[294] Roy A. Maxion and Tahlia N. Townsend. Masquerade detection using truncated command lines. In *Proc. of Int'l Conf. on Dependable Systems and Networks*, pages 219–228. IEEE Computer Society, 2002.

[295] Tim Menzies, Jeremy Greenwald, and Art Frank. Data mining static code attributes to learn defect predictors. *IEEE Trans. on Software Engineering*, 33(1):2–13, 2007.

[296] Ryszard S. Michalski. Knowledge acquisition through conceptual clustering: A theoretical framework and an algorithm for partitioning data into conjunctive concepts. *Journal of Policy Analysis and Information Systems*, 4(3):219–244, September 1980.

[297] Ryszard S. Michalski and Robert E. Stepp. An application of AI techniques to structuring objects into an optimal conceptual hierarchy. In *Proc. of Int'l Joint Conf. on Artificial Intelligence (IJCAI)*, pages 460–465, 1981.

[298] Shin-ichi Minato. Zero-suppressed BDDs for set manipulation in combinatorial problems. In *Proc. of 30th International Design Automation Conf.*, pages 272–277, 1993.

[299] Shin-Ichi Minato. Zero-suppressed BDDs and their applications. *Int'l Journal on Software Tools for Technology Transfer (STTT)*, 3(2):156–170, 2001.

[300] Shin-Ichi Minato. Finding simple disjoint decompositions in frequent itemset data using zero-suppressed BDD. In *Proc. of IEEE ICDM Workshop on Computational Intelligence in Data Mining*, pages 3–11, 2005.

[301] Shin-Ichi Minato, Takeaki Uno, and Hiroki Arimura. LCM over ZB-DDs: Fast generation of very large-scale frequent itemsets using a compact graph-based representation. In *Proc. of Pacific-Asia Conference on Advances in Knowledge Discovery and Data Mining (PAKDD)*, pages 234–246, 2008.

[302] Konstantinos Morfonios and Yannis E. Ioannidis. CURE for cubes: Cubing using a ROLAP engine. In *Proc. of Int'l Conf. on Very Large Data Bases (VLDB)*, pages 379–390, 2006.

[303] Konstantinos Morfonios and Yannis E. Ioannidis. Supporting the data cube lifecycle: the power of ROLAP. *VLDB Journal*, 17(4):729–764, 2008.

[304] Hiroyuki Morita, Takanobu Nakahara, Yukinobu Hamuro, and Shoji Yamamoto. Decision tree-based classifier incorporating contrast pattern. In *IEEE Int'l Symp. on Consumer Electronics (ISCE)*, pages 858 – 860, 2009.

[305] Maybin K. Muyeba, Muhammad S. Khan, Spits Warnars, and John A. Keane. A framework to mine high-level emerging patterns by attribute-oriented induction. In *Proc. of Int'l Conf. on Intelligent Data Engineering and Automated Learning (IDEAL)*, pages 170–177, 2011.

[306] Takanobu Nakahara, Touken Kin, and Katsutoshi Yada. Analysis of the impact of media contact on the purchase process. In *Proc. of SIAM International Workshop on Data Mining for Marketing at SDM*, pages 55–61, 2011.

[307] Sébastien Nedjar. *Cubes Emergents pour l'analyse des renversements de tendances dans les bases de donnees multidimensionnelles*. PhD Thesis, Universite de la Mediterranee, 2009.

[308] Sébastien Nedjar. Exact and approximate sizes of convex datacubes. In *Proc. of Int'l Conf. on Data Warehousing and Knowledge Discovery (DaWaK)*, pages 204–215, 2009.

[309] Sébastien Nedjar, Alain Casali, Rosine Cicchetti, and Lotfi Lakhal. Emerging cubes for trends analysis in OLAP databases. In *Proc. of Int'l Conf. on Data Warehousing and Knowledge Discovery (DaWaK)*, pages 135–144, 2007.

[310] Sébastien Nedjar, Alain Casali, Rosine Cicchetti, and Lotfi Lakhal. Upper borders for emerging cubes. In *Proc. of Int'l Conf. on Data Warehousing and Knowledge Discovery (DaWaK)*, pages 45–54, 2008.

[311] Sébastien Nedjar, Alain Casali, Rosine Cicchetti, and Lotfi Lakhal. Emerging cubes: Borders, size estimations and lossless reductions. *Inf. Syst.*, 34(6):536–550, 2009.

[312] Sébastien Nedjar, Alain Casali, Rosine Cicchetti, and Lotfi Lakhal. Reduced representations of emerging cubes for OLAP database mining. *Int'l J. of Business Intelligence and Data Mining*, 4(3/4):267–300, 2009.

[313] Sébastien Nedjar, Alain Casali, Rosine Cicchetti, and Lotfi Lakhal. Cubes fermés / quotients émergents. In *EGC 2010 – Extraction et gestion des connaissances*, volume RNTI-E-19 of *Revue des Nouvelles Technologies de l'Information*, pages 285–296. Cépaduès-Éditions, 2010.

[314] Sébastien Nedjar, Rosine Cicchetti, and Lotfi Lakhal. Extracting semantics in OLAP databases using emerging cubes. *Information Sciences*, 2011.

[315] Oscar Newman. *Defensible Space; Crime Prevention Through Urban Design*. Macmillan Pub. Co., 1973.

[316] Thanh-Son Ngo, Mengling Feng, Guimei Liu, and Limsoon Wong. Efficiently finding the best parameter for the emerging pattern-based classifier PCL. In *Proc. of Pacific-Asia Conf. on Knowledge Discovery and Data Mining (PAKDD)*, pages 121–133, 2010.

[317] Siegfried Nijssen and Joost N. Kok. A quickstart in frequent structure mining can make a difference. In *Proc. of ACM Int'l Conf. on Knowledge Discovery and Data Mining (KDD)*, pages 647–652, 2004.

[318] Petra Kralj Novak, Nada Lavrac, Dragan Gamberger, and Antonija Krstacic. CSM-SD: Methodology for contrast set mining through subgroup discovery. *Journal of Biomedical Informatics*, 42(1):113–122, 2009.

[319] Petra Kralj Novak, Nada Lavrac, and Geoffrey I. Webb. Supervised descriptive rule discovery: A unifying survey of contrast set, emerging pattern and subgroup mining. *Journal of Machine Learning Research*, 10:377–403, 2009.

[320] Kok-Leong Ong, Wee-Keong Ng, and Ee-Peng Lim. Mining multi-level rules with recurrent items using FP'-Tree. In *Proc. of Third Int'l Conf. on Information, Communications and Signal Processing (ICICS)*, 2001.

[321] Tomonobu Ozaki and Minoru Etoh. Correlation and contrast link formation patterns in a time evolving graph. In *Proc. of IEEE ICDM Workshops: Workshop on Contrast Data Mining and Applications*, pages 1147–1154, 2011.

[322] Balaji Padmanabhan and Alexander Tuzhilin. Small is beautiful: discovering the minimal set of unexpected patterns. In *Proc. of ACM Conf. on Knowledge Discovery and Data Mining (KDD)*, pages 54–63, 2000.

[323] Jin Hyoung Park, Heon Gyu Lee, and Jong Heung Park. Real-time diagnosis system using incremental emerging pattern mining. In *Proc. of 5th Int'l Conf. on Ubiquitous Information Technologies and Applications (CUTE)*, pages 1–5, 2010.

[324] Jin Hyoung Park, Heon Gyu Lee, Gyo Yong Sohn, Jin ho Shin, and Keun Ho Ryu. Emerging pattern based classification for automated non-safe power line detection. In *Proc. of Int Conf Fuzzy Systems and Knowledge Discovery (FSKD)*, pages 169–173, 2009.

[325] Srinivasan Parthasarathy and Mitsunori Ogihara. Exploiting dataset similarity for distributed mining. In *Proc. of IPDPS Workshops*, pages 399–406, 2000.

[326] Nicolas Pasquier, Yves Bastide, Rafik Taouil, and Lotfi Lakhal. Discovering frequent closed itemsets for association rules. In *Proc. of Int'l Conf. on Database Theory*, pages 398–416, 1999.

[327] Dhaval Patel, Wynne Hsu, and Mong-Li Lee. Discriminative mutation chains in virus sequences. In *Proc. of IEEE Int'l Conf. on Tools with Artificial Intelligence (ICTAI)*, pages 9–16, 2011.

[328] Zdzislaw Pawlak. Rough sets. *Int'l J. of Computer and Information Sciences*, 11:341–356, 1982.

[329] Zdzislaw Pawlak. Rough classification. *Int. J. Hum.-Comput. Stud.*, 51(2):369–383, 1999.

[330] Zdzislaw Pawlak and Andrzej Skowron. Rough sets: Some extensions. *Information Sciences*, 177(1):28–40, 2007.

[331] Zdzislaw Pawlak and Andrzej Skowron. Rudiments of rough sets. *Information Sciences*, 177(1):3–27, 2007.

[332] Jian Pei, Jiawei Han, and Laks V. S. Lakshmanan. Pushing convertible constraints in frequent itemset mining. *Data Min. Knowl. Discov.*, 8(3):227–252, 2004.

[333] Jian Pei, Jiawei Han, and Runying Mao. Closet: An efficient algorithm for mining frequent closed itemsets. In *Proc. of ACM SIGMOD Workshop on Research Issues in Data Mining and Knowledge Discovery*, pages 21–30, 2000.

[334] Emanuele Perola and Paul S. Charifson. Conformational analysis of drug-like molecules bound to proteins: an extensive study of ligand reorganization upon binding. *Journal of Medicinal Chemistry*, 47:2499–2510, 2004.

[335] Emanuel F Petricoin III et al. Use of proteomic patterns in serum to identify ovarian cancer. *Mechanisms of Disease*, 359:572–577, 2002.

[336] Matthai Philipose, Kenneth P. Fishkin, Mike Perkowitz, Donald J. Patterson, Dieter Fox, Henry A. Kautz, and Dirk Hähnel. Inferring activities from interactions with objects. *IEEE Pervasive Computing*, 3(4):50–57, 2004.

[337] Minghao Piao, Heon Gyu Lee, Gyoyong Sohn, Gouchol Pok, and Keun Ho Ryu. Emerging patterns based methodology for prediction of patients with myocardial ischemia. In *Proc. of Int'l Conf. on Fuzzy Systems and Knowledge Discovery (FSKD)*, pages 174–178, 2009.

[338] Roman Podraza and Krzysztof Tomaszewski. KTDA: Emerging patterns based data analysis system. In *Proc. of XXI Fall Meeting of Polish Information Processing Society*, pages 213–221, 2005.

[339] Guillaume Poezevara, Bertrand Cuissart, and Bruno Crémilleux. Discovering emerging graph patterns from chemicals. In *Proc. of Int'l Symp. on Foundations of Intelligent Systems (ISMIS)*, pages 45–55, 2009.

[340] Guillaume Poezevara, Bertrand Cuissart, and Bruno Crémilleux. Extracting and summarizing the frequent emerging graph patterns from a dataset of graphs. *Journal of Intell. Inf. Syst.*, 37(3):333–353, 2011.

[341] Lech Polkowski. *Rough Sets: Mathematical Foundations*. Physica-Verlag, Heidelberg, Germany, 2002.

[342] Xiaoyuan Qian, James Bailey, and Christopher Leckie. Mining generalised emerging patterns. In *Proc. of Australian Conf. on Artificial Intelligence*, pages 295–304, 2006.

[343] Yongsong Qin, Shichao Zhang, Xiaofeng Zhu, Jilian Zhang, and Chengqi Zhang. Estimating confidence intervals for structural differences between contrast groups with missing data. *Expert Syst. Appl.*, 36(3):6431–6438, 2009.

[344] J. Ross Quinlan. Induction of decision trees. *Machine Learning*, 1(1):81–106, 1986.

[345] J. Ross Quinlan. *C4.5: programs for machine learning.* Morgan Kaufmann, 1993.

[346] Zahid H. Qureshi. A review of accident modelling approaches for complex socio-technical systems. In *Proc. of Australian Conf. on Safety-Related Programmable Systems*, volume 86, pages 47–59, 2007.

[347] Rafal Rak, Lukasz A. Kurgan, and Marek Reformat. A tree-projection-based algorithm for multi-label recurrent-item associative-classification rule generation. *Data and Knowledge Engineering*, 64(1):171–197, 2008.

[348] Kotagiri Ramamohanarao. Contrast pattern mining and its application for building robust classifiers. In *Proc. of Int'l Conf. on Algorithmic Learning Theory (ALT)*, page 33, 2010.

[349] Kotagiri Ramamohanarao. Contrast pattern mining and its application for building robust classifiers. In *Proc. of Discovery Science*, page 380, 2010.

[350] Kotagiri Ramamohanarao and James Bailey. Discovery of emerging patterns and their use in classification. In *Proc. of Australian Conf. on Artificial Intelligence*, pages 1–12, 2003.

[351] Kotagiri Ramamohanarao and Hongjian Fan. Patterns based classifiers. In *Proc. of World Wide Web*, pages 71–83, 2007.

[352] A. Rauzy. Mathematical foundations of minimal cutsets. *IEEE Transactions on Reliability*, 50(4), 2001.

[353] J. E. Ridings, M. D. Barratt, et al. Computer prediction of possible toxic action from chemical structure: An update on the DEREK system. *Toxicology*, 106(1-3):267–279, 1996.

[354] J. Rissanen. Modeling by shortest data description. *Automatica*, 14(5):465–471, 1978.

[355] Stanislaw Romanski. Operations on families of sets for exhaustive search, given a monotonic function. In *Proc. of Third Int'l Conf. on Data and Knowledge Bases: Improving Usability and Responsiveness (JCDKB)*, pages 310–322, Jerusalem, Israel, 1988.

[356] Richard Rudell. Dynamic variable ordering for ordered binary decision diagrams. In *Proc. of Int'l Conf. on Computer Aided Design*, pages 42–47, 1993.

[357] Inmaculada Fortes Ruiz, José L. Balcázar, and Rafael Morales Bueno. Bounding negative information in frequent sets algorithms. In *Proc. of Discovery Science*, pages 50–58, 2001.

[358] Andrew Rusinko, Mark W. Farmen, Christophe G. Lambert, Paul L. Brown, and S. Stanley Young. Analysis of a large structure/biological activity data set using recursive partitioning. *Journal of Chemical Information and Computer Sciences*, 39:1017–1026, 1999.

[359] Khalid E. K. Saeed, Heon Gyu Lee, Wun-Jae Kim, Eun Jong Cha, and Keun Ho Ryu. Using emerging subsequence in classifying protein structural class. In *Proc. of Int'l Conf. on Fuzzy Systems and Knowledge Discovery (FSKD)*, pages 349–353, 2009.

[360] Ozlem Sahbaz and Bill Hillier. The story of the crime: functional, temporal and spatial tendencies in street robbery. In *Proc. of 6th Int'l Space Syntax Symp.*, 2007.

[361] Amit Satsangi and Osmar R. Zaïane. Contrasting the contrast sets: An alternative approach. In *Proc. of Int'l Database Engineering and Applications Symp.*, pages 114–119, 2007.

[362] Claude E. Shannon. A mathematical theory of communication. *Bell System Technical J.*, 27:623–656, 1948.

[363] Rong She, Fei Chen, Ke Wang, Martin Ester, Jennifer L. Gardy, and Fiona S. L. Brinkman. Frequent-subsequence-based prediction of outer membrane proteins. In *Proc. of ACM Int'l Conference on Knowledge Discovery from Data (SIGKDD)*, pages 436–445, 2003.

[364] Shashi Shekhar and Yan Huang. Discovering spatial co-location patterns: A summary of results. In *Proc. of Int'l Symp. on Advances in Spatial and Temporal Databases (SSTD)*, pages 236–256, 2001.

[365] Leming Shi and Weida Tong et al. Cross-platform comparability of microarray technology: Intra-platform consistency and appropriate data analysis procedures are essential. *BMC Bioinformatics*, 6(S-2), 2005.

[366] Jin-Ho Shin, Bong-Jae Yi, Young-Il Kim, Heon-Gyu Lee, and Keun Ho Ryu. Spatiotemporal Load-Analysis Model for Electric Power Distribution Facilities Using Consumer Meter-Reading Data. *IEEE Trans. on Power Delivery*, 26(2):736–743, 2011.

[367] Peter Shoubridge, Miro Kraetzl, Walter D. Wallis, and Horst Bunke. Detection of abnormal change in a time series of graphs. *Journal of Interconnection Networks*, 3(1-2):85–101, 2002.

[368] Mondelle Simeon and Robert J. Hilderman. Exploratory quantitative contrast set mining: A discretization approach. In *Proc. of IEEE Int'l Conf. on Tools with Artificial Intelligence (ICTAI)*, pages 124–131, 2007.

[369] D. Singh et al. Gene expression correlates of clinical prostate cancer behavior. *Cancer Cell*, 1(2):203–209, 2002.

[370] Andrzej Skowron and Jerzy Grzymala-Busse. From rough set theory to evidence theory. *Advances in the Dempster-Shafer theory of evidence*, pages 193–236, 1994.

[371] Noam Slonim, Nir Friedman, and Naftali Tishby. Unsupervised document classification using sequential information maximization. In *Proc. of ACM SIGIR Int'l Conf. on Research and Development in Information Retrieval*, pages 129–136, 2002.

[372] Vassiliki Somaraki, Deborah Broadbent, Frans Coenen, and Simon Harding. Finding temporal patterns in noisy longitudinal data: A study in diabetic retinopathy. In *Proc. of Industrial Conf. on Data Mining*, pages 418–431, 2010.

[373] Hee Seok Song, Jae Kyeong Kim, and Soung Hie Kim. Mining the change of customer behavior in an internet shopping mall. *Expert Syst. Appl.*, 21(3):157–168, 2001.

[374] Sarah Song and Michael A Black. Microarray-based gene set analysis: a comparison of current methods. *BMC Bioinformatics*, 9:502, 2008.

[375] Arnaud Soulet and Bruno Crémilleux. Adequate condensed representations of patterns. *Data Min. Knowl. Discov.*, 17(1):94–110, 2008.

[376] Arnaud Soulet, Bruno Crémilleux, and Marc Plantevit. Summarizing contrasts by recursive pattern mining. In *Proc. of IEEE ICDM Workshops: Workshop on Contrast Data Mining and Applications*, pages 1155–1162, 2011.

[377] Arnaud Soulet, Bruno Crémilleux, and François Rioult. Condensed representation of emerging patterns. In *Proc. of Pacific-Asia Conf. on Knowledge Discovery and Data Mining (PAKDD)*, pages 127–132, 2004.

[378] Arnaud Soulet and C. Hébert. Using emerging patterns from clusters to characterize social subgroups of patients affected by atherosclerosis. In *Proc. of Discovery Challenge Workshop co-located with ECML/PKDD'04*, 2004.

[379] Tomasz F. Stepinski, Wei Ding, and Christoph F. Eick. Discovering controlling factors of geospatial variables. In *Proc. of ACM SIGSPATIAL Int'l Symp. on Advances in Geographic Information Systems (GIS)*, 2008.

[380] Tomasz F. Stepinski, Josue Salazar, and Wei Ding. Discovering spatio-social motifs of electoral support using discriminative pattern mining. In *Proc. of 1st Int'l Conference on Computing for Geospatial Research & Application (Com.Geo)*, 2010.

[381] Tomasz F. Stepinski, Josue Salazar, Wei Ding, and Denis White. Estate: Strategy for exploring labeled spatial datasets using association analysis. In *Proc. of Int'l Conf. on Discovery Science*, 2010.

[382] Gerd Stumme, Rafik Taouil, Yves Bastide, Nicolas Pasquier, and Lotfi Lakhal. Computing iceberg concept lattices with TITANIC. *Data Knowl. Eng.*, 42(2):189–222, 2002.

[383] Qun Sun, Xiuzhen Zhang, and Kotagiri Ramamohanarao. Noise tolerance of EP-based classifiers. In *Proc. of Australian Conf. on Artificial Intelligence*, pages 796–806, 2003.

[384] Robert Susmaga. Parallel computation of reducts. In *Proc. of Int'l Conf. on Rough Sets and Current Trends in Computing (RSCTC)*, pages 450–457, 1998.

[385] Roman W. Swiniarski and Andrzej Skowron. Rough set methods in feature selection and recognition. *Pattern Recogn. Lett.*, 24(6):833–849, 2003.

[386] Nobuyuki Takahashi, Atsushi Takizawa, Naoki Katoh, and Wonyong Koo. Analysis of Kansei evaluation on entrance halls of rental office buildings by CAEP. *Journal of Architecture and Planning*, 74(640):1403–1410, 2009.

[387] Atsushi Takizawa. Classification and feature extraction of criminal occurrence points using CAEP with transductive clustering. In *Procedia - Social and Behavioral Sciences 21, Int'l Conf.: Spatial Thinking and Geographic Information Sciences*, 2011.

[388] Atsushi Takizawa, Fumie Kawaguchi, Naoki Katoh, Kenji Mori, and Kazuo Yoshida. Risk discovery of car-related crimes from urban spatial attributes using emerging patterns. *KES Journal*, 11(5):301–311, 2007.

[389] Atsushi Takizawa, Wonyong Koo, and Naoki Katoh. Discovering distinctive spatial patterns of snatch theft in Kyoto City with CAEP. *Journal of Asian Architecture and Building Engineering*, 9(1):103–110, 2010.

[390] Atsushi Takizawa, Kazuma Yoshida, and Naoki Katoh. Applying graph mining to discover substructures of room layouts which affect the rent of apartments. In *Proc. of IEEE Int'l Conf. on Systems, Man and Cybernetics (SMC)*, pages 3512–3518, 2007.

[391] Paul K. Tan and Thomas J. Downey et al. Evaluation of gene expression measurements from commercial microarray platforms. *Nucleic Acids Research*, 31(19):5676–5684, 2003.

[392] Fung Michael Tang. *Sequence classification and melody tracks selection*. Master of Philosophy Thesis, University of Hong Kong, 2001.

[393] Tsuyoshi Taniguchi and Makoto Haraguchi. Discovery of hidden correlations in a local transaction database based on differences of correlations. *Eng. Appl. of AI*, 19(4):419–428, 2006.

[394] Emmanuel Munguia Tapia, Stephen S. Intille, and Kent Larson. Activity recognition in the home using simple and ubiquitous sensors. In *Proc. of Second Int'l Conf. on Pervasive Computing*, pages 158–175, 2004.

[395] Lothar Terfloth. Calculation of structure descriptors. In Johann Gasteiger and Thomas Engel, editors, *Chemoinformatics*, pages 401–437. Wiley-WCH, Weinheim, Germany, 2003.

[396] Pawel Terlecki. *On the Relation between Jumping Emerging Patterns and Rough Set Theory with Application to Data Classification*. PhD Thesis, Institute of Computer Science, Warsaw University of Technology, 2009. Winner of Polish Prime Minister's Award for PhD thesis.

[397] Pawel Terlecki. On the relation between jumping emerging patterns and rough set theory with application to data classification. *Trans. on Rough Sets XII*, 12:236–338, 2010.

[398] Pawel Terlecki and Krzysztof Walczak. Local reducts and jumping emerging patterns in relational databases. In *Proc. of Int'l Conf. on Rough Sets and Current Trends in Computing*, pages 358–367, 2006.

[399] Pawel Terlecki and Krzysztof Walczak. Jumping emerging pattern induction by means of graph coloring and local reducts in transaction databases. In *Proc. of Int'l Conf. on Rough Sets, Fuzzy Sets, Data Mining and Granular Computing*, pages 363–370, 2007.

[400] Pawel Terlecki and Krzysztof Walczak. Jumping emerging patterns with negation in transaction databases - classification and discovery. *Inf. Sci.*, 177(24):5675–5690, 2007.

[401] Pawel Terlecki and Krzysztof Walczak. Local table condensation in rough set approach for jumping emerging pattern induction. In *Proc. of ICCS Workshop*, Sheffield, UK, 2007. Springer-Verlag.

[402] Pawel Terlecki and Krzysztof Walczak. On the relation between rough set reducts and jumping emerging patterns. *Inf. Sci.*, 177(1):74–83, 2007.

[403] Pawel Terlecki and Krzysztof Walczak. Attribute set dependence in reduct computation. *Trans. on Computational Science*, 2:118–132, 2008.

[404] Fadi A. Thabtah. A review of associative classification mining. *Knowledge Eng. Review*, 22(1):37–65, 2007.

[405] Roger Ming Hieng Ting. *Mining Minimal Contrast Subgraph Patterns*. Masters Thesis, The University of Melbourne, 2007.

[406] Roger Ming Hieng Ting and James Bailey. Mining minimal contrast subgraph patterns. In *Proc. of SIAM Int'l Conf. on Data Mining (SDM)*, 2006.

[407] Roberto Todeschini and Viviana Consonni. *Handbook of Molecular Descriptors*. Wiley-WCH, Weinheim, Germany, 2000.

[408] Chieh-Yuan Tsai and Yu-Chen Shieh. A change detection method for sequential patterns. *Decision Support Systems*, 46(2):501–511, 2009.

[409] George Tzanis, Ioannis Kavakiotis, and Ioannis P. Vlahavas. Polyadenylation site prediction using interesting emerging patterns. In *Proc. of IEEE Int'l Conf. on Bioinformatics and Bioengineering (BIBE)*, pages 1–7, 2008.

[410] George Tzanis, Ioannis Kavakiotis, and Ioannis P. Vlahavas. PolyA-iEP: A data mining method for the effective prediction of polyadenylation sites. *Expert Syst. Appl.*, 38(10):12398–12408, 2011.

[411] Luis G. Valerio Jr. In silico toxicology for the pharmaceutical sciences. *Toxicology and Applied Pharmacology*, 241(3):356–370, 2009.

[412] Laura J. van't Veer and Hongyue Dai et al. Gene expression profiling predicts clinical outcome of breast cancer. *Nature*, 415:530–536, 2002.

[413] Vladimir Naumovich Vapnik. *Statistical learning theory*. Wiley, 1998.

[414] G. D. Veith, B. Greenwood, R. S. Hunter, G. J. Niemi, and R. R. Regal. On the intrinsic dimensionality of chemical structure space. *Chemosphere*, 17(8):1617–1644, 1988.

[415] Adriano Veloso, Wagner Meira Jr., Márcio de Carvalho, Bruno Pôssas, Srinivasan Parthasarathy, and Mohammed Javeed Zaki. Mining frequent itemsets in evolving databases. In *Proc. of SIAM Int'l Conf. on Data Mining (SDM)*, 2002.

[416] Jilles Vreeken, Matthijs van Leeuwen, and Arno Siebes. Characterising the difference. In *Proc. of ACM Conf. on Knowledge Discovery and Data Mining (KDD)*, pages 765–774, 2007.

[417] C. S. Wallace and D. M. Boulton. An information measure for classification. *The Computer J.*, 11(2):185–194, 1968.

[418] Haijun Wang, Yaping Lin, Xinguo Lu, and Yalin Nie. A novel EPA-KNN gene classification algorithm. In *Proc. of 4th Int'l Symp. on Neural Networks (ISNN)*, pages 1254–1263, 2007.

[419] Huixia Wang, Xuming He, Mark Band, Carole Wilson, and Lei Liu. A study of inter-lab and inter-platform agreement of DNA microarray data. *BMC Genomics*, 6(1):71–79, 2005.

[420] James Z. Wang, Jia Li, and Gio Wiederhold. SIMPLIcity: Semantics-sensitive integrated matching for picture libraries. *IEEE Trans. on Patt. Anal. and Machine Intell.*, 23:947–963, 2001.

[421] Jianyong Wang and George Karypis. HARMONY: Efficiently mining the best rules for classification. In *Proc. of SIAM Int'l Conf. on Data Mining (SDM)*, pages 205–216, 2005.

[422] Ke Wang and Salvatore J. Stolfo. One Class Training for Masquerade Detection. ICDM *Workshop on Data Mining for Computer Security* (DMSEC), 2003.

[423] Ke Wang, Chu Xu, and Bing Liu. Clustering transactions using large items. In *Proc. of ACM Conf. on Information and Knowledge Management (CIKM)*, pages 483–490, 1999.

[424] Ke Wang, Senqiang Zhou, Ada Wai-Chee Fu, and Jeffrey Xu Yu. Mining changes of classification by correspondence tracing. In *Proc. of SIAM Int'l Conf. on Data Mining (SDM)*, 2003.

[425] Liang Wang, Yizhou Wang, Tingting Jiang, and Wen Gao. Instantly telling what happens in a video sequence using simple features. In *Proc. of IEEE Conf. on Computer Vision and Pattern Recognition (CVPR)*, pages 3257–3264, 2011.

[426] Liang Wang, Yizhou Wang, and Debin Zhao. Building emerging pattern (EP) random forest for recognition. In *Proc. of Int'l Conf. on Image Processing (ICIP)*, pages 1457–1460, 2010.

[427] Lusheng Wang, Hao Zhao, Guozhu Dong, and Jianping Li. On the complexity of finding emerging patterns. *Theor. Comput. Sci.*, 335(1):15–27, 2005.

[428] Zhou Wang, Hongjian Fan, and Kotagiri Ramamohanarao. Exploiting maximal emerging patterns for classification. In *Proc. of Australian Conf. on Artificial Intelligence*, pages 1062–1068, 2004.

[429] Geoff I. Webb. Multiboosting: A technique for combining boosting and wagging. *Machine Learning*, 40(2):159–196, 2000.

[430] Geoffrey I. Webb. Discovering significant patterns. *Machine Learning*, 71(1):131, 2008.

[431] G.I. Webb, S. Butler, and D. Newlands. On detecting differences between groups. In *Proc. of ACM Conf. on Knowledge Discovery and Data Mining (KDD)*, pages 256–265. ACM, 2003.

[432] Daniela M. Witten and Robert Tibshirani. A comparison of fold-change and the t-statistic for microarray data analysis. *Analysis*, 2007.

[433] Ian H. Witten and Eibe Frank. *Data Mining: Practical machine learning tools and techniques.* Morgan Kaufmann, 2nd edition, 2005.

[434] Tzu-Tsung Wong and Kuo-Lung Tseng. Mining negative contrast sets from data with discrete attributes. *Expert Syst. Appl.*, 29(2):401–407, 2005.

[435] Stefan Wrobel. An algorithm for multi-relational discovery of subgroups. In *Proc. of European Conf. on Principles and Practice of Knowledge Discovery in Databases (PKDD)*, pages 78–87, 1997.

[436] Baohua Wu, Lei Duan, Zhonghua Yu, Changjie Tang, and Jun Zhu. Birth defects detection algorithm based on emerging patterns. *Journal of Computer Applications*, 31(4):885–889, 2011.

[437] Xindong Wu, Chengqi Zhang, and Shichao Zhang. Efficient mining of both positive and negative association rules. *ACM Trans. Inf. Syst.*, 22(3):381–405, 2004.

[438] Dong Xin, Jiawei Han, Xiaolei Li, Zheng Shao, and Benjamin W. Wah. Computing iceberg cubes by top-down and bottom-up integration: The starcubing approach. *IEEE Trans. Knowl. Data Eng.*, 19(1):111–126, 2007.

[439] Dong Xin, Zheng Shao, Jiawei Han, and Hongyan Liu. C-cubing: Efficient computation of closed cubes by aggregation-based checking. In *Proc. of IEEE Int'l Conf. on Data Engineering (ICDE)*, page 4, 2006.

[440] Zhengzheng Xing, Jian Pei, Guozhu Dong, and Philip S. Yu. Mining sequence classifiers for early prediction. In *Proc. of SIAM Int'l Conf. on Data Mining (SDM)*, pages 644–655, 2008.

[441] Hui Xiong, Shashi Shekhar, Yan Huang, Vipin Kumar, Xiaobin Ma, and Jin Soung Yoo. A framework for discovering co-location patterns in data sets with extended spatial objects. In *Proc. of SIAM Int'l Conf. on Data Mining (SDM)*, 2004.

[442] Jingfeng Xue and Yuanda Cao. Application and research of aggregation emerging pattern in intrusion detection. *Computer Application and Software*, 22, 2005.

[443] Jingfeng Xue, Changzhen Hu, Kunsheng Wang, Rui Ma, and Jiaxin Zou. Metamorphic malware detection technology based on aggregating emerging patterns. In *Proc. of Int. Conf. Interaction Sciences*, pages 1293–1296, 2009.

[444] Xifeng Yan, Hong Cheng, Jiawei Han, and Philip S. Yu. Mining significant graph patterns by scalable leap search. In *Proc. ACM Int'l Conf. on Management of Data (SIGMOD)*, pages 433–444, 2008.

[445] Xifeng Yan and Jiawei Han. gSpan: Graph-based substructure pattern mining. In *Proc. of IEEE Int'l Conf. on Data Mining (ICDM)*, pages 721–724, 2002.

[446] Yiling Yang, Xudong Guan, and Jinyuan You. CLOPE: a fast and effective clustering algorithm for transactional data. In *Proc. of ACM Int'l Conf. on Knowledge Discovery and Data Mining (KDD)*, pages 682–687, 2002.

[447] Ying Yang, Xindong Wu, and Xingquan Zhu. Mining in anticipation for concept change: Proactive-reactive prediction in data streams. *Data Min. Knowl. Discov.*, 13(3):261–289, 2006.

[448] Yanfang Ye, Tao Li, Qingshan Jiang, and Youyu Wang. CIMDS: Adapting postprocessing techniques of associative classification for malware detection. *IEEE Trans. on Systems, Man, and Cybernetics, Part C: Applications and Reviews*, 40(3):298–307, 2010.

[449] Eng-Juh Yeoh, Mary E Ross et al. (incl. Jinyan Li, and Limsoon Wong). Classification, subtype discovery, and prediction of outcome in pediatric acute lymphoblastic leukemia by gene expression profiling. *Cancer Cell*, 1(2):133–143, 2002.

[450] Xiaoxin Yin and Jiawei Han. CPAR: Classification based on predictive association rules. In *Proc. of SIAM Int'l Conf. on Data Mining (SDM)*, 2003.

[451] Jin Soung Yoo and Shashi Shekhar. A join-less approach for mining spatial co-location patterns. *IEEE Trans. on Knowledge and Data Engineering (TKDE)*, 18, 2006.

[452] Hye-Sung Yoon, Sang-Ho Lee, and Ju Han Kim. Application of emerging patterns for multi-source bio-data classification and analysis. In *Proc. of Int'l Conf. on Natural Computation (ICNC)*, pages 965–974, 2005.

[453] Kui Yu, Xindong Wu, Wei Ding, and Hao Wang. Causal associative classification. In *Proc. of IEEE Int'l Conf. on Data Mining (ICDM)*, 2011.

[454] Larry T. H. Yu, Fu-Lai Chung, Stephen Chi-Fai Chan, and Simon M. C. Yuen. Using emerging pattern based projected clustering and gene expression data for cancer detection. In *Proc. of Asia-Pacific Bioinformatics Conf. (APBC)*, pages 75–84, 2004.

[455] Xiaohui Yuan, Bill P. Buckles, Zhaoshan Yuan, and Jian Zhang. Mining negative association rules. In *Proc. of IEEE Symp. on Computers and Communications (ISCC)*, pages 623–628, 2002.

[456] Lofti Zadeh. Fuzzy sets. *Information Control*, 8:338–353, 1965.

[457] Reza Zafarani and Huan Liu. Social computing data repository at ASU, http://socialcomputing.asu.edu, 2009.

[458] Osmar R. Zaïane, Jiawei Han, and Hua Zhu. Mining recurrent items in multimedia with progressive resolution refinement. In *Proc. of 16th Int'l Conf. on Data Engineering (ICDE)*, pages 461–470, 2000.

[459] Mohammed Javeed Zaki and Ching-Jui Hsiao. Efficient algorithms for mining closed itemsets and their lattice structure. *IEEE Trans. Knowl. Data Eng.*, 17(4):462–478, 2005.

[460] Jilian Zhang, Shichao Zhang, Xiaofeng Zhu, Xindong Wu, and Chengqi Zhang. Measuring the uncertainty of differences for contrasting groups. In *Proc. of AAAI Conf. on Artificial Intelligence*, pages 1920–1921, 2007.

[461] Shaoyi Zhang, Kotagiri Ramamohanarao, and James C. Bezdek. EP-based robust weighting scheme for fuzzy SVMs. In *Proc. of Australasian Database Conf. (ADC)*, pages 123–132, 2010.

[462] Shichao Zhang. Detecting differences between contrast groups. *IEEE Trans. on Information Technology in Biomedicine*, 12(6):739–745, 2008.

[463] Xiuzhen Zhang. *Emerging Patterns: Efficient Constraint-Based Mining and the Aggregation Approach for Classification*. PhD Thesis, University of Melbourne, 2001.

[464] Xiuzhen Zhang, Guozhu Dong, and Kotagiri Ramamohanarao. Exploring constraints to efficiently mine emerging patterns from large high-dimensional datasets. In *Proc. of ACM Conf. on Knowledge Discovery and Data Mining (KDD)*, pages 310–314, 2000.

[465] Xiuzhen Zhang, Guozhu Dong, and Kotagiri Ramamohanarao. Information-based classification by aggregating emerging patterns. In *Proc. of Intelligent Data Engineering and Automated Learning (IDEAL)*, pages 48–53, 2000.

[466] Xiuzhen Zhang, Guozhu Dong, and Kotagiri Ramamohanarao. Building behaviour knowledge space to make classification decision. In *Proc. of Pacific-Asia Conf. on Knowledge Discovery and Data Mining (PAKDD)*, pages 488–494, 2001.

[467] Xiuzhen Zhang, Guozhu Dong, and Limsoon Wong. Using CAEP to predict translation initiation sites from genomic DNA sequences. Technical report, CSSE-TR2001/22, University of Melbourne, 2001.

[468] Yuhai Zhao, Guoren Wang, Yuan Li, and Zhanghui Wang. Finding novel diagnostic gene patterns based on interesting non-redundant contrast sequence rules. In *Proc. of IEEE Int'l Conf. on Data Mining (ICDM)*, pages 972–981, 2011.

[469] Wojciech Ziarko. Probabilistic rough sets. In *Proc. of Int'l Conf. on Rough Sets, Fuzzy Sets, Data Mining, and Granular Computing (RSFD-GrC)*, pages 283–293, 2005.

Index

Printed and bound by CPI Group (UK) Ltd, Croydon, CR0 4YY

23/10/2024

01778003-0001